# WHITEHALL

*Also by Colin Brown*

FIGHTING TALK: THE BIOGRAPHY OF JOHN PRESCOTT

# WHITEHALL

*The Street that Shaped a Nation*

COLIN BROWN

**SIMON &
SCHUSTER**

London · New York · Sydney · Toronto

A CBS COMPANY

First published in Great Britain by Simon & Schuster UK Ltd, 2009
A CBS COMPANY

1 3 5 7 9 10 8 6 4 2

Simon & Schuster UK Ltd
1st Floor
222 Gray's Inn Road
London WC1X 8HB

www.simonandschuster.co.uk

Simon & Schuster Australia
Sydney

Map on p. ix © Liane Payne

A CIP catalogue record for this book is available
from the British Library.

ISBN: 978-1-84737-077-8

Typeset in Granjon by
Ellipsis Books Limited, Glasgow

Printed and Bound in Great Britain by
CPI Mackays, Chatham ME5 8TD

To the memory of my brother, Peter (1945–2009)

# CONTENTS

Map    *ix*

*Foreword and Acknowledgements*    *xi*

Introduction   The Seabird Shore    1

1   The Cardinal's Court    13

2   Henry VIII's Palace of White Hall    43

3   Queen Elizabeth I's Whitehall    69

4   Blood at the Banqueting House    93

5   Pepys's Whitehall    122

6   Downing Street    153

7   Nelson and the Admiralty    183

8   Dover House – the Most Notorious Address in London    210

9   Wellington and Horse Guards    237

10   Pam's Palace – the Foreign and Commonwealth Office    258

11   The War Office – from Haig to Hoon    281

12   The Cabinet Office and the Treasury    301

13   Scotland Yard    312

14   Winston and Whitehall    324

*Postscript*    *347*

*Notes*    *349*

*Picture Credits*    *358*

*Index*    *361*

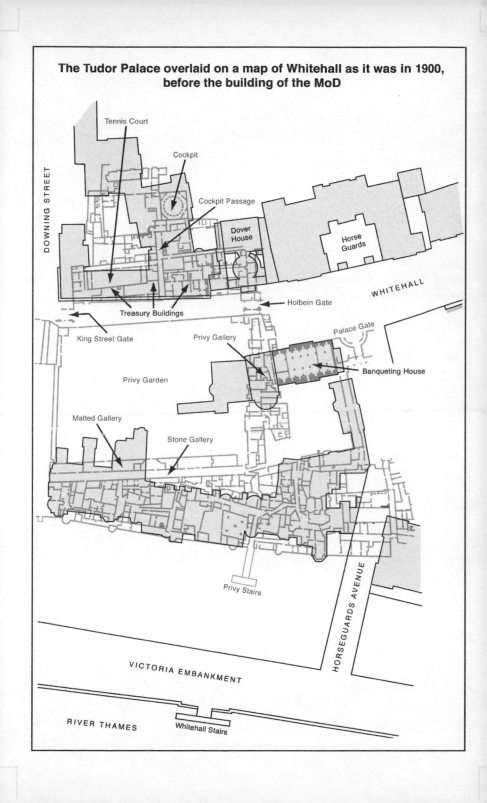

## The Tudor Palace overlaid on a map of Whitehall as it was in 1900, before the building of the MoD

Tennis Court

Cockpit

Cockpit Passage

Dover House

Horse Guards

DOWNING STREET

WHITEHALL

Holbein Gate

Treasury Buildings

King Street Gate

Privy Gallery

Palace Gate

Banqueting House

Privy Garden

Matted Gallery

Stone Gallery

Privy Stairs

HORSEGUARDS AVENUE

VICTORIA EMBANKMENT

RIVER THAMES

Whitehall Stairs

# Foreword and Acknowledgements

This book is the biography of the most important street in Britain, with a name that still resonates with power 500 years after it was first christened Whitehall. As a political correspondent, Westminster has been my 'beat' for thirty years, and Whitehall has been my backyard. No other street in Britain contains more landmarks of our island's history than Whitehall but even I had no idea what surprises lay behind the bland façades of the ministries where the so-called bowler-hat brigade pushed their pens: the Admiralty Board Room with its wind clock still in working order to tell the Sea Lords which way the wind was blowing; the captains' waiting room where Nelson's body lay in state before his funeral and where the humble Yorkshire clockmaker, John Harrison, waited interminably for the Board of Longitude to give him his prize; Henry VIII's wine cellar deep in the bowels of the Ministry of Defence main building; the remains of Henry's indoor tennis court at the Cabinet Office; Lady Caroline Lamb's bedroom on the first floor at Dover House, the Scotland Office, where she conducted an affair with Lord Byron, the poet, that scandalized even liberal Regency society; and the secret Tudor passage to Downing Street where countless political figures have followed in the footsteps of Henry VIII.

The germ of the book arose when I was researching my biography of John Prescott, the former Labour Deputy Prime Minister, and was taken inside some of the historic settings at the Admiralty in which he conducted Cabinet committee meetings. The treasures of Whitehall are rarely open to the public, and I wanted to bring them to a wider audience, by providing a guide to the buildings and a narrative of the lives of those who played out their dramas, triumphs and failures here. Today Whitehall is synonymous with the government departments and the battalions of civil servants who work there. But this is not a book about the civil service – I can safely leave that to the definitive account, *Whitehall* by Professor Peter Hennessy. This is the story of our island race, its naval history, its empire, its conquests and its decline, encapsulated in one small corner of the capital that I have called *Whitehall*.

In researching this book, I owe a debt of gratitude to Stephen Coomber of the Cabinet Office; Simon Thurley of English Heritage; the London Topographical Society; Sam Keayes of the Ministry of Defence press office; Bob Evans from the Corporate Memory Branch of the MoD; John Williams; Colin White, Director of the Royal Naval Museum at Portsmouth Historic Dockyard; historian Alison Weir; Mari Takayanagi of the Parliamentary Archives; Dr Andrea Clarke, Curator of Early Modern Historical Manuscripts at the British Library; John Battersby of HM Treasury; Kate Crowe of the Foreign and Commonwealth Office; Terry Charman, Sarah Clarke and staff at the Cabinet War Rooms, the Imperial War Museum; Karen Watts, Senior Curator of Armour at the Royal Armouries York; Nick Humphrey of the Victoria and Albert Museum; Jane Roberts, Librarian and Curator of the Print Room, the Royal Collection Trust, Windsor Castle; Mike Jones and Katherine Stanton at Simon & Schuster; the many historians on whose research I have drawn; and my long-suffering wife, Amanda.

Colin Brown
Blackheath, June 2008

*Introduction*

# THE SEABIRD SHORE

*EDWARDUS PRIMUS SCOTTORUM MALLEUS HIC EST*
*PACTUM SERVA*
Inscription on the tomb of Edward I, Westminster Abbey
('Edward I Hammer of the Scots Keep the Faith')

Edward I, the ruthless 'Hammer of the Scots', persecutor of the Jews and conqueror of the Welsh, was stricken with grief. It was early December, and Edward rode at the head of a melancholy procession carrying a coffin across the streams and through the mud of the rutted track to his royal palace at Westminster. They were on the last leg of their journey and could see the great north window, steeples, arches and flying buttresses of Westminster Abbey that had been raised at vast expense by his father, Henry III. The Abbey loomed, grey and austere, above the thatched roofs of a hamlet on the muddy banks of the Thames near Westminster that had been known since Saxon times as Enedehithe – *Seabird Shore*.[1] They were bringing home the body of Edward's devoted Queen, Eleanor of Castile, to her last resting place behind the Abbey's high altar. Eleanor had been with Edward on the Crusades, borne him fifteen children, and had been a source of strength to the King throughout his years of carrying the crown of England, but she had succumbed to 'winter sickness', probably malarial fever contracted on a summer visit to Gascony. On a progress north, almost certainly to pray for relief from her illness at the shrine of St Hugh in Lincoln Cathedral, Eleanor's condition suddenly worsened and she died in the house of a knight in the village of Harby near Lincoln on 28 November 1290. She was forty-nine and had prepared for death, issuing instructions for her heart to be given to the care of the Black Friars in London.

After the journey home, her body was entombed in the holiest corner of the Abbey, by the shrine of St Edward, the King known for his piety as Edward the Confessor. Henry III believed in the power of St Edward, and though the name was no longer fashionable, being Old English, he had christened his eldest son after the saint as a sign of his devotion. In 1254, Edward had been married to Eleanor to seal an alliance with her Spanish family and to settle a dispute over Henry III's lands in Gascony, on the west coast of France. She was a few weeks short of her thirteenth birthday and he had just turned fifteen but Edward had grown to love his wife deeply and at the places where her funeral cortège stopped each night of their journey, he ordered a cross to be erected to her memory, twelve in all. The last of the Eleanor crosses was erected at Charing, the hamlet within sight of Westminster by the Strand that was to become known as Charing Cross and the starting point for all measurements from London.

The muddy road from Charing to Westminster along which her body travelled for the last time is now known as Whitehall. Her tomb lies in a dark corner of the Abbey but the gloom is lifted by a glowing effigy of Eleanor, cast in bronze and covered in gold by London goldsmith William Torel in 1291. It shows Eleanor as she was in her younger life, a slender and beautiful woman lying serenely with her hair cascading over a pillow covered in the lions and castles of Leon and Castile, her hand gently holding the neck cord of her cloak. When Edward died in 1307, aged sixty-eight, from dysentery in a windswept settlement at Burgh by Sands, Cumbria, his body too was brought back to Westminster to lie in his coronation robes near his wife by the shrine to Edward the Confessor. Even today, the austerity of Edward's plain black sarcophagus is striking, but it is more famous for the inscription: *EDWARDUS PRIMUS SCOTTORUM MALLEUS HIC EST PACTUM SERVA* – 'Edward I Hammer of the Scots Keep the Faith'. The flaking words, which are barely legible now, were probably painted on the side of Edward's tomb in the sixteenth century, but it is believed they repeated an earlier message. It is normally translated as 'Keep the Faith' but, according to Marc Morris in his biography of Edward, it may be more accurately rendered as 'Keep the Troth' for it was more than an exortation to remain faithful to their cause. The year before Edward died, he had suffered a series of reverses at the hands of the Scots and held a feast in the great hall at Westminster at which his supporters swore an oath to avenge the rebellion of the Scottish leader Robert Bruce. The words on his tomb are a warning to keep that vow.[2]

When Edward laid his wife's body in her tomb, Westminster was already a place of ancient power. It had been the centre of England's ecclesiastical, judicial and political power for 300 years but its origins extended beyond the conquest by the Normans and beyond the Saxon settlements along the river. There had been a religious settlement at Thorney Island since the year 600, and before that it was probably the site of a Roman pagan temple. The river at Westminster was wider and more sluggish than it is today, which made it fordable and a favourite crossing place for travellers who may have paused at Thorney Island, one of the few dry points on the marshy north bank of the Thames, to pay their religious homage, before taking the track around the bends in the river to the Saxon market town and port, Lundenwic, or north to the old Roman road, Watling

Street. Thorney Island was enclosed by two tributaries of the Tyburn River, creating the ground on which the Abbey and the Palace of Westminster now stand. Peter Ackroyd, the expert on the history of London, suggests that nearby Tothill Fields was an ancient centre for ritualized power, and around 960 a small Benedictine monastery was founded by King Edgar and St Dunstan at the place regarded by fearful travellers who paid their tributes there as 'terrible Westminster', for the sense of holy terror[3] that they felt in this hallowed place.

King Edward the Confessor, after a religious vision, moved his entire court from Winchester to a new palace at Thorney Island and in 1060 ordered the existing abbey to be reconstructed in the Romanesque style, with rounded arches and massive towers which have survived in the undercroft in the cloisters, once used as the domestic quarters for the monks and now the Abbey's museum. Its height was limited by its semicircular arches, the extent of the architectural technology known to the Romans, but it must still have awed the Saxon people who lived in modest houses by the river. It became known as the 'West Minster', to distinguish it from the 'East Minster', St Paul's in the city. The invention of load-bearing flying buttresses and pointed archways led to the creation of the great soaring Abbey we see today with its pinnacles, towering walls, windows and arches pointing to heaven. It was started in 1245 for Henry III in an age of great cathedral building which saw Gothic architecture taken to a high art in France, with cathedrals at Amiens, Evreux and Chartres. Henry III dedicated the rebuilding of West Minster to its creator, Edward the Confessor, who had reinforced its ancient powers with holy relics including sand from Mount Sinai, soil from Calvary, pieces of the Cross, blood from Christ's side, St Paul's finger, and hair from St Peter. Edward was too ill to attend the reconsecration of his great Abbey on 28 December 1065 and died in January 1066, to become the first in a long line of monarchs to have their bones buried at Westminster. Harold Godwinson seized the crown, but by Christmas 1066 he too was dead, killed by an arrow in the eye at the battle against the Norman invaders by the coast near Hastings. Remnants of King Harold's defeated army may well have splashed across the ford in the river at Westminster on their stocky Saxon mounts before the Norman army of William arrived in full cry to make the Conqueror the first monarch in an almost unbroken line lasting a thousand years to be crowned in the Confessor's Abbey.

With the Normans came the first recognizable vestiges of the civil service that was to become synonymous with the rutted track called Whitehall. The houses along the track to Westminster that became known as King Street also quickly grew with its importance. A settlement of eighty-six households was listed in the Domesday Book of 1086. William Rufus built the great hall at Westminster, and the Abbey monks granted the land along the river at Enedehithe to Gerin, an administrator to Henry II. His house and land passed to Henry II's Treasurer Richard FitzNigel, one of the first of the civil servants of Whitehall. FitzNigel recorded that he used a chequered cloth like an abacus on a table five feet by ten to count taxes due to the King from the accounts set down in the Domesday Book. It is the reason the chief finance minister at the Treasury in Whitehall is still known as the Chancellor of the Exchequer.

Hubert de Burgh, one of the most powerful men in England (men who were to make Westminster and Whitehall the power centre of England for the next thousand years), built his house close to the royal court by the Thames on the land where the Ministry of Defence now stands. De Burgh was King John's chief minister and powerbroker with the barons. He remained loyal to the King, but persuaded him to sign the treaty limiting the Sovereign's powers, known as Magna Carta. When de Burgh died in 1243 he left his house near Westminster to the Black Friars as a penance for not fulfilling a pledge to go on a Crusade, though he could never be accused of cowardice – he had fought the French to a standstill at the sieges of Chinon Castle in France and Dover Castle. It was granted by the Black Friars to the See of York, and would be home to successive Archbishops of York for the next three centuries as York Place. King Street and the Strand, linking Charing to the old city of London, were about 200 yards from the river to avoid flooding, and became the site of other ecclesiastical residences, including those of the Bishops of Durham, Norwich and Arundel. As the power of the church declined, these houses were taken by courtiers, including the Dukes of Buckingham and Northumberland, whose titles survive today in the street names of the area. York Place grew in importance, however, as four Archbishops of York between 1426 and 1529 were also Chancellors to the King.

Six years after Queen Eleanor's death, Edward (nicknamed Longshanks because he was six feet two inches tall) began to rebuild the Royal Palace of Westminster, but it was damaged by fire, a fatal hazard in timber-framed buildings that was repeatedly to affect the development of Whitehall. Edward I decamped to York Place, which was convenient for his official duties with his council in Westminster. Edward must have enjoyed the house by the river because after he had married again he built lodgings there for his new Queen, Margaret, as there were none for a wife for the celibate Archbishop.[4] And it was not to be the last time that a monarch would covet the riverside mansion owned by the See of York – it was seized in 1529 by Henry VIII to create his own Palace of White Hall. The road on which Eleanor's funeral cortège passed, known as King Street, was dotted with cottages and low tenements belonging to the Abbey, housing servants and courtiers who earned their living from the Church and the Crown at Westminster. It was fast becoming an urban landscape by the end of the fifteenth century, but there were still meadows where cattle grazed at St James's Fields – now St James's Park – and a path wound its way east through the fields to a willow marsh where osiers, branches of the narrow-leaved shrubs of the willow family, were cut for wicker baskets and for wooden laths. These would have been prized for use locally in medieval wattle-and-daub house construction, similar to our modern-day lath-and-plaster technique. The path met King Street at the field known as Steynour's Croft; being slightly higher ground, this was better drained and drier. The firm ground was good for horses, which led to it being used as the site for the Tudor Tilt Yard, later to become Horse Guards Parade. Across the road was the gatehouse of York Place, where the rush-hour traffic roars into Horse Guards Avenue today. 'The Green' was also located at this spot on Whitehall. This patch of land – facing the court gate of the later Royal Palace of White Hall – became important as the place where royal proclamations were made, from the reign of Edward VI in 1547 until the reign of William and Mary in 1689. When the palace and the court gate burned down in 1698, the practice continued on the railings of Horse Guards, until the Coronation in 1953.[5] There was a white cross outside York House and posts across King Street nearby, marking the boundary of St Margaret's parish; this is still marked today in black and white lettering on the underside of the archway in Horse Guards.

In 1514, one of Henry VIII's most subtle courtiers, Thomas Wolsey, was rewarded for his services and sycophancy to the Crown by being made Archbishop of York. King Street, when Wolsey arrived, was a bustling and busy thoroughfare, with tenements, brewhouses and shops – there was a clockmaker and a book shop. Painstaking research by historians Gervase Rosser and Simon Thurley has enabled us to repopulate the street with the characters that were living there in Wolsey's time.[6] A London developer called John Millyng had built seven cottages and a barn on Steynour's Croft by 1490, producing rents of £8 a year (£3,917 a year at 2007 prices, but about the same as the annual income of a builder). Dr Richard Duck, Wolsey's treasurer and dean of his chapel at York Place, lived in a large house on Steynour's Croft. Along the street, there were pub signs everywhere, to help identify places for the illiterate. Next to Dr Duck's house, walking towards Westminster, was the sign of the Bell, which was owned by Westminster Abbey. The Bell and its tenements were leased to the Russells, who were carpenters and craftsmen, and earned their living from the Abbey and the King's Royal Palace at Westminster. Richard Russell had two sons, one a carpenter and the other, William, a chandler, who had a workshop near King Street where he made candles, a staple commodity for the Abbey, Wolsey's mansion and the Westminster village. William Russell had also become a landlord, subletting the nine cottages next to the Bell for a yearly profit of £6 15s. Next door to the Bell was Rose Yard, occupied by a Mr Tull, and tenements in Rose Alley where the Cabinet Office now stands were occupied by Messrs Wyatt, Dixon and Lytton. Across the street at this point – now obliterated by the Ministry of Defence main building in Whitehall – a lane ran down to a wharf by the river. It was known as Endive Lane, and the monks of Westminster collected £6 a year (£2,938 at 2007 prices) there from eleven cottages that had been built as part of a charitable endowment from the Abbey. Along with other properties, they were sublet for around £25 a year (£12,243 at 2007 prices) to small businesses, turning Endive Lane into a thriving community of workshops: there was a butcher, a baker, a pin maker, a spurrier (spur maker), a cobbler, a tiler, porters from the wharf, watermen – who earned their living like today's London cabbies – and Wolsey's laundry that discharged its dirty water into the river.

Beyond Endive Lane was Lamb Alley, an ancient right of way to the river, roughly on the line of the current Richmond Terrace, where ministerial cars for the Department of Health are parked today. At the head of the Alley, which ran down to a quay, was the Lamb brewhouse, which was leased to leading pillar of the community John Pomfrett, a local churchwarden. Next door, the Red Lion brewhouse – near the site, though not in the same building, as the current Red Lion on Whitehall – was leased by John Henbury. Henbury and Pomfrett became embroiled in a violent dispute about access to the quay at the end of Lamb Alley. Pomfrett leased the Alley from Henbury, on condition that he erected a gate at its entrance and paid the fees he collected from tolls to Henbury. But Pomfrett kept the money and ordered his men to attack Henbury's men if they argued. Their row was due to be settled in court but the dispute was overtaken by a greater crisis that enveloped them both in 1529, when Henry VIII stripped Wolsey – by now a Cardinal – of his high office as Lord Chancellor of England, and appropriated all Wolsey's property, even though it was owned by the Church. Henry and his future queen, Anne Boleyn, set about buying up all the land surrounding Wolsey's mansion to turn it into the greatest royal palace in Europe, covering twenty-three acres. The King acquired St James's Field, as far as St James's Hospital (now St James's Palace) for hunting and the whole of the waterfront encompassing Wolsey's York Place from Charing Cross to Lamb Alley. It included Scotland Yard to the north and to the south Endive Lane and a watercourse known as Clowson Stream that emptied into the Thames roughly where the east wall of the MoD main building is today. The properties on the west side of King Street including the Bell, which was owned by Westminster Abbey, the Rose owned by the Assumption Guild, the Axe, and the houses of the people who served Wolsey, were all swallowed up in the purchase. Pomfrett, Henbury, Dr Duck and their neighbours the Russells were swept aside, and would have been swept from history but for the fact that their names were preserved in the account books of the King's exchequer, which had to pay them compensation for his land grab. Their story was published in the *The London Topographical Record* (vol. XXVI, London Topographical Society, 1990). John Henbury, brewer of the Red Lion, was paid £168 (£64,394 at 2007 prices). William Russell, yeoman and waxchandler of the Bell, received £128 (£49,062). John Russell, carpenter, tenant of the Bell, received £33 6s 8d (£12,777). John Bennett, listed as a 'citizen and grocer of London', who inherited from John Pomfrett received £68 13s 4d (£26,336). The papers for the compulsory purchase of the land owned by Dr Duck were listed as missing, though it is known his house and its grounds became the wood yard, where the Russells may have continued to work. It is not known what happened to these people, as the community was displaced.

There are plenty of theories about why the palace that Henry built on the site of Wolsey's mansion became known as Whitehall but nobody is sure. An Act of Parliament of 1535 gave legal approval to Henry's seizure of the medieval village around York Place and extended the special status and privileges of the old palace at Westminster – made uninhabitable by a fire – to Henry's new palace in Whitehall, but the legislation referred to the new complex as the Palace of Westminster. It may have become known as White Hall because Wolsey's great hall, which dominated the skyline for centuries later, was built of white ashlar stone. However, Mr Thurley, the outstanding expert on the Tudor Palace of Whitehall, has established from the results of archeological excavations on the site in 1939 that the gable end of the hall was decorated in a black and white chequerboard design – a favourite motif of Wolsey's harking back to his boyhood in Ipswich – which scientific analysis showed was achieved by using black 'paint' made with shavings and dust from a smithy. Mr Thurley told me: 'The term White Hall is interesting as it often refers to a building of stature and importance. It may have something to do with the colour but equally it might be a generic term conferring status. I don't think the hall itself ever looked particularly white. The gable end was black and white, certainly from smithy dust.'[7]

Shakespeare, by the time he came to pen his play about the life and wives of Henry VIII half a century later, clearly saw the change of name from York Place to Whitehall as a deliberate act of political rebranding, to wipe out the memory of Wolsey and assert the authority of the King. As a political observer, I tend to agree with Shakespeare. It was like Tony Blair and his 'courtier' Peter Mandelson rebranding *New* Labour to distinguish it from its past.

Edward I's memorial to his Queen remained standing at Charing Cross until 1643, the year after civil war broke out in England, when the octagonal cross with eight statues of Eleanor was thrown down and destroyed by Parliament's forces as a symbol of monarchy along with most of the other eleven Eleanor crosses. Three have miraculously survived at Hardingstone and Geddington, both in Northamptonshire, and at Waltham Cross, Hertfordshire. Charing Cross – then a small cobbled area in front of the King's mews – was a popular site for punishment with stocks for public pillorying. After the Restoration, the spot where Eleanor's Cross had stood was chosen for the execution of some of those who had signed the death warrant for the King. In 1676, the monarchists defiantly erected a lively equestrian statue of Charles I where the regicides had been hung, drawn and quartered in agony. The statue had been commissioned during his lifetime in 1633 from a Huguenot, Le Sueur, and hidden throughout the Civil War. Today, Charles still sits jauntily on his horse on the same spot. It is now on a little road island, surrounded by a sea of traffic, looking down to the scene of his own execution, outside the Banqueting House.

It was not the end of the story of the Eleanor crosses, however. In 1862, a Victorian Gothic version of the Eleanor Cross was made by Edward Barry (son of Sir Charles Barry, architect of the Houses of Parliament) as part of the surge in interest in medieval design.

It was erected outside the new steam railway station at Charing Cross on the Strand, where it stands today ignored by commuters rushing to their offices in Whitehall.

# 1

## THE CARDINAL'S COURT

'O wavering and new fangled multitude! Is it not a wonder
to consider the inconstant mutability of this uncertain world!'
George Cavendish, *A Life of Wolsey*

When Cardinal Thomas Wolsey, Lord Chancellor of England,
stepped onto the landing stage by the Thames at York Place for the
last time, he could hardly believe his eyes. The river was full of
small craft loaded with spectators. There were hundreds of small
boats of all kinds sailing up and down the Thames – his gentleman-
usher, Cavendish, called it 'waffeting' – outside his palatial residence
near Westminster, keeping pace with the flow of the river to witness
his departure. There was something of a carnival atmosphere among
the boaters who had flocked to see Wolsey step from the jetty of
his great house to his private barge, and for a fleeting second he
must have imagined they had turned out in a show of support. Great
figures are always the last to know what the public really think of

them and, surrounded by courtiers, Wolsey was as isolated as anyone in high office from the views of the ordinary people in the city. But, as the well-fed figure in the crimson robes of a cardinal went down the stairs, and stepped gingerly into his gilded barge, it became clear the crowds were not there to cheer him, but to jeer him. They had turned out in their small flotilla of boats because they believed the Cardinal was going to meet his fate at the sharp end of an executioner's axe on Tower Green. Cavendish, his faithful servant, later described the spectacle in his account of Wolsey's life, one of the first great political biographies of England:

> At the taking of his barge, there were no less than a thousand boats full of men and women of the City of London, waffeting up and down the Thames, expecting my lord's departing supposing that he should have gone directly from thence to the Tower. Thereat they rejoiced . . .

The crowds were soon disappointed. For when his bargemen pushed off from Whitehall Stairs at York Place, instead of gliding downriver to the Tower and his execution, the barge turned right across the fording place at Westminster, beyond the Abbey and the old royal palace, and headed upriver to Esher, where Wolsey had another of his many mansions. Henry VIII, who had once regarded Wolsey as a mentor, had stripped the Lord Chancellor of his seals of office, seized his ecclesiastical property including York Place and Hampton Court (even though they belonged to the Church) and would confiscate his personal fortune, but he had allowed Wolsey to keep his head, for now.

Wolsey – pronounced *Wulcy* – had used his high office in the church to amass personal wealth that would amount to the equivalent of £11 billion today.[1] It was a staggering fortune, which would have eclipsed even the personal fortune of the Russian oligarch, Roman

Abramovich, the owner of Chelsea FC. Such incomparable wealth had made him many enemies, and an object of envy, even of the King. The crowds in their flotilla of small boats wanted to see him brought to his knees.

Cavendish, writing when a Catholic Queen – Mary, Henry's daughter by Katherine of Aragon – was on the throne and it was safe to do so, bewailed the fickleness of public opinion:

> O wavering and new fangled multitude! Is it not a wonder to consider the inconstant mutability of this uncertain world! The common people always desire alterations and novelties of things, simply for the strangeness of the case; which afterwards gives them small profit and commodity ... for the inclination and natural disposition of Englishmen is, and has always been, to desire alteration of officers who have been thoroughly fed with sufficient riches and possessions by long holding of their offices. And they being put out, then comes another hungry and lean officer in his place, that bites nearer the bone than the old. So people be ever pillaged and despoiled by hungry dogs, through their own desire for change and new officers.[2]

The courtier's words echo down over four centuries to Margaret Thatcher's tearful farewell from Downing Street. It was the Conservative, and later Ulster Unionist, MP Enoch Powell who said that 'all political careers end in failure', now often misquoted as 'tears'. It was also Powell who told the woman the Russians had called the 'Iron Lady' that she would prove of what metal she was made when she faced the Falklands War in 1982. The Conservative Prime Minister whom Powell had admired proved the accuracy of his maxim after she was stabbed in the back by her own Cabinet in 1990. 'It was treachery,' she later said. 'Treachery with a smile on its face.' Her armour-plated Daimler swept out of the gates of

Downing Street for the last time on 28 November 1990, only a few hundred yards from where Wolsey's barge carried the Cardinal away to his fate. Like Wolsey, she was bemused at being brought down and as she left the Iron Lady was caught in the flashlight of a newsman's camera, red-eyed, blinking back the tears at the unfairness of life. But when Wolsey made his final exit from Whitehall, he feared his life was in peril.

In Wolsey's time, the river was wider and the tidal flow far less than the current six knots, making it easier to navigate for small boats using mainly oarsmen for power. The west bank of the river was up to 400 feet further west than the Victoria Embankment, and the remains of Wolsey's river wall lie under the east wall of the Ministry of Defence main building in Whitehall. The river in Wolsey's day would have spread across the Victoria Embankment and the dappled lawns of Whitehall gardens, and lapped up to the east wall of the MoD, submerging the statues of the moustachioed Lord Trenchard who conceived the RAF, Lord Portal who became Chief of the Air Staff in 1941, permanently looking to the skies for enemy bombers, and the golden-winged figure celebrating the Fleet Air Arm. Here, the sucking mud of the river would be exposed at low tide, near the short covered jetty where Wolsey's barge would have docked. The Thames was the main artery of Tudor London, which, like Venice, had been built to face the river. Each of the great houses along the river bank had its own river entrance or water-gate and covered jetty with stairs to the Thames where private barges could safely tie up to discharge or collect their passengers. At York Place, there was an ancient public right of way through the great main gate east to a public jetty, later known as Whitehall Stairs, which would have stretched out into the river roughly where the ornamental shrubbery grows by the statue of William Tyndale in Victoria Embankment Gardens on the east side of Whitehall Court.

The public right of way had existed for so long that, like King

Street, Henry VIII felt he could not abolish it when he took over the land for his Palace of White Hall. If you were to stand today on the small traffic island near the Banqueting House at the junction of Horse Guards Avenue and Whitehall and look towards the Thames, you would be standing in the centre of Henry's enlarged gateway looking along the public pathway that passed through the main courtyard of the Palace, and some service yards to a public wharf and the Whitehall Stairs. The wharf was also used as a service entrance to the royal palace for the bulk delivery of cargo including wood and coal in small lighters, or cargo vessels. The private barges which landed at Henry's private river gateway, known as the Privy Bridge, to the south of Whitehall Stairs were long rowing boats, with ornate glazed cabins at the back for their rich occupants – Prince Frederick's gilded royal barge of 1732 survives in the National Maritime Museum at Greenwich – and were usually pulled by up to eight oarsmen in the livery of their owners. Servants wore the livery of their masters and most of Wolsey's servants wore rich scarlet to match the Cardinal's robes.

When he first took possession of York Place one hot summer's day in August 1514 as Archbishop of York, it was already handsome, having been extended fifty years earlier by George Neville, brother of the 'Kingmaker' Richard, Earl of Warwick. Neville was made Lord Chancellor and Archbishop of York under Yorkist rule before the Wars of the Roses that brought the Tudors to power, and between 1465 and 1476 Neville doubled the size of York Place. When Wolsey arrived, it was almost identical to the Archbishop of Canterbury's London residence, Lambeth Palace, half a mile upstream on the south side of the river, with a gatehouse leading to a hall, a chapel with a cloister, a lesser hall for the archbishop's public duties, and a suite of more private rooms overlooking gardens.

But York Place was not grand enough for Wolsey. He hurriedly set about an ambitious expansion, made more pressing by the celebrations to accompany the receipt of his cardinal's hat in 1516. The ageing Archbishop of Canterbury, William Warham, was troubled that the ambitious cleric at York Place was intent on replacing him, and could use his influence on the King to bring that about. But Wolsey, like a power-hungry politician, was not interested in Warham's title. He saw the way to absolute power over the Roman Catholic Church in England was to become the personal representative of the Pope in Britain, a position he secured within two years of arriving at York Place. The hat was brought by papal messenger to Britain, but Wolsey – ever the showman – ensured that it was brought to York Place with full ceremonial honours worthy of a coronation.

In a burst of building, he ordered York Place to be improved with a new great chamber, his privy chamber was updated with a fashionable bay window, and he improved the chapel which stood in the line of Horse Guards Avenue at the junction with Whitehall Court. In 1519 Wolsey began to acquire more land, buying up the leases on the tenements belonging to the Abbey to the south of York Place, King Street to the west, and to the north, the land called 'Scotland' that had traditionally been reserved for Scottish Kings summoned to the royal palace at Westminster. Having removed some of the houses and unsightly tenements that backed on to his property to the south of York Place, Wolsey created a pleasant orchard as far as Endive Lane. The two principal structures remained Neville's great hall and the thirteenth-century chapel, but the star attraction of Wolsey's ecclesiastical palace was an elegant long gallery by the river, where Wolsey could stroll with his courtiers, admire the tapestries, and do his plotting. Wolsey's gallery was 250 feet long and 23 feet wide and, according to Simon Thurley, was the 'ultimate sixteenth-century status symbol'.[3] Wolsey's builders had to build over the river, offering spectacular views of the Thames through mullioned and leaded lights on one side and the inner courtyard gardens on the other. Mario Savorgnano, the Venetian Ambassador, reported there were 'windows on each side, looking on gardens and rivers . . . the ceiling being marvellously wrought in stone with gold and the wainscot of carved wood representing a thousand beautiful figures'.

Halfway along Wolsey's gallery was a small chamber with a bay window known as the Gilt Chamber, probably for its rich decoration. At the gallery's northern end, a large chamber with a bay window over the river was used as his council chamber. He finished the work on York Place in 1528 by rebuilding the hall with a new, larger chamber built of brick and rendered with white lime plaster, decorated with a chequerboard pattern. Wolsey also resited the chapel, which had faced east over the river. The new chapel ran north to south, alongside his new hall.

Wolsey was at the zenith of his powers. His ecclesiastical palaces at Whitehall and Hampton Court eclipsed those of Henry VIII, spurring the court laureate, John Skelton (1460–1529) to pen these dangerously mocking lines.

> Why come ye nat to court?
> To whyche court?
> To the kynges court?
> Or to Hampton Court?
> The kynges court
> Shulde have the excellence;
> But Hampton Court
> Hath the pre-emynence!
> And York's Place,
> With 'My lordes grace',
> To whose magnifycence,
> Is all the confluence,
> Suits and supplycacyouns,
> Embassades of all nacyons.

From 1517 until 1529, Wolsey *was* the Government of England. As the Cardinal of England and the Lord Chancellor, he was both the Church and the Law and had 'supplications' – appeals for legal redress – with petitions to resolve personal grievances presented to him at York Place. Sebastian Giustiniani, another Venetian ambassador, in a secret report to his government on Wolsey reported that the 'Cardinal of York' was 'the beginning, the middle and the end' of power behind the throne in England.

Each day of the legal term, the gates were thrown open for a regal procession as the Lord Chancellor and his servants dressed in the Cardinal's crimson colours travelled to the Star Chamber at Westminster to preside over the highest court in the land, dispensing justice and protecting the monarch from libel. The Star Chamber – named after the ceiling in the Westminster chamber, which was decorated with stars – had the flexibility to impose penalties on those who had not broken laws but had offended society or the King, and it became a byword for arbitrary punishment.

Wolsey earned his patronage from Henry VIII with a combination of astute statesmanship, powers of persuasion (he was noted for his 'filed tongue and ornate eloquence' by his peers on his irresistible climb to power), a mastery of palace politics (he broke the power of the younger courtiers, cronies of the King known as the 'minions', when they threatened his influence over Henry), and a subtle understanding of Henry, the man. He was a restraining hand on the young King Henry when to have allowed him to rush into wars against France or Spain would have proved ruinous. The popular view of Henry as a bloated tyrant banqueting on chicken legs as portrayed in Hollywood movies by Charles Laughton and Keith Michell ignores the fact that he was once a young and very lusty monarch dazzled by the heroic tales of chivalry and Arthur and his Knights of the Round Table. The portrayal of the young Henry is probably nearer to the picture presented by

Jonathan Rhys Meyers in the 2007 television series *The Tudors*. He was the archetypal playboy king, who lusted for wars, glory and women. He also had a passion for sports such as tennis and the tilt, and he was powerfully built, being more than six feet tall. As a boy Henry liked to mix with professional jousters. Historian David Starkey in his book on the politics of Henry's court compares him to an autograph hunter hanging around his heroes at a Premier League football club.[4]

Wolsey helped Henry pull off propaganda coups: a skirmish during an English siege in France in 1513 – where a force of French horsemen turned on their heels and fled showing their spurs – was turned into a great English victory as the Battle of the Spurs. But Henry VIII wanted to eclipse the glory of Henry V at Agincourt, and his astute Lord Chancellor rightly saw that there were limitations to even his skill as a spin doctor. Henry was facing the might of France under Francis I and Spain ruled by Charles V, the Holy Roman Emperor, who was also the nephew of Henry's Queen, Katherine of Aragon. Wolsey persuaded the King that England may not be able to win outright military victories on the field of battle, but she could hit above her weight with diplomacy. In 1520, Wolsey engineered his most famous diplomatic coup as the architect of an Anglo-French summit that became known as the Field of the Cloth of Gold after the vast glittering tented city that was created to house around 12,000 people attending the event, from 7 June to 24 June, outside Calais, then an English possession. There were gold-coloured jousting pavilions, and a canvas and glass palace with gold fountains that poured claret for the king's followers to sup at will. Wolsey accompanied Henry and his Queen at the head of an impressive 6,000-strong army of knights, ladies, courtiers and servants for the summit with Francis I, who was accompanied by an equal number of French attendants. Francis, like Henry, was in his twenties, tall, strong and athletic, and had a reputation for his prowess at kingly sports. The entertainments included jousting and a Breton-style wrestling match (similar to Cumberland wrestling). Henry and Francis grappled with each other at wrestling and Henry was embarrassingly thrown by the French king.

As with modern-day summits, the promises of peace and unity lasted no longer than the canvas palace in which they were signed. Wolsey quickly arranged for Henry to sign an alliance with Katherine's nephew, Charles V, who declared war on France later that year. However, Wolsey had succeeded in making his youthful monarch (his 29th birthday was four days after the summit) appear to the rest of Europe as a Renaissance king who, like Francis I, could choose peace rather than war. He gave England a seat at the European diplomatic table when its financial resources and its forces were too small to compete with the two superpowers of the age.

At home, Wolsey used his consummate skills as a showman to entertain Henry, who was living in relative discomfort, having been forced by a fire in Westminster Palace in 1512 to decamp with his Queen and their court across the river to the medieval Lambeth Palace. The lusty young Henry frequently left his ageing queen at Lambeth and came calling with his retinue of male friends on Wolsey's mansion over the river for banquets with the ladies of the court at the Cardinal's expense.

Wolsey's confident world exploded in 1527, when Henry's court was convulsed by his sudden, all-consuming passion for one of the Queen's ladies-in-waiting, a woman who was to become Wolsey's nemesis – Anne Boleyn.

At New Year 1527, the year in which the 'Great Matter', as it was to become known, would soon break upon the court, Henry crossed the Thames in his royal barge from Lambeth with a group of his favourite courtiers in search of entertainment at Wolsey's palace. They were dressed outlandishly in masks and ornate silken shepherd's smocks to gatecrash a New Year's banquet being thrown by Wolsey in his great hall.

The scene was described by Cavendish, Wolsey's faithful retainer. The Cardinal was relaxing in a throne, bearing the coat of arms of the Archbishop of York, in his Presence Chamber, looking down contentedly on the trestle tables where lords and ladies of Henry's court were enjoying a lavish banquet in the flickering candlelight. Then a noise like thunder outside stopped the babble of conversation and Wolsey ordered two of the most senior courtiers, Lord Sandys, the Lord Chamberlain to the King, and Sir Henry Guildford, the King's Comptroller of the Royal Household, to go and discover the cause of the noise. For Wolsey, the sound of cannon being fired was a carefully prearranged signal for the start of an elaborate piece of play-acting on his guests. Looking through a window of Wolsey's palace on to the Thames, the courtiers, who also must have been in on the subterfuge, saw a score of visitors disembarking from a barge at the Cardinal's Privy Stairs by the river. They were lit by torchbearers and all were wearing coloured masks of gold or silver. The two courtiers returned to the banqueting hall and loudly informed Wolsey that there was a party of visitors arriving and they appeared to be foreign princes who could only speak French. Wolsey told them to bring the visitors in where they could join 'all these noble personages sitting merrily at our banquet'.

The strangers made a courtly entrance to the banquet two by two. Cavendish said the visitors were

> . . . all in garments like shepherds made of fine cloth of gold and fine crimson satin paned and caps of the same, with visors of good proportion, their hairs and beards either of fine gold wire or else of silver and some being black silk; having 16 torchbearers, besides their drums and other persons attending upon them with visors, and clothed all in satin of the same colours.

This exotic party of princely gatecrashers was accompanied 'with such a number of drums and fifes as I have seldom seen together at one time in any masque', Cavendish added. The masked intruders went to Wolsey's throne and saluted him 'very reverently'. The Lord Chamberlain acted as their French interpreter. He said the visitors, hearing the 'triumphant banquet' and the assembly of 'such a number of excellent fair dames, could do no less, presuming on your good grace, but to repair hither to view as well their incomparable beauty, as to accompany them at mumchance (a game of dice) and then afterwards to dance with them, and so to have of them acquaintance'.

Then the masquers, said Cavendish

... went first and saluted to all the ladies as they sat, then returned to the worthiest and there opened a cup full of gold with crowns and other pieces of coin, and set divers pieces to cast at. Thus in this manner they diced with all the ladies and gentlewomen, and to some they lost, and from some they won. And this done, they returned to the Cardinal, and with great reverence, pouring down all the crowns in the cup, which were about two hundred crowns. 'At all!' quoth the Cardinal, and so cast the dice, and won them all at a cast: whereat was great joy made.

It is not surprising that the Cardinal, in spite of his wealth, showed 'great joy' at his good fortune. The crowns he won with a single throw of the dice would now be worth about £60,000.

The Lord Chamberlain told the Cardinal that there was one among them who was a 'noble personage' who would disclose himself, if Wolsey could pick him out. The game, Wolsey knew well, was to pick out the King.

The Cardinal arose from his great chair and studied the 'foreigners' with great care. He eyed one man, who was of large build, over six feet tall, with a fine black beard. Wolsey chose him with a great flourish, and offered him his great chair. But the Cardinal had picked Sir Edward Neville, one of the King's courtiers, who Cavendish said was

> ... a comely knight of a goodly personage, that much more resembled the King's person in that mask than any other.
>
> The King, hearing and perceiving the Cardinal so deceived in his estimation and choice, could not forbear laughing, but plucked down his visor and Master Neville's also and dashed out with such a pleasant countenance and cheer that all noble estates there assembled, seeing the King to be there amongst them, rejoiced very much.

Shakespeare, who knew a good story when he read it, incorporated Cavendish's account half a century later when he came to write *King Henry the Eighth*. With poetic licence, Shakespeare has Anne Boleyn make her courtly debut in Act One at Wolsey's banquet. In fact, Anne had made her debut at the court of Henry VIII five years earlier, but it is true to say this was the year in which she captivated Henry:

**Wolsey:** Say Lord Chamberlain,
     They have done my poor house grace, for which I pay 'em
     A thousand thanks and pray 'em take their pleasures.
    *(They choose ladies. The King chooses Anne Bullen).*
**King:** The fairest hand I ever touch'd! O beauty,
     Till now I never knew thee!
    *(Music. Dance)*

After the revellers are told in Shakespeare's play that the King is in their midst, concealed by a mask, Wolsey correctly picks out Henry, who then removes his mask and conspiratorially asks the Lord Chamberlain about the girl.

**King:** My Lord Chamberlain,
> Prithee come hither: what fair lady's that?

**Chamberlain:** An't please your Grace, Sir Thomas Bullen's
> daughter – The Viscount Rochford – one of her
> Highness' women.

**King:** By heaven, she is a dainty one.
> Sweet heart,
> I were unmannerly to take you out
> And not to kiss you . . .

Henry and Anne then exit to the sound of trumpets, but the groundlings at the Globe knew how the tragedy would unfold. It was safe for Shakespeare to portray Anne as the prize being pursued by the King, as the playwright was writing when her daughter, Elizabeth I, was on the throne. Within a few months of Wolsey's New Year banquet in 1527, the real drama – the 'Great Matter' of the King's divorce from Katherine to marry Anne Boleyn – exploded onto the court, and was to test Wolsey's powers to destruction.

Anne had returned to England from France and made her debut at court in an elaborate masque hosted by Wolsey at York Place in 1522 to celebrate the diplomatic betrothal of the infant Princess Mary, aged six, to Katherine's 22-year-old nephew Charles V, then the most powerful figure in Europe. Katherine, then thirty-six, was in good spirits for the celebrations for her nephew's wedding. Charles had yet to arrive in England but the festivities were laid on for his ambassadors around Shrove Tuesday, 4 March 1522, and lasted several days. As usual they started with a tournament in the tiltyard to give the King the opportunity to show off his horsemanship. The court was abuzz with speculation after Henry had ridden a horse in the tilts with a silver tabard or coat, known as a comparison, bearing the mysterious courtly message, 'She has stolen my heart'. The court gossips eagerly wanted to know: who?

Katherine, like the rest of the court, must have been well aware that Harry had fathered a son by his mistress, Elizabeth Blount. But at the York Place festivities, she may have noticed a cooling in his affections for Mistress Blount.

It was to be Elizabeth's last public appearance with Henry, for the King's eye had already fallen on someone else, the prettier of the two 'Bullen' sisters, Mary.

The Boleyns were the daughters of one of Henry's most experienced courtiers, Sir Thomas Boleyn, and his wife, Lady Elizabeth Howard, a member of the powerful Howard dynasty and daughter of the Duke of Norfolk. The two sisters were ladies-in-waiting to the long-suffering Katherine. The two Boleyn daughters were cast as two of the damsels in distress in a romantic pageant entitled *Chateau Vert* in Wolsey's great hall, which had been transformed by his master of the revels and the carpenters into a wooden castle, painted green. It had three towers, and on each of them flew a banner dedicated to the Arthurian ideal of courtly love: a broken heart, a heart cupped in a maiden's hand, and a heart being turned by a lady's hand.

The chronicler Edward Hall described the scene:

The castle was occupied by ladies with strange names: Beauty, Honour, Perseverance, Kindness, Constancy, Bounty, Mercy and Pity. All eight ladies wore Milan-point lace gowns made of white satin and each had her name embroidered in gold on her headgear and Milan bonnets of gold encrusted with jewels. Underneath the fortress were more ladies whose names were Danger, Disdain, Jealousy, Unkindness, Scorn, Sharp Tongue and Strangeness, dressed like Indian women. Then eight lords entered wearing cloth of gold hats and great cloaks made of blue satin. They were named Love,

Nobleness, Youth, Devotion, Loyalty, Pleasure, Gentleness and Liberty. This group, one member of which was the King himself, was led in by the man dressed in crimson satin with burning flames of gold. His name was Ardent Desire and the ladies were so moved by his appearance that they might have given up the castle, but Scorn and Disdain said they would hold the fort . . .

The lords ran to the castle at which point there was a great sound of gunfire, and the ladies defended it with rose water and comfits.

The lords replied with dates, oranges and other pleasurable fruits, and eventually the castle was taken. Lady Scorn and her companions fled. Then the lords took the ladies by the hands and led them out as prisoners, bringing them down to floor level and dancing with them, which pleased the foreign guests immensely. When they had danced their fill, everyone unmasked themselves. After this, there was an extravagant banquet.

Mary Boleyn played Kindness and Anne played Perseverance, which was to prove prophetic. Afterwards, Henry led the dancing with twenty-four masked courtiers. They included his jousting partner and brother-in-law, Charles Brandon, first Duke of Suffolk. They had fallen out when Brandon married the King's sister Mary without his consent, but were now reconciled.

Henry later conquered Mary Boleyn's defences, but having had sex with her, began to pursue her sister. Anne may have caught Henry's eye, but she must have been blissfully unaware of it, because the following year she fell in love with Lord Henry Percy, an aide to Wolsey, and the son of the Earl of Northumberland. Percy was in the habit of frequenting the Queen's chamber, and chatting up her maids-in-waiting, who included Anne, and they foolishly told friends they were engaged to be married. Henry ordered Wolsey discreetly to investigate the rumours of a relationship between Anne and Percy, and to break it off. It was not the first time the Cardinal had been ordered to act as Henry's pimp. Wolsey had already arranged for Elizabeth Blount to be married off to Gilbert Tailboys, the wealthy young heir to estates in Lincolnshire and Somerset, when the King dropped her for Mary Boleyn. Cavendish gave an eyewitness account of how Percy was summoned to York Place by Wolsey.

Wolsey found young Percy surprisingly deaf to his advice to break off his engagement to Anne Boleyn and told the youth:

> I marvel not a little at thy peevish folly, that thou wouldst tangle and engage thyself with a foolish girl yonder in the court, I mean Anne Boleyn. Dost though not consider the estate that God hath called thee unto in this world? For after the death of thy noble father, thou art most like to inherit and possess one of the most worthiest earldoms of this realm. Therefore, it would have been most meet and convenient for thee to have sued for the consent of thy father in that behalf and also to have the made the King's highness aware thereof; requiring then his princely favour . . .

When the appeal to Percy's sense of social standing failed, Wolsey lied, saying the King had promised Anne to someone else. Percy, in tears, apologized, but refused to give her up, saying that, as Anne had noble parents, he thought the match was a good one, and naively pleaded with Wolsey to help him achieve it, saying his conscience could not let him break it off now because they had told so many of their friends.

Exasperated, Wolsey warned the boy he would be disinherited by his father, and summoned the Earl to York Place for a brisk discussion, which took place in Wolsey's long gallery, overlooking the Thames. The Earl then sat down on a bench normally used by waiters at the end of the gallery and called his son to him. He bluntly ordered Percy to do his duty, and forget Anne. The warning was stark enough to destroy any rebellious thoughts in Percy, who was quickly married off to one of the Earl of Shrewsbury's daughters.

In Whitehall there is a time-honoured saying about revenge: 'Don't get mad, get even'. Cavendish claimed that, from that moment on, Anne was determined to get even with Wolsey: 'Mistress Anne Boleyn was greatly offended with this, saying that if it lay ever in her power she would work the Cardinal as much displeasure as he had done her.'

If true, it also revealed the ruthless side of Anne. She was taking on the most powerful man in England below the King. As Lord Chancellor, Wolsey was the head of the English courts, and, as cardinal, he was the Pope's representative in England. Politically, he was also one of the most astute figures in Henry's court, but he proved no match for Anne.

Wolsey had also made enemies during his rise to power, and they resented the vast riches he had amassed from the church. Wolsey enjoyed the trappings of state, but he also understood the importance of pomp. His regal procession to Westminster to preside over civil and criminal appeals in the Court of Chancery and the Star Chamber was intended as a show of power – the common people expected it, and were in awe of it. But he was no fool. He rode to Westminster seated on a humble mule as a mark of his piety. However, being Wolsey, there was nothing poor about his appearance. The mule was covered in a coat of scarlet, and the saddle had gilt stirrups.

> After mass, he would return into his private chamber again, and being advised of the noblemen and gentlemen and other persons attending in his chambers outside, he would issue out into them, apparelled all in red, in the habit of a cardinal – either of fine scarlet or else of crimson satin, taffeta, damask or caffa [a rich silk cloth], the best that could be got for money.
>
> And upon his head a round pillion, with a neck of black velvet

set to the same in the inner side; he had also a tippet of fine sables about his neck. He held in his hand a very fair orange, whereof the meat or substance within was taken out and filled up again with the part of a sponge, wherein was vinegar and other confections against the pestilent airs. This he most commonly smelt unto, when passing among the press or else when he was pestered with many suitors.

There was also borne before him, first the great seal of England, and then his cardinal's hat, by a nobleman or some worthy gentleman, right solemnly, bareheaded. And as soon as he entered into his presence-chamber, he found there – attending his coming to await upon him to Westminster Hall – noblemen and other worthy gentlemen of his own household. Thus he passed forth with two great crosses of silver borne before him; with also two great pillars of silver and his sergeant-at-arms with a great mace of silver gilt. Then his gentlemen-ushers [including Cavendish] cried, and said: 'On, my lords and masters! Make way for my Lord's Grace!' Then he was mounted, with his cross bearers and pillar bearers also upon great horses trapped with red scarlet, then marched he forward with his train and appurtenances having about him four footmen with gilt pole-axes in their hands. And thus he went until he came to Westminster Hall door.

To run the mansion, Wolsey employed a small army of nobles, servants and scribblers at York Place, which Cavendish estimated amounted to at least 500 people. Each day three tables were laid out in his chamber for Wolsey's three principal officers – a steward, who was always a doctor or a priest; a treasurer, a knight; and the comptroller, an esquire – who each carried a white wand as a mark of their office. The official titles and positions in the Royal Household are still carried today by government whips in the Commons and Lords – the deputy chief whip is also the Treasurer of Her Majesty's

Household; other whips include Comptroller of HM Household; and the Chief Whip in the Lords is the Captain of the Honourable Corps of Gentlemen-at-Arms while the Deputy Chief Whip in the Lords is the Captain of the Queen's Bodyguard of the Yeomen of the Guard, who wear tunics similar to 'Beefeaters' at the Tower for official ceremonies, and inspect the cellars of Parliament on the eve of every state opening to check for another Gunpowder Plot. The whips still carry the white wands of office when they are on royal duties, to the amusement of left-wing Labour MPs such as Dennis Skinner, who loudly offered to chalk the 'snooker cue' of one whip when he marched into the Commons chamber. A whip still pens a report by hand to the monarch at the end of each day on the proceedings in Parliament, and when the Queen carries out the state opening of Parliament, a whip is held as a 'hostage' at Buckingham Palace until her safe return from Westminster.

Wolsey's 'army' of servants had uniforms of crimson red to match his status as a cardinal, and several wore gold chains of office, including his head cook. His staff included a cofferer, who looked after the treasure in the wooden coffers in his hall, three marshals, two yeomen ushers, two grooms and an almoner who handed out alms – the Tudor equivalent of welfare benefits – to the community. There was a village of servants running the hall kitchen, his private kitchen, pantry, larders, scalding house, and stables where he had a muleteer to look after his mule and sixteen grooms of his stable, each keeping four geldings, making a small cavalry of sixty-four horses. There were six servants in the ewery, for supplying water for washing; three in the chandlery, the store for the candles; two in the wafery, where cakes, biscuits and sacramental wafers were baked; a master and ten pages in the wardrobe of beds; a yeoman and two grooms in the bakehouse; one in the garner – the granary; and in the Cardinal's all-important wine cellar, he employed three yeomen, two grooms and two pages, beside a 'gentleman for the month'. At the gatehouse he had two tall yeomen and two grooms to act as porters, and a yeoman of his barge. In his chapel Wolsey employed a dean, a vice-dean, a repeater of the choir, a gospeller, a pisteller – a reader of the epistle – twelve singing priests, twelve choirboys, sixteen adult choristers and a children's nanny.

All these comforts were to be put at hazard by the question of the King's divorce. Henry ordered Wolsey, as the Pope's legate, to procure his divorce from Katherine. For two years from 1527 Wolsey expended all his political guile and diplomacy on seeking a papal annulment of the King's marriage. Quite why Henry was so besotted with Anne Boleyn was a mystery to most courtiers.

'Madame Anne is not one of the handsomest women in the world, she is of middling stature, swarthy complexion, long neck, wide mouth, bosom not much raised, and in fact has nothing but the English King's appetite, and her eyes, which are black and beautiful and take great effect,' one Venetian diplomat acidly reported home. Hans Holbein, the court painter, produced an unflattering miniature of Anne, recently authenticated by David Starkey, showing her with a hint of a double chin. She may have been no great beauty, but she was vivacious, self-assertive and loaded with that indefinable quality we know as sex appeal. Having returned with the airs of the French court, Anne was fluent in French and the height of fashion in Henry's court. She had been schooled in other courtly French arts including, it was claimed around the English court, lovemaking, like her older sister Mary, who was known by the Francis I as his 'English mare' on account of the number of times he had 'ridden' her. Above all, she was young, and capable of bearing Henry a male heir. There are still disputes about her age but, when the crisis hit the court, Anne was probably twenty-six, Henry thirty-six. Katherine was forty-one and beyond the normal age of childbearing in Tudor England. Anne benefited from the advice of her father Thomas, at fifty an astute courtier who had been a diplomat to Henry's father, and who had already seen his other daughter bedded by the King. Anne understood that Henry had no need for another bastard son by one of his mistresses. It was only by a legitimate son, born in a marriage recognized by Rome, that he could hand the crown to a future king. That was to be Anne's leverage on Henry to divorce the Queen.

The more she said 'No' to his attempts to bed her, the more passionately Henry pursued her. So great was his passion, he later accused Anne of 'bewitching' him. Wolsey said Henry never liked writing letters but now he frantically poured out steamy letters of desire for Anne. Seventeen of Henry's love letters, written in French, survive and some are surprisingly explicit: 'Wishing myself, especially an evening, in my sweetheart's arms, whose pretty dukkys [breasts] I trust shortly to kiss. Written with the hand of him that was, is, and shall be yours by his will HR.'

They are now in the Vatican library, where they were probably collected as evidence that his desire for a divorce was driven by his lust, rather than religious conscience about marrying Katherine, who had been his brother's wife.

Henry was persuaded by Anne that Wolsey was working against them and together they studied the scriptures, of which Henry was already something of a scholar, to find a way out of his marriage. Tutored by the humanist Thomas More before he fell in love with Anne, Henry had published an attack on the heretical theories of Martin Luther called *Defence of the Seven Sacraments*, for which the Pope had rewarded him with the title 'Defender of the Faith', which the monarch still holds today. Recruiting a previously obscure theologian at Cambridge, Thomas Cranmer, Henry and Anne seized on the biblical law of Leviticus, which appeared to condemn marriage between a man and his brother's wife: 'It is an unclean act . . . they shall be childless.' Before she married Henry, Katherine had been forced into a diplomatic marriage to his older brother, Arthur. She had married Henry after Arthur died. Convinced he was cursed by a judgement of God's law, Henry demanded Wolsey annul his marriage, and when he failed to deliver, in spite of having grown up treating Wolsey as a father figure, Henry cast him aside.

Wolsey had been born the son of a wealthy Ipswich butcher. He had proved a precocious scholar and went up to university at Cambridge at fifteen, making him a figure of interest at the university where he was known as the 'boy bachelor'. But after a brilliant start, he had languished as a tutor in the city until a little local difficulty – he was allegedly held in the stocks for drunkenness by a justice of the peace, Sir Amyas Poulet – compounded by criticism from his peers for his extravagance in the building of the Magdalene Tower forced Wolsey to find his fortune in a different direction, and he chose the Church. Wolsey later had his revenge on Poulet when he became the Treasurer of the Middle Temple in London. Wolsey ordered Poulet not to leave his lodgings in the Temple without permission for six years.

By 1529, all Wolsey's guile had failed him. An arch-pragmatist, Wolsey had played for time but Henry was enflamed with sexual desire for Anne and was persuaded by her that, instead of working for a solution with Rome, Wolsey, who had jointly convened an ecclesiastical court with Pope Clement's legate Cardinal Lorenzo Campeggio to hear the King's case for an annulment, was part of the problem. Henry and Anne travelled north with most of the court including the Boleyn faction to Grafton in Northamptonshire where the King went hunting with his bride-to-be. Anne's allies warned her that Henry had been seen speaking privately with Wolsey and, according to Cavendish, she berated Henry, saying, 'There is never such a nobleman within this realm that if he had done half so much as the Cardinal had done, he were well worthy to lose his head.'

Henry mockingly said, 'Why then, I perceive that you are not the Cardinal's friend.'

Anne angrily replied, 'Forsooth, Sir! I have no cause, nor any other that loves your Grace, if you consider well his doings.'[5]

The Boleyn faction were alarmed when Wolsey and Campeggio followed them to Grafton for one last private appeal for more time. Bets were laid by courtiers on whether Henry would see Wolsey after he arrived. Henry surprised the Boleyn family and their allies by agreeing to meet Wolsey for lengthy private talks at the country house where they were staying, and bade Wolsey and Campeggio a fond farewell in front of the court, but Campeggio was due to return to Rome and Wolsey knew privately the game was up. For once, his 'filed' tongue had failed to persuade the King, and Wolsey returned to York Place a broken man. He prepared for the Michaelmas legal term to begin as if it was 'business as usual' but there were rumours swirling around his court that the King's messengers, the Duke of Suffolk (Henry's best friend) and the Duke of Norfolk would be arriving soon at the gates of York Place. He went with his retinue to Westminster and sat for the last time in the Court of Chancery, then spent the next day at York Place waiting for the King's men. Suffolk and Norfolk duly arrived with a verbal demand for his great seal and for him to vacate York Place. He sent them away, questioning their authority, said Cavendish:

> 'Yes,' quoth he, 'that is not sufficient for me, without a further commandment of the King's pleasure. For the great seal of England was delivered me by the King's own person, to enjoy during my life, with the administration of the dignity and high office of chancellorship of England: for my surety whereof, I have the King's letters patent to show'.

Within twenty-four hours the King's men returned to York Place, with their orders in writing from Henry, and Wolsey knew it was over. He surrendered the great seal and, he believed, his life. He ordered his staff to assemble all his riches, the plate, the tapestries and the jewels, on tables in his palace, and went to the Privy Stairs where the barge was waiting to take him away for the last time.

As the oars gently pushed the barge beyond the ford at Westminster, Wolsey caught the last glimpse of his palace from the river, with the dying sun glinting on the windows, the turrets and the chimney pots. Landing at Putney, he still feared the worst when he saw a rider approaching. It was Sir Henry Norris, one of Henry's most trusted courtiers, who had ridden from the King at Windsor to tell Wolsey the King wished him to be 'of good cheer'. As a token, the King had sent him a gold ring set with a rich stone, which had been used between them before as a signal of trust. Wolsey was so relieved that he jumped off his mule and almost kissed the ground.

'He quickly alighted from his mule, all alone, as though he had been the youngest person amongst us, and straightway kneeled down in the dirt upon both his knees, holding up his hands for joy,' wrote Cavendish.

Henry, however, stripped Wolsey of his most prized possessions: Hampton Court, Esher, two other fine country houses (the More and Tittenhanger in Hertfordshire), his college at Oxford and even Wolsey's unfinished tomb at Windsor, but York Place was the property that Anne wanted most, as her palace. All were owned by the Church, and were confiscated illegally by Henry, who was now clearly bent on destroying the power of the Pope in England.

On 26 October Henry handed Wolsey's great seal of England to the reluctant Sir Thomas More and made him Lord Chancellor.

A few weeks later, on 2 November 1529, Henry and Anne were rowed from his royal palace at Greenwich to Westminster for the opening of what was to become the Reformation Parliament. Parliament later that month arraigned Wolsey on treason charges (carrying the death penalty) for taking orders from a foreign power, Rome. The King at first ensured that his old friend and mentor, now in his mid-fifties, would not face trial, though allowed him to be arrested a year later.

Parliament went on in 1534 to assert the authority of the King over the Pope in the Act of Supremacy that was to pave the way for an autonomous Church of England and the lasting break with Rome.

However, Henry had other pressing business. He wanted to inspect his new house at Westminster with his bride-to-be and his powerful future mother-in-law, Elizabeth Howard. The royal barge docked at the Privy Stairs where Wolsey had made his humiliating exit, and Henry, with Anne on his arm, retraced the steps he had gaily taken only two years earlier to gatecrash Wolsey's New Year party.

The glittering array of gold and silver they discovered as they walked through Wolsey's cherished long gallery was 'almost incredible', even to the eyes of the Tudor prince, said Cavendish. On the walls of the gallery were cloths of gold and silver, rich brocade and tapestries. Wolsey's staff had dutifully laid out on trestle tables an Aladdin's hoard of all his treasures including the cardinal's copes, the clerical vestments, which Wolsey had ordered to wear when he visited the colleges he had endowed at Christchurch in Oxford and at Ipswich. In sixteenth-century England, valuable and often imported materials were highly prized, and they found an array of 'rich stuffs of silk, velvet, satin, damask, caff[a], taffeta, grograine, sarcenet, a thousand pieces of fine Holland cloth'. But it was Wolsey's collection of gold and silver plate that must have astonished even Henry.

Then had he two chambers adjoining the gallery, the one called the gilt chamber and other called most commonly the council chamber. In each were set two broad and long tables upon trestles, whereupon was set such a quantity of plate of all sorts as was almost incredible. In the gilt chamber was set out upon the tables nothing but all gilt plate; and a cupboard standing under a window was garnished wholly with plate of clean gold, whereof some was set with pearl and rich stones. And in the council chamber was set all white plate and parcel gilt. And under the tables in both the chambers were set baskets with old plate, which was not esteemed but for broken plate and old, not worthy to be used. And books containing the value and weight of every parcel were laid by them ready to be seen . . .

To Anne, possession of York Place must have been worth more than all the gold and silver. Built for a succession of archbishops, it had no separate wing for a wife. She would temporarily occupy living quarters under Wolsey's library, but moving the palace and the court here would leave the King with little option but to live with Anne as his Queen. If Henry was determined to move in, it was conclusive evidence that he did intend to marry her. A fire destroyed most of the Tudor palace in 1698.

What traces remain of Wolsey's palace were revealed and painstakingly recorded when the construction work began on the site for the Ministry of Defence in 1938. The archeologists had precious little time, scraping and digging in the trenches sometimes during the lunch breaks of the workers on the building site. They found walls, and floors where Henry and his mistress had walked, which established the layout of the lost palace. The archaeologists were annoyed that they had no time to look for traces of the earlier Saxon settlement before the site was closed for ever. Before it disappeared under tons of concrete, they revealed how in Henry's time the builders had been ordered to create a new river wall, up to 100 feet further east – into the river – than Wolsey's, reclaiming

4,000 square feet from the Thames. It was a massive structure running 500 feet south from the privy kitchen (roughly where Horse Guards Avenue is today) to Lamb Alley to the south.

There is, however, a remarkable survival from Wolsey's palace under the MoD: Wolsey's wine cellar. It is a jaw-dropping moment to walk down three flights of stairs, under pipes, ducting and ventilators, to the basement of the MoD main building, to be confronted suddenly by a side wall of Wolsey's wine cellar, made up of distinctive small Tudor bricks and heavy-cut stone that Wolsey would have recognized. It is as if the cellar had been preserved as a time capsule, to transport the visitor from a basement set in the 1950s to the 1500s of Wolsey's time. There is a short flight of steps, worn by the tread of Wolsey's grooms of the wine cellar, leading into a handsome brick-vaulted cellar measuring 56 feet long by 24 feet wide and 20 feet high. The arched roof is supported by four stone octagonal pillars that throw out the ribbed brick ceiling with a boss in the centre of each. At the far end is another door on the left that must have led out into the cloister near the north side of the Presence Chamber. Historian David Starkey in his Channel 4 series *Monarchy* says it was almost certainly above this cellar in Wolsey's Great Hall that on 17 May 1527 the Cardinal opened the first secret trial of Katherine's marriage to the King without Katherine's knowledge. Henry was confident that the Cardinal would find the marriage invalid, but Wolsey adjourned the trial indefinitely on 31 May, on the grounds of the difficulty of the case. He may have wanted the Pope Clement VII to make the final ruling but his delay was fatal, because within two days news reached London that the troops of Katherine's nephew, Emperor Charles V, had sacked Rome. The Pope had taken refuge in a castle, but was in effect the Emperor's prisoner, leaving Wolsey little hope of persuading the Pontiff to annul Katherine's marriage to Henry. It is remarkable to walk in the cellar today and imagine the secret trial being conducted by Wolsey above the vaulted ceiling. In fact, the secret trial was held a short distance from the cellar's present position under the MoD. The cellar which survived the fire at Whitehall Palace in 1698 had been incorporated into Cromwell House when it was built for Sir George Byng in 1722. The house had been taken over for Government use in the early twentieth century and Wolsey's cellar, which stood at ground level, had been used as the canteen for the staff of the Department of Transport. But when construction of the MoD began after the Second World War, the cellar was unfortunately in the way of a new road, Horse Guards Avenue, and, like the house, would have been demolished for the road building had not Queen Mary of Teck, Queen Elizabeth II's grandmother, intervened. She marshalled public support for this relic of Wolsey's palace to be preserved. An engineers' report said:

> In 1946 when work on the office building restarted, the decision to retain the Crypt was re-examined. Economy of floor space and an uninterrupted corridor on the ground floor were of paramount importance and the decision was finally taken to obtain full use of the ground-floor space in the neighbourhood of the Crypt, and to avoid the unsightly projection from the Horse Guards Avenue face of the new building, by moving the Crypt bodily to another position . . .[6]

In an amazing feat of engineering, the entire crypt, slimmed down for transportation to 800 tons by removing over 200 tons of brickwork from the structure, was braced with steel and painstakingly moved on steel rollers while a hole was dug amid the foundations of the MoD, then it was pushed west again, before being carefully inched into the basement of the MoD on screw jacks. It is now 9 feet 8 inches further to the west and 18 feet 9 inches lower than its starting point.

These days it is used for social events for the military brass hats, civil servants and charities. The elaborate fare of the sumptuous banquets over which Wolsey presided have been replaced by bottles of red Australian shiraz and bowls of crisps.

And Wolsey? Having retired in some style to his See in York, he was charged with treason in 1530, as he had feared, and was being escorted back to London to his inevitable execution at the Tower when he was taken ill at Leicester. He died of natural causes on 29 November 1530 and was buried at Leicester Abbey, now Abbey Park. In Queen Victoria's reign, a woollens manufacturer in Leicester was looking for a brand name and seized on the city's historical associations with the Tudor cardinal buried in the local churchyard. So it was that Wolsey, once the most powerful name in the country after Henry VIII, became synonymous with a brand of 'unshrinkable' socks.

# 2

# HENRY VIII'S PALACE
# OF WHITE HALL

You must no more call it York Place: that is past;
 For since the Cardinal fell that title's lost.
'Tis now the King's and called Whitehall.
 Shakespeare's *King Henry the Eighth,* Act Four, Scene I

Standing in a small room of the Holbein Gate over King Street before the cold break of day on 25 January 1533, Henry VIII was becoming irritated. Outside the frosted windows, hardly anyone in the palace was stirring. The sun was breaking in milky streaks over the chimneys beyond the River Thames in the east.

Beside Henry, forty-one, stood Anne, ten years younger, regally dressed, and flushed with pleasure that she had finally got her wish to become Henry's legitimate wife. Also in the room was a small gathering of their closest servants: Sir Henry Norris and Thomas Heneage, from Henry's privy chamber; and Anne Savage, an attendant of Anne's. They were here to act as witnesses at their wedding, but Dr Rowland Lee, the King's chaplain, was prevaricating and Henry wanted him to get on with it.

'Sir, I trust you have the Pope's lycence both that you marry and that I may join you together in marriage?' the worried priest is said to have asked.

He reminded Henry that if he did not have the licence from the Pope, they could all be excommunicated for what they were about to do.

Playing the amiable bully, Henry told him:

Why Master Rowland, think you me a man of so small faith and credit, you, I say, that do well know my life past and even now have heard my confession? Or think you me a man of so small and slender foresight and consideration of my affairs that unless all things were safe and sure I would enterprise this matter?

I have truly a lycence but it is reposed in another sure place whereto no man resorteth but myself, which, if it were seen should discharge us all.

With growing impatience, Henry added: 'But if I should, now that it waxeth towards day, fetch it, and be seen so early abroad, there would rise a rumour and talk thereof other than were convenient. Go forth in God's name and do that which appertaineth to you. I will take upon me all other danger.'[1]

The gatehouse may seem an odd location for one of the most important weddings in the history of Britain, and academics still argue about the exact location of the ceremony, but there is good documentary evidence, backed up by circumstantial evidence, to fix it in the Holbein Gate. The gateway acted as a footbridge between the two halves of Henry's expanded palace and remained a famous landmark in the capital for 200 years, though not a trace of it remains in Whitehall today. It stood across the north carriageway of Whitehall where red London buses queue on their way to Trafalgar Square, near the northern end of the Cabinet Office.

The main source for the account of Henry's clandestine and bigamous marriage to his pregnant mistress is Nicholas Harpsfield, the last Catholic Archdeacon of Canterbury. He is hardly an impartial historian. He was one of the fiercest critics of the divorce, which made Mary, Henry's daughter by Katherine of Aragon, a bastard. When Mary, a devout Catholic, was on the throne, Harpsfield acted as a judge against Protestants and helped to send many to be burned at the stake, in a persecution that created 300 martyrs, and earned the Queen the title (celebrated today in vodka and tomato juice) of 'Bloody Mary'. He was acting as Mary's Catholic propagandist when he described the wedding scene in his *Treatise on the Pretended Divorce between Henry VIII and Katherine of Aragon*. Harpsfield called the marriage 'cursed and incestuous' – a reference to the King reputedly having had sex with both Boleyn sisters and even Anne's powerful mother, Elizabeth Howard. Henry denied it, saying, 'Never with the mother . . .' However, that does not mean that the basic thrust of his account is not accurate.

It is a second, anonymous manuscript in the Sloane collection at the British Library that firmly places the marriage ceremony in the unlikely setting of the Holbein Gate. The manuscript, entitled *The life of Kinge Henry the 8th from his fallinge in love with Anne Bulloigne to the death of Queene Katheren, his wife*, is on parchment, and now quite faded. Written in English in a gentle flowing hand, the unknown writer says Henry VIII and Anne 'Bulloigne of London' married 'at York House which people have called Whitehall'. The marriage took place 'in the highest chamber which is over the West Gate'.[2] Andrea Clarke of the British Library manuscript section told me it dated from around a hundred years after the events, but the details of who was there have been corroborated by other accounts and there are good reasons why Henry may have wanted the ceremony to be conducted in a room above the bridge across King Street.

Firstly, by marrying Anne above the gateway, Henry was ensuring secrecy. It had to be a clandestine marriage, because he had *not* completed his divorce from his first wife, and Anne was barely six weeks pregnant. Convinced she would at last become Queen, Anne had given way to Henry's demands for sex, probably in Calais in September 1532,[3] and in early January 1533 she told Henry she was expecting his child. Henry, in a flurry of excitement, consulted his astrologers and they confirmed it was to be a boy. Henry could not wait any longer for the wedding to take place because Anne's pregnancy would soon be all too visible, but it was essential to have the ceremony now so that when his son was born, the longed-for heir to the Tudor crown would be legitimate. The anonymous author of the Sloane manuscript confirmed that had 'more men known', they would have 'harshly kept counsel with the King'. Henry did have a licence from Pope Clement to marry Anne, providing he had secured a declaration from the Pope's inquisitors that the marriage to his Queen, Katherine of Aragon, was void.[4] By marrying Anne before he had legally divorced Katherine, Henry was taking a huge political gamble. There was a threat that it could provoke Katherine's Spanish cousins to declare war on his crown. He must also have been unsure how England, then still a Catholic country, would react to the removal of their popular Catholic Queen and the schism it would bring with Rome, which would cast the whole country into damnation.

Secondly, the Holbein Gate was also convenient. It was a few paces away from the King's inner sanctum, his private rooms in the Privy Gallery running up to the Holbein Gate.

Henry and Anne had spent Christmas 1529 together at Henry's palace by the river at Greenwich like a pair of young lovers, planning to turn Wolsey's mansion into a sprawling palace over both sides of King Street, bigger than Versailles or the Vatican, with a sports complex on the west side linked by the Holbein Gate. Henry agreed to refurbish and expand Wolsey's living quarters by the river for Anne, according to one account, 'to please the lady who prefers that place for the King's residence to any other'. But for his own privy lodgings, Henry ordered a new gallery to be constructed at right angles to Wolsey's long gallery along the riverside. Running east to west from the river to King Street, the King's new Privy Gallery would form the spine of the new royal palace and it would carry all his private rooms, his bedroom, his dining chamber, and his bath in one elongated set of apartments at first-floor level. However, both to save money and to rub salt into Wolsey's wounds, Henry was persuaded by his Privy Council, many of whom had old scores to settle against Wolsey, to tear out the timber-framed long gallery from Wolsey's house at Esher while the Cardinal was still there, and ship it to Whitehall for his own apartments.

Cavendish wrote:

> The council had put into the King's head that the new gallery at Esher, which my lord had late before his fall newly set up, should be very necessary for the king to take down and set it up again at Westminster; which was done accordingly, and stands at this present day there. The taking away thereof before my lord's face was to him a corrosive, which was invented by his enemies only to torment him.

Records show land at the house on the site today occupied by Horse Guard was owned by Dr Duck, Wolsey's treasurer, and was used as a wood yard while Henry's gallery was reassembled. Simon Thurley says the nineteen-foot-wide Esher Gallery was probably erected to the east of the Holbein Gate running towards the river, where it met a cross-house. A new gallery, much wider at thirty feet, continued east towards the river. In all, the Privy Gallery was at least 200 feet long. As Henry walked towards the gatehouse, his privy bedrooms and meeting rooms were off to the left overlooking a new great ornamental garden on the Westminster side. There was a flight of stairs about halfway along the gallery down to the lower garden gallery and the garden itself. Known as the Adam and Eve stair, because of a large painting of the biblical scene from the Garden of Eden at the head of the stairs, it had four bay windows, two large and two small, carved in timber and allowed the King to take a stroll among the sculptures of fantastic beasts that were placed on plinths among the rose beds. The cross-house for the stairs also accommodated a chimney for a fireplace and a garderobe (a Tudor toilet) for the King.

Throughout the interior of the palace the walls and pillars were decorated in ornamental designs called grotesque-work, which was clearly shown in the background to a dynastic painting by an unknown artist called *The Family of Henry VIII*, which also gave a fleeting glimpse of the garden and its beasts on poles.

Construction of the Holbein Gate started in 1531 and there are documentary accounts of how the builders put up a canvas 'tent' like modern developers to keep the rain off and avoid the work being delayed. There are doubts about whether Hans Holbein was involved at all – he was home in Basle at the time work started – but he was back in London about the time it was completed, and he was certainly capable of the commission, designing everything from decoration on daggers and armour, to jewels, plate, triumphal arches and a fireplace for the palace, in addition to his magically fresh portraits of Henry's court. The Holbein Gate was two storeys high, with octagonal turrets at the four corners – almost identical to the Tudor entrance to St James's Palace in Pall Mall. The archway for the twin gates was squared off, probably to allow a flat floor to be laid more easily for the room and passage above to cross over to

Parkside. There were smaller gates on either side for pedestrians. The King's coat of arms was set over the gateway and it was decorated on each side by four terracotta roundels carrying the faces of prominent Tudor figures, including his father Henry VII and Henry VIII himself. The span of the gateway was not much more than a carriage in width.

A 1647 sketch by Wenceslaus Hollar, *View of Whitehall from King Street,* shows Henry's Privy Gallery was carried at first-floor level to the Holbein Gate through what appears to be a terraced row of four Tudor town houses, each with a gabled end, pierced by a window, with a large window beneath, and a door and smaller lean-tos attached to the ground floor. The gateway was decorated in a black-and-white chequerboard effect with 600 tons of knapped flint, commandeered from Wolsey's quarry in Ipswich, that Wolsey had used all over York Place, probably a nostalgic throwback to his boyhood in the town. A small army of thirty-one painters was set to work in October 1531 decorating the plasterwork of the gallery exterior with ornamental floral designs, black-and-white checks, set off occasionally by a splash of bold primary colours with Henry's red Tudor rose. In the Presence Chamber, all signs of Wolsey were removed, and a stone dragon – another Tudor motif signifying his family's Welsh connections – was put on the wall to support Henry's coat of arms, which were gilded.

The buildings for the sports complex, known as Parkside, were mostly in red Tudor brick, in contrast to the chequer-work on the other side of the street, making it look to visitors very much a palace of two halves. The overall appearance, says Simon Thurley, was 'essentially chivalric and heraldic and relied on the use of military forms, bright colours and strong silhouettes'. Drawings of the palace attributed to Ralph Agas, the woodcut from John Foxes' *Acts and Monuments* showing the cloistered Preaching Place in the King's Privy Garden, the detailed Greatorex map of the palace of 1670 and the sketch of the palace from the river by Anthonis van den Wyngaerde, all show that the palace, in Thurley's view, was 'far more ordered and less confused than the impression gained from later sources. Indeed, it is important to view Tudor Whitehall as an architecturally coherent composition.'[5] Exposed brickwork was painted with red ochre, with the mortar joints picked out in red, and elsewhere the timber-framed buildings were painted black and white, the theme carried through in the knapped flint and chalk squares that gave parts of the palace its chequerboard effect. Internally, the galleries would have been covered with rich hangings, ceilings were patterned with gilded geometrical fretwork, floors were painted, walls were covered in frescoes, and the windows glittered with stained glass.

One of Henry's first priorities was to build a new river wall as part of his enlargement of the palace, and create a grand new river entrance to the south of the Whitehall Stairs where Wolsey had made his exit a couple of years before. The new Privy Stairs had a covered jetty with the King's royal crest above the front to leave visitors in no doubt whose palace this was. Wolsey's old long gallery was extended to a new house by the river as private lodgings for Henry's daughter, Princess Mary. Behind this gallery, running roughly parallel to it, Henry built another, longer gallery, called the Stone Gallery. It stretched south to the old boundary marked by Lamb Alley with a gallery above it, called the Matted Gallery, the ceiling of which was painted by Holbein. Queen Elizabeth I held a banquet in the Stone Gallery in 1559 for a visit by the Duke of Montmorency, Constable of France, when according to a contemporary account it was decorated with wreaths of sweet-smelling fresh flowers and 'hung with gold and silver brocade'. The writer said it was 'divided into three apartments in the centre of which was the table prepared for her Majesty and at a short distance from it another for ambassadors. There was also a table fifty-four paces in length for other lords gentlemen and ladies.'

Between the two galleries, over the coming years, Henry constructed a smaller Queen's Gallery overlooking the river, which led out of the Queen's privy lodgings next to the gallery to the Privy Stairs that extended into the river. The King also acquired the 830-acre St James's Fields from Eton as a deer park for hunting, and on the site of St James's leper hospital he built St James's Palace, which is still the main royal court of Britain to which all foreign diplomats are assigned. Originally, the windows on the south side of the King's Privy Gallery overlooked an orchard, which occupied the large space between the street and the Stone Gallery by the river. In 1538, the King acquired more land to the south of Lamb Alley and in 1545 moved the orchard further south, with a fountain added in 1570 as the centrepiece. The King's Privy Garden had originally been to the north of the Privy Gallery in a small quadrangle that became known as Pebble Court after it was covered over. But after the orchard was moved, a new great ornamental garden was created below the south windows of the Privy Gallery. The new Privy Garden was largely unchanged fifty years later when it was described during Elizabeth's reign by the traveller and writer Leopold von Wedel:

We walked into the Queen's garden. In it there are 34 high painted various animals of wood with gilt horns placed upon columns. On these columns are further banners with the Queen's coats of arms. In the centre of the garden is a beautiful fountain and thereto a large gnomon [sundial blade] which shows the hours in thirty different ways. Between the herbaceous plants that are set in the garden there are beautiful pleasant grassy walks. The plants are artistically set out in various ways and surrounded by hedges trimmed in the form of seats. By this garden, there is an orchard beneath whose trees fragrant herbs are planted.

But Henry's pride and joy appears to have been his recreation complex catering for most of the Tudor pastimes. And the Holbein Gate was the key to Henry's design for his new palace – it carried his Privy Gallery across the ancient public thoroughfare between Charing Cross and Westminster, enabling him to cross over to his sports centre without setting foot in King Street. Inspired by the tennis courts at Richmond Palace where he grew up, Henry built four courts, two open and two covered.

The game in the open courts – today covered by a service road and small eco-garden with a pond to the side of Number Ten Downing Street – was similar to the tennis played at Wimbledon today, but played on a court paved with Purbeck stone. The game played indoors was very different to lawn tennis, more akin to a form of squash, and very vigorous. A great indoor tennis court, or 'play', was built running alongside the street towards Westminster, where the Cabinet Office stands today. The rectangular building was 88 feet long by 26 feet wide and had a pitched roof with octagonal towers 65 feet high at the four corners, decorated in chequered knapped flint. Although it was later converted into lodgings it remained a landmark in Whitehall until it was demolished in 1846. The interior was painted black and there were windows sixteen feet high to let in light for the court. At the south end there was a viewing gallery where courtiers could lay bets on the outcome of the matches. The ball was whacked across a net against walls up to eighteen feet off the ground, buttresses and pentices (low-roofed internal galleries) with an unpredictable bounce to fox an opponent. The rackets, made with sheep gut, would have been recognizable today. The game is now called 'real' tennis and is still played in a few special indoor courts in the United States, Australia, France and the UK, including at the Queen's Club and the Oratory School in London. The term real tennis may have been a corruption of the title 'Royal' tennis from Tudor times, but experts in the sport claim it was first used in the nineteenth century to distinguish the game from lawn tennis. The word 'tennis' is believed to have been imported from the French shouting '*Tenez!*' (take it) when they served.

Henry – tutored by professionals hired by his father at Richmond Palace – was a powerful player. He played tennis stripped to his 'slops' – drawers – and wore a black velvet tennis coat to throw over his shoulders as he walked over to the matches or back to his Privy Gallery. When he twisted an ankle in a game in 1527, he had a black slipper made to match his tennis outfit. 'It was the prettiest thing in the world to see him play, his fair skin glowing through a shirt of finest texture,' the Venetian Ambassador enthusiastically reported. 'He sits his horse well, jousts, wields the spear, throws the quoit, and draws the bow admirably. He plays at tennis most dextrously. He has an air of royal majesty such has not been witnessed in any other sovereign for many years.'

A century later, the great indoor court was converted into apartments, with floors and ceilings inserted where the ball had crashed around the lofty walls. Charles II had a tennis court laid out in his Privy Garden at Whitehall. He used the sport to lose weight and Pepys recorded the Merry Monarch had lost over four pounds after one match. It remained in use until the eighteenth century – a copy of *St James's Chronicle* for 3–5 March 1708 recorded a match of six games between Madam Bunell and Mr Tomkyns, and Madam Bunell won four.

Henry's sports complex also boasted an octagon-shaped cockpit for blood sports, which stood behind the present Cabinet Office building. It was later converted into a theatre and then used as the site for a new Treasury building, which led to the term 'The Cockpit' being used in the seventeenth century as 'Downing Street' is today to describe the centre of power in Whitehall. Henry also created a tiltyard – now covered by Horse Guards Parade – for tournaments and bear-baiting, one of the most popular sports at the beginning of the sixteenth century. Bear-baiting today is regarded as barbaric and the philosopher Erasmus remarked on the number of bears kept for the purpose when he visited London in 1510, but the Tudors enjoyed the spectacle of the animal fighting off dogs, sometimes killing them with its paws. Bears had their legs fastened to a post by a chain to be attacked by dogs, which would try to tear out the animal's throat. It was not intended that the bears would be killed but it was bloody, vicious, and drew large crowds. Bear-baiting at Whitehall was in the open tiltyard, but as a mark of its popularity with the public, a 1572 map of London from the *Civitates Orbis Terrarum* by Braun and Hogenberg shows a ring with seating, similar to the later Globe Theatre, dedicated to 'bearbayting' at Southwark, near London Bridge.

Elizabeth I did not attend cockfights, which was regarded during her reign as a preserve for men, but she enjoyed bear-baiting so much that she had her own team of bears and a royal Master of Bears. Her great court favourite Lord Robert Dudley staged bear-baiting for her enjoyment as part of the spectacular entertainments when she visited Kenilworth, his sumptuous castle in Warwickshire, in 1575. Robert Laneham, Clerk of the Council Chamber Door, recorded the 'finer' points of the sport:

> The Bear with his pink eyes leering after his enmiez approach and the nimbleness of the Dog to take hiz avauntage, and the fors and experiens of the Bear to avoid the assaults. If he were bitten in one place, how he would pynch in an oother to get free, and if he were onez taken then what shyft with byting, clawing and roring, tossing and tumbling he would work to wynd himself awaie, And when he was loose, to shake his ears with the blud and slaver about his phizonomie was a pittance of a goodly relief . . .

The Holbein Gate joined a new gallery that overlooked the tiltyard, from which it took its name, but it was also known as the Bear Gallery in Elizabeth I's day when it was used by the Queen for watching the baiting of her bears. Sometimes they were blindfolded and whipped for entertainment, and when Tudor tastes tired of the bears, a monkey could be tied to the back of a pony to torture it for the amusement of the people. The lower classes were banned from playing tennis, bowls or skittles, but the Queen was so alarmed that bear-baiting was falling in popularity that laws were introduced to protect it. Bear-baiting normally took place on Thursdays and the Privy Council ordered the Mayor of London to ban plays on Thursdays, saying the 'players do use to recite their plays to the great hurt and destruction of the game of bear-baiting and like pastimes which are maintained for Her Majesty's pleasure'.

Bear-baiting continued into the Stuart era. James I held a banquet for Juan Fernández de Velasco, Constable of Castile, in the Presence Chamber on 19 August 1604 as part of peace negotiations with Spain, at which the King presented Velasco with a melon and half a dozen oranges grown in England. After the toasts, they took their places at the windows of a room overlooking an inner square where a platform was raised, according to a contemporary account in W. B. Rye's *England as Seen by Foreigners*, 'and a vast crowd had assembled to see the King's bears fight with greyhounds. This afforded great amusement. Presently, a bull, tied to the end of a rope, was fiercely baited by dogs. After this certain tumblers came who danced upon a rope and performed various feats of agility and skill on horseback. With this ended the entertainment of the day.'

A second gateway completed in 1532 crossed King Street from the corner of the King's Privy Garden, near the site now occupied by Gwydyr House, home of the Welsh Office, to join Henry's Parkside sports complex roughly where the north corner of Downing Street is today. The Holbein Gate and the King Street Gate were only about a hundred paces apart, but they created an impressive fortified way from the King's palace at Whitehall to the Church's ancient power base at Westminster. The short narrow road between the two gatehouses would become known as The Street. To the south, King Street continued to Westminster and emerged on what is now Parliament Square, roughly opposite where St Margaret's Church stands today. A second road, Parliament Street, ran parallel to King Street, separated by two blocks of houses. King Street was finally wiped off the map of London when the last block of houses was demolished to make way at the end of the nineteenth century for the public office now occupied by the Treasury and HM Revenue and Customs, and for the widening of Parliament Street. A small plaque on a balustrade by the side of the Treasury in Great George Street marks the spot where King Street joined Parliament Square and is all that is left of a thoroughfare that existed for 500 years.

The King Street Gate was regarded as less handsome than the Holbein Gate; it was built of stone with two storeys and circular towers at the corners topped by domes. There was a central opening for vehicles flanked by two side passageways for pedestrians.

Between the two gateways, on the Parkside, a passageway ran from east to west with tennis courts springing off it on either side. This was known as Cockpit Passage and ran parallel to the present Downing Street. There was a two-storey gallery at the end of Cockpit Passage to allow courtiers to watch the games below. The wall of this tennis gallery has survived with a large mullioned Tudor window without glass. Here Anne Boleyn, Henry's sister Mary and her husband, Charles Brandon, the Duke of Suffolk, would have looked down on the spectacle and wagered their purses on the outcome. The window today overlooks a side door – the tradesman's entrance – to Number Ten Downing Street where political editors queue up each month for the regular press conference in which the Prime Minister bats questions back and forth with the media.

Brandon was one of Henry's best friends, and the King's most celebrated opponent in the tiltyard. He had infuriated Henry and risked a charge of treason when he married Henry's sister Mary without the King's explicit approval, after being entrusted with escorting her back from France following the death of her elderly husband, Louis XII. But jousting was too important to allow a dynastic rift to stand in the way of their sport. The tiltyard was about 160 yards long and 30 yards wide, running roughly from Dover House to the side of Admiralty House, with a neck-high fence running along to prevent head-on collisions. It was originally canvas and called by its Continental name, the *teld*, which later corrupted into *tylt*. The yard was protected from the public road by a wall with a gateway near the Holbein Gate that was watched by a gatekeeper to the park. Warhorses used in the jousts were similar to the hunters used by the Horse Guards today and were trained to canter with the right foreleg leading to slant the rider towards his rival thundering at him on the other side of the tilt. They were known as destriers, a name derived from the Anglo-Norman *destrer* and *dextrarius*, the Latin for right-handed.

The prowess of a knight could be judged by the number of lances he broke, or 'courses' he ran, and Henry and Brandon regularly ran into double figures against each other. The Venetian Ambassador was among the thrilled spectators in the Tiltyard Gallery who reported seeing the King 'running upwards of thirty courses, in one of which he capsized his opponent [Brandon], who is the finest jouster in the Kingdom, horse and all. He then took off his helmet and came under the windows where we were, and talked and laughed with us to our very great honour, and to the surprise of all beholders.'

Lances were made hollow to limit the damage to participants and reduce the risk of fatal wounds in the joust, but it could be a perilous sport. Another of Henry's friends was killed by a splinter from a lance that shattered and shot through his visor into his eye, penetrating his brain. Amazingly, given how fragile they were, one of Brandon's lances has survived. Weighing twenty pounds, and fourteen and a half feet long, it is on show today at the armoury in the Tower of London.

Knights set up tents around the tiltyard, or the park, and notices were nailed on a tree announcing the types of combat to be offered. Henry invited challengers from all over Europe to one of his tournaments at Whitehall. They were popular spectator sports as well as a way of showing off a knight's fighting skills, but they were not open to all-comers. Challengers had to approach the heralds, who decided whether they were socially fit to fight the knights who had made the courtly offer to do battle. There were three main forms of combat: the Joust, where they charged each other, left-hand to left-hand, with lances on horseback; the Tourney, where knights fought on foot or horseback with swords, maces or halberds; and the Barriers, where knights on foot hammered each other with axes, two-handed swords, maces and spears across the tilt to test their parrying skills.

The armour was light, similar to that in use today for ceremonial duties at Horse Guards. Brian Harwood, a former Guards officer and historian of Horse Guards, says a modern Household Cavalryman still has to mount his horse from the ground unaided in full cuirasses – body armour with a breastplate and back plate – to pass his training. Henry imported highly skilled Flemish and German armourers to create the finest armour for tournaments. The Tower of London armoury has on show a suit of armour made in 1515 for use in jousts. It was decorated with gilt brass initials H and K, for Henry and Katherine of Aragon, entwined with true lovers' knots. The decoration was carried out by the King's harness gilder, Paul van Vrelant, and was engraved and stippled with scenes from the lives of St George and St Barbara, the patron saints of England and Aragon, with roses and pomegranates, the badges of their royal households. As late as 1540, when he was forty-nine,

Henry ordered the finest suit of armour that the craftsmen could create. Measuring this suit of armour showed that his waist had ballooned from a medium thirty-four inches to a gross fifty-two inches. The massive suit of armour was delicately etched and gilded by Holbein, but the most eye-catching feature is Henry's majestic shiny steel codpiece. Such a strike may have caused pain, but would not have scored a point. One point was awarded for a hit above the waist, two for a hit on the head, and three for unhorsing the opponent, but points were deducted for hitting the opponent's horse (minus one) and the tilt (minus two).

Tournaments in Elizabeth's reign opened with a colourful parade carrying dress shields of papier mâché, known as *impresa*. A bill for the Earl of Rutland still survives showing he paid £15 for a chariot with a trumpeter (about £6,600 at 2007 prices, and more than a year's income then for a skilled builder). Champions of the tilt in Elizabeth I's reign could display their *impresa* on the walls of the Shield Gallery that led to the Privy Stairs by the river. This spectacular show of toy shields and its convenience for the river made the Shield Gallery a popular place for courtiers to meet and gossip about court life for more than a century.

Anne and her ladies could watch Henry and Brandon and the other knights from the safety of the Tiltyard Gallery, which ended in twin towers and a staircase to the park. There were also temporary stands erected for spectators alongside the tiltyard.

After their marriage, Anne was allowed a household of 200 staff at Whitehall Palace, and they included a young girl called Jane Seymour, who was to prove her own nemesis. Anne, already acting the Queen before she was crowned, dressed her servants in her own special livery of blue and purple, and on their doublets they bore her new embroidered motto, *La Plus Heureuse* ('The Happiest').[6] Anne's new coat of arms – a white falcon, with a crown and sceptre, standing on a tree stump covered with Tudor roses – replaced the

K and the pomegranate. It was erased from the palace after Anne's execution, but has survived in odd places, including one of her prayer books.

The clandestine marriage in the gatehouse may not have been the wedding of which Anne must have dreamed, but her coronation on 1 June 1533 was everything she could have hoped for. She was six months pregnant, with Henry merrily planning for the birth of a male heir at last, when she was crowned Queen at Westminster Abbey by Thomas Cranmer, using the historic crown of Edward I. The ceremony was followed by a feast in Westminster Hall.

The building work at Whitehall Palace was still going on and the new Queen moved to Greenwich where, three months later, between 3 p.m. and 4 p.m. on Sunday, 7 September, against the predictions of Henry's astrologers, Anne gave birth to a girl, to be christened Elizabeth. In the sixteenth century astrology – now generally regarded as entertainment in newspapers – was taken seriously as a mathematical science on a par with astronomy. One of Henry's most famous astrologers who may have been to blame for the misreading of the stars was a German mathematician, Nikolaus Kratzer, a friend of Sir Thomas More and Hans Holbein. Kratzer was introduced to the court by More and employed by Wolsey as a maths teacher at Oxford University; he was appointed by Henry VIII as his astrologer, clockmaker and map-maker. A portrait of his friend surrounded by mathematical instruments was painted by Holbein and is now in the Louvre Museum in Paris. A copy is in the National Portrait Gallery in London.

At Westminster, Henry secured parliamentary approval for an Act to legalize his seizure of Church property for the Crown at York Place. With Wolsey gone, Henry relied on others in his court at Whitehall; these were less capable of holding down the rival factions, driven by jealousy and religion, vying for power in the corridors of Tudor power at Whitehall. After a fall from his horse that left him with a debilitating wound in his leg that would not heal, and developed into an ulcer, Henry gradually tired of sports, and of his troublesome wife who had failed to deliver him a son. Around the Whitehall court there were whispers that the King had fallen in love with Jane Seymour. She was the antithesis of Anne – demure, obedient and plain. In the spring of 1536 Thomas Cromwell, Wolsey's brilliant protégé, who had turned bureaucracy into an art form after replacing his master as the King's key adviser, produced trumped-up charges against the Queen, based on the flirtatious language of courtly love taken to its extremes. Anne was accused of treason through incest with her own brother, George, Lord Rochford, and adultery with four courtiers. The purge began suddenly on Sunday, 30 April 1536 with the arrest of some of the Boleyn faction at Greenwich. George was arrested at Whitehall, probably trying desperately to reach the King to plead his innocence. Henry had gone to ground in the palace, and remained incommunicado from the Boleyn family. Anne, imprisoned in the Beauchamp Tower at the Tower of London, carved a white falcon, a symbol from her coat of arms, in the wall of her prison cell, and followed her brother to the block on 19 May 1536. The Tower wardens today have a bloodthirsty line in describing her death for the amusement of the tourists at the spot where she died: 'A swordsman was brought from France at her request. She had a particularly thin neck and swept her hair up out of the way. After she finished her prayers, he hit her this ways [indicates sideways slicing stroke]. If you had blinked you would have missed it. He held up her head, with the blood pumping from the stump and her feet banging against the floor . . . and said in a heavy French accent, "So perish all the King's enemies".'

It is not far from the awful, bloody truth. Henry was at Whitehall Palace when he heard the distant thunder of guns that signalled that his second Queen was dead. He had been in an alarmingly merry mood for days, because he was in love again, this time for real. Wearing white mourning clothes, he made his exit by the Privy Stairs to his barge shortly after Anne died, and was rowed to the Strand to meet Jane. Ten days later, on 29 May, they were married by Cranmer at Whitehall Palace in the Queen's Closet, where Anne's falcon badge had been discreetly removed and replaced by Jane's coat of arms – a phoenix rising from the flames above a castle – and her motto: 'Bound to obey and serve'.

At 2 a.m. on 12 October 1537, and after a long labour, Jane did her duty, and delivered to Henry the son and male heir he had longed for. Delirious with relief, Henry ordered a 2,000-gun salute at the Tower, free wine in the city, bells to be rung in every parish, and merry rejoicing across the land for Prince Edward. However, his joy turned to grief twelve days later when Jane died from complications – puerperal fever – as a result of infection caused by the difficult birth and Tudor gynaecology. Childbirth was always attended by midwives, who were trained by surgeons, but often were relatives of the mother, and hygiene was at its most basic. Women could expect to be pregnant almost every year, and lose their children at birth or soon afterwards. If there were no complications in the delivery, infection was a constant threat to the mother, making death in childbirth commonplace. Caesarean operations were known, but without anaesthetics, apart from alcohol, they were fatal. Jane Seymour was supposed to have died after a Caesarean operation, according to a popular song in which she said to the surgeon: 'Rip open my two sides, and save my baby'. But this is believed to be a myth. Like many women, she died from septicaemia. Henry later was to say she was the only wife he truly loved and, for once genuinely grief-stricken, he retired to his darkened Privy Gallery at Whitehall Palace to mourn. Having got the son he wanted, Henry ordered Holbein to paint a great mural on the wall of the Privy Chamber to celebrate the Tudor dynasty, which he now believed was secure. The original was a massive twelve feet by nine feet and showed Henry in his most famous pose: standing immense, huge legs spread apart, hands on hips, his tunic thrust wide open with his codpiece jutting out, and his left hand resting on a dagger, defying the world. It is claimed that men who stood before the portrait would quake with fear at the prospect of meeting the monarch in the flesh. Karel van Mander, though writing a century later, was still awed at the painting. He said Henry 'stood there, majestic in his splendour . . . so lifelike that the spectator felt abashed, annihilated in his presence'. Only a small copy survives by the Flemish artist, Remigius van Leemput, an assistant of Van Dyck. It was commissioned by Charles II and is now kept at Hampton Court.

The mural contained four full-length portraits – a break with tradition – of the Tudor dynasty: Jane Seymour, Henry's mother Elizabeth of York, both on the right, with himself and his father Henry VII on the left. They flank a hubristic monument to the two Tudor kings. An inscription asks: which is the greater, the father who brought peace to his nation after the Wars of the Roses or the son, who asserted the authority of monarchy over Rome?

> If it pleases you to see the illustrious images of heroes, look on these: no picture ever bore greater . . . The former often overcame his enemies and the conflagrations of his country and finally brought peace to its citizens. The son, born indeed for greater things, removed the unworthy from their altars and replaced them by upright men. The arrogance of the Popes has yielded to unerring virtue and while Henry VIII holds the sceptre in his hand, religion is restored and during his reign the doctrines of God began to be held in his honour.

Henry's dynastic mural was destroyed in the palace fire in 1698. In another portrait, which was the centrepiece of a Tate Britain exhibition of Holbein's work in 2006, Henry is dressed in magnificent cloth of silver and of gold, his shirt collar embroidered with gold thread. Holbein used powdered gold in his paint and for the background the expensive ultramarine pigment more usually used for his miniature portraits. In the small portrait of Henry, which was clearly intended to be handled and studied closely, power exudes from every pore, but the artist's honesty could not avoid him depicting Henry's less appealing side. Holbein captured his overbearing, hot-tempered, vain, mercurial nature through Henry's porcine eyes and the cruel little mouth with the cupid-bow lips that appear ready to bark out to the painter: 'Enough!' Henry was dangerous to be near, and must have been a difficult sitter for Holbein, in spite of his genius. The artist resolved the problem by using the same drawings over again for his portraits of the King. But the stars of the Holbein exhibition were the 'snapshot' portraits of the knights and ladies, some anonymous, that seem as fresh and alive today as the day when they were drawn. Towards the end of his life, Henry commissioned an unknown artist to create a second great dynastic painting to show his family reunited and the arguments about the succession resolved, by the positioning of his children in order of precedence – Edward with him in the centre, then Mary, Elizabeth and, off to the left, Jane Seymour. His other wives, including Anne Boleyn, were not part of the picture. It is this painting, now in the collection at Hampton Court, which also carries a tantalizing glimpse of the Whitehall Palace. It clearly shows its richly gilded interior and, through two open doorways, the viewer can see the geometrical Privy Garden with carved beasts on the top of poles. By one doorway there is a gardener with a monkey on his shoulder.

In his declining years, Henry became reclusive and at times morose, retiring for days to secret rooms within the area of his bedchamber and the Holbein Gate, to contemplate his life, his six wives, and his historic split from Rome. The gatehouse became his main place of work and study of religious books. An inventory of 1547 taken shortly after his death says Henry kept 'vii instruments of astronomye hanging uppon the wall' in the Holbein Gate – he had given up his belief in astrology years before, but he still studied the stars. He also brought in books from his great library and a collection of maps, a globe, looking glasses, nine terracotta statues, armour, a javelin and other oddities that interested him. There was also a secret jewel house, and a private wardrobe.

When he came downstairs to eat in the Great Hall, he sought comfort in drink and vast quantities of food. The French ambassador, Charles de Marillac, said the King was 'stout' and 'daily growing heavier'. His great walnut bed was enlarged to truly king-size dimensions – seven feet wide and seven feet six inches long – to accommodate his bulk. A handwritten note by Henry in a Book of Psalms that he read in the bedchamber in the Privy Gallery reveals his mood. The verse was from Psalm 37 and read: 'I have been young, and now am old . . .' Alongside it, Henry wrote in the margin: *'dolens dictum'* (a painful saying).

As he became more immobile from his leg ulcer Henry took to a wheelchair, or 'tramm', which he kept in his private 'chairhouse' in the Holbein Gate, from which he could watch the jousting in the nearby tiltyard, where he had once been a star.

Henry VIII died at Whitehall at about 2 a.m. on 28 January 1547, at the age of fifty-five. Shortly before he breathed his last, he whispered: 'All is lost.' By the time Cranmer had arrived from across the river at Lambeth, he was no longer capable of speech.[7]

Having been the scene of the wedding that was to provoke the schism with Rome that still exists today, it could be said that the Holbein Gate was one of the most important buildings in England, but not a single trace now remains of the great west gateway in Whitehall. To ease traffic congestion in the seventeenth century, the King's former gallery buildings that jutted out from the south of the Banqueting House to connect Henry's great Holbein Gate to his palace were demolished and cleared away. The traffic continued to meander around the gateway, leaving it broken off from the palace, high and dry like a black and white elephant on the west side of the street, but it was not until 1759 that the Holbein Gate itself was finally torn down for road widening. The King Street gate – never much loved by Londoners – had been demolished thirty-six years earlier.

Fragments of the Holbein Gate may have survived outside the capital, however. Horace Walpole recorded that William, Duke of Cumberland, son of George II, and Ranger of Windsor Park and Forest, 'intended to re-edify it but never did'. However, Mr Slingsby, one of the stonemasons then employed by the King at Windsor, said, 'on the taking down the Gate it was begged and obtained' by Cumberland 'with the intention to erect it at the end of the Long Walk'. Thomas Sandby produced drawings, now in the Royal Library, of *The Old Gate, Whitehall,* for the gatehouse to be erected in its former glory with two additional wings on either side at Snow Hill in Windsor Great Park. When the Snow Hill plan was abandoned, many of the stones from the old gatehouse were 'by the Duke's direction worked up by Mr Slingsby . . . in several different buildings erected by the Duke in the Great Park there. A medallion from it is in one of the fronts of a keeper's lodge near the head of the Virginia Water (Virginia Water Lodge).' A similar medallion was put in another cottage, built about the year 1790 in the Great Park, and accessible from the road from Peascod Street. Some roundels were taken to Hampton Court Palace in Queen Victoria's reign and two can be found, although disguised, embedded in the great gatehouse. No other remains were found of the Holbein Gate at Windsor despite concerted efforts during the twentieth century.[8]

There are other traces of Henry's sporting complex hidden behind the bland walls of Whitehall. A window and the northeast tower of the great tennis court that Hollar depicted has miraculously survived inside the wall of the Cabinet Office building. The tower has lost its top twenty feet, but it is a heartstopping experience to walk out of a plain passage painted in the buff colours of civil service envelopes on the top floor of the Cabinet Office to see the distinctive black-and-white chequered Tudor tower standing preserved inside the building, with a clear drop to the ground floor, forty feet below. In Henry's day, where civil servants push pens today, he would have thrashed about the court below, dripping in sweat. But the most complete relic of Henry's palace is the passage that Henry used to reach his sports halls. The gallery, Cockpit Passage, is still in daily use by civil servants including the Cabinet Secretary Sir Gus O'Donnell, who has his desk in the Cabinet Office. For the Tudor passageway where Henry walked with Anne Boleyn and his court is also part of a secret route into Number Ten Downing Street. Visitors not wishing to be seen entering by the media stationed outside in the street can do so by slipping in through the front door of the Cabinet Office at 70 Whitehall. These have included the Sinn Fein leader, Gerry Adams, for private talks with Tony Blair when the Northern Ireland peace initiative was at risk of breaking down, and Alastair Campbell, Mr Blair's former 'spin doctor', who returned to Number Ten after he retired to offer advice to Mr Blair a year before he stepped down, and to his successor Gordon Brown, when disastrous opinion poll results caused a crisis of confidence in his leadership in the summer of 2008. Visitors have to go through the security doors – they look like space-age Perspex pods – and up sixteen stone steps to Cockpit Passage, which is unmistakably Tudor with small red bricks and a large stone fireplace that would have warmed Henry on his way to the courts. In Henry's day, it would have been plastered and hung with tapestries, and the ceiling would have been gilded. At the end of the passage is another flight of steps down to more civil service offices, but tucked away on the left is the 'secret' security door to a further passage, which emerges near the Prime Minister's den inside Number Ten.

In 2012 the sporting ghosts of Henry's Palace of Whitehall may be stirred again. Tons of sand are to be laid two feet deep on Horse Guards Parade, the site of Henry's tiltyard. Where Henry jousted with Charles Brandon, teams of women in skimpy bikinis will compete for an Olympic gold medal in beach volleyball.

# 3

# QUEEN ELIZABETH I's WHITEHALL

'I have already joined myself in marriage to a husband, namely the Kingdom of England.'

Elizabeth to Parliament

On a chill winter morning, on 12 February 1554, Henry's daughter Elizabeth was told she was being taken to Whitehall and she was terrified. Six months earlier, she had ridden to London to greet her half-sister Mary in the city after Mary had defeated the attempted Protestant coup d'état by one of Edward VI's leading councillors, John Dudley, the Duke of Northumberland, to put the sixteen-year-old Lady Jane Grey on the throne and marry her to one of his sons. Now Elizabeth was implicated in another Protestant plot against the Catholic Queen and was carried in a litter from Hatfield by an escort force of 200 horsemen in Mary's red tunics. As they set off for the city, Lady Jane Grey, who had been Queen for just nine days, stepped on to a scaffold at Tower Green and was beheaded, just as Elizabeth's mother, Anne Boleyn, had been on the same spot eighteen years before.

Elizabeth was twenty years old, wise beyond her years, and well versed in the dangers of bloody Tudor politics. She had been ill but the Queen, a zealous Catholic, suspecting a ruse, had insisted on her being carried to Whitehall in a litter if necessary. They made slow progress, averaging six miles a day, and it was not until 23 February that they clattered through Smithfield on the eastern edge of the old city, through Fleet Street and Charing Cross to her mother's former palace, where Mary was waiting. As her litter bounced through the streets of London, the princess, dressed all in white, had the curtains drawn back and showed the people a look of defiance – 'lofty, scornful and magnificent' – but in her heart, she must have been quaking with fear.

A power struggle had followed Henry's death, and the premature death of his son Edward VI (it is a popular myth that Henry had syphilis and passed it on to Edward, a sickly child, but there is no medical evidence to support it) by his third wife, Jane Seymour. This had already led to the execution of Elizabeth's former guardian, the fatally ambitious Thomas Seymour, Jane Seymour's dashing brother. Driven partly by ambition, he had married Henry's widow and sixth wife, Katherine Parr, into whose care Elizabeth had been placed as a teenager. Katherine was an old flame of Seymour's, but he engaged in frolics and games with Elizabeth, including entering her bedchamber in his nightclothes and slapping her buttocks, that today would be seen as sexual abuse. But his most deadly flaw was his lack of judgement. Seymour's older brother Edward, Lord Hertford, had been made the boy king's Protector when Henry VIII died, and had been created Lord Somerset. Thomas had the title of Lord High Admiral, but it was not high enough for him – he hatched a plot to capture the young king in his bedchamber, was discovered and beheaded.

Elizabeth needed all her guile to survive the Seymour plot, but Queen Mary was being urged to rid herself of her Protestant rival by some of her most senior courtiers, including Stephen Gardiner, the Lord Chancellor, and Simon Renard, ambassador to Charles V, the Holy Roman Emperor. Renard had arrived in London to arrange the marriage between the Queen and the Emperor's only son, Philip. The Lady Jane conspirators were held for treason in the Tower of London and for six months Mary had delayed their execution, until her impending marriage with the Catholic heir to the Spanish throne sparked a more reckless Protestant uprising in Kent led by Sir Thomas Wyatt. The rebels were spurred on by a fear that the Spanish prince would bring with him the horrors of the Spanish Inquisition for Protestants like themselves in England. In late January, they had marched to London and headed towards the city, but some split off and stormed towards the gates of Whitehall. Mary anxiously watched the commotion in Whitehall from the Privy Gallery by the Holbein Gate. The rioters were a ragtag army but caused such panic in the guardroom in the courtyard at Whitehall that the Captain of the Guard and Lord Chamberlain, Sir John Gage, fell over in his haste to run away, fouling his garments in the mire, until someone had the presence of mind to close Wolsey's old court gate and lock them out.

The rebels headed off to join their comrades in the city, where they had expected a riotous welcome. However, people showed for a second time within a year that, though they might not want a return to the old religion, they would not rise up against their rightful Queen. Wyatt's rebels found the city gates barred to them. They were forced abjectly to surrender outside the old coaching inn, the Bell Savage on Ludgate Hill. In a remarkable show of clemency, Mary had the rebels brought to the tiltyard where Henry Machyn, an undertaker looking for business, noted in his diary: 'All the Kent men bound with cords two and two together went through London to Westminster. At the Tilt, the poor persons kneeld down in the mire and the Queen's grace looked out from the Gate and gave them all pardon.'

The main plotters were taken to the tower but Mary was persuaded that the rebellion had proved that it was too dangerous to let Lady Jane live. Her execution left only one person who could threaten Mary's hold on the Crown – Elizabeth.

There was circumstantial evidence that Elizabeth knew about the Wyatt plot. Wyatt had sent her a letter that had been intercepted by Mary's spies, but the Privy Council needed more evidence to prove her guilty of treason and so had her brought to Whitehall to secure it. Elizabeth was taken to a remote corner of the palace, near the Privy Garden, so she could be held securely to limit the risk of an armed rescue attempt by her followers. Wyatt, thirty-three, was tortured to admit her involvement in his plot but he stoically refused to implicate Elizabeth, to the frustration of some of the council who wanted her out of the way. Their best chance was to trick Elizabeth into some form of confession. She proved more than their equal. On 17 March, two days after Wyatt's trial in the Great Hall at Westminster, the council came to see Elizabeth where she was under house arrest in the palace apartments. She denied the charges of treason with Wyatt but was told that the Queen was determined she would go to the Tower. That word filled Elizabeth with dread. The next day, a Saturday, the Marquess of Winchester and the Earl of Sussex, both trusted members of the council, stepped into her lodgings in the palace to take her by barge to the Tower, no doubt in the hope of breaking her resistance. Elizabeth was desperate to delay the journey for as long as possible, and she begged Winchester and Sussex for permission to write a letter appealing for an audience with the Queen. Her escorts reluctantly agreed, and she sat down in Whitehall and penned the remarkable letter pleading for her life that still exists in the royal archive. Her writing for once betrayed her nervous state. With many crossings-out and corrections, Elizabeth reminded Mary that she had promised that Elizabeth would not be condemned without answer and proof of her guilt. She urged Mary to fulfil her promise by seeing her before she was sent to the Tower. The letter took a long time to compose, and as she carefully assembled her arguments, the tide in the river turned.

Elizabeth confronted head-on the advice she knew her half-sister would be receiving from some of her councillors – that if she were not removed now, the Queen would never be secure. Then she daringly referred back to the Seymour scandal. By mentioning Seymour, Elizabeth was taking a huge risk, but she was playing for the highest stakes. She said Seymour's brother, the Duke of Somerset, had been placed in a similar position as the Queen was now, because, when he was Lord Protector of England in charge of Edward VI, he had to decide whether to approve the execution of his own brother. Somerset, who was also later to be executed, had refused to hear his brother's pleas for mercy and had regretted it. She wrote:

> In late days I heard my lord Somerset say that if his brother had been suffered to speak with him, he had never suffered.
>
> But persuasions were made to him so great that he was brought in belief that he could not live safely if the Admiral lived. Though these persons are not to be compared to your majesty, yet I pray God the like evil persuasions persuade not one sister against another . . .

Over the page she added: 'I humbly crave to speak with your highness which I would not be so bold as to deceive if I knew not myself to be so dear as I know myself to be true. And as for the traitor Wyatt, he might peradventure write me a letter but [Elizabeth inserted] *on my faith* I never received any . . .'

Then she struck eleven lines in ink diagonally across the page to prevent anyone forging a confession in the space above her signature. She concluded: 'I humbly crave but only one word of answer from yourself.' And she signed herself, *Elizabeth,* with four loops of her quill under the E.

Mary refused to see her but, with the tide running out, it was too late to go to the Tower. The next day, Palm Sunday, Elizabeth was finally taken by barge from Whitehall Palace, which she must have felt was her final journey to the Tower, as it had been her mother's. As she was led out through the Privy Garden towards the Privy Stairs to the barge, she looked up at the windows hoping to see Mary in the Privy Gallery to make a final mute appeal, but it was in vain. She now faced her most terrifying test of nerve, and it took all her father's indomitable spirit and her mother's political guile to survive the ordeal and the charges of treason. Some historians, including Christopher Hibbert in his 1991 biography *The Virgin Queen*, describe in detail how she was taken in through the Traitors' Gate with Kat Ashley, her faithful but simple servant, in driving rain. The scene was meticulously enacted in the television series *Elizabeth R*, in which actress Glenda Jackson, later to become a Labour MP, played Elizabeth with all the fiery intelligence she must have possessed.

Ms Jackson told me that for the filming she had been required to sit defiantly on the steps at the Traitors' Gate entrance while the London Fire Brigade poured thousands of gallons of water over her to simulate rain. 'I said to Kat [played by Rachel Kempson], we must be the only two people who have nearly drowned while sitting on land.'

However, later accounts now suggest the tide was running out again by the time Elizabeth had splashed in the rain from Whitehall to the Tower, huddled in the cabin of the royal barge. The river was so low the barge scraped the bottom in the shallows when it ran under London Bridge. By the time they reached the Tower, the Thames was too low to go through Traitors' Gate. Instead, her barge docked by Tower Wharf and she was taken in across the drawbridge in the rain with Kat Ashley. But there is no doubt that Elizabeth outwitted her gaolers. When Elizabeth arrived at the gates of her prison, she declared: 'Here landeth as true a subject, being prisoner, as ever landed at these steps.' Boldly she told the yeomen warders lined up to receive her: 'Oh Lord! I never thought to have come here as a prisoner, and I pray you all bear me witness that I come in as no traitor but as true a woman to the Queen's Majesty as any as is now living.' Several warders knelt in supplication, and one said: 'God preserve your Grace.'

Elizabeth also exploited divisions within the Queen's council, and raised doubts about the legality of what they were intending to do. Above all, as the feared King's Protestant daughter, she was held in high esteem by the people, and she knew how to mobilize her popularity. As she was shut up in the Bell Tower, in the corner by the Lieutenant's lodgings, the Earl of Sussex warned his companions: 'Let us take heed, my Lords, that we go not beyond our commission, for she was our King's daughter.'

Unable to prove her guilt, and fearful of the consequences of killing her, after two months Mary freed Elizabeth from the Tower on 19 May 1554, into house arrest at Woodstock. Mary had her confidence restored after her wedding to Philip and allowed Elizabeth to return to her beloved Hatfield to await events.

Elizabeth's patience was rewarded when Mary died in 1558 after a phantom pregnancy that modern historians believe was probably a huge ovarian cyst that could have caused blood poisoning. Horsemen returned to Hatfield, but this time to deliver Mary's black enamelled engagement ring, the signal that Elizabeth was now Queen, provoking her to fall to her knees on the turf and utter her famous quotation from the Psalm 118: 'This is the Lord's doing; it is marvellous in our eyes.'

Within six hours of Mary's death the joint Houses of Parliament went to Whitehall Palace to proclaim Elizabeth Queen. It was 17 November 1558, a date she would celebrate each year at Whitehall for the rest of her life.

Elizabeth quickly established a daily routine at Whitehall. She occupied the Privy Gallery range, intended for the King, and left vacant the rooms by the river intended for a consort. She was not, she said, 'a morning woman'. Rising late, sometimes when the rest of her court had had breakfast, she sat in her 'night-stuff' looking through the window as her ladies helped her with her toilet, brushing her hair, and dressing her – she had an immense wardrobe, and particularly liked silk stockings – before she went for a brisk walk around the palace gardens. An inventory showed she had 102 French gowns, 100 loose gowns, 67 round gowns, 99 robes, 127 cloaks, 85 doublets, 125 petticoats, 56 outer skirts, 126 kirtles and 136 stomachers to choose from, and a valuable collection of jewellery, including jewelled watches, bracelets, rings and necklaces. She breakfasted in her Privy Chamber.

She was notorious for changing her mind and, to the irritation of her long-suffering Secretary of State William Cecil, whom she ennobled as Lord Burghley, the Queen immersed herself in council business, carefully reading council letters presented to her for signature by messengers on bended knee. She then might chair meetings of her council in a room off the Privy Gallery, often displaying the flashes of fiery temper and tantrums she had inherited from her father and Anne Boleyn. Henry had moved the council from Wolsey's old Turk's Gallery overlooking the Thames to a larger first-floor room off the north side of the principal Privy Gallery overlooking the Preaching Place; this was probably for his greater convenience when he found walking difficult, as it was a few steps from his private apartments, near to the south corner of the Banqueting House today. The Preaching Place had been set up in 1548, the year after Henry's death, in the centre of the then Privy

Garden, for Elizabeth's pious Protestant half-brother, Edward. The Preaching Place was a square, cobbled courtyard, open to the skies, surrounded by a two-storey loggia, which was supported on columns and had a balustrade on the balcony above. In the centre was the covered pulpit; vast crowds would gather to hear hell-and-damnation sermons, while Elizabeth and her nobles sat in the window of the first-floor council chamber, which overlooked the preacher. Elizabeth may have resisted her half-sister's efforts to convert her to Catholicism, but she did enforce religious doctrine herself. In 1560, Lent was strictly observed: carts of meat could be confiscated during fasting for forty days by royal proclamation sealed by Elizabeth.[1] When the fasting was over, the feasting would begin in the Great Hall or the Presence Chamber, where Wolsey had entertained his guests.

When Elizabeth was away from Whitehall, her private rooms were open to viewing and they were a spectacular sight. Visiting ambassadors and diplomats would usually enter up the staircase from the Parkside and cross via the Holbein Gate to be taken into the Privy Gallery range by a palace custodian. Leopold von Wedel recorded:

> First he led us up a staircase into a passage which runs alongside the tilt-yard. The passage has a ceiling most beautifully ornamented with gold and is carpeted underfoot. On the walls hang fine paintings among them Edward, the present Queen's brother . . . Likewise the face of Moses is portrayed there . . . Near it hangs the Passion. It has the appearance of being painted on glass. Everything is studded with gold.[2]

One portrait of Edward VI looked distorted until the visitors viewed it through a small hole or 'O' cut into a plate on a bar by the painting, which resolved the distortion into a formed face. This altered perspective – used by Holbein in the skull in the enigmatic

*The Ambassadors' Secret* – fascinated Shakespeare, who visited the palace and toyed with the idea of perspective in Act Two of *King Richard the Second*: 'Like perspectives, which rightly gazed upon show nothing but confusion; eyed awry distinguish form.'

The ceiling of her bedchamber was gilded but a number of visitors remarked on how dark it was, lit only by a single window. Helen Mirren's portrayal of Elizabeth in *Elizabeth I* for Channel 4 in 2005 captured the drama of life in the elongated setting of the Privy Gallery, and the extraordinary – to modern eyes – interiors of the Whitehall Palace. The film sets which show the Queen's apartments with dark walls, decorated with golden stars and blood-red splashes of Tudor roses are accurate for the time. But the most striking aspect of the palace would have been the magnificent rich wall hangings and tapestries, before hanging paintings became the norm, although the tapestries were too prized to be used permanently like wallpaper. Nick Humphrey at the Victoria and Albert Museum told me: 'There was a good deal of continuity during Elizabeth's reign, especially in terms of creating an effect of magnificence through co-ordinated colour and texture – most lavishly through luxury textiles.'

The Queen also had an exotic bath and Baron Waldstein described how 'the water pours from oyster shells and different kinds of rock'. The next room, on the east side of the bedchamber, according to Waldstein, held musical instruments, which she liked to play, including an Elizabethan organ and a virginal, and she kept up her father's interest in science and mechanical objects – there were 'numerous cunningly wrought clocks in all sizes'. Then came the library where diarist John Evelyn discovered a century later a wide variety of books that had been presented to successive monarchs:

> . . . few histories, some traveles, and french bookes, Mapps and sea [charts], entertainments and pomps, buildings and pieces relating to the Navy; some mathematical instruments. But what was most

rare were 3 or 4 Romish Breviaries with a greate deal of Miniature and Monkish Painting and Gilding, one of which is most exquisitely don, both as to the figures, Grotescs and Compartiments, to the uttmost of that curious art. There's another in which I find written by the hand of Henry VII, his giving it to his deare daughter Margarite, afterwards Queene of Scots, (mother of our K James and greate greate Grandmother to the successive Kings uniting the two Kingdomes) in which he desires her to pray for his soule, subscribing his Name at length . . . An ancient woman who made these lodgings cleane and had all the keyes let me in at pleasure, for a small reward, by the meanes of a friend.[3]

The remaining rooms towards the river were the dining chamber, and a dressing chamber that held an expensive collection of costumes for the Queen.

After chairing the council, dinner would be served at noon in the Privy Chamber at the end of the Privy Gallery range. The Privy Chamber, according to accounts of the day, was decorated with a gilded ceiling and pictures of the wars that Elizabeth had waged, including no doubt the destruction of the Spanish Armada. This was her private chamber, near the great hall where Wolsey had entertained her father. According to Hentzner's *Travels in England*, 'The Queen dined and supped alone, with very few attendants and it was very seldom that anybody, native or foreigner, was admitted at that time, and then only at the intercession of somebody in power.' But there was an elaborate performance before she was served in the chamber. While she was at prayers in the ante-chapel, the table cloth was laid with great veneration, as if she were there, with servants kneeling three times; the salt cellar, plate and bread were laid out with equal reverence; an unmarried lady – a countess – in a dress of white silk prostrated herself three times before rubbing the plates with salt and bread; then the yeomen of the guard – the tallest and strongest that could be found – arrived clothed in scarlet with a golden rose upon their backs bringing in at each turn a course of twenty-four dishes, served on golden plate; these dishes were received by a gentlemen of the yeomen and placed upon the table where the lady taster gave to each of the guards a mouthful to test for poison. As the dinner was brought in, it was accompanied by twelve trumpets and two kettledrums, which 'made the hall ring for half an hour together'. At the end of this ceremony, a number of unmarried ladies appeared who 'with particular solemnity, lifted the meat off the table and conveyed it into the queen's inner and more private chamber, where, after she had chosen for herself, the rest went to the ladies of the Court'.

In the afternoon, her public duties began. She met diplomats at formal receptions in the Presence Chamber, which would be packed with diplomats and her courtiers, all vying for her eye. There would be an orchestra playing, and space would be cleared for entertainments, where she indulged her love of courtly music and elaborate Elizabethan dance. She was renowned for dancing up to six galliards, coquettishly inviting her favourites to dance with her, as she smiled and nodded, and stepped haughtily to the music. And in the evening there were more lavish banquets and sometimes, as a treat, she watched the daring plays of Shakespeare performed in Whitehall by the playwright and his company of actors, the Chamberlain's Men. In his account of a year (1599) in the life of Shakespeare, the historian James Shapiro says the plays were put on in the great chamber, which was 60 feet long by 30 feet wide with a ceiling 20 feet high; it had a wooden floor and a fireplace, and was decorated with rich tapestries.[4] The Office of the Revels supervised the lighting and scenery and acted like a royal censor, removing offending material from plays. There was a Sergeant Painter to oversee any more decoration and hordes of pages to clear the hall and bring in the throne chair where the Queen would sit.

By this date, the Queen was old, but Shakespeare was in his prime. He had tired of accommodating in his plays the farcical antics of one of the company's stars, Will Kemp, the Tudor equivalent of a stand-up comedian, who played Falstaff. Elizabethan plays traditionally ended with a ribald 'jig', a free-for-all comedy routine at which Kemp excelled. For the royal command performance at Whitehall, Shakespeare was to make his own speech at the end of the play. Shapiro believes we can now read Shakespeare's remarks because they were preserved at the end of Part 2 of *King Henry the Fourth* by accident by the printers with the text for Kemp's 'jig'. Shakespeare apologized to the Queen for presenting 'a displeasing play' in the past – he does not identify it – with the hope that he has now delivered a better one:

> First, my fear; then my curtsy; last my speech. My fear is your displeasure; my curtsy, my duty; and my speech, to beg your pardons. If you look for a good speech now, you undo me, for what I have to say is of my own making and what indeed I should say will, I doubt, prove my own marring. But to the purpose, and so to the venture. Be it known to you, as it is very well, I was lately here in the end of a displeasing play, to pray your patience for it, and to promise a better. I meant indeed to pay you with this, which, if like an ill venture it come unluckily home, I break, and you, my gentle creditors, lose. Here I promised you I would be, and here commit my body to your mercies. Bate me some and I will pay you some and, as most debtors do, promise you infinitely. And so I kneel down before you; but indeed, to pray for the Queen.'

The whole audience would have had no option but to fall to its knees to pray at that point.

Elizabeth liked to work late into the night, even after such entertainments as a performance by Shakespeare and his band of players, and – like later Prime Ministers with their cabinet secretaries – would sometimes summon Cecil to her privy chamber to work after midnight.

Unlike her spendthrift father, Elizabeth was parsimonious from necessity, and Whitehall went largely unchanged during her forty-four-year reign apart from the building of a wooden banqueting house in April 1581. She was then thirty-seven and under immense political pressure from Parliament to marry. This expenditure she approved in order in May that year lavishly to entertain her French suitor in marriage, Henry, the snub-nosed Duc d'Alençon, whom she called her 'Frog'. He was the brother to the King of France, Henry III, and it was clearly getting serious – it was his second visit in two years. The new entertaining hall was hurriedly constructed alongside the court gate on King Street, where the later neoclassical Banqueting House of Inigo Jones now stands on Whitehall.

The Great Hall could not be taken over by the Office of Revels for entertaining the Queen's French suitors and their courts because it was on the processional route to the Queen's lodgings, and was regarded as too old-fashioned. The new banqueting house was an immense space, and its roof was supported by thirty great wooden masts, each of which were estimated to be forty feet high, but – like the tents at the Field of the Cloth of Gold – it was not meant to be permanent. It had canvas walls painted to look like stone but 292 glass windows. Holinshead's *Chronicles* in 1587 recorded:

> The banquet house made in manner and form of a long square 332 foot in measure about, 30 principalls made of great masts, being XL foot in length apeece, standing upright; between every eny of these masts X foot a sunder and more. The walls of this howse was closed with canvas, and painted all the outsides of the same most artificially with a work called rustick, most like unto stone. This house hath 292 lights of Glas.'

Elizabeth's courtiers were expected to lavish flamboyant flattery on the Queen, even as she advanced into middle age, and the pageants that were put on by her revel masters had not changed from those enjoyed by her father at Wolsey's expense. Before the romantic overtures from her 'Frog', the Queen was treated to a courtly pageant rich in allegory at the tiltyard. She was hailed by her courtiers as a 'fortress of perfect Beautie' at a pageant of the same name in 1581 for the French marriage embassy, and a chorus led by Desire sang to her:

> Yield, yield, O yield, ye that this fort do hold,
> Which seated is in Honour's spotless field
> Desire's great force no forces can withhold
> Then to Desire's desire, O yield, O yield ...

It proved so popular with the public that the stands in the tiltyard collapsed. She was seen strolling with her 'Frog' in the gallery at Whitehall Palace after dinner on Accession Day. The French Ambassador, Michel de Castelnau, asked if he might tell the French King that they were to be married. Elizabeth kissed the Duke on the mouth, took a ring from her hand and placed it on his finger, and said: 'You may tell his Majesty that the Prince will be my husband.'[5] Her 'Frog' gave her a ring in return. Mendoza, the Spanish Ambassador, who would soon be sent home in a diplomatic rift leading eventually to the Armada, reported, 'Shortly afterwards, the Queen summoned the ladies and gentlemen from the Presence Chamber into the [Privy] Gallery, repeating to them in a loud voice in [Anjou's] presence what she had just said.'

Her behaviour shocked some of her courtiers, and the prospect of the Virgin Queen 'yielding' to her French 'Frog' was anathema to many of her subjects, including John Stubbs and William Page, the author and publisher of a nationalist tract against the alliance, who each had a hand chopped off on a block outside Whitehall Palace in punishment. Showing no remorse, Page bravely said: 'I have left there a true Englishman's hand.' The public sympathy they gained reinforced Elizabeth's doubts about her faltering marriage plans. The morning after her unequivocal commitment to marry the Duc d'Anjou, Elizabeth, after a sleepless night, called it off. Anjou tore the ring she had given him off his finger and threw it to the ground.

The episode soured international relations, but also showed the English had developed a strong sense of their own national identity under their Protestant Queen Elizabeth. The constant threat of a Catholic invasion from either France or Spain was heightened when spies employed by her intelligence chief, Francis Walsingham, uncovered a serious Catholic plot to assassinate Elizabeth at Whitehall, and put Mary, Queen of Scots, on the throne. Elizabeth took the traumatic decision to sign the warrant for Mary's execution at Fotheringhay Castle, Peterborough, which, as the daughter of another beheaded queen, haunted her for the rest of her life.

Then came the Spanish Armada of 130 ships carrying 17,000 soldiers. It sailed from Lisbon on 30 May 1588 and Britain, not for the last time, faced invasion. Elizabeth wanted to go to the south coast, where the Spanish were expected to land, but was persuaded by Robert Dudley, Earl of Leicester, her devoted favourite and Master of Horse, to travel by her private barge from the steps at Whitehall to review her pathetically small army of troops at Tilbury. Dressed in a steel corselet – an armoured breastplate – over a white velvet riding dress, and carrying a small silver staff, she rode a white charger from which she made one of her most famous speeches. There is no doubt about the stirring words she used, because it was also circulated in printed form to be repeated to the troops out of earshot:

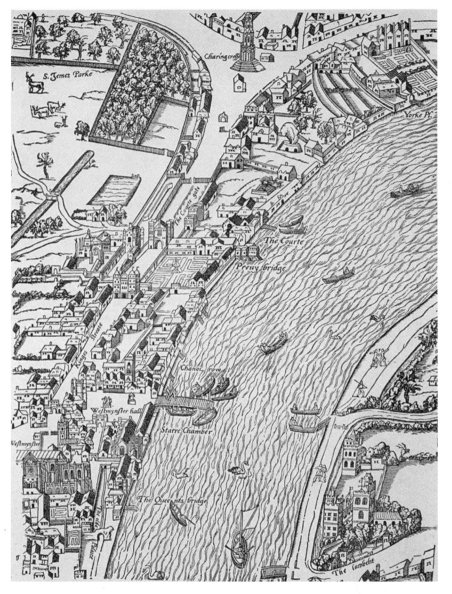

The Royal Palace of Whitehall *c*.1560. This was copied in 1633 from an original woodcut map of London called *Civitas Londinium* attributed to Ralph Agas.

Henry VIII's wine cellar. It survived the fire that destroyed the Palace of Whitehall in 1698 but in 1948 was moved and lowered on screw-jacks into the basement of the Ministry of Defence Main Building, where it is used today for receptions.

Cockpit Passage, used by Henry VIII and his court to reach the Cockpit and the indoor tennis courts, where he played 'real tennis'.

An exterior wall of Henry VIII's tennis courts has survived behind the Cabinet Office. The line of mullioned windows follow the path of Cockpit Passage to a 'secret' entrance to Number Ten Downing Street.

The northeast tower of the former Tudor tennis court inside the Cabinet Office.

The glittering interior of the Banqueting House, Inigo Jones's classical masterpiece for James I, completed in 1622. Charles I walked through this hall onto the scaffold outside the windows on the right, where he was beheaded.

The execution of Charles I took place outside the Banqueting House at about 2 p.m. on 30 January 1649. Pepys was in the crowd which gave a collective groan when the severed head was held up by the executioner.

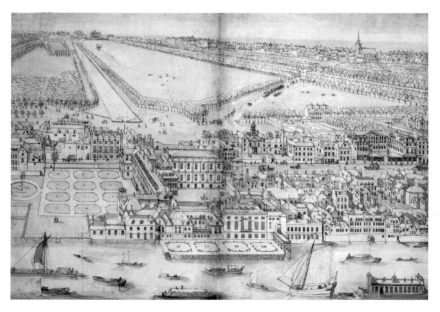

Whitehall Palace c.1698 by Leonard Knyff shortly before the fire destroyed most of the buildings. Queen Mary's steps survived and can be seen in the gardens by the MoD building today.

Queen Mary's steps, part of Wren's terrace and the bases of the portico, a pillared walkway, were uncovered with the foundations of the Tudor Royal Palace in 1939 when work started on the building of the MoD.

The Tudor foundations of the Royal Palace of Whitehall revealed in 1939.

The dining room of Admiralty House, official residence of the First Lord of the Admiralty, where Nelson dined after the Battle of Nile and treated his wife Fanny with 'contempt'.

The Board Room of the Admiralty completed in 1726. The wind dial on the right, one of the hidden gems of Whitehall, is attached to a weathervane on the roof to show the Sea Lords which way the wind was blowing.

A bust of Lord Nelson wearing the Chelengk, or diamond Plume of Triumph, from the imperial turban given to him by Sultan Selim III of Turkey for his victory at the Battle of the Nile.

I know I have the body of a weak and feeble woman but I have the heart and stomach of a King and of a King of England too, and think foul scorn that Parma or Spain or any Prince of Europe should dare to invade the borders of my realm . . .

She was still at Tilbury when a messenger arrived with news that the Armada had been scattered and the crisis was over. At the thanksgiving service, the Queen rode in procession from Whitehall to St Paul's in a chariot pulled by two white horses, like a goddess of war, and there were days of festivities in the tiltyard.

As she grew into old age, pageantry became more important than jousts, although they were still enjoyed. One eyewitness account describes:

My Lord Robert Dudley and my Lord Hunsdon the challengers, and they all wear in skarffes of whyt and blak boyth the heraldes and trumpeters and defenders with others in skarffes of red and yellow sarsenett.

Ever more elaborate pageants were held at the tiltyard to mark important events in the Elizabethan calendar, including her succession day, and her birthday, a tradition maintained today with the Trooping of the Colour on the same spot at Horse Guards Parade. The pageants included the Tourney of the Inner Temple, the jousts to celebrate a wedding of courtiers, jousts between ten married men and ten bachelors, and more jousts to celebrate the victory over the Spanish Armada every August.[6]

Elizabeth required every knight taking part in the tournament to present her with a papier mâché shield, an *impresa*, which was more than just a chivalric coat of arms; it was supposed to contain a witty hidden message, with a Latin motto. The Earl of Rutland paid Shakespeare forty-four shillings to produce a shield for him – a huge sum at the time when a labourer might earn four pence a day. Shakespeare later included the theme of knights presenting their shields with their clever mottos in *Pericles*, whose own shield bore a 'withered branch that's only green at top' and the Latin motto *in hac spe vivo* – which roughly translated means 'I live in hope' (II. ii. 43–4).

Elizabeth created an extraordinary cult of herself as an object of adoration, to reinforce the image of wealth, authority and power. She was slender, red-haired, witty, learned and flirtatious. She expected handsome gifts, especially at New Year: a surviving account from 1 January 1588 shows they ranged from a gold, diamond and ruby necklace with matching earrings from Sir Christopher Hatton (one of her court favourites who gave his name to the jewellery market in London), to a macaroon from her master cook. She was meticulous about ritual and style, and there was a legally enforced pecking order in the richness of clothes – only duchesses, marquises and countesses could wear clothes adorned with gold or sable fur. Her maids of honour were kept in black and white, but the Queen wore striking colours of red to match her hair, or yellow with brilliant embroidery with cascades of pearls (then prized as much as precious jewels), and, in her old age, sumptuous black dresses embroidered with pearls and silver. An alabaster complexion symbolized wealth and to achieve it women would use a white foundation, known as ceruse, made from white lead, powdered eggshells and vinegar. Women tried to copy Elizabeth's red hair, resorting to red wigs when the dyed hair thinned and, as Elizabeth's hairline receded, plucked ever more vigorously to look like the Queen. Eyes were brightened with drops from the deadly nightshade plant also known as belladonna – the Italian for 'beautiful lady' – because it constricted the muscles in the eye to dilate the pupils, making the eyes look bigger and more attractive. It is also claimed that when Elizabeth's teeth became blackened, due to her sweet tooth, women in the court even followed by blacking their own. She also used golden toothpicks, which appeared in her inventories.

Male courtiers, including Hatton, whom she nicknamed her 'lids' while Robert Dudley was her 'eyes', were expected to indulge her in elaborate exaggerated flattery, however wrinkled she appeared, in return for enormously profitable offices and favours. In the later years of her reign, they took to wearing miniature portraits of the Queen to show their devotion – even her sombre Secretary of State Burghley wore a medallion of the Queen in his hat. They avoided marriage or married in secret to remain her favourite at court. The swashbuckling seafarer, Sir Walter Raleigh, whom she lightly mocked by calling him 'Water', was sent to the Tower for marrying one of her favourite ladies-in-waiting, Bess Throckmorton, and Elizabeth was furious when she discovered that Dudley, her favourite courtier with whom she was rumoured to have had an affair, had secretly married the beautiful Lettice Knollys, Countess of Essex and Mary Boleyn's granddaughter. Elizabeth vented her anger when Lettice arrived with her retinue at the Whitehall court: 'As but one sun lights the East, so shall I have but one queen in England!'

Dudley adopted Lettice's son by her first marriage, Robert Devereux, the Earl of Essex, and there were court rumours he had been the real father. The boy was handsome, headstrong, ambitious and disastrously spoiled by the Queen, who was thirty-three years his senior.

After Dudley's death, Elizabeth, old, black-toothed and white-faced, maintained an extraordinary, passionate relationship with Essex, whom she called her 'wild horse'. It was an apt nickname, and his ambition proved untameable. He had become a national hero after a successful raid on the Spanish port at Cadiz and he hotly opposed peace with the Spanish. At one meeting in the council chamber Burghley, alarmed by Essex's histrionics, pushed a warning note to him across the table – a practice still common today among ministers in the Cabinet. It was a psalter open at the Psalm 55: 'The bloody and deceitful men shall not live out half their day . . .' But it had little effect on Essex.

Old and infirm, Burghley engineered the succession of his son, Robert Cecil, as the Queen's Secretary of State. Elizabeth had nicknames for her courtiers and unkindly dubbed Robert Cecil, whom she never liked as much as his father, 'Pygmy'. Essex, however, was convinced that Cecil was leading a faction against him in favour of a compromise over Spain.

Courtiers at Whitehall Palace had become used to the Queen's angry outbursts, shouting profanities such as 'God's death!' at her own ministers, but her anger increased as she came to realize that Essex could not be reined in. Thirsting for more glory, he persuaded Elizabeth to allow him to lead a series of military attacks on the Spanish. They were badly handled, but his downfall came after he was put in charge of a force of 17,000 English troops in 1599 to subdue an Irish rebel leader, Hugh O'Neill, Earl of Tyrone, who had been in contact with Philip II of Spain, threatening a fresh invasion of England through Ireland. Instead of concentrating an attack on O'Neill as the Queen repeatedly demanded, Essex prevaricated and allowed his force to be humbled by disease. Essex defied the Queen's orders and met O'Neill on horseback in the shallows of the River Lagan to agree an armistice before sailing with a small force back to England. The Queen was furious, had Essex put under house arrest, and told one of his messengers: 'By God's son, I am no Queen. This man is above me.'

Burning with injustice at his treatment, and convinced of his own popularity with the people, Essex later gathered a handful of young cronies from the court (including his openly gay friend, the Earl of Southampton), and at the head of a force of 200 followers went by river to the city to raise support for a palace coup. Spies had been keeping a watch on Essex's house in the Strand and the guard was reinforced around the Whitehall court gate when his plans to storm the palace were leaked, but the reinforcements were not needed. Essex failed to gain supporters and, after a short siege at Essex House, Essex and Southampton surrendered their swords and were taken to the Tower. Southampton and the rest were spared but on 24 February 1601 Elizabeth, now aged sixty-seven, reluctantly signed the death warrant for Essex for treason. Later that day, the Queen buried her grief with an entertainment at Whitehall. The Chamberlain's Men, who included Shakespeare and Richard Burbage, put on a comedy for her at Whitehall Palace, *The Merry Wives of Windsor*, the hilarious farce in which Falstaff woos the wives of two Windsor merchants. The next day, Ash Wednesday, wearing black and a red waistcoat, Essex was beheaded on Tower Green. It took three strokes of the axe to sever his head.

Approaching her seventies, she still enjoyed blood sports at the tiltyard in Whitehall where, a quarter-century before, her knights Robert Dudley and George, Earl of Cumberland, had fought for her favour.

'Her Majesty says she is very well,' Sir Robert Sidney's agent, Rowland White, wrote to Sir Robert, later Earl of Leicester. 'This day she appoints a Frenchman to do feats upon a rope in the conduit court; tomorrow she has commanded the bears, the bull and the ape to be baited in the Tilt-yard. Upon Wednesday she will have "solemne dancing".'

Elizabeth had transformed England from the turbulence of the succession to stability, and had seen off the threat of Catholic invasion by the Spanish. In 1601, both Houses of Parliament, 141 members, crowded into the Presence Chamber at Whitehall, less than half a mile from where the ceremony takes place today, to hear the Queen's Speech on bended knee. She was sixty-eight and in good health, though some may have guessed this was to be her final speech to them, and would go down as the 'Golden Speech':

> Of myself I must say this: I never was any greedy, scraping grasper, nor a strait fast-holding Prince, nor yet a waster. My heart was never set on any worldly goods . . . To be a King and wear a crown is a thing more glorious to them that see it than it is pleasant to them that wear it . . .

She died in 1603 at Richmond aged sixty-nine without an heir. The Tudor Age died with her, but even in death her body served a purpose for the stability of the State. It was placed inside a lead coffin and taken down the Thames by barge to Whitehall, where she lay in state. A life-size effigy of the Queen was dressed in her royal robes and placed on top of the coffin, remaining on show as a visual display of monarchy in the capital while her successor, James I, the first of the Stuart kings, made his progress from Scotland to London. Her tomb in Westminster Abbey carries an effigy of how she would have looked in old age – hawk-nosed, gaunt and terrifyingly regal.

## Whitehall Farce

Whitehall has also become synonymous with a form of entertainment that Elizabeth I would probably have recognized – farce. Playing the fool in Tudor Whitehall was deadly serious. There was a long tradition of fools, dwarfs and jesters in the households of the rich and the best were highly prized for their wit. Cardinal Wolsey sent his own Fool called Patch to Henry VIII after the King had spared his life as a token of his affection, saying, 'Surely, for a nobleman's pleasure he is worth a thousand pounds.' Patch wanted to stay with his master, but settled down under the guidance of Henry's jester, Will Somers.

When crowds refused to remove their hats at Anne Boleyn's

coronation parade, Anne's Fool chided them: 'I think you all have scurvy and dare not uncover your heads.' They shouted back 'Witch' and 'Harlot' and made a punning joke of the Henry and Anne initials, 'Ha Ha'.

Poking fun at the Royal Court could be dangerous. 'Archy' Armstrong, jester to James I who came with the King from Scotland and remained to entertain the court under Charles I, was sentenced on 11 March 1637 'to have his coat pulled over his head and be discharged the King's service and banished the King's court'. His crime was ridiculing Archbishop Laud, the Archbishop of Canterbury, after the Scottish rebellion against the Book of Common Prayer, saying: 'Who's the fool now?'

The court jesters faded away, but the long tradition of farce was revived in the 1950s in Whitehall by the comic actor Brian Rix. His live television performances from the stage of the Whitehall Theatre when television was in its infancy made Whitehall synonymous with farce. He spanned nearly two decades and became a household name in Britain with a string of hit comedies, *Reluctant Heroes*, *Dry Rot*, *Simple Spymen*, *One for the Pot* and, in the Cold War 1960s, *Chase Me Comrade*, classically involving Rix in mix-ups over rooms, slamming doors, scantily clad maids, and trousers falling around his ankles. His autobiography was called *My Farce from My Elbow*, but he was given a life peerage in 1992 for his charitable work. He is the president of the charity Mencap, and was an active member of the House of Lords. Lord Rix's many books include a history of farce such as *Life in the Farce Lane*. He can trace the roots of farce to Shakespeare and Ben Jonson, and also to the fools who used to entertain at the Whitehall Palace. Playwright Ray Cooney, known as 'the master of farce' drew the comparisons with Elizabethan theatre: 'What Shakespeare does with kings, I do with taxi drivers.'

The art deco Whitehall Theatre opened its doors in September 1930 and during the war became famous with the troops for a 1942 revue called *Whitehall Follies* starring stripper Phyllis Dixey. Fiona Richmond, a vicar's daughter who became a sex goddess, also bared all in *Pyjama Tops,* a show that ran for five years after the curtain finally came down on the Brian Rix farces at the theatre in 1969. Farce briefly returned to the Whitehall Theatre (now the Trafalgar Studios) in 1981 with the comedy *Anyone For Denis?* starring the late John Wells. It lampooned Prime Minister Margaret Thatcher's loyal husband and escort, Denis, with a script loosely based on the *Dear Bill* letters Wells co-wrote with Richard Ingrams in the satirical magazine *Private Eye*. It ran for more than a year, and Mrs Thatcher sat in the stalls one night with Denis to see what all the fuss was about. She was not amused.

# 4

# BLOOD AT THE
# BANQUETING HOUSE

He nothing common did or mean
Upon that memorable scene,
But with his keener eye
The axe's edge did try;
Nor called the Gods, with vulgar spite,
To vindicate his helpless right,
But bowed his comley head
Down, as upon a bed.

From *An Horatian Ode upon Cromwell's
Return from Ireland*, Andrew Marvell

Still in the first flush of Labour's election victory in 1997, Tony Blair
had a royal duty to perform: a toast to Queen Elizabeth II and
Prince Philip on their Golden Wedding anniversary.

Three months earlier, on Sunday 31 August, the youthful Prime

Minister had spoken movingly about the death of their daughter-in-law, Diana, Princess of Wales, describing her as the 'People's Princess'. It was a phrase that appeared to bear the imprint of former *Daily Mirror* journalist Alastair Campbell, the Prime Minister's head of communications and chief 'spin doctor', although he denied it, but Blair was judged to have 'spoken for the nation'. England, for a nation that prided itself on its stiff upper lip, was in the grip of an extraordinary emotional outpouring of grief for the pop-star princess who had been, by popular opinion, wronged by the Royal Family. It resulted in a dangerous public backlash against the House of Windsor. Campbell's Downing Street 'spin' machine had found the Palace hopelessly outdated and wooden in its response to Diana's death, and took on the role of saving the Royal Family from itself by populist touches, such as flying the flag of Buckingham Palace at half-mast, to show to the public it 'cared'. Blair's support for the monarchy at the Banqueting House was part of the 'fightback' strategy.

By November, as Blair stood to deliver his toast to the Golden Wedding anniversary, the New Labour spin machine was in overdrive to restore the popularity of the monarchy: 'I know too, contrary to some of the hurtful things that were said at the time, how moved you were by the outpouring of grief which followed,' he said.

And in a sound bite that was designed to catch the headlines the next day, he added: 'I am proud as proud can be to be your Prime Minister today offering this tribute on behalf of the country. You are our Queen. We respect and cherish you. You are, simply, the Best of British.'

His remarks in retrospect may sound like a bad line from a cheap greetings card but they were part of 'Cool Britannia', the campaign by the image makers to sell 'Modern Britain' to the world – including the British monarchy – before the fiasco of the Millennium Dome was to knock the new shine off New Labour. Here was a Labour

Prime Minister at the flood of his popularity defending the House of Windsor from the murmurings of the people. And yet, only a Prime Minister with a view of history that started on his own election day could have ignored the historical importance of the venue – Inigo Jones's brilliant Palladian building, the Banqueting House in Whitehall – for the defence of monarchy as an institution. Sources at the Palace have confirmed to me that the venue was chosen by Downing Street. 'It wasn't us,' I was told. For it was outside the windows that lit the Queen's luncheon, on 30 January 1649, that King Charles I was executed and England's Republic was born.

The Banqueting House in Whitehall was one of the outstanding monuments to the modern age that was ushered in by the Stuart kings. It had been built on the site of the old Queen's banqueting hall that was in a dilapidated state in April 1603 when James I arrived at Whitehall Palace for the first time from Holyrood. He arrived already bearing the crown of Scotland as James VI to assume the crown of England and create a new united Britain. King James was an intellectual who lent his name to a revised version of the Bible in English that was to have a profound and lasting impact on the development of the English language.

Courtiers at Whitehall Palace were used to the earthy language of Elizabeth – she once told a courtier when he bowed to her after absenting himself for farting: 'My Lord, I had forgot the fart' – but they feared worse when they heard exaggerated reports from Scotland of his behaviour. He was said to have bawdy tastes, and shockingly uncouth manners, a thick Scots accent, a rich vocabulary in obscene jokes, and a predilection for young men. Their fears seemed to be realized when, as the public crowded round his carriage as he made for Whitehall, he exploded: 'God's wounds – I will pull down my breeches and they shall also see my arse!'.[1] With his slovenly dress and his sloppy table manners – he ate with an open mouth and spilled his food down his beard – his English courtiers could hardly believe this was the great-great-grandson of Henry VII and Elizabeth of York, and the son of the beautiful Mary, Queen of Scots, and dashing Lord Darnley. But he had a quick, shrewd mind, and remarkable education, and the English looked to his arrival with relief. Like countless political leaders since her reign, Elizabeth I's final years in power were marked by disillusionment among her people at rising prices and unpopular taxes, leading to protests and harsh suppression. In James they saw a committed Protestant, who guaranteed a line of succession with the two sons produced by his Danish Queen, Anne – Henry and Charles.

Historian David Starkey focuses on his statecraft in his book *Majesty*, describing how James adopted a very modern strategy on receiving the crown by summoning three major conferences on peace, religion and union with Scotland in an attempt to reach compromises on each. The religious conference at Somerset House on the Strand enraged the Protestant extremists, who did not wish to enter a peace treaty with the Roman Catholic powers in Europe, where Protestant persecution was continuing, nor did it satisfy the Roman Catholic fundamentalists who were enraged that the Catholic negotiators had failed to extract a commitment to religious tolerance for Catholics in England. Starkey suggests it was this failure that led an English Catholic clique, including a conspirator called Guido Fawkes, to take direct action by attempting to blow up King James and the Parliament with him.

Sir Thomas Knyvett is known to history as 'the man who uncovered the Gunpowder Plot'. In fact, Knyvett was the keeper of the keys to the royal palace of Whitehall, and acted on a tip-off in an anonymous letter to Lord Monteagle warning the Catholic peer not to attend the State Opening on 5 November because of a 'terrible blow' against Parliament. Knyvett delayed his search until the night of 4 November to try to catch the conspirators in the act. The Clerk of the House, Ralph Ewans, made a marginal note in the records for the next day's business:

> This last night, the Upper House of Parliament was searched by Sir Thomas Knyvett and one Mr Johnson [Fawkes's assumed name], servant to Mr Thomas Percy, was there apprehended, who had placed 36 barrels of gunpowder in the vault under the House with a purpose to blow it and the whole company [up] when they should here assemble.

Sir Thomas was rewarded with a peerage and, as a mark of trust, he was also made Warden of the Royal Mint. Four plotters were sentenced to death by hanging, drawing and quartering (brief hanging, castration, and disembowelling alive before being beheaded, and chopped into four sections). They were executed in St Paul's churchyard, and four others including Fawkes were put to a bloody death at Old Palace Yard in front of the Parliament building they tried to blow up. The search for the barrels is re-enacted today before every State Opening of Parliament by the Queen's Bodyguard of the Yeomen of the Guard, the oldest military corps in existence, created after Bosworth by Henry VII. All they will find today is the MPs' rifle range[2] and stores of furniture.

Having survived the Gunpowder Plot, life at the Palace of Whitehall under James I seemed to be one long party. James revelled in bawdy drunken parties, and practical jokes. The Earl of Pembroke (one of the King's favourites who had grace-and-favour apartments near the Cockpit in the palace) did not like frogs, so the King put one down his neck. The King disliked pigs so Pembroke put a pig in the King's bedroom at Whitehall. Masques would turn into drunken orgies – at a re-enactment of King Solomon's Temple, the Queen of Sheba was so drunk that she stumbled and dropped 'wine, cream, jelly, beverages, cakes, spices and other good matters' over James's brother-in-law, King Christian IV of Denmark, who was also so drunk he collapsed unconscious on the floor. James I also appalled old courtiers with his love for beautiful boys, and none more so than George Villiers, whom he dubbed 'Steenie', because his angelic looks reminded the King of Saint Stephen. He showered money, land and titles on Steenie, making him the Marquess of Buckingham.

In 1606, the King's Men, including Shakespeare, put on the first performance of *King Lear* in Elizabeth's old Banqueting House at Whitehall Palace. The play tells of a king who split his kingdom three ways between his daughters, an allegorical message that would not have been lost on James, who was seeking to consolidate his three kingdoms of England, Wales and Scotland into one nation. His Queen, Anne of Denmark, also had a passion for lavish amateur theatricals at the palace and James ordered a new banqueting house on Whitehall to indulge her passions for masques. The masques were a cross between a ball, an amateur play and a fancy-dress party, offering the audience, including the King and Queen, the chance to dance, play-act and dress up. They were always underscored by a strong moral message of the divine role of kings in bringing order to chaos. The sets were painted and designed by Inigo Jones. Jones was from a humble background – he was born in Smithfield in 1573 – but he was a talented painter and gained the sponsorship of the Earl of Arundel, a connoisseur of fine art, who paid for him to go to Italy to study art and architecture. The scripts were written by the greatest playwright of the day, Ben Jonson. Jones and Jonson were, however, bitter rivals, and Jonson would make Jones the butt of some of his biting wit in his plays. Queen Anne adored dressing up and would appear in the plays, provocatively costumed and covered in precious jewels costing thousands of pounds. Jonson and Jones put on *The Mask of Beauty* for the opening of the new

Banqueting House in 1609. It included a scene of Hell complete with smoke and flames, before Jones's ingenious set was magically transformed into the jewel-encrusted House of Fame.

James I was dissatisfied with his new building because it had too many pillars, nine down each side creating a centre aisle, which probably restricted the view of the entertainment. The Banqueting House was used primarily for masques such as the entertainment to celebrate the investiture of Prince Henry – Charles's precociously talented elder brother – as Prince of Wales in 1610, followed by dinner in the great hall. The Tudor great chamber was used for plays, and the first production of Shakespeare's *The Tempest* was staged at Whitehall in 1611. But the new Banqueting House was principally made of wood, and burned down on 12 January 1619 as a result of two careless cleaners, who were too frightened to raise the alarm after accidentally setting light to some scenery. A letter written by a courtier nine days later to a Dr Ward described the event:

> I doubt not but you heard of the great mischance by fire at Whitehall ten days past which burnt all the Banqueting-house and was feared the whole house of Whitehall would also have been consumed; but my Lord Chamberlain and his brother being present, whose industry, pains and great providence, all the time, through the abundance of water brought and pulling down of some places (God be thanked!) prevented any more hurt. The fire arising by the neglect of some heedlessness of two men that were appointed to sweep the room, and having candles, firing some oily clothes of the devices of the masque (which the King had commanded should all remain to be again at Shrove-tide), that fire inflaming suddenly about to the roof, which the two men, not able to quench, and fearing to be known that they did it, shut the doors, parting away without speaking thereof, till at last, perceived by others, when too

late and irrecoverable. The two, since confessing the truth, are put
to prison.

The fire also destroyed important documents including Parliamentary
Bills signed by Henry VIII, Edward VI, Mary I, Elizabeth I and
James I and kept in vaults under the building in the Signet and
Privy Seal Offices. James ordered a new, finer building to replace
the Banqueting House by Inigo Jones, despite the death of his Queen
only a month after the fire. Jones by now had become the country's
leading theorist on classical architecture. This time it would be in
fireproof stone.

It is difficult to appreciate through modern eyes the shock – and,
to many Londoners, the outrage – that the Italianate Banqueting
House had on the London public, which loved and revered the
traditional Tudor buildings that still dominated the skyline of the
city and Palace of Whitehall. Where the Tudor buildings of Whitehall
were warm red brick, or black-and-white checks, haphazard and
homely, with detailing painted gaily in primary colours, the
Banqueting House was cold stone and appeared wholly alien to
English cultural heritage. However, it was not as grey and austere
as it looks today. Professor Max Hutchinson, the architectural
commentator, said the lower levels were clad in soft yellow
Oxfordshire stone, now so loved in the Cotswolds and Bath, with
grey Portland stone only at the top.[3]

'Inigo Jones used three types of stone in the building – at the
lower level it was Oxfordshire stone, in the middle it was Northants
stone, and only the balustrade at the top was made out of Portland.
It looked like a cake,' he said.

'The Banqueting House we see today is clad entirely in Portland
stone. John Soane, the classical architect who built the Bank of
England, clad it in Portland stone in 1830. He was a supreme classicist,
a Greek revivalist and didn't believe it was perfect enough.'

Portland stone was used later in the Victorian period to lend grace to the principal buildings of empire around Whitehall. Hutchinson approved, though it has left Whitehall looking as bland and faceless as the bureaucracy it houses.

'There is no point in building government buildings out of brick. They would look like houses – in the same way as Ten Downing Street looks humble. It is almost a non-government building. When we build grand buildings – the symbols of empire, bureaucratic dominance and control, we build them out of Portland stone,' said Hutchinson.

Inside, the Banqueting House was hung with fine tapestries – the windows were bricked up and not glazed until after Cromwell and the Commonwealth – and must have been darker than the Elizabethan hall with the hundreds of windows it replaced. Jones had studied the theories of Andrea Palladio in Italy, and owned a copy of his book on architecture. His first major commission was the Queen's House at Greenwich, and he designed Covent Garden, but his lasting masterpiece is the Banqueting House. It cost £15,618 – the equivalent of £2.2 million today – and was finished in 1622. It is also now obscured from view by a plane tree, which perhaps should share the same fate as Charles I. Using the form of a basilica – an ancient Roman meeting hall – as a template, he followed Vitruvius's rule that it should be twice as long as it was wide. However, James objected to the use of central columns and an aisle like its predecessor, and that plan was scrapped in favour of the existing huge interior space. The exterior was influenced by a design Jones had seen for a palace in Venice. Using the foundations of its predecessor, which had been built on top of the Elizabethan Banqueting House, the new building was 120 feet long and 53 feet wide. It had a balcony to allow more people in to see the festivities but once it was opened it took on a more formal role as a Presence Chamber for state occasions, with a throne at the south end. These occasions included garter feasts, ennoblements, diplomatic receptions, joint addresses to the two Houses of Parliament, the traditional banquet for St George's Day, touching the afflicted for the king's evil (scrofula, a disfiguring form of skin disease affecting the neck, particularly in children) and the washing of feet on Maundy Thursday, a tradition that continued until William III.

Charles had always looked up to his older brother Henry, and never expected to inherit the crown. But Henry had died suddenly and on their father's death the unlikely sibling succeeded to the throne as Charles I. He had been taken on a farcical tour of Europe by Steenie, wooing princesses in the French and Spanish courts, which only served to prove that Charles was shy and inept in lovemaking. But having inherited the crown, the charms of hapless Charles were reinforced by power and a marriage was quickly arranged with one of the princesses on whom he had spied, the French Princess Henrietta Maria. They were married at Notre Dame in Paris on May Day 1625. They were both diminutive – she was likened to a little bird, and despite the later heroic portraits by Van Dyck of Charles I in dashing black armour on a horse he was only five feet four inches tall and suffered from rickets, the vitamin deficiency that causes bandy legs. Just how short Charles was may be measured from his surviving suits of armour on show in the Tower, but that can be misleading. A small suit of English armour in the Royal Collection that once belonged to Charles I, dated about 1630, is only 37.5 inches tall but it was probably a demonstration piece.

Charles and Maria hit it off together, but almost before the wedding bells had died, the strains in their marriage became the talk of the Whitehall court as Henrietta Maria, a devout Roman Catholic, asserted herself. She would speak only French, and surrounded herself with French ladies-in-waiting, and, worse,

French priests. Charles remonstrated with her, to no avail, and became convinced that his marriage was being undermined by the 'maliciousness' of the French priests he called the 'monsieurs'. Indignant at her indifference to him and his court, on 26 June 1626, he stormed into the Queen's private chambers in Whitehall Palace to have it out with her. Her ladies had been dancing 'un-reverently' and watched in shocked silence as he told her she should leave them for a private conversation. She said there was nothing he could say that could not be said in front of her attendants. Charles seized her by the hand and dragged her from her lodgings, through the Privy Gallery and into his private chamber overlooking the orchard. He locked the door and, in a rage, said he would no longer tolerate her French retinue and they were to be sent home. She flew into a tantrum, burst into tears and then furiously smashed a window in his privy chamber with her hand. People below in the garden were astonished to hear her shouts before she was pulled away by Charles, bruising her hand and tearing her dress, but after the histrionics died down she agreed to his demands to expel most of her French attendants.

The priests and the ladies-in-waiting were jeered when they boarded their barge at the Privy Stairs of Denmark House, the Palladian mansion now renamed Somerset House on the Strand, which had become Crown property after the execution of Edward Seymour, the Duke of Somerset, on 2 January 1552. London had become a stronghold for English nationalist Protestantism and the Gunpowder Plot of 1605 was still fresh in people's minds, but in spite of the public fears of popery, Charles and Henrietta Maria patched up their differences and returned to married bliss in the Palace of Whitehall, supported by 1,700 staff.

When Charles was not supervising the masques, he was passing time playing golf, swimming, riding and hunting. He commissioned Rubens to paint the ceilings of the Banqueting House in honour of his father, at a cost of £3,000 – equivalent today to £423,456. The Rubens paintings on the ceilings – recently restored to their original glory – were a symbol of the Stuart dynasty, depicting *The Union of the Crowns of Scotland and England by the accession of James I of England and VI of Scotland*, while *The Apotheosis of King James I* celebrated the unshakeable Stuart belief in the divine right of kings. In June 2008, historian David Starkey led a £6 million campaign to rescue an oil sketch for the ceiling by Rubens for the nation, saying its loss would be a 'betrayal' of Britain's heritage. It had been in a private collection in England for 200 years, but the finished painting was one of the last things Charles I saw before being beheaded. 'In January 1649, the King solemnly walks through, under the ceiling and the apotheosis of his father and his dynasty to his own martyrdom,' said Starkey. However, the paintings made the Banqueting House unusable as a theatre because of the need for bright torch lights that would have damaged them. A separate building was used at the back of the Banqueting House as the palace theatre, and Henry's old Cockpit was later converted for use as a theatre.

Charles had been brought up by his father to believe in the divine right of kings, which James had set out in a book, *The Trew Law of Free Monarchies,* and had little regard for Parliament, which he called only when he needed to raise finance through taxes. When he needed money to wage war on the Scots he summoned Parliament in 1640, but the Commons, led by Puritans such as John Pym, the MP for Calne, Wiltshire, refused to grant money until the King had addressed their grievances about the State and the Church. Charles summoned both Houses of Parliament to the Banqueting House on 23 January 1641. Speaking from the throne, he astonished and wrong-footed his critics in Parliament by promising a 'Reformation'. He agreed to some of their key demands – an end to his use of tax-raising powers without their approval, reform of the courts, and a return to the church of Queen Elizabeth (hinting at an end to popish practices) – and called for a return to the 'politics of affection'. But the era of *New* Charles was not to last, and when it ended the distrust was greater than ever.

There was panic in London's streets at Christmas 1641, after news had been spread of a bloody Catholic uprising in Ireland, and a mob jeered the King outside the gates of Whitehall Palace. Charles now faced more demands from MPs for his powers to be curtailed in what became known as the 'Grand Remonstrance' by Parliament. In their private lodgings at Whitehall Palace, Henrietta Maria and Lord Digby, a friend of the Queen, urged the King to arrest the five leading agitators in Parliament but, torn by indecision, he prevaricated until on 30 January 1642 he was goaded into action by the Queen. The main source for much of the detail of what happened at Whitehall is the Venetian Ambassador Giovanni Giustiniani, who had spies in the palace. The Queen accused Charles of cowardice, shouting at him: 'Go, you poltroon! Go and pull those rogues out by their ears or never see my face again.'

He was fired up by her words, but still hesitated, which gave the MPs enough time to prepare for his arrival at Westminster. At about 3 p.m. he marched into the Guard Chamber off the great court at Whitehall, and told the surprised palace guards: 'Follow me, my most loyal liege-men and soldiers.' He strode out into the great court, followed by a considerable force of his men, through the court gates and into King Street, where he commandeered a private carriage to take him the short journey down King Street to Parliament, hurriedly followed by the guards, Prince Charles (his son and heir), the imperious sixty-year-old Earl of Roxburgh, and the Prince's cousin, the Elector Palatine. Charles got out of the carriage at Palace Yard and swept through Westminster Hall at the head of over 400 armed troops. They mounted the wide stone staircase to St Stephen's

Chapel, where the Commons was in session, seated in the pews. Roxburgh truculently lounged against the open door to show the force behind him, and an officer cocked a pistol at the MPs as Charles marched into the chamber. Sweeping off his hat, he said to the Speaker, William Lenthall: 'Mr Speaker, by your leave I must for a time make bold with your chair.'

The King sat down in the Speaker's chair and asked for the five MPs. 'Is Mr Pym here?' There was a sullen, shocked silence. He turned to the Speaker and repeated the question. Speaker Lenthall fell on one knee and, in a remark still often repeated in Parliament, replied: 'Sire, I have neither eyes to see nor tongue to speak in this place but as the House is pleased to direct me . . .'

The King said: ''Tis no matter. I think my eyes are as good as another's.' On his way out, he added: 'All my birds have flown . . .'

The five – John Pym, John Hampden (who had earlier been fined for refusing to pay Ship Money tax when it was extended to inland towns), Denzil Holles, William Strode and Sir Arthur Haselrig – escaped across the river. They were never arrested but, by the time the King had returned to Whitehall Palace, London was in uproar at the attack on the parliamentary privilege of free speech.

Charles's attempt to arrest the MPs – and Parliament's defiant response – is re-enacted every time the Queen opens Parliament in the ceremony of Black Rod, who walks to the chamber of the Commons from the Lords to request the presence of MPs for the Queen's Speech to be read, and has the door ceremoniously slammed in his face. It may look like a comic scene from Gilbert and Sullivan but it is deadly serious.

So it proved for the King. Barricades were erected in the city and chains thrown across the streets to stop a charge by the King's horse guards, who were contemptuously called *Cavelieros* or Cavaliers after the Spanish horsemen who had been responsible for routing Protestants in Europe. Charles, his Queen and the royal children boarded a barge at Whitehall's Privy Stairs and fled to Hampton Court on 10 January. As the sixteen oarsmen stroked their way past Westminster in the frosted air, Charles looked back through the windows at the stern of the barge and caught a glimpse of the towers and the gilded weathervanes of Whitehall Palace. He would not see it again until he returned as a prisoner seven years later.

A key factor in the King's decision to quit London was that the city's armed militias, formed of apprentices, had sided with Parliament. The capital defended itself from the Royalist forces by throwing up a defensive ring, with batteries including one in the Privy Gallery facing north towards Charing Cross to deliver fire along Whitehall against any Royalist attempt to recapture the palace. The gun remained there through the Restoration of the monarchy – it was taken down in 1685 for the rebuilding of the Privy Gallery but was restored within three years. The new battery occupied the whole length of a wall from the Banqueting House to the Holbein Gate as illustrated in an engraving by H. Terason in 1713 showing the muzzles of cannon aimed into the street. It was only demolished for road widening in 1723.

The immediate cause of the Civil War was the King's refusal to sign the Militia Bill handing power over England's military forces to the Puritan-dominated Parliament. Having marched to Hull to seize the city's military supplies stored there against a Scottish rebellion, Charles was rebuffed and retreated to the Royalist stronghold of York, where he was presented with nineteen propositions by Parliament for a settlement, including its control of the army, which he rejected. Charles's banner was unfurled in driving rain on 22 August 1642 in a field outside Nottingham and for the next three years England was racked by civil war. Initially, the Royalist forces had a success at Edgehill Ridge on Sunday 23 October 1642 where the cavalry of the Roundheads – named because of their close-cropped hair – were broken by the Royalist cavalry under the dashing command of the 23-year-old Prince Rupert of the Rhine, younger brother of the Elector Palatine and a nephew of King Charles.

The successful charge by Prince Rupert's cavalry against the less adventurous Parliamentary forces had convinced Oliver Cromwell, a farmer and MP for Huntingdon, Cambridgeshire, then in his forties, that the Parliamentary army needed to be organized on more professional lines.

In a letter to the commander of the Roundhead cavalry, fellow Parliamentarian John Hampden, Cromwell wrote:

> Your troopers are most of them old decayed servingmen and tapsters; and the Royalist troopers are gentlemen's sons, younger sons and persons of quality; do you think that the spirits of such base and mean fellows [as ours] will ever be able to encounter gentlemen that have honour and courage and resolution in them?

It was to lead to the creation of the Parliamentary New Model Army, with promotion by ability not blood, under Cromwell as Lieutenant-General and Sir Thomas Fairfax as Commander-in-Chief, and ultimately to the decisive defeat of King Charles's forces on 14 June 1645 at the Battle of Naseby. In the Royalist retreat, the Roundheads caught up with the baggage train, slashed the women camp followers, and captured correspondence between Henrietta Maria and the King discussing the recruitment of foreign Catholic forces to come to their aid, information that would be used against Charles at his trial.

Charles and his broken army escaped, and Charles plotted to go to Scotland for assistance. In August 1645 some of his leading supporters, including Wenceslaus Hollar, the court artist and tutor to the King's children, retreated to a Royalist stronghold at Basing

House. Hollar was responsible for many of the drawings of Whitehall, including a landscape of Whitehall Palace from the River Thames circa 1660 and a portrait of the young Charles after the style of Sir Anthony van Dyck (now at the Metropolitan Museum of Art, New York) with the Banqueting House in the background, underlining its importance. It was belittled by the Roundheads as the 'Queen's dancing barne' but its architect Inigo Jones was among the defenders at Basing House who were overwhelmed by Cromwell's guns after a siege lasting two months. The bloody end of the siege is depicted in one of the Civil War murals in the Central Lobby of the House of Commons. It shows a woman defending her father before she was put to the sword, and terrified priests about to be killed. The dead included William Robbins, an actor-comedian in Queen Henrietta's Men. Jones, a grey-haired old man of seventy-one, was stripped and allowed to leave wrapped in a blanket.

The King was taken prisoner in Scotland and reunited with his children at Hampton Court, but while Charles prevaricated over the negotiations, he planned his escape at night through a tunnel to the river.

Charles fled to Carisbrooke Castle on the Isle of Wight, but he was betrayed and imprisoned again. Even in captivity, Charles summoned Inigo Jones and the architect's pupil John Webb to plan the comprehensive rebuilding of Whitehall into a classical palace to eclipse Versailles and the Louvre for his return. They planned to replace the rambling Tudor village in Whitehall with an immense rectangular palace, on classical Palladian lines, like the Banqueting House, with four fine matching frontages running 900 feet along the river, the park and the sides. There was a variety of schemes, including one that would incorporate the Banqueting House with a series of hidden squares, one with a circular space as fine as the Crescent at Bath. The ancient public thoroughfare through Whitehall would have been moved to the riverside while the King's privy apartments would face the park. Framed engravings of the designs for the new palace, thought now to be the work of Webb, were printed a hundred years later and are displayed in an obscure corner of the Commons committee corridor, where it adjoins the press gallery, largely ignored.

While the King played with paper palaces, Whitehall was deserted and the courtyards overgrown. William Lithgow, a Scottish traveller, wrote in 1643:

> What shall I say, I found the street-enravelled court, before Whitehall Gate guarded also with a Court du Guard, a noveltie beyond novelties and what was rare, I found grasse growing deep in the royall Courts of the King's House, which indeed was a lamentable sight.

The result of the King's trial in Westminster Hall was never in doubt – though it was difficult to recruit the panel of fifty-nine judges, some of whom may have been physically forced to sign the death warrant. At Westminster Hall on 27 January 1649, Charles Stuart was found guilty as a 'Tyrant, Traitor, Murderer and a Public Enemy' and condemned to be executed 'by the severing of his head from his body ... In the open streete before Whitehall upon the morrow'. Cromwell's authorization said:

> To Colonell Francis Hacker, Colonell Huncks and Lieutenant Colonell Phayre and to every one of them.
> At the High Court of Justice for the tryinge and judginge of Charles Steuart Kinge of England is and standeth convicted attaynted and condemned of High Treason and other high Crymes, And sentence uppon Saturday last was pronounced against him by this Court to be put to death by the severinge of his head from his

body Of whch sentence execucion yet remayneth to be done, These are therefore to will and require you to see the said sentence executed In the open Streete before Whitehall upon the morrowe, being the Thirtieth day of this instante moneth of January, betweene the houres of Tenn in the morninge and Five in the afternoone of the same day wth full effect. And for soe doing this shall be your sufficient warrant And these are to require all Officers and Souldiers and other good people of this Nation of England to be assisting unto you in this service . . .

That night, instead of being taken to a residence in the Palace of Westminster known as the Cotton House, where he was normally held, King Charles I was carried in a sedan chair down King Street, lined by troops on either side, to the familiar surroundings of his palace at Whitehall for the last time. The next day, after prayers in the chapel, he was taken to St James's to be with his children for a final farewell. It was a heart-rending scene: his daughter Elizabeth was weeping uncontrollably and would not be soothed when Charles said: 'Sweetheart – you will forget this . . .'

'I will never forget it whilst I live,' she said. That night she wrote a graphic account of it, in her childish hand:

> He bid me tell my mother that his thoughts had never strayed from her and that his love should be the same to the last . . . He doubted not but the Lord would settle his throne upon his son and that we should be all happier than we could have expected to have been if he had lived.

He had a sterner message for young Harry, then only eight, whom he sat on his knee. 'Heed my child what I say – they will cut off my head and perhaps make thee a King.' Henry looked 'very steadfastly' at his father.

But mark what I say – you must not be a King so long as your brothers Charles and James do live; for they will cut off your brothers' heads (when they can catch them) and cut off thy head too at last; and therefore, I charge you, do not be made a King by them.

The boy promised he would be 'torn in pieces first'. Charles kissed them both and Elizabeth left in floods of tears after asking for one more kiss. She died a year later at Carisbrooke. The next day, Tuesday 30 January, Charles awoke shortly after 5 a.m. and opened his curtain to stir Sir Thomas Herbert, his Gentleman of the Bedchamber, who had slept the night on a pallet-bed by his side. The King told Sir Thomas, 'I will get up having a great work to do this day. This is my second marriage day . . .'

Charles took the precaution of asking for thick underclothes to avoid giving the impression that he was shivering through fear, rather than the cold of a January day. 'Let me have a shirt more than ordinary, by reason the season is so sharp as probably make me shake, which some will imagine proceeds from fear. I would have no such imputation . . . I fear not death. Death is not terrible to me; I bless my God I am prepared,' he said.

It was in such a bold frame of mind that he dressed neatly, in grey stockings and a rich red striped silk waistcoat, covered by a black cloak decorated with the Garter jewel of St George, an onyx surrounded by diamonds. At the thump on the door from Colonel Hacker and the guards at 10 a.m. sharp, the King walked across St James's Park to his execution, with his dog Rogue running about by his side. There were several companies of foot soldiers drawn up in the park, and a guard of halberdiers before him and behind, with drummers thumping out a dull beat as they walked. As he strolled through Spring Garden, the King pointed out a tree that his brother Henry had planted more than thirty years before. He climbed the wooden staircase up to the Tiltyard Gallery, through the Holbein Gate to the Privy Gallery. He had to wait almost four hours in his chambers off the Privy Gallery with his faithful priest, William Juxon, Bishop of London, before the order came for him to proceed to the scaffold.

We cannot be sure where exactly Charles lay down to meet his end, as publication of drawings of the execution was banned in Britain by Cromwell, and the only ones that exist were produced abroad. But there is good documentary evidence to suggest that the scaffold was erected outside the windows of the Banqueting House (but he did not step through the windows because they were bricked up at the time). He walked through the Great Hall, where he and the Queen had enjoyed the masques, under the immense Rubens ceiling with its cherubs, seven feet in length, to the northern end where he went down a short flight of stone steps to the first landing, then out into the sunlight through a door that had been opened in the wall, finally to face his executioners.

There is a small bust of Charles I over the doorway outside the Banqueting House to mark the spot where he is believed to have stepped out onto the scaffold. There is still a dispute over the names of his executioners – it was said the common executioner had refused to do the job. There were two men, both wearing black masks and false beards. The scaffold was draped in black cloth and surrounded by Cromwell's soldiers, with a dense crowd of thousands of onlookers. He handed his 'George' to Bishop Juxon for the Prince of Wales, saying, 'Remember'. The gem has since disappeared. David Chandler of the Sealed Knot, the society dedicated to research into England's Civil War and the 'Martyred King', told me: 'Some say it is lost; others that it is at Windsor; there is even an American claim of possession.'

The executioner's block was short, unlike those used at Tower Green, and Charles was forced to lie down to put his neck on it, rather than adopt the usual kneeling position. He asked whether it could be raised but was told by the executioner, 'It can be no higher, Sir.' It had been decided to force him to lie flat out so that it would be easier to kill him, if he struggled. This detail underlined the serious fears that Cromwell and his ruling council had about a disturbance at the execution. Cromwell's drummers around the scaffold were also ordered to drown out the short speech that the King made on the scaffold. Archbishop Usher was among those eyewitnesses who could not bear to watch the final scene. He had gone up on the leads on the roof of Wallingford House, which stood across King Street on the site of Admiralty House and was built by Sir Francis Knollys, one of Elizabeth I's favourite courtiers, in 1572 then passed to his son, Viscount Wallingford. One report said: 'When his Majesty had done speaking, and had pulled off his cloak and doublet and stood stripped in his waistcoat and that the villains in vizards [false beards] began to put up his hair, the good Bishop, no longer able to endure so horrible a sight, grew pale and began to faint . . .'

Witnesses were shocked to see that the King's hair and beard were grey and he seemed suddenly to have grown old. Strands of hair were pushed up under a white cap to avoid deflecting the axe from his neck. He lay down, telling his executioner to strike when he gave the sign – his arms outstretched. In one blow, his head was sliced off and a groan went up from the crowd. As a gush of blood spurted out of the severed neck, the second executioner lifted up the King's head and exclaimed, 'Behold the head of the Traitor!'

Philip Henry, an Oxford undergraduate, recorded in his diary:

On the day of his execution, which was Tuesday, January 30, I stood amongst the crowd in the street before Whitehall gate where the scaffold was erected, and saw what was done, but was not so near as to hear any thing. The blow I saw given, and can truly say with a sad heart, at the instant whereof, I remember well, there was such a grone by the Thousands then present as I never heard before and desire I may never hear again. There was according to Order one Troop immediately marching from Charing Cross to Westminster and another from Westminster to Charing Cross purposely to master the people, and to disperse and scatter them, so that I had much ado amongst the rest to escape home without hurt.

Another in the crowd that Tuesday was a schoolboy who had played truant from St Paul's school to witness the execution. Young Samuel Pepys, just fifteen, went back to school and told his young friends that if he had to preach a sermon on the King, his text would be: 'The memory of the wicked shall rot'.[4] It was ten years before he began his great diary in a house in Axe Yard, Whitehall, not far from the spot he had stood that day. Pepys would also play a part in the restoration of Charles II to the throne, but he was reminded later by one of his former schoolfriends that he was a 'great Roundhead' at school.

Within weeks, Parliament officially abolished the monarchy and established the English Commonwealth to stop the dead King's son, Charles, succeeding to the Crown, declaring: 'The office of the King in this nation is unnecessary, burdensome and dangerous to the liberty, society and public interest of the people.' However, abolishing the monarchy was easier said than done. Cromwell initially refused to live in the palace himself, and instead used the palace buildings as administrative offices – the forerunner of the present Whitehall civil service – for his military regime, including the Board of Ordnance, the Treasurer of War, the Wagonmaster General, the Judge Marshall, the Military Secretary, the Physician, Adjutant General, the Quartermaster General and the commissary supply staff. Cromwell's own office was by the Cockpit, next to his intelligence chief, known as the Scoutmaster General, an enterprising republican called George Downing, who later built the street named after himself on the Cockpit site.

In 1654, after defeating an attempt by Charles II to regain the throne, Cromwell took the title of Lord Protector and, as Head of State, moved into the Royal Palace of Whitehall. Parliament petitioned Cromwell with the offer to take on the Imperial Crown of England, with the intention of trying to bind him to their wishes, like the king he had executed.

On 31 March 1657, the Speaker and members of Parliament met Cromwell at the Banqueting House to present a 'humble petition and advice' that he should become King of England. In May, he summoned Parliament again to the Banqueting House, this time formally to reject their offer. On 26 June he was reinstalled as Lord Protector in a ceremony richly reminiscent of a coronation, except for the crown. It took place in Westminster Hall with Cromwell seated in the ancient throne of kings that had been brought from Westminster Abbey; but within fourteen months, he was dead.

The Puritans had torn down statues and smashed the Tudor stained glass in the Chapel, but John Evelyn noted in his diary on 11 February 1656: 'I ventured to go to Whitehall, where of many years I had not been, and found it very glorious and well-furnished as far as I could safely go, and was glad to find they had not much defaced that rare piece of Henry VII etc done on the walls of the King's privy chamber.'

However, during Cromwell's Protectorate, a commission had been set up to disperse the King's treasures and works of art. Charles I was described by Sir Roy Strong as the 'greatest connoisseur king ever to sit on the English throne' and the 400 pages of items for sale reveals just how rich the Palace of Whitehall was during his reign. The inventories, said Sir Roy, 'leave one with a sense of desolation': there were superb tapestries, gold-bespangled cloths of state, richly upholstered furniture, embroidered cushions, clocks, ornate silk carpets depicting fabulous fish and ships, chairs, stools, beds – the 'backdrop for the lives of the rulers of Tudor and Stuart England' – all sold or disposed of by the Puritans. But the greatest losses were the paintings: twenty-one Titians hung in the King's privy lodgings at Whitehall Palace; paintings by Correggio, Tintoretto, Durer, Rubens and, of course, Holbein the court painter, went for £100 (equivalent to £10,546 at 2007 prices) or £200 each (about £21,000); Leonardo da Vinci's *St John* was sold for £140 (£14,764). Three rooms were filled with the treasures, including Bernini's celebrated bust of the King, and the Spanish Ambassador was sent over to 'traffic in the purchase of the rich goods and jewels of the rifled Crown' – he filled twenty-four chests with the valuables. Most are still in the Prado, while Europe's other great museums have the rest of the royal collection. Of the Titians, four are in the Louvre, three in the Prado, one in Vienna, one in Antwerp, two in private collections, leaving only three in the present royal collection.[5]

Royal plate was melted down, and the Crown Jewels, including the crown of Edward the Confessor, were seized from the Jewell House by Westminster Abbey and destroyed. Then the Roundheads turned to the disposal of the King's royal residences. There was a move to sell the Palace of Whitehall to pay the army the money they were owed, but in 1660 Parliament, longing for political stability, agreed on the Restoration of the monarchy and abandoned the sale. Evelyn noted in his diary for 1 November 1660 that the King's cabinet room – where he kept his collection of treasures in cabinets – had survived the Commonwealth. The cabinet room at Whitehall was built by Inigo Jones for King Charles I, about halfway along the length of the Privy Gallery facing south to the Privy Garden.

It was the King's inner sanctum and may be why the principal meeting room at Downing Street, and its group of ministers, became known as the Cabinet.

> I went with some of my relations to Court to show them his Majesty's cabinet and closet of rarities, the rare miniatures of Peter Oliver after Raphael, Titian, and other masters which I infinitely esteem; also that large piece of the Duchess of Lennox done in enamel by Pettitot, and a vast number of agates, onyxes and intaglios, especially a medallion of Caesar, as broad as my hand; likewise rare cabinets of *pietra commessa* [inlaid marble]; a landscape of needlework, formerly presented by the Dutch to King Charles I. There I saw a vast book of maps in a volume near 4 yards large; a curious ship model: and among the clocks, one that showed the rising and setting of the sun in the zodiac, the sun represented by a face and rays of gold, upon an azure sky, observing the diurnal and annual motion, rising and setting behind a landscape of hills, the work of our famous Fromantel [sic][6]; and several other rarities.[7]

Cromwell had died at Whitehall of a malarial fever in September 1658 and for two years the King's apartments in the palace stood empty once more, although most of the adjoining lodgings were filled with ministers, senior government officials, civil servants and hangers-on.

Arguments still rage over the cause of the Civil War and the execution – Marxists see it as a precursor of the French and Russian revolutions; Whigs saw it as an assertion of the rights of Parliament; 1960s Revisionists as a collision of circumstances, powered by the break-up of the kingdoms, an accident waiting to happen to a weak king; others that it was a religious war; and powerful new theories have been advanced that it was, to paraphrase Harold Wilson in the seamen's dispute, a tightly knit group of politically motivated men, a Puritan Junto, an aristocratic elite, who were determined to grab back power from an imprudent King – a theory advanced by John Adamson in *The Noble Revolt: The Overthrow of Charles I*.[8] Lawrence Stone, a former Marxist turned 'old-fashioned Whig', pinned his colours to the revolutionary mast in *The Causes of the English Revolution* in the 1970s while Conrad Russell, a Liberal Democrat peer, challenged the view that a revolution had taken place and saw religious divisions as one of the causes. As a political observer, I would also look to men like Pepys who supported Cromwell, then, when he was gone, backed the restoration of King Charles II. The changing opinions of men like Pepys suggests that, by the time of his execution outside the Banqueting House, there had been a total collapse of trust in Charles I, but not in the institution of monarchy. It is a balancing act that is still going on today.

Why was the Banqueting House in Whitehall chosen for the execution rather than the more traditional Tower Green? Historians suggest there were practical reasons – it was a small square where a disturbance could easily be put down by Cromwell's men. It was also convenient for his place of imprisonment at St James's. But that does not seem convincing. A figure of Cromwell's political awareness surely calculated on the importance of the execution taking place against the backdrop of the Banqueting House. This was not merely the hated Stuart's 'dancing barne' but a lasting monument to Stuart power. Beheading Charles outside the Banqueting House in Whitehall was a potent message to Royalists that monarchy was dead, as full of meaning as if the Allies had shot Adolf Hitler at the Nazi stadium in Nuremberg.

England's only republic lasted just eleven years. The young clerk Sam Pepys noted: 'Everyone now drinks the King's health without any fear, whereas before it was very private that a man may do it.'

The death warrant for Charles I became a curse for those who had signed it. The original, with its fifty-nine red wax seals and signatures is held in the parliamentary archives in the Victoria Tower above the House of Lords. A recent memorandum in the House of Lords Record Office confirms the date of execution was changed, as were the names of Cromwell's officers who were empowered to carry out the sentence: 'Colonell ffrancis Hacker and Colonell Huncks and Lieutenant Colonell Phayre . . .' were inserted on top of the originals whose names were scraped off the parchment. The Lords' archives memorandum says that it may have been a correction for an error, but it broadly supports the more convincing argument that those originally chosen refused to carry it out. They were wise to be cautious. On 13 October 1660 Pepys noted:

> To my Lord's in the morning, where I met with Capt Cuttance. But my Lord not being up, I went out to Charing cross to see Maj.- Gen Harrison hanged, drawn and quartered – which was done there – he looking as cheerfully as any man could do in that condition.
>
> He was presently cut down and his head and his heart shown to the people, at which there was great shouts of joy . . . Thus it was my chance to see the King beheaded at Whitehall and to see the first blood shed in revenge for the blood of the King at Charing cross.

Though dead and buried, Cromwell did not escape the retribution against the regicides. Cromwell's exhumed and decapitated head was put on a spike at Westminster Hall, where it was displayed for the twenty-five years of Charles II's reign.

Today a facsimile of the King's death warrant is displayed in a case at the Palace of Westminster in the Royal Gallery, where the Queen prepares for the procession at the State Opening of Parliament.

It is no more than a mile from where Charles I was beheaded, and may have been put on show as a symbol of the fallibility of monarchy or as a reminder to republicans that we have been down that road before.

# PEPYS'S WHITEHALL

'A most malicious bloody flame, as one entire arch of fire
. . . of above a mile long. It made me weep to see it.'

Samuel Pepys, September 1666

Samuel Pepys and his new bride, Elizabeth, huddled against the chill as they crossed Parliament Yard to begin their married life in a cold garret in the old Elizabethan palace in Whitehall. Elizabeth Marchant de St Michel was beautiful, but poor, and barely fifteen years of age, while Pepys was twenty-two. They had exchanged their marriage vows at their parish church, St Margaret's, in the shadow of Westminster Abbey, on 1 December 1655, but it had been a civil ceremony. Religious ceremonies had been banned for the previous two years by Cromwell's Puritan Protectorate. Richard Sherwyn, a justice of the peace and secretary to the Treasury Commissioners, for whom Pepys worked, had officiated.

It was an inauspicious time to get married for a clerk who relied on stability at Whitehall for a living. It was six years after the execution of the King, and England was still getting used to life in a republic. First there had been the 'Commonwealth' but two years previously, Oliver Cromwell had dismissed Parliament (in an ironic echo of the last action by the King he helped to overthrow) and replaced the Commonwealth with his own military dictatorship, which he called a Protectorate. Cromwell had taken over the old Cockpit lodgings for offices, not far from where Pepys lived in his garret. These were dangerous, unpredictable days for anybody trying to survive in Whitehall, but at least Pepys had a job, and he had prospects, provided he kept his nose clean. He was a clerk to one of Cromwell's chief officers of the navy, Edward Montagu, and had been given lodgings near Montagu's apartments in the palace, in a turret of the King Street Gate. Montagu lived alongside the old King Street Gate in a gallery overlooking two great gardens on either side – the former King's ornamental Privy Garden covering two acres to the north and his bowling green on the south side, which had been an orchard during the reign of Henry VIII.

However, in January 1656, within a month of Pepys's wedding, Montagu was promoted by Cromwell to General-at-Sea and joint commander with Admiral Blake of the navy. Pepys's fortunes rose with his master's and he was soon able to afford to move out of the garret room with his wife and take on the lease of half a house on the west side of King Street, where the Foreign Office now stands. It was in Axe Yard, within a few minutes' walk of Montagu's apartments. Axe Yard was a cul-de-sac of twenty-five houses, reached through a narrow entrance off King Street by the Axe tavern. Some of the houses at the end of the street were grand and had elevated views across St James's Park, but they did not include the house that Mr and Mrs Pepys rented.

Among his duties was deciphering the notes from an intelligence source in the Hague, the Protectorate's ambassador, George Downing,

123

who had been a neighbour of Pepys when he was Cromwell's Scoutmaster General, in charge of intelligence. Pepys regarded Downing as a 'perfidious rogue' with plenty of justification.

Pepys prospered, but when Cromwell died suddenly in September 1658, everything changed. Montagu supported the succession of Cromwell's son, Richard, but Richard was weak, and was forced out of office within eight months, leaving England perilously close to anarchy without strong leadership. Montagu distanced himself from the republican zealots who seized control, and engaged in secret negotiations with agents of the exiled Charles II while commanding a fleet in the Baltic. This was a highly risky game and, in October, England was faced with the nightmare of plunging once more into civil war as the army took control of the government, dismissing the Rump Parliament of only fifty members. Montagu, suspected of being a Royalist traitor, was stripped of his peerage and his lodgings at the palace by the ruling council. He retreated to his country estate in Hinchingbrooke for his own safety to await events, leaving Pepys to fend for himself. These were perilous days for them both, but Pepys kept Montagu informed with intelligence. On New Year's Day 1660, a former Royalist-turned-Roundhead, General George Monck, commander of Parliamentary forces in Scotland, made a decisive move and switched sides again, leading his army south across the Tweed into England to make a show of strength.

It was on that historic day that Pepys, twenty-six, sat down at his desk in his little house in Axe Yard and began to write a personal diary to jot down his intimate view of the great events that were unfolding before him, mixed with Whitehall gossip and frank confessions about his private life. He began on the first page with a condition check on his family life and the state of nation: his wife had started her periods again, after an absence of her 'terms' for seven weeks, wrecking their hopes she was with child – they were never to have children, which put a strain on their marriage; meanwhile, in Westminster, the resumed Rump Parliament had sent its swordbearer to General Monck to support a free and full Parliament.

My own private condition . . . esteemed rich, but endeed very poor, besides my goods and my house and my office, which at present is somewhat uncertain. Mr Downing master of my office.

January 1. Lords day. This morning (we lying lately in the garret) I rose, put on my suit with great skirts, having not lately worn any other clothes but them.

In spite of his republican sympathies, Pepys grew to love being a Whitehall insider, his access to the royal family, court gossip and political intrigue, which he recorded in his diary. On 6 March he noted:

Shrove-Tuesday. I called Mr Sheply and we both went up to my Lord's lodgings at Mr Crew's where he bade us to go home again and get a fire against an hour after – which we did at Whitehall, whither he came; and after talking with him and I about his going to see, he called me by myself to along with him into the garden where he asked me how things were with me . . . And asked whether I could without too much inconvenience go to sea as his Secretary, and bade me think of it . . . He told me also that he did believe the King would come in and did discourse with me about it and about the affection of the people and the City – at which I was full glad . . . I went to the Bell where was Mr's Eglin, Veezy, Vincent a butcher, one more, and Mr Tanner, with whom I played upon a vial and he the viallin after dinner, and were very merry, with a special good dinner – a leg of veal and bacon, two capons and sausages and fritters with abundance of wine.

He also confided to his diary that Montagu disclosed there were moves to bring back Richard Cromwell as the Protector, but he did not think they would last. There was an alternative plan to install Charles II as King, but Montagu said he would have to conduct himself 'very soberly and well' to bring it off.

Charles II, in exile in Holland, did just that. He offered his services to Parliament in a cleverly crafted letter to the Speaker of the Commons – the Declaration of Breda – offering religious toleration and a continuation of stable government from the Lord Protector.

And Pepys was soon to rise again with his master's fortunes. On 2 May 1660, Pepys noted that Parliament had passed the vote to restore the monarchy – 'the happiest May-day that hath been many a year'. Montagu was ordered to The Hague to bring back Charles, this time as King. On 11 May he set sail from the Downs in Cromwell's flagship *Naseby*, with the figure of Cromwell removed from the prow and tactfully renamed the *Royal Charles*. He took with him his talented clerk Pepys, who was promoted as the Admiral's Secretary and Treasurer to the Fleet. On their return, Montagu was rewarded with honours, including being made Earl of Sandwich, a title chosen because the fleet he was commanding in 1660 was lying off Sandwich before it sailed to bring Charles II back. It was the fourth earl, a workaholic, who became synonymous with the snack, but, had Montagu opted to name himself after the naval harbour in Hampshire as he originally planned, the sandwich might have been known as a 'Portsmouth'.

Life for Pepys in 1660 under Sandwich's patronage had never been better. He had quickly resigned his post as an Exchequer clerk under Downing, whom he did not trust, and in June was made Clerk of the Acts to the Navy Board, which was a hugely responsible post for a young man – the chief civil servant for the navy. The board was responsible not for fighting, but for making sure that Britain had a fighting navy at its call – victualling the fleet, repairing ships, managing the dockyards, ordering, designing, building and repairing ships. Under the King's brother, James, the Duke of York, as Lord High Admiral, the Navy Board included the Treasurer, Sir George Carteret, the Surveyor, Sir William Batten and Sir William Penn (father of the founder of Pennsylvania), one of two general commissioners. Pepys's job also carried with it a handsome salary of £350 a year (£37,774 at 2007 prices) and a house in Seething Lane, in the heart of the old City of London, where the Navy Board met. He frequently visited the Palace of Whitehall and met the King. On 3 September 1660, a Monday, he wrote:

> About noone, my Lord having taken leave of the King in the Shield Gallery (where I saw with what kindnesse the King did hugg my Lord at his parting) I went over with him and saw him in his Coach at Lambeth and there took leave of him, going to the Downes. In the afternoon with Mr Moore to my house to cast up our Privy Seal accounts . . .

As a senior civil servant in charge of navy finances, Pepys now had his own powers of patronage that he would exploit for his other great passion – sexual conquests, which he called *vaincues* from the French for vanquished women. While Pepys had joiners laying new floorboards in his house in Seething Lane, he exploited the emptiness of his house in Axe Yard to add another conquest to his list: Diana, the daughter of Mrs Crisp, one of his neighbours, who had caught Pepys's eye when she was serving drinks to himself and the Earl of Sandwich at a dinner party at her mother's house in Axe Yard.

> September 4 1660:
> Did many things this morning before I went out – as looking over the Joyners, who are flooring my dining roome – and doing business with Sir Wms. Both [Batten and Penn] at the office. And so to

White-hall and so to the Bullhead where we had the remaynes of our pasty . . . From thence to my Lord's and dispatcht Mr Cooke away with the things to my Lord. From thence to Axeyard to my house; where standing at the door, Mrs. Diana [Crisp] comes by, whom I took into my house upstairs and there did dally with her a great while, and find that 'nulla puella negat' [the girl refuses nothing].

One of his favourite pubs was the Leg on King Street, the narrow road from the King Street Gate to Parliament Yard.

October 2 1660:
With Sir Wm. Pen by water to Whitehall . . . At Whitehall I met with Captain Clerk, and took him to the Leg in King Street, and did give him a dish or two of meat, and his purser that was with him, for his old kindness to me on board. After dinner I to Whitehall, where I met with Mrs. Hunt, and was forced to wait upon Mr. Scawen at a committee to speak for her husband, which I did. After that met with Luellin, Mr. Fage, and took them both to the Dog, and did give them a glass of wine.

The Leg was one of many inns around the alleyways in this corner of Whitehall. Pepys's routine would take him to Whitehall most days to conduct naval business with Lord Sandwich before going to Westminster, or taking a barge downriver to the naval docks at Deptford, where he would sometimes have his pleasure of Bagwell's wife while her cuckolded husband, William, a ship's carpenter, was out:

December 20 1664:
alone avec elle je tentoy a faire ce que je voudrais, et contre sa force je la faisoy, bien que pas a mon contentment. [alone with her I did what I would and against her will I was well contented]

Pepys would be regarded as a predatory monster today, but his sexual appetite was no worse than others around the court, especially the King's. Charles II sired at least fourteen children by nine mistresses and most were found lodgings at the palace. His first task on arriving at Whitehall, however, was to look after his own comfort. Charles I had moved the King's bedchamber from the western end of the Privy Gallery near the Holbein Gate, where it had been since Henry VIII's day, to the eastern end, nearer the ceremonial rooms. Charles II, following the French fashion, ordered a magnificent state bedchamber to be created to act as a ceremonial focal point where he could dine and allow an audience for foreign diplomats. The bed was treated with veneration, screened by a gilded rail. The floor of the new chamber also copied French style and was in marquetry. The great bed was covered in crimson damask, and there were 'flying boys' holding up the drapery to the bed, which was put in an alcove. He also needed a bed to sleep in, and this was located in a new room in the Turk's Gallery, which ran a short way in front of the Matted Gallery on the first floor along the Thames, where the MoD building is today. The Duke of York also had his apartment in the Matted Gallery and so had direct access to the royal bedchamber.

Charles was disarmingly charming and, unlike his rigidly doctrinaire father, untroubled by promises or principles. Historian David Starkey in *Monarchy* said the 'only rigid thing about Charles II was his male member . . .' John Evelyn, the other great diarist of his age, described one evening at his court at Whitehall Palace, with obvious distaste:

The King sitting and toying with his concubines, Portsmouth, Cleveland, and Mazarine, etc; a French boy singing love songs in that glorious gallery; whilst about twenty of the great courtiers and other dissolute persons were at basset [a card game resembling Faro] round a large table, a bank of at least £2,000 in gold before them, upon which two gentlemen who were with me made reflections with astonishment.' [1]

The King was also careful to give the people what they had missed under the dull rule of Cromwell – some magic with his Majesty. Within weeks of the Restoration, he reinstated the tradition of the laying on of hands, to cure the sick, in the Banqueting House. Evelyn recorded on 6 June 1660:

> His Majestie began first to Touch for the Evil according to costome: Thus, his Majestie sitting under his State in the Banqueting House: the Chirurgeons [barber surgeons] cause the sick to be brought or led up to the throne, who kneeling, the King strokes their faces or cheekes with both hands at once: at which instant, a Chaplaine in his formalities, says, 'He put his hands upon them and he healed them'.

Charles II was forever ordering alterations to the layout of the old Tudor palace, and lavished expenditure on his mistresses, but did little for the Queen's apartments. Paintings of the period show that the palace was a sublime mix of Tudor buildings, with haphazard rooftops and towering chimneys; the dominant colour was the warm red of the Tudor brickwork. However, Charles II shared his father's ambitions for the complete modernization of Whitehall to match the French court at the Louvre or Versailles, and discussed his grand design with Evelyn, as the diarist noted on 28 November 1664:

> Being casualy in the Privy Gallery at White-hall, his Majestie gave me thanks (before divers Lords and noble men) for my Book of Architecture and Sylva ... then caused me to follow him alone to one of the Windows; he asked me if I had any paper about me un-written, and a Crayon; I presented him with both and then laying

it on the Window stoole, he with his owne hands, designed to me the plot for the future building of White-hall together with the Roomes of State, and other particulars, which royal draft, though not so accurately don, I reserve as a rarity by me.

Charles commissioned Christopher Wren, who had been promised an appointment as the King's surveyor of works, to prepare detailed plans for rebuilding Whitehall in its entirety in the style of the Renaissance Banqueting House. Wren travelled to Paris to see the Louvre and meet Bernini, Europe's most famous living architect and sculptor. It was Wren's only recorded trip abroad and he returned full of ideas for turning Whitehall into a Renaissance masterpiece in the fateful year of 1666.

While Wren was away, the King and the court fled the palace and London for Oxford because the Great Plague of 1665 was at its height in the city. Pepys recorded on 29 June:

By water to Whitehall, where the Court is full of waggons and people ready to go out of town. This end of town every day grows very bad with the plague ... Home, calling at Somerset House where all were packing up, too; the Queen-mother[Henrietta Maria] setting out for France this day ...

Henrietta Maria, Charles I's widow, never returned, and died in France four years later.

On Sunday 2 September 1666, fire broke out in the city, and swept through the old wooden Tudor buildings with their thatched roofs, destroying everything in its path, including St Paul's. Driven by an easterly wind, the fire spread west towards Whitehall, throwing sparks high into the air. Realizing the danger late on the first day of the fire, Pepys took a boat from the Tower to Whitehall, where the Sunday service in the Chapel Royal was under way:

There to the King's closet in the chapel, where people came about me and I did give them an account dismayed them all; and word was carried in to the King so I was called for and I did tell the King and the Duke of York what I saw, and that unless his Majesty did command houses to be pulled down, nothing could stop the fire. They seemed much troubled and the King commanded me to go to my Lord Mayor from him and command him to spare no houses but to pull down before the fire every way . . .

Pepys took a coach to the city and found the mayor, Sir Thomas Bludworth, exhausted after being up all night. 'Lord, what can I do?' he asked Pepys. 'I am spent! People will not obey me. I have been pulling down houses but the fire overtakes us faster than we can do it.' Pepys walked on into the city and his vivid account of the fire is the great set piece of the diary, but it is the little details that are so telling. Pigeons singed their wings, and were burned; people threw goods into boats on the river, and into the water; pitch and tar ran hot, and burst into flames. Returning to Whitehall, Pepys went into St James's Park, where his wife had gone for safety, and then they took a boat on the river from Whitehall Stairs. 'With one's face in the wind you were almost burned with a shower of firedrops,' he noted.

At Bankside, on the south side of the river, they retreated to a little alehouse opposite the Three Cranes in the city where they could see the whole panorama of London on fire. By a remarkable coincidence, Evelyn recorded in his own diary standing on the same spot to view the fire the next night. It was, said Pepys, 'a most horrid malicious bloody flame, not like the fine flame of an ordinary fire . . . an arch of fire from this to the other side of the bridge, above a mile long. It made me weep to see it.'

On the evening of 4 September, the third day of the fire, he dug a pit in his garden at Seething Lane with Sir William Penn and 'put our wine in it, and I my parmesan cheese . . .'

The fire which Pepys was told had started in the King's bakers in Pudding Lane reached as far west as Fleet Street, but after three days it finally burned itself out, and remarkably the Palace at Whitehall remained unscathed. However, the skyline of London was altered for ever, and Wren's plans for Whitehall were shelved while he threw himself into designs for a new city reborn on classical lines that, too, would never be built.

Rumours swept Whitehall that Catholics or the Dutch were to blame for the fire. On 7 November 1666, Pepys was told by the Duke of York, 'they have it at Court that a fatal day is to be expected shortly of some great mischief in the remainder of this week, whether by Papists or what, they are not certain'. The anxiety in the Court that a catastrophe worse than the Great Fire was about to befall London was increased two days later when fire broke out at the Horse Guards, the bastion against an attack on the palace. Pepys had hoped the growing alarm would prove to be 'foolery' but noted in his diary on 9 November 1666 he was was making merry with friends, dancing and singing at Mrs Pierce's in the City, when 'comes news that Whitehall was on fire – and presently more particulars, that the Horse guard was on fire. So we run up to the garret and find it so, a horrid great fire and by and by we saw and heard part of it blown up with powder. The ladies begun presently to be afeared – one fell into fits. The whole town is in alarme. Drum beats and trumpets and the guards every where spread, running up and down the street . . .'

Pepys added:

And I begun to have mighty apprehensions how things might be at home, and so was in mighty pain to get home, and that encreased all is that we are in expectation, from common fame, this night, or to-morrow, to have a massacre, by the having so many fires one after another, as that in the City, and at same time begun in

133

Westminster, by the Palace, but put out; and since in Southwarke, to the burning down some houses; and now this do make all people conclude there is something extraordinary in it; but nobody knows what. By and by comes news that the fire has slackened; so then we were a little cheered up again, and to supper, and pretty merry.

The *London Gazette* applauded 'the timely help which his Majesty and His Royal Highness caused to be applied' by having buildings blown up to prevent the fire from spreading. The damage was limited to the buildings where hay was stored, and the blame for the fire was placed on a 'drunken groom in the hayloft' at Horse Guards, but Pepys's account illustrated the hysteria taking hold in Whitehall.

However, the Great Fire did not entirely extinguish the King's ambitions for Whitehall. Wren commissioned Ralph Greatorex, a mathematical instrument maker and surveyor, to carry out a detailed survey of the Whitehall Palace as the first step towards the creation of a new palace on the site. Greatorex produced an annotated map, the most comprehensive that we have today, of precisely who lived where in the rambling royal household. With a surveyor's disinterest in the King's private affairs, Greatorex identified the lodgings of Her Majesty the Queen, Catherine of Braganza (to the right of the Privy Stairs by the river), and those of the King's mistress, Lady Villiers (whose apartments were off The Street, now the site of the Welsh Office at Gwydyr House). Barbara Villiers, the Countess Castlemaine, later the Duchess of Cleveland, was one of his most celebrated mistresses by whom the King fathered three sons – the Dukes of Southampton, Grafton and Northumberland, and three daughters, including the Countess of Sussex. The Palace of Whitehall appeared to be filled with the King's progeny and they populated the House of Lords for three centuries: there were apartments for James Scott, the Duke of Monmouth and Buccleuch, born in the Hague to Lucy Walters, who was Charles's mistress at the time of his marriage to Catherine; Louise-Renée de Kéroualle, later the Duchess of Portsmouth, who bore him a son, the Duke of Richmond; and Catherine Pegge, whom he met in Spain, whose son by him, the Earl of Plymouth, was known as 'Don Carlo' because he was so dark-skinned. His liaison with an actress, the feisty, witty Eleanor 'Nell' Gwyn, the erotic icon of Restoration theatre, produced two sons, who were also given titles, the Duke of St Albans and Lord Beauclerk.

Nell was reputedly born in the coalyard of Drury Lane, sold oranges as a child and delighted in calling herself the King's whore, but she was an accomplished comedic actress. She captivated Pepys as Florimel in Dryden's *Secret Love*: 'So great a performance of a comical part was never, I believe, in the world before ... so done by Nell her merry part as cannot be better done in nature.'[2] Pepys even had a portrait of Nell, naked and voluptuous, as Cupid on his desk at the Admiralty in Seething Lane.

The King also had to provide rooms for his brother, James, the Duke of York, and his wives, Anne (who died in March 1671) and Mary of Modena, who later became Queen. Lodgings were also allocated to his cousin, Prince Rupert, who had been a dashing failure in the Civil War, until his death in 1682. Most were accommodated in the central part of the palace, off the Stone Gallery and the Matted Gallery above it, overlooking the Thames, where the MoD sits today.

One of the largest features in Greatorex's bird's-eye view of Whitehall is the Privy Garden. It was divided into sixteen irregular rectangles, each containing a statue of marble or bronze, most of which were later removed to Hampton Court, and it had a complex sundial set up on a stone pedestal by Edmund Gunter, the professor of astronomy at Gresham College for James I, to flatter his interest in science. King Charles II banned the Earl of Rochester from the palace after he drunkenly knocked the dial down, cursing its phallic shape. Charles II, a patron of the arts and sciences, had seven clocks in his bedroom, with another in an antechamber that also gave the direction of the wind. He had a laboratory for alchemy next door to his bathroom, which had a sunken bath, a square pool seven feet long and seven feet wide. A screen was provided outside in the Privy Garden to avoid the King's nakedness being seen by visitors. The bathing room on the ground floor below the Privy Gallery was also fitted with a feather bed, wall hangings and soft furnishings. The King's lodgings were surrounded by the rooms for his closest courtiers: James, Duke of York; Prince Rupert; the Duke of Richmond; and palace officials such as the Lord Chamberlain, the Maids of Honour and the Countess of Suffolk, who all had rooms off the Stone Gallery. There was reputed to be a secret passage from the King's apartments to the quarters of the Maids of Honour for his assignations.

To the left of the Privy Stairs by the Thames, Greatorex's map simply lists the lodgings of Mr Chiffinch, but this was the home of the man at the centre of 'back stairs' intrigue, the spider at the heart of the Whitehall web. William Chiffinch was the Keeper of the King's privy closet and the King's jewels, the only servant allowed to enter the bedchamber unbidden, and the Keeper of His Majesty's Back Stairs, an important role when the Thames was still one of the main thoroughfares of London. As such, he was the unofficial 'gatekeeper' to the royal household, which put him in a powerful position. His wife is reputed to have been paid £1,200 a year for her duties (£139,140 at 2007 prices), which included escorting women from the river stairs for assignations with the King.[3] Chiffinch also acted as an amateur spy for the King. He is said to have stayed sober while he plied contacts with drink, through the use of drugs known as the 'King's Drops' that were concocted in the King's laboratory. Frequent visitors to the back stairs of the palace who knew him well included Nell Gwyn, who would dine with friends in his apartments beside the river. He also had more mundane duties to perform, as the *London Gazette*, 16–19 July 1673, testified:

> A small liver coloured Spanish bitch lost from the King's lodgings on the 14th instant, with a little white on her breast and a little white on the tops of her hind feet. Whoever brings her to Mr Chiffinch's lodgings at the King's Back Stairs, or to the King's Dog-Keeper in St James's Park shall be very well rewarded for their pains.

But intrigue was clearly in the Chiffinch blood. He died in 1688, aged eighty-six, but his daughter Barbara married Edward Villiers, and their son became the Old Pretender. Their grandson became famous as 'Bonny Prince Charlie', the tragic Stuart 'King' over the water.

Like Westminster's corridors of power today, the King's privy chamber at Whitehall remained the 'chief staple of news'. Macaulay recorded in his *History of England*:

> Whenever there was a rumour that anything important had happened or was about to happen, people hastened thither to obtain intelligence from the fountain head. The galleries presented the appearance of a modern club room at an anxious time. They were full of people enquiring whether the Dutch mail was in, what tidings the express from France had brought, whether John Sobieski had beaten the Turks, whether the Doge of Genoa was really at Paris. These were matters about which it was safe to talk aloud. But there were subjects concerning which information was asked and given in whispers. Had Halifax got the better of Rochester? Was there to be a Parliament? Was the Duke of York really going to Scotland? Had Monmouth really been summoned from The Hague? Men tried to read the countenance of every minister as he

went through the throng to and from the royal closet. All sorts of auguries were drawn from the tone in which His Majesty spoke to the Lord President, or from the laugh with which His Majesty honoured a jest of the Lord Privy Seal; and in a few hours, the hopes and fears inspired by slight indications had spread to all the coffee houses from St James's to the Tower.

In this respect, little at Whitehall has changed today, apart from the buildings. Across King Street, around the Cockpit, rooms were allocated to the Duke of Albemarle, the elderly General Monck, in recognition of his service to the Crown, and the Duke of Ormonde, a close ally of the King when he was in exile, who was given the Tiltyard Gallery. The extensive apartments, in the former Great Close Tennis Court – roughly where the Cabinet Office now standards – were divided horizontally and given three chimney stacks, two new staircases and a range of sash windows overlooking King Street and the palace beyond the Holbein Gate. Greatorex lists them under the name of the King's bastard son by Lucy Walters, the Duke of Monmouth.[4] After the restoration, Monmouth was elevated to Cromwell's former post as Commander-in-Chief of the army but was fatally to overplay his hand in the Monmouth Rebellion.

The Greatorex map shows that most of the old tiltyard, where Henry had jousted, had been replaced with the headquarters of the Horse Guards by Charles II in 1663. Their presence was reassuring for the King, who was becoming increasingly unnerved by the London mob that rioted at the slightest whiff of popish plots. The growing hostility to the court was increased by the humiliation of the navy under the command of the Duke of York, when the flagship in which Montagu had brought the King back to England, the *Royal Charles*, was seized by the Dutch in a daring raid on its base in Chatham. Pepys, in happier times, records going on to the 'leads', the roof, of the palace with the Duke of York and King

Charles for a picnic and hearing the sound of the guns at sea in a battle against the Dutch fleet. Now he noted: 'The people make nothing of talking treason in the streets openly; as that they are bought and sold and governed by Papists and that we are betrayed by people around the King and shall be delivered up to the French and I know not what.'

During Easter Week of 1668, the anti-Catholic feeling around Whitehall led to the so-called Bawdy House Riots. A group of Puritan extremists protested against the brothels in the city as a symbol of the immorality of Charles's 'popish' court and to vent their anger at the way their own Protestant beliefs had been put down. In 1673 Parliament passed the Test Act excluding Catholics from high office – leading to the 'Exclusion Crisis' when the King's younger brother James was forced to surrender his post as Lord High Admiral because he was a Catholic. This also raised the question of who was to inherit the Protestant throne? In 1678, the hysteria around Whitehall reached fever pitch with the 'Popish Plot' – a convincing fraud pulled off by a charlatan and fantasist Titus Oates, who claimed that a high-placed clique of Catholics was plotting to seize the crown. It was in this atmosphere that an angry mob shouted 'Catholic whore' at a carriage thinking it was carrying the King's Catholic mistress, the Duchess of Portsmouth. Nell Gwyn leaned out of the window and said, 'Pray, good people, be civil. I am the Protestant whore!'[5]

Charles was so unnerved by the mood of the London mob that he abandoned his ambitious plans for the Palace of Whitehall and decided instead to move the court to the safety of Winchester, for the first time since Edward the Confessor. In 1682, as a precaution, he discreetly ordered Wren to build him new lodgings away from the road at Whitehall and near the river, moving into the Duke of York's lodgings while the work was carried out. Charles II kept colourful caged birds for amusement, and a volary or aviary became the fashion. Wren produced a fine new red-brick town house facing the river on the site of Charles II's aviary, and the apartments over the Privy Stairs were known as the Volary. The house had two wings stretching down to the river, with its back to Whitehall, forming a U with a small courtyard in the middle. Each of the wings had two floors, with four large windows on each floor. The Volary lodgings were finished four months behind schedule in October 1682 and the King had to wait until May 1683 for the delivery of fine new furniture to match the apartments, which stretched from the Matted Gallery through the withdrawing room, the anteroom, the official bedchamber, the eating room, the cupola room, and the back stairs near the river, to his little bedchamber with a window giving views over the river. On 5 February 1685 the King was suddenly taken ill while entertaining his 'harem' of mistresses as his courtiers relaxed, playing cards, and retreated to his bed.

Writing for a Victorian audience, Macaulay – borrowing heavily from Evelyn's diaries – said the King had been 'toying' with three women 'whose charms were the boast, and vices the disgrace, of three nations': Barbara Villiers (Macaulay sniffily referred to her by her married name, Barbara Palmer), Duchess of Cleveland; the Duchess of Portsmouth; and Hortensia Mancini, the Duchess of Mazarin. With the King on his deathbed, the court gates of the palace were shut, and family members gathered round the ailing Charles in his bedchamber. They included his three illegitimate sons by the Duchess of Cleveland, his son by the Duchess of Portsmouth, and the Duke of St Albans, the illegitimate son of Nell Gwyn.

'Do not let poor Nelly starve,' he whispered to his brother James, before falling into a coma. James kept the promise – she was granted the lease on her house in Pall Mall, which remains the only private property in the street, though it is now a fashionable suite of offices and was until recently the headquarters of a shipping line. Before he succumbed, the Queen sent apologies for being too distressed to be at his bedside. 'She asks my pardon, poor woman! I ask hers, with all my heart,' he said. He apologized for the delay, but he died the next day.

Charles II converted to Catholicism on his deathbed, and the crown was passed to his heir, James II, his younger brother, a devout Catholic. But Charles's bastard son, the Protestant Monmouth, who had been exiled in Holland, was persuaded by Protestants at home to make his move. He had the common touch, which made him popular with the people, and declared himself king. He landed with a tiny force in Devon, intent on the overthrow of James by popular uprising but the people were too shrewd to want another bloody civil war. They refused the call to Monmouth's banner and his pathetically small army was routed at the Battle of Sedgemoor. The Monmouth rebellion led to 320 of his followers being executed after the Bloody Assizes of Judge Jeffreys. Monmouth did not need to be tried because an Act of Parliament had been rushed through declaring him guilty of treason, but he pleaded for his life on his knees before James. Monmouth was beheaded at the Tower on 15 July; it took four blows of the headsman's axe to finish the job.[6]

James II, who had lived in Catholic Brussels after his exclusion, promised religious tolerance, but proved too Catholic for the imbedded Protestant tastes in London. Within six months, his Whitehall court faced a crisis over a demand by Parliament – panicked by the suppression of Protestants in France by Louise XIV – for James to remove the Catholic officers of his professional army. The Test Act, which barred Catholics from office, became a test of the King's strength against the exclusionists who did not want England to become Catholic. It was the pregnancy of his second wife, Mary of Modena, that proved the catalyst. His two Protestant daughters by his first marriage, Anne and Mary, who had married the Protestant William of Orange, believed the pregnancy was false: when a boy was produced at St James's on 10 June 1688, christened

James Francis, there were claims the Catholic heir to the throne was a changeling.

James II left his own mark on Whitehall Palace, in spite of his short tenure as king. Before his accession in 1685, he had decided to modernize the Privy Gallery in which he was to live by pulling down the 150-year-old wooden-framed Tudor buildings that had been familiar to Henry VIII and Elizabeth I and replacing them with a handsome range in the Renaissance style. The new Privy Gallery by Sir Christopher Wren was 200 feet long and three storeys high, with garrets above and faced with brick and Portland stone, as described by Evelyn in his diary on 18 October 1685:

> The King was now building all that range from east to west by the court and garden to the street and making a new chapel for the Queen whose lodgings were to be in his new building, as also a new Council Chamber and offices next to the south end of the Banqueting-house.

It was lavishly decorated – the Queen's great bedchamber had a chimney piece with ornate carving by Grinling Gibbons and a ceiling painted by Verrio. Portland stone was used for the great staircase with an iron balustrade. Landings were decorated with black and white marble. The Roman Catholic chapel, opened on Christmas Day 1686, was also faced with brick and ornamented with Portland stone to match the exterior of the new Privy Gallery. Verrio painted the chapel walls and ceiling and Grinling Gibbons designed a magnificent altarpiece, which is now in Westminster Abbey. A richly carved pulpit by Gibbons was given to the Danish Church in Wellclose Square in 1696 after the restoration of Protestantism as the authorized religion in Britain, and it was sold at auction in 1869, possibly to a church in the south of England; its current whereabouts are unknown. The chapel's organ was presented by Queen Mary II to St James's Church, Piccadilly, in 1691.

William of Orange amassed an impressive armada for the second great invasion of Britain comprising 15,000 troops, 4,000 horses, 700 transport ships, 60 battle ships, and a printing press to subdue his new subjects with propaganda. James was so unnerved by the threat to his crown that he ordered a weathercock to be erected on the north side of the Banqueting House to warn him whether there was 'a Protestant wind' (blowing from the east to hasten the arrival of the Dutch fleet) or a 'Catholic wind' (blowing from the west to push the Dutch back to port). A golden weathercock still swings in the wind above Whitehall today, showing E and W on its golden tips, although the one bearing a cross that James studied so anxiously has been replaced. In the autumn of 1688, the weathercock showed an easterly wind, and with it, on 5 November, came the third invasion of England.

William landed with his formidable force at Torbay, an area of strong Protestant sympathies. Unlike Monmouth, William, the son of Mary Stuart, the eldest daughter of Charles I, and the Dutch Protestant Prince William II, quickly gathered enough support to force James to abdicate. Prince George of Denmark and the outstanding general of his day, John Churchill, both flew to his banner. In desperation, James II imprisoned their wives – Anne, his own daughter, and her best friend and courtier, Sarah Churchill – in Whitehall. They both escaped and a doorway that opens from the Cabinet Office into Treasury Passage – which bisects the site of the former Cockpit – is said to be the route used by them for their exit from Cockpit Lodgings. Treasury Passage can still be seen from the north corner of Horse Guards Parade. It used to be a convenient public thoroughfare to Downing Street but is barred to the public today for obvious security reasons. It runs right under the internal passage from the Cabinet Office to Downing Street and is lit by large gas lamps. There are black metal hoops in the corners to prevent Regency 'muggers' waiting in the shadows for their victims.

On a visit to the Cabinet Office, I was told that 'Queen Anne's bath' was in the attic, a remnant of her house arrest at Whitehall. A lift took us up to the top floor, and another flight of steps to the attic where, under the dusty eaves, we found a large square stone object that looked like a sink with a hole in the base. Was this Queen Anne's bath? It was impossible to tell, but it was quite easy to imagine Anne being held prisoner there.

The Queen, Mary of Modena, escaped with her infant son from the Privy Stairs at Whitehall by boat on 10 December 1688, dressed as a laundrywoman. The next day James II followed, tossing the mould for his Great Seal into the River Thames as he left the palace, to avoid it being used to ratify his surrender of the crown, or the nomination of William as his successor.[7] But James was even incompetent about his escape. After crossing the river, he rode to north Kent and tried to get across the Channel to Catholic France, but was spotted by Kentish fishermen and brought back. He was then released by loyal guards, returned to Whitehall, and made a hapless attempt to meet William's army and do battle, but after having a series of heavy nosebleeds he retreated to the palace to await his fate. He was in his privy bedchamber at midnight when William's troops came in force to the Whitehall Palace gatehouse and gave him the ultimatum to quit the capital, which he did on 23 December, escaping with William's connivance at last to France. The 1688 invasion that brought William and Mary to Whitehall Palace as joint rulers – unique in English history – was hailed as the Glorious Revolution. It was the second great change in the course of English history, as significant in its own way as the invasion of 1066 or the Roman conquest.

The accession of William and Mary heralded the beginning of a modern age of government. William ruled, but accepted, in the Declaration of Rights, Parliament's right to decide on taxation, and to keep a standing army. This Bill of Rights also ended the right of the King to determine the religion of his country. From now on, the king and queen would have to be Protestant. It also heralded the end of Whitehall as the monarch's principal royal palace in the capital.

Wren had been commissioned by James II to replace the Queen's lodgings by the river with a new Renaissance-style building to house withdrawing rooms for her. This building was never fully occupied by her, but it dramatically altered the face of Tudor Whitehall from the river, and brought Renaissance harmony to the core of the palace.

However, William, an asthmatic, disliked the riverside fogs and the damp morning mists that clung about the palace, so he bought Nottingham House on the edge of Hyde Park, which William and Mary quickly turned into the sort of palace they had enjoyed in Holland – not great, but fine. It was renamed Kensington Palace and they left Whitehall abandoned for all but ceremonial occasions.

The neglected Palace of Whitehall was still used to house hundreds of courtiers and suffered a series of serious fires. After two fires, in 1661 and 1662, all those with lodgings in the palace were ordered to keep a leather bucket full of water for every chimney, but that did not prevent a disaster on 9 April 1691, as recorded by Narcissus Luttrell, a bibliographer:

> About 8 at night happened a dismall fire at Whitehall. It began in the duke of Gloucester's lodgings, late those of the Duchess of Portsmouth, occasioned (as said) by the carelessness of a maid in burning of a candle from a bunch of candles, and leaving the others lighted, quickly set fire to the buildings; it burnt violently for several hours and consumed the greatest part of the Stone Gallery on both sides, that towards the privy garden and that towards the Thames, wherein were the lodgings of the lord Devonshire, Heer Overkirks,

Lord Monmouths etc; they blew up several times before it could be stopped.

After the fire, Wren was commissioned to replace the destroyed buildings with a new range by the river, including a riverside garden terrace for Queen Mary II, against Henry VIII's river wall. It was 70 feet long and 280 feet wide, and centred on Henry's Privy Stairs, which was replaced with a curved flight of steps to the river at either end of the terrace. At its northern end, Wren designed an Italianate portico leading to the stone river staircase to protect the Queen from rain. Mary II, one of the leading gardeners of her age, planned to plant out her terrace as a parterre. The new buildings and the gaps left by the fire were included in a remarkable bird's-eye view of Whitehall drawn by Leonard Knyff in 1695–7, which is now in the British Museum.

Mary's sudden death from smallpox at Kensington Palace in December 1694 brought work on her lodgings to a halt. Prior to her funeral at Westminster Abbey, her coffin was laid in the Great Bedchamber at Whitehall facing the Privy Garden. The lead-lined coffin is said to have been so heavy that it broke the stairs when it was carried down into Pebble Court. In 1939, when the excavations were made for the MoD building, the north corner of Wren's terrace was uncovered. The bases for the pillars that supported the cover over the walkway to allow the Queen to remain dry on her way to her barge can still be seen on the top step. The stone staircase with part of the garden terrace was left open to public view on the Embankment by the side of the MoD, providing a rare sight of the Palace of Whitehall.

At around 4 p.m. on 2 January 1698, a far more serious fire broke out when a careless maid (who was Dutch and probably one of the staff brought to London with William) in Colonel Stanley's lodgings next to the Earl of Portland's house left linen drying by an open fire which caught alight.

One contemporary account said:

> It not only consumed the line but had seized the hangings, wainscots, beds and whatnot, and flamed and smoke in such a violent manner, that it put all the inhabitants thereabouts into consternation, as well as confusion, not knowing whence it proceeded, insomuch that the unhappy Dutch woman could not return; so that in an instant (as it were) the merciless and devouring flames got such an advantage that, not withstanding the great endeavours used by the water-engines, numerous assistance, and blowing up houses to the number of about twenty, it still increased with great fury and violence all night, till about eight of the clock next morning, at which time it was extinguished after it had burnt down and consumed (according to modest computation) about one hundred and fifty houses, most of which were lodgings and habitations of the chief of the nobility. Such was the fury and violence of this dreadful and dismal conflagration, that its flames reduced to ashes all that stood in its way from the Privy Stairs to the Banqueting House and from the Privy Gardens to Scotland Yard, all on that side except the Earl of Portland's house and the Banqueting House, which were preserved, though much damnified and shattered.

Evelyn, never a dramatist like Pepys, briefly noted in his diary:

> Excessive cold weather and piercing winds . . . White-hall utterly burnt to the ground, nothing but the walls and ruines left.

When the smoke cleared, the whole of the Tudor part of the great riverside palace lay in smouldering ruins, and along with it went all the Tudor treasures: the Presence Chamber and the Great Hall where Wolsey had welcomed the King and his party of masked gatecrashers, the chapel, the dynastic mural painted for Henry VIII by Holbein, and the new Privy Gallery range designed by Wren for James II. About twelve people were reported to have been killed, including the Dutch maid who caused it, and a painter who was killed trying to reach goods from the river when a piece of iron fell on his head from the burning building, 'and beat out his brains'. The southern end of the Banqueting House still shows traces of the fire, but the Cockpit side of Whitehall survived unscathed, as did a few other prominent features of the old palace including the Holbein Gate and the Court Gate. The Court Gate remained until 1765 when it was found to be in such a bad condition that it had to be pulled down. A new gateway had to be put up three years later following a spate of robberies inside the old palace yard. It remained there until 1813 when it was moved to the City of London Brewery.

After the fire, William abandoned Whitehall for St James's and Kensington Palace, and let most of the land on leases to noblemen to build private houses on the site of the former palace. William converted the Banqueting House into a chapel, to replace the destroyed Chapel Royal, which is how it remained for 200 years until it was used as the museum of the Royal United Services Institute (RUSI), which today has its headquarters in the next-door building to the south.

The RUSI site was used after the fire as the office of the state lottery to store the wheels that were used for randomly selecting the winners. Instead of the plastic balls used in the modern version, the Restoration lottery used two large wheels, six feet in diameter. Tickets were placed in the hollow rims more than a foot wide and were freely mixed up when the wheels were turned. Two small boys, usually drawn from Christ Church Hospital, were given the task of drawing the tickets randomly sorted by the wheels. A clerk stood between the wheels to ensure there was no cheating, and managers shouted out the winners, one boy drawing out the numbers from one wheel while the other at the same time drew out tickets from the second wheel containing the prizes of up to £20,000 or blanks. The draw was an annual event, and continued from 9 a.m. until 2 p.m. It was sanctioned by Parliament as a means of raising revenue. The first lottery in England took place in 1569 and the practice continued until 1826, and was then revived by John Major, the Tory Prime Minister who succeeded Margaret Thatcher in 1990. The lottery office was pulled down in 1792 to make way for stables for the Duke of York, when he lived across the road at York House, now the Scotland Office.

By the Georgian period, the area occupied by Whitehall Palace had become one of the most prestigious private addresses in London, where Whig ladies entertained politicians and royalty. But, when the private leases ran out towards the end of the nineteenth century, they reverted to the Crown and were taken over for public offices, which paved the way for the modern Whitehall as a street dominated by government departments. However, this trend had already started in 1694–5 with the creation of the first purpose-built office in England, to house the Admiralty, on the site of Wallingford House.

Immediately after the fire, the ruins of Wolsey's chapel were used for archery. Houses which had survived the fire in Whitehall Court – the former courtyard of the palace beyond the Court Gate which stood to the north of the Banqueting House – were taken over by new tenants and gradually replaced by fine houses, including a London residence for Earl Gower. Gower House was later taken over by Lord Carrington in 1803, and Carrington House remained a landmark until being pulled down in 1886. Vanbrugh, the architect of Blenheim Palace (granted by a thankful nation to John Churchill, the first Duke of Marlborough, for his victory against the French), built his own town house in Whitehall Court. It was ridiculed by Swift as a 'goose pie' because it was small and squat.

There were more fine houses between the Banqueting House and the river, including Fife House, where Lord Liverpool lived as Prime Minister. The Earl of Portland had an extensive mansion that incorporated the ornate riverside garden laid out on the terrace by Wren for Queen Mary II. Nearby, Cromwell House was built to the north of the Banqueting House in 1722 for Sir George Byng, a naval hero who became First Lord of the Admiralty – his name is remembered now for his unfortunate third son, Admiral John Byng, who was court-martialled and shot on the deck of his ship for failing to 'do his utmost' at the battle of Minorca in the Seven Years War. The builders of Cromwell House – demolished in the early twentieth century to make way for Horse Guards Avenue – incorporated Wolsey's wine cellar in the ground-floor plan. Early in the nineteenth century, a row of fine houses called Whitehall Gardens was built with leafy gardens running down to the river from a line formerly taken by Henry VIII's Stone Gallery. Several had elegant bow windows, and they became homes for leading statesmen. No. 1 Whitehall Gardens was the home of the society hostess Lady Townsend in the reign of George II and subsequently became the headquarters of the Liberal Club; No. 2 became the home of Disraeli when he was Prime Minister; Sir Robert Peel, the Home Secretary who created the police or the 'Peelers', lived at No. 4 and died there from injuries sustained after falling from his horse on Constitution Hill on 2 July 1850.

Montagu House, the town mansion of the Duke of Buccleuch, a major landowner in Scotland, stood next door to Gwydyr House, now the Welsh Office, on the site of the old palace gardens. It was demolished in the 1930s and is now the site of the car park for the Ministry of Defence. Montagu House was 144 feet long and 88 feet wide with elevated roofs above each wing rising to a height of 90 feet, and was taken over by the Ministry of Labour before it was pulled down for the construction of the MoD building.

To the north of Scotland Yard, Northumberland House was one of the last survivors of the great aristocratic mansions which lined the river but, despite having fine state rooms by Robert Adam, all that is left is its name – it was demolished in the 1870s to make way for Northumberland Avenue, linking Trafalgar Square to the Embankment. Vanburgh's 'pill box' also was pulled down to make way for the modernization of Scotland Yard.

The fine houses, the elegant rooms, and the leafy gardens were all swept away by the Victorian and Edwardian planners in their eagerness to create a street of offices for the twentieth-century army of civil servants, the bowler-hat brigade. But to the south of the former Privy Garden, a fine terrace of Georgian houses, Richmond Terrace, which now face the MoD and its car park, managed to survive the planners, the Luftwaffe and Geoffrey Rippon, who proposed demolishing it after the war as part of another grandiose plan to rebuild the whole of Whitehall (see Postscript). Charles II had given the land to the Duchess of Portsmouth, Louise-Renée de Kéroualle, mother of their illegitimate son who became the first Duke of Richmond. For a time in the eighteenth century, Richmond House was a privately sponsored art school under the patronage of one of the Duke's heirs. Cipriani, the painter, taught there and in 1746 Canaletto painted a breathtakingly detailed view from the Duke's windows looking down Whitehall. The painting, like a photographic snapshot, captured in detail the view across the Privy Garden to the Banqueting House and the Holbein Gate in the distance, with Montagu House to the right by the river. Richmond House burned down in 1791 and was replaced by Richmond Terrace. Residents of Richmond Terrace later included William Huskisson, a member of Wellington's Cabinet who fell out very publicly with the Duke, but who is remembered now for being the first man to be killed by a steam locomotive, Stephenson's *Rocket*. Poor Huskisson, a Liverpool MP, was attending the opening of the first railway line between Liverpool and Manchester in 1830 and was walking across the line to speak with Wellington, no doubt preoccupied with what he was going to say to the Duke, when he was hit by the steam engine. He died of blood loss from horrific injuries to one of his legs.

No. 3 Richmond Terrace became the campaign headquarters of Whig and Liberal supporters of the Great Reform Bill. It later passed to Sir Charles Wood, son-in-law of Earl Grey, who was created Viscount Halifax in 1866. There is a tradition that an apprentice was whipped soundly at Richmond Terrace as part of the ceremony of 'beating the bounds' of St Margaret's Parish. That may disturb the present tenants of Richmond Terrace, the Department for Health. Behind the amber bricks and rusticated Bath stone façade, the terraced houses were knocked together in 1984–6 in an award-winning refurbishment to create modern offices for headquarters staff and ministers. The vantage point that was used by Canaletto for his view of Whitehall is now enjoyed by the Secretary of State for Health from his private office at the corner of Richmond House on Whitehall.

# 6

# DOWNING STREET

Few thought he was even a starter
There were many who thought themselves smarter
But he ended PM
CH and OM
An Earl and a Knight of the Garter

> Clement Attlee (about himself),
> Prime Minister 1945–51

Downing Street has borne witness to most of the momentous events in British history, from the first news of the loss of America to the colonists and victory at Waterloo, to rejoicing by Lady Thatcher at the retaking of South Georgia in the war for the Falkland Islands, and a very nearly successful attempt by the IRA at the mass assassination of John Major and his Cabinet. It has survived jerry-builders, planners and the Luftwaffe. Throughout it all, the small town house off Whitehall has remained a domestic retreat for most of the fifty-two Prime Ministers who have served there.

It is perhaps ironic, therefore, that the street takes its name from the man Pepys regarded as a 'perfidious rogue' who became a byword in New England for duplicity – Sir George Downing. Downing was born in 1623 into a prominent East Anglian family of Puritans who had grown increasingly restless with England under Charles I. When George was old enough to go to college, he was taken by his parents to Salem, Massachusetts, to join some family and friends who had earlier fled Norfolk for a new life in New England. They included George's uncle, John Winthrop, the first governor of the state. Downing went to the new university established with the benefaction of a Puritan minister, John Harvard, and became one of its first graduates. Young George breathed in the New England oxygen of independence and republicanism that was to be set down a hundred or so years later in *The Rights of Man* by Tom Paine, but grew dissatisfied with a small salary of four pounds a year as a teacher of junior pupils at Harvard. It was worth £608 at 2007 prices and was less than half what a skilled builder could earn in England.

He sailed to the West Indies as a preacher but, after the Civil War broke out in England, returned to his old country to join the Parliamentarians as a chaplain to the regiment of Colonel John Okey, who had sponsored his education in New England and whom he was to betray when he changed sides on the Restoration of the monarchy.

Downing, having won Cromwell's confidence as an intelligence agent, abandoned the church and became one of Cromwell's most trusted spy chiefs, rising to the title of Scoutmaster General with Whitehall offices alongside Cromwell in the Cockpit Lodgings. It was here that he must have eyed the land that was to bear his name, even though it was occupied by the home of one of Cromwell's aunts and the mother of the leading Parliamentarian John Hampden.

Downing acquired the lease on the land in 1654, but three years later he was sent to The Hague as an ambassador to spy on Mary Stuart, the daughter of Charles I. She had married William of Orange and had given birth to a son, later to succeed to the crown as King William III. Downing knew that the exiled Charles II frequently visited his sister in The Hague so John Thurloe, the Secretary of State, ordered Downing to report back to Whitehall on all he heard. His dispatches were deciphered by Samuel Pepys, who had been hired by Downing as a Treasury clerk in Whitehall. He was paid a tenth of the £500 salary (about £70,000 today) Downing, a Teller of the Exchequer, was allocated for his staff of junior clerks, with Downing pocketing the rest. Pepys had good reason to fear for his own neck when Cromwell suddenly died and his ineffectual son Richard was deposed. Downing, through his spying on the exiled royalists in The Hague, must have known that Pepys's master in charge of Cromwell's Navy, Montagu, had made contacts with them. But Downing was also keen to save his own neck, and judged the wind was blowing in favour of the Restoration. Jettisoning his republican principles, Downing quickly shifted his allegiance to the exiled Charles II on whose family he had been spying. He turned one of his spies, a Royalist exile, Tom Howard, brother of the Earl of Suffolk, whom he had blackmailed, into a double agent to win the future King's trust, and got Howard to write to his Royalist allies saying Downing was a reformed character. Howard wrote that Downing had been taken as a boy to New England, 'where he was brought up and had sucked in principles that since his reason had made him see were erroneous and that he never was in arms but since the King's death, nor had never taken oath or engagement of any kind'. Almost all of this was untrue but Charles was sufficiently won over by his promises to be convinced that he owed Downing for helping him return to London in safety. He rewarded Downing with a knighthood in May 1660 for his services in the Restoration. Just how ruthless Downing was prepared to be became clear when he betrayed three former allies, including his old mentor John Okey, to gain favour with the new regime. Okey was among the fifty-nine to have signed the death warrant of Charles I and were wanted for regicide. Staying in The Hague, Downing traced Okey, John Barkstead (an MP and major general in Cromwell's army) and Miles Corbet (a Puritan MP and the last to sign the death warrant) to Delft, bribed a Dutchman, who believed Downing was their friend, and had them arrested. Downing proudly boasted of their capture. They were sitting 'by a fyere side with a pipe of tobacco and a cup of beere', he wrote:

> Immediately they started to have gott out at a back Doore but it was too late, the Roome was in a moment fulle. They made many excuses, the one to have gott liberty to have fetch his coate and another to goe to privy but all in vayne.'[1]

They were all brought back to the Tower of London, tried for regicide, and were hung, drawn and quartered at Tyburn. On the scaffold, Okey said he forgave Downing, whom he had treated like a son, though he 'did pursue me to the very death'. Downing's reward for his betrayal of his former friends was a baronetcy to go with his knighthood and promotion in Whitehall as secretary to the commissioners for the Treasury. In New England, the name of Downing became synonymous with betrayal, but in Restoration London, he prospered.

Downing could have given Machiavelli lessons in treachery but he was an accomplished diplomat and a brilliant administrator. He brought back with him from The Hague a knowledge of an accounting system that was to form the basis of the modern Treasury. He was already rich when John Evelyn recorded his disgust of Downing in his diary for 12 July 1666:

There was added to the Commission (of His Majesty's Ordnance) now Sir Geo Downing (one that had ben a greate ... against his Majestie but now insinuated into favour and from a pedagogue and fanatic preachr not worth a groate, becoming excessive ric).

A house on the Crown land, where Downing was to make himself richer with speculative building, had been leased previously to one of Queen Elizabeth's most trusted servants, Sir Thomas Knyvett, the Keeper of the Palace of Whitehall. She had granted him the lease for his lifetime, but after entering the service of James I following the death of 'Good Queen Bess', the Stuart king moved Knyvett out to make way for Prince Charles – the future King Charles I. Knyvett was given compensation of £20 a year for life (£2,993 a year at 2007 prices) and the lease of another nearby property, the half-timbered brewery house known as the Axe. After uncovering the Gunpowder Plot in 1605, Knyvett was rewarded by the King with a peerage and extension on the Axe lease for a further sixty years after his death so his descendants could continue living there. When he died, Knyvett House passed to Sir Thomas's niece, Elizabeth Hampden, whose son John was one of the five MPs whom Charles I tried in vain to arrest at the Commons. Elizabeth Hampden lived there through the Civil War, near enough to the Banqueting House to have heard the collective groan of the crowd at the King's decapitation. During his Protectorate, Cromwell ordered his civil servants to draw up a detailed list of all the King's assets for sale to pay off his troops, including Hampden House. A Roundhead bureaucrat produced this description of the property, which, apart from the spelling, could have come from a modern estate agent's window:

Consistinge of a Large and spacious hall, wainscoted round, well Lighted and Paved with brick Pavements, two parls whereof one is Wainscoted round from seeling to ye floor, one Buttery, one seller, one large kitchen well paced with stone and well fitted . . . above stayres in the first story one large and spacious dyneinge Roome, wainscoted round from seelinge to the floore . . . and fitted with a fair Chimney with a foot pace for Paynted Tylein the same. Also 6 more Roomes and 3 closetts [sitting or reading rooms] in the same flore all well lighted and seeled. And in the second story 4 garretts.

Hampden House was never sold while Elizabeth survived, perhaps because of Cromwell's family connection to the Hampdens, but in 1654 – four years before Cromwell's death – Downing persuaded the Protector (it is not clear how) to give him the title to the land when Knyvett's old lease ran out. Even Downing, however, had to observe the niceties of Knyvett's lease on the valuable land at Whitehall and it was not until 1682 that he finally got his hands on it. At the Restoration, Cromwell's confiscation of the land was cancelled and it passed back to the Crown. But Downing again used his powers of persuasion and royal patronage to successfully plead with the King that it had been granted to him during Cromwell's Protectorate, not as a payment for a service to the military dictator, but as a settlement for a debt he was owed. He was given the lease for 99 years to

. . . all that messuage or house in Westminster, with all the courts, gardens and orchards thereto, situate between a certain house or mansion called the Peacock in part and the common sewer in part of the South side and a gate leading to King Street called the New Gate in part, and an old passage leading to a court called Pheasant Court in part, and an old passage leading from the great garden to St James's Park in part, on the North side, and abutting on King Street on the East side and upon the wall of St James's Park on the West side.[2]

Downing demolished Hampden House and the Peacock, another inn that stood between the old Cockpit area and the tiltyard. Downing may have been rich, and old – he died two years later in Cambridgeshire – but it did not stop him penny-pinching for a quick return. He put up a cul-de-sac of fifteen terraced houses, but the foundations were hopelessly inadequate for the boggy ground, built on a raft of timbers that rotted with the wet over the years. His jerry-built houses had to repaired several times over the next three centuries and massively underpinned in the 1960s when Downing Street was in danger of collapsing. Instead of a regular brick façade, Downing's bricklayers had in places cut the skin of the bricks to imitate neat mortar lines. The current Number Ten was No. 5 in Downing's scheme, which is how it would have been known to the world, but for later renumbering. Being on slightly higher ground, it overlooked a much finer house, on the site of part of the old Cockpit Lodgings, with an L-shaped garden that is in use at Number Ten today. The house was owned by the Countess of Lichfield, the illegitimate daughter of Charles II and his mistress Barbara Villiers. In an early example of Nimbyism – Not In My Back Yard – the Countess complained to her father that the new buildings were overshadowing her house. Charles II wrote back sympathetically with a note for the King's Surveyor, Christopher Wren, to build up the wall 'as high as you please'. Lichfield House looked onto the parade ground for the Horse Guards and, after the Lichfields vacated it, was taken over by Lord Overkirk, William III's Master of Horse.

Robert Walpole's appointment as First Lord of the Treasury, and de facto Prime Minister, in 1721 was a milestone towards modern Cabinet government and the emergence of the embryonic party system. Hitherto, the relations between the first minister and the monarch had been little altered since the Tudor period when the Secretary to the Council was someone who had to take notes and carry out the monarch's wishes, hence the title of Secretary of State bestowed on members of the Cabinet today. However, with the arrival of the Hanoverian George I, who spoke poor English and was more concerned with his affairs back home in Hanover, Walpole became Prime Minister in all but name – that title was not officially recognized until 1905 and his official title 'First Lord of the Treasury' still remains on the famous brass letter box of Number Ten.

While he had the confidence of George I, Walpole had to use all his cunning to carry a majority among the two loose political groupings in Parliament: the Whigs, who supported constitutional monarchy, trade, Protestant nonconformists, and large aristocratic landowners who had most to gain from a weakened monarchy; and their opponents, the Tories, who supported the King, the Church of England, and the lesser gentry. The Tories were regarded as the 'court party'. Although both sides were too loosely formed to be compared to a modern political party, the Tories would eventually become the Conservative Party while the Whigs transformed into the Liberals.

Walpole, a Whig, had inherited wealth and a country estate at the age of twenty-four. He was short and fat, but also entertaining company and, though George II did not like him, he captivated Caroline, the King's wife. He was also wise – it was Walpole who had warned against the investment in the South Sea Company in South America, that was to be known as the 'South Sea Bubble', and had rescued the nation from the financial crash that followed. He was avaricious, amassing vast riches from land, and had magnificent houses in Norfolk and Richmond, Surrey, where he loved to hunt. When George II offered him the small town house in Downing Street as a personal gift to use as his London home, he refused, saying he would only accept it if it were taken as a gift to the nation for use by his successors. This rare act of philanthropy was conditional, however, on Downing Street being fitted out to his liking. Walpole complained that the house was too small and, having secured more property through the King, commissioned his architect William Kent to merge it with the former Lichfield House at the back that overlooked Horse Guards Parade. Kent was a follower of the Palladian fashion and had designed the palatial interiors for Walpole's handsome country seat, Houghton Hall in Norfolk, where Walpole lived in sumptuous style to equal the monarchy. He was already working on the first Treasury building for Walpole when he took on the commission to convert Number Ten. Numerous staircases in the two houses in Downing Street were torn out and replaced by one elegant stone staircase with a scrolled iron balustrade. Kent could have retained the entrance to the former Lichfield House, which would have given the Prime Minister today a far grander entrance across Horse Guards Parade for world leaders to arrive at Downing Street. But he opted instead for the pokier entrance on Downing Street because it was more discreet and convenient for Walpole to get to Parliament. This arrangement made Number Ten little more than an entrance hall to the complex.

Downing Street today is overshadowed by the Foreign Office and is cold even in summer, as any journalist who has waited outside Number Ten can testify. When Walpole and his wife Catherine Shorter, a merchant's daughter from Kent, moved into Downing Street in 1735, it must have been sunnier in summer, but they lived in the former Lichfield House at the back overlooking Horse Guards Parade. The Walpoles used the White Room – which Tony Blair has said was his favourite – as their sitting room and the Terracotta Room as the dining room. Catherine died in 1737, only two years after moving to Downing Street, and her son, the writer Horace Walpole, composed the eulogy on her tomb in Westminster Abbey. Walpole and Catherine had led separate lives under the same roof for years, and there were doubts he was the father of her children, while he enjoyed the company of several mistresses, including Maria

'Molly' Skerrett. Within a few months of Catherine's death, Walpole, in his sixties, married Molly, who was twenty-six years his junior. She was soon to die after a miscarriage, but Walpole at the age of sixty-four found solace in another mistress, the sister of the governor of the state of Carolina. Walpole held office for twenty-four years, making him still the longest-serving Prime Minister. The tenants of Number Ten who followed Walpole included the outrageously dissolute Sir Francis Dashwood, who occupied Number Ten as Chancellor of the Exchequer for ten months while he was also running the Hellfire Club in the ruins of a Cistercian Abbey at Medmenham.

In 1766, William Pitt, already an inspired war leader, became First Lord of the Treasury, as Lord Chatham, but it was too late. His two years in power were dogged by dispute, illness and failure. He had opposed George III's campaign against the American colonists but ten years after leaving office, with his health broken, on 17 April 1778, he collapsed while speaking in the Lords. His son, also called William, who was to eclipse him helped to carry his father to Downing Street but the old man died a month later at his home in Hayes Place, Bromley. He was sixty-nine.

Pitt was succeeded by his rotund Tory opponent Lord North, one of George III's cronies, who is remembered now for having lost the American colonies. North enjoyed living in Downing Street and came to relish its comforts as a respite from the American War of Independence, which was to prove his downfall. It took six weeks for news of the British surrender at Yorktown on 14 October 1781 to reach London. When the disaster was broken to North in Number Ten on 25 November, it hit him 'as he would have taken a ball in his breast ... he opened his arms, exclaiming wildly, as he paced up and down the apartment during a few minutes, "O God! It is over!" Words which he repeated many times under emotions of the deepest consternation and distress.' He was subsequently forced out of office, and Downing Street, the following March.[3] But North left his mark on some improvements, including the chequered tiled floor in the entrance hall, the lamp above the front door to Number Ten and the brass lion's-head doorknob.[4]

Armed with prodigious skills of oratory which his father had forced into him, William Pitt became an MP at twenty-one, Chancellor at twenty-three and in 1783 First Lord of the Treasury at the age of twenty-four – the youngest Prime Minister there is ever likely to be. While he was at Number Ten, Pitt the Younger went on through two terms to guide Britain through the French Revolution, the Napoleonic Wars and the return to stability after North's disasters over the American War of Independence.

He had been an admirer of the older, equally gifted, Charles James Fox but broke with him decisively when Pitt accepted office as Chancellor of the Exchequer in July 1782 and Fox resigned from the Whig Government. Fox and Pitt could have been allies but from that moment became arch-rivals for the rest of their political careers. Their historic clashes, across two decades, were fuelled by a surrogate family feud between George III, who backed Pitt, and the King's wayward son, the Prince of Wales, who supported Fox. Samuel Johnson, a Foxite, described it as 'a struggle between George the Third's sceptre and Mr Fox's tongue'. But Pitt's tongue was a match for Fox in their epic debates, and a remarkable political maturity helped him keep his rival on the opposition benches. Pitt made Fox appear opportunistic, and used the power of public opinion to remain in office. In those days, debating skills really mattered – Pitt was trained in classical oratory at his father's insistence – and the loose political groupings, before the advent of the party machines, made it possible to swing votes with the power of rhetoric. His fame as a speaker was assisted by the advent of parliamentary reporting by William Cobbett for a growing provincial readership as towns and the middle classes expanded with the coming Industrial Revolution.

Pitt never married and had riotous parties with his close friends, including William Wilberforce, later to become an anti-slavery campaigner after a bout of depression and conversion to evangelical Christianity. The Foxites were based in Brooks's club in Pall Mall and poked fun at young Pitt with libellous ditties which suggested he was gay, including 'On the Immaculate Boy': ''Tis true, indeed, we oft abuse him; because he bends to no man; but slander's self dares not accuse him; of stiffness to a woman . . .'

Pitt described Number Ten as 'the best summer town house possible' and his sister Harriet moved in as a companion for him before her marriage to one of his closest friends, Edward Eliot. She helped organize his social life at Downing Street. He spent twenty years – longer than any other Prime Minister – at Number Ten, where he plotted the course of parliamentary reform, the rise of free trade based on Britain's naval supremacy, and with it, growth in national prosperity. Pitt also created the most famous space in Number Ten – the Cabinet Room – by knocking a wall down to merge Walpole's study and a waiting room into one large room. This also explains why the room is dominated by pillars that were put in to take the load. In spite of his sister's help, Pitt was notoriously disorganized with his paperwork. The Foreign Secretary Grenville was urged by Count Woronzow, the Russian envoy, not to leave his letters with Pitt 'for he will not be able to find them again a day later among the immense mass of papers which reach him from all sides and encumber all his tables and desks'.[5] The delicate desk that Pitt covered in papers still stands in the corner of the Terracotta Room upstairs. Herbert Asquith used it to write to Kaiser Wilhelm II of Germany before the outbreak of the First World War and Chamberlain penned a letter to Hitler from here in his attempt at appeasement with the Nazis before the Second World War.

In its Georgian heyday, Downing Street was never able to compete with the Foxite salons of Georgiana, Duchess of Devonshire, at Devonshire House in Piccadilly or Lady Melbourne at nearby

Melbourne House – now the Scotland Office – as a social hub of life around Whitehall. Pitt preferred the company of his close friends, and was forced to court George III between his bouts of madness. At university, Pitt had been advised by a doctor to drink port for his health and had become used to downing copious amounts of the fortified wine. He became noted as a 'three-bottle man', although William Hague, in his biography of Pitt, calculated that Georgian port bottles were smaller and it would have been equivalent to one and two-thirds of a bottle today.[6] Pitt died in 1806 at the age of forty-six, a year after the battle of Trafalgar and the death of Nelson, safe in the knowledge that Britain had been preserved from invasion by the French.

After Pitt, Downing Street's role diminished as successive Prime Ministers preferred to live in their own London town houses. The Duke of Wellington lived there only while he awaited the refurbishment of Apsley House, his house on the corner of Hyde Park. Queen Victoria's first Prime Minister, Lord Melbourne, lived a few steps away in Whitehall at what is now called Dover House, and only used Downing Street during business hours.

William Ewart Gladstone, the father of the Liberal Party, who served four terms as Prime Minister between 1868 and 1894, was offered Dover House – the Duke of York's former 'palace' – as his main residence, but turned it down on the grounds that Dover House was too grand, and he would have to 'receive', that is entertain and host parties. Instead, he lived at Number Ten where he also pursued his charitable works for 'fallen women'. In his biography of Gladstone, the late Roy Jenkins shed new light on Gladstone's repressed sexuality via his diaries in which he recorded his night-time searches for particular prostitutes, and his use of flagellation. Gladstone confessed his guilty feelings to his diary, drawing a whip after some of his night-time meetings.[7] Jenkins gave Gladstone the benefit of the doubt, insisting there was no evidence that he used the prostitutes to assist him in his flagellation sessions for his own sexual gratification. Today's media would not be so generous in believing the Prime Minister would simply take them 'back to their rooms for long conversations'. Even his Cabinet colleagues thought it was odd when calling late at Number Ten on some important issue 'to find the Drawing Room still filled with cheap scent or even to pass a prostitute in the hallways as she was being shown out by the butler'.

Gladstone was disliked by Queen Victoria, who noted he had a 'weird look in his eyes' when she appointed him for the last time. She complained: 'He addresses me as though I were a public meeting.' She sent him a telegram – unencrypted so the world could know its contents – after the fall of Khartoum and the death of General Gordon, saying, 'All this might have been prevented and many precious lives saved by earlier action.' She preferred the brilliant wit of Gladstone's hated opponent, Benjamin Disraeli, who made her an Empress (of India) and was in return elevated to the peerage as the Earl of Beaconsfield.

Disraeli may have brought sparkle to the job, but he found the rooms in Number Ten in a 'dingy and decaying' condition when he arrived in Downing Street as Prime Minister in 1868, aged sixty-three. Disraeli preferred to stay at his town house across Whitehall at 2 Whitehall Gardens, the row of elegant houses that had been built on the site of the former Tudor Palace of Whitehall with gardens running down to the Thames. Disraeli's house had a steep flight of steps to his front door, which proved too difficult for 'Dizzy' in his old age, and he moved into Downing Street in 1877, nine years after taking office. Grumbling about the dilapidated state of Number Ten, where the state rooms had been neglected for three decades, he persuaded the Treasury to pay for renovations to the hall, stairs and first-floor rooms. But he had to pay out of his own pocket for his private rooms to be made habitable, including £105 3s 6d (about £7,100 at 2007 prices) for a bath with hot and cold running water.

Gladstone regarded the telephone as 'most unearthly' but still had the first one installed in Number Ten. At the age of eighty-four he decided to retire from office, and on 1 March 1894, bade an emotional farewell to his Cabinet. He said, 'God bless you all,' and walked out of the room, leaving them to file out 'much as men walk away from the graveside', some in tears, which earned them the popular title of the 'Blubbering Cabinet'.

The work of Downing Street in the twentieth century gradually increased, and offices overlooking the garden were taken over for secretaries, known as the 'garden girls', and the legendary women who staff the Number Ten telephone switchboard, collectively known as 'Switch'. They can patch through calls across the world. One former Number Ten official told me he still rings up for a number when he is stuck, and they still recognize his voice. He is discreetly 'patched' through without confidences being broken. Sometimes their ability to track ministers down can be disconcerting. One former Conservative employment minister told me 'Switch' tracked him down to a Swiss mountain hotel when he was on a skiing holiday so he could be informed that he was being sacked from the government.

During the Second World War, Winston Churchill was forced to evacuate his Cabinet to a bunker under the Treasury (now known as the Cabinet War Rooms) for the remainder of the conflict after a bomb fell near Number Ten in the Blitz on London. He secretly lived with his wife Clementine in two rooms of what is now the corner of the Treasury, which became known as the Number Ten 'annexe'.

Sir Edward Heath and Lady Thatcher both liked to 'live above the shop'. Heath brought in his grand piano to the White Room, which had been used as a retreat by Prime Ministers since the 1940s. It was also the room in which Liberal Sir Henry Campbell-Bannerman died on 22 April 1908 – the only Prime Minister to die in Downing Street. His last words were: 'This will not be the end of me . . .'

By the late 1950s, the war damage and the sinking foundations of the Georgian house at Number Ten had left the timbers in such a perilous state that a carpenter was kept permanently in place to ease the windows open and make running repairs. A survey showed that repairs over the centuries to shore up the shoddy foundations laid by Downing's builders had failed, and there was a serious risk of the building falling down. Options were drawn up, including complete demolition, but that was discounted by the aristocratic Conservative Prime Minister Harold Macmillan on the grounds of the property's historical importance. Macmillan brought in the architect Raymond Erith to carry out a sensitive restoration and rescue the buildings from collapse. It was the greatest change since Kent's overhaul, but you would hardly know it today. A committed classicist out of favour with the modernists of the era, he painstakingly stripped back the building to its brick bones, and set about a sympathetic restoration so his mark could barely be seen, apart from occasional adornments such as two Romanesque pillars in a courtyard which appear half-buried underground. The work lasted from 1958 to 1963 and cost over £1 million (about £15 million at 2007 prices). One change he brought about was in the colour of the door. Violet Bonham-Carter, Asquith's daughter, noted in *Country Life* magazine in March 1941 that the door had been dark green. Now it was permanently fixed in the nation's psyche as black, like the new brickwork in Downing Street, which was a lovely honey colour, but was dirtied to match the previous soot-black appearance. It was restored again to its 'sooty' appearance when it was re-pointed in the summer of 2008.

Lady Thatcher commissioned the architect Quinlan Terry to refurbish the three main state rooms and he repaid the compliment by having a straw-carrying thatcher carved into the plasterwork of the Terracotta Room as a lasting memorial to her. The thatcher figure is near the door to the Pillared Room. Terry said: 'She thought the rooms were boring. The best of the three was the Pillared Room and she wanted the rooms to be more imposing. She wanted pictures of achievers, like Nelson, Wellington, and she felt that, after the Falklands War, the time had come to do something mildly triumphalist and confident.'[8]

However, according to Cherie Blair, it was too ornate for one heritage expert who wanted to remove the gilding and return the interior decoration to its 'pure Kent' look. It was so elaborately done, however, that it would have cost a fortune to remove, she said.[9]

The largest of the three state rooms, the Pillared Room, is said to be haunted. Several staff in Number Ten report having seen or heard a woman in a Victorian long dress and pearls. Despite her ethereal presence, it is used when international agreements are being signed, or for receptions. This is where the England Rugby Union team were entertained after winning the World Cup in 2003.

The small dining room, or Breakfast Room, was used by Prime Ministers and their families for their meals until the flat upstairs was renovated. There is a small galley kitchen next door that has been used by some of Britain's top celebrity chefs such as Rick Stein and Nigella Lawson, daughter of the former Tory Chancellor, Lord Lawson. It was used on 29 April 2002 by Rick Stein, famous for his fish dishes, to cooked roast turbot for a glittering banquet to celebrate the Queen's Golden Jubilee. Guests at the evening hosted by Tony Blair included the four other surviving Prime Ministers of her then fifty-year reign – Lord Callaghan, Sir Edward Heath, Lady Thatcher, and John Major – in addition to members of the families of all her other Prime Ministers, including Sir Winston Churchill's daughter, the widow of Sir Anthony Eden, and the son of Harold Macmillan.

The state dining room is still used for banquets and the Prime Minister's monthly press conferences. Tony Blair would enter through the small dining room, and would usually be handed a mug of tea from the kitchen by one of the staff, before facing the press with his 'Hi, guys' greeting.

Every Friday, when the Prime Minister is usually away at Chequers, his official country retreat in Buckinghamshire, private tours are arranged of the building and they begin in the entrance hall. I joined a group of Whitehall junior civil servants and Labour Party members for one tour. The first requirement for all visitors to Number Ten, including ministers, is to remove all portable phones, which could be used as a homing device for terrorist bombs. They are placed in a chest of drawers on the left of the entrance next to a campaign chest owned by the Duke of Wellington. In another corner of the hall, on the right as you go in, is a Chippendale porter's chair with a huge black leather hood. It was once used outside when men sat on watch in the street. The hood was intended to protect the watchman from draughts and it has a drawer beneath for hot coals to heat the seat. The scratches on the leather were caused by the guards' pistols, but today police officers stationed inside the door carry Heckler-Koch 9mm MP5 sub-machine guns. The door opens mysteriously before visitors can reach the brass knocker because a bank of television screens inside can tell the porter who is arriving. There is a grandfather clock by Benson of Whitehaven in the corner, whose chimes so irritated Winston Churchill when he was Prime Minister he had the musical machinery turned off.

A door to the left of the entrance hall leads to a waiting room and Number Eleven, the Chancellor's official residence. Cherie Blair noted that the long corridor between Number Ten and Eleven still had a dividing line where she had put in a new carpet, but the parsimonious Chancellor Brown had refused to do so because of the cost. Brown lived up to his prudent image by throwing out the threadbare carpet in the elegant first-floor entertaining rooms of Number Eleven, where he held receptions, but instead of replacing it he left the boards in his reception rooms bare. Brown was also an avid fan of modern British art and proudly showed examples on his wall. In common with other twentieth-century Prime Ministers, Sir Edward Heath begged and borrowed fine paintings for the walls of Number Ten. Heath was regarded as socially very stiff in office, but became a great raconteur in old age, particularly of anti-Thatcher stories, and once told me he had been loaned the fine Impressionist paintings that adorned the walls of Number Ten during his time there by Armand Hammer, the financier and philanthropist. 'Armand phoned me one day and said, "Sir Edward, I think you've had that Renoir too long. I'll get you another one",' Heath told me with a chuckle. Now most of the paintings are from the government store or on loan from national galleries.

The corridor from the front door of Number Ten, through Number Eleven, also connects to the house at the end of the Downing Street cul-de-sac, No. 12, traditionally the Chief Whip's office. No. 12 was burned down in 1879 and remained a single storey, opening up views of St James's Park for a time, until it was rebuilt in 1962 with the major restoration of Downing Street. Alastair Campbell commandeered it for the Downing Street press office after Labour came to power in the 1997 general election when he was Tony Blair's director of communications. He turned the elegant rooms into an open-plan newsroom, filled with computers, and I interviewed him in his airy private office at the height of the so-called 'Cheriegate' affair when Cherie Blair was forced tearfully to apologize in public for giving misleading statements about her property investments. Campbell had a Burnley FC football shirt on a coat hanger, and his running kit dumped under his desk. His successor under Gordon Brown, Mike Ellam, moved back into the room to the right of the front door of Number Ten that had been used by Sir Bernard Ingham and Sir Christopher Meyer. It was into this room with the bow window that a handful of daily newspaper journalists used to cram for the regular morning 'eleven o'clock' briefing when I first joined the Westminster press pack, known as the lobby, in 1978. A few years earlier, Joe Haines, then Wilson's press chief, had ended the meetings, leading to a cartoon which is still in the press gallery at the Commons, of Haines slamming the door on the leading lobby journalists of the day, including Walter Terry of the *Sun* and Gordon Greig of the *Daily Mail*. Relations were never easy with Number Ten and the media. When Blair took power, Campbell moved his morning lobby briefings to a basement briefing room and, instead of going through the front door, the lobby was made to queue at the tradesman's entrance at the side, putting us firmly in our place.

For two or three years, Blair enjoyed a honeymoon period with the media, but Campbell became so frustrated with his inability to get his message across with an increasingly hostile lobby that he invited a wider range of journalists to his daily 11 a.m. briefings, including those from foreign papers. This required a bigger briefing room, and they were moved out of Number Ten to the Foreign Press Association in Carlton Terrace. The 11 a.m. briefings with the Prime Minister's official spokesman are now held in a room at the Treasury overlooking St James's. Ellam kept No. 12 as the press office. But in mid-2008 Gordon Brown established a 'War Room' there. The press office moved to Number Ten and the Prime Minister's special advisers moved to No. 12. Brown had a desk there with a 'hub and spokes' command structure to handle the crisis in his own leadership. In 2007, the total number of staff on the Number Ten payroll was 236, comprising 215 in the Prime Minister's office, 9 in the Number Ten Policy Unit, 6 in the Strategic Communications Unit and 6 Number Ten press officers.

The long corridor running to the back of the building that can be glimpsed from outside when the door is opened leads directly to the Cabinet Room, overlooking the gardens. There are a few anterooms where private meetings between ministers anxious to use the opportunity to sort out an inter-departmental row can be held 'in the margins' of the Cabinet meetings, which Brown moved from Thursday to Tuesdays at 9 a.m. Cabinet ministers habitually gather outside the Cabinet Room until they are summoned inside. Margaret Thatcher used a claxon hooter to order her ministers to enter the Cabinet Room.

Harold Macmillan, a wily politician, introduced the bow-shaped table in the Cabinet Room to keep eye contact during meetings with his ministers, who still use the twenty-three chairs from Gladstone's Cabinet. The Prime Minister's chair is the only one with arm rests and he sits with his back to the fireplace. The Cabinet Secretary sits to his right. Each minister has his own place around the table according to the Cabinet pecking order, so that when they are reshuffled they have to move chairs. John Prescott, as Deputy Prime Minister, sat to Blair's left, but when Harriet Harman was elected to his post as deputy leader of the Labour Party, Prescott's chair was occupied by the justice secretary, Jack Straw. The Chancellor traditionally sits opposite the Prime Minister, and the more junior Cabinet ministers are at the end of the table. Walpole's portrait hangs in pride of place over the fireplace. Harold Wilson had a clock put in so he could see the time without looking at his watch. A smoking ban was introduced by the Labour Prime Minister Clem Attlee in 1945, even though he smoked a pipe, but was later ignored by Churchill during his last term as Prime Minister. It was also in the Cabinet Room that Churchill recorded some of his defiant wartime speeches for the BBC.

There are two bookcases to the right of the Cabinet table as you go in, containing books by politicians, and it was here that Gerry Adams, the leader of Sinn Fein, found the Ulster Unionist leader, David Trimble, perusing a volume during a lull in their talks that eventually brought peace to Northern Ireland. 'What are you reading?' asked the bearded Adams. 'Cromwell,' smiled Trimble, in the knowledge that Cromwell, who was ruthless in quelling nationalist unrest, was one of the great enduring hate figures for Irish Republicans.

To the right of the Cabinet Room is the famous staircase displaying portraits of the past Prime Ministers. Winston Churchill is the only Prime Minister to have two portraits on the staircase, including one by the photographer, Yousef Karsh, who according to our guide took the cigar out of Churchill's mouth to produce the famous stern-but-statesmanlike 'grumpy' look. The staircase is famous for another reason today – the guide on the day I visited said he is always asked whether it was where they shot Hugh Grant's dance scene to 'Jump' by Girls Aloud in the film *Love Actually*. In fact, the film-makers used a mock-up of Downing Street, but it was very accurate.

While they were next-door neighbours, the Blairs moved into the flat above Number Eleven after selling their Islington home because it was bigger than Number Ten and they had a young family. That left Brown, then a bachelor, with the smaller flat over Number Ten. The flat above Number Eleven has a large, comfortable living room where the Blairs would try to tidy up Leo's toys when he was a baby, but VIP visitors were still likely to find themselves tripping over building blocks and bits of Lego when seeing the Prime Minister. It was reserved as the Blairs' private place, which Cherie jealously guarded, and only a few visitors were allowed a peep inside. They included a Roman Catholic priest who conducted private mass there for Cherie before Tony converted to the faith. There are spacious bedrooms overlooking Horse Guards Parade and St James's Park that would make it the most sought-after location in London if it ever came on to the market, except for one drawback – the crash and bang of the guards bands every day in early summer, practising for Trooping the Colour.

Harold Wilson's widow Mary said in an interview in the *Daily Mail* in 2007 that she hated the house in Downing Street. 'Everybody who has lived there seems to. I missed my real home, where I was cook, mother and gardener,' she said. When Wilson won the first of the two 1974 general elections to begin his second stint as PM, they stayed in their flat in Lord North Street rather than move back into 'that little flat upstairs' in Number Ten.

It is the domesticity of Downing Street that has jarred with its role as the nerve centre of government. Alongside the homeliness, it bristles with hi-tech equipment, which includes a transatlantic video link to the White House. Lady Avon, the widow of Sir Anthony Eden who was politically destroyed by the Suez crisis, once complained that the Suez Canal flowed through her living room. The Prime Minister can be feeding the baby one moment, and the next speaking to the President of the United States. The video link is in the basement, where the lobby journalists used to be briefed, and was in constant use between Blair and Bush during the Iraq War.

Downing Street has been the home of successive Prime Ministers and the epicentre of power in Whitehall since Robert Walpole's arrival in 1735, but questions are now being asked about how long the town house can remain the headquarters of government in the twenty-first century?

Unlike the White House or the Kremlin, Number Ten was not purpose-built for the head of state. It lacks the space required for a modern government complex, which is available in the West Wing, for instance, and the apartment 'above the shop' is small compared to the Residence assigned to the President of the United States at the White House. And, unlike the Oval Office, the presidential office in the White House, there is no fixed place for the Prime Minister to work. Margaret Thatcher used a room upstairs as her inner sanctum, where she could kick off her shoes, take a glass of whisky and relax with close confidants or senior civil servants she could trust, including her foreign-policy guru Sir Charles Powell, (brother of Jonathan, who later became Chief of Staff to Tony Blair). Cherie Blair describes how, on the night of the state banquet hosted by the Blairs for the former Prime Minister, Lady Thatcher revisited her old study and was horrified to find it had been turned into a bare, neglected office. 'What have you done to my lovely room?' Lady Thatcher said. 'It is appalling.' Cherie swore to restore it, and the work was completed shortly before she and Tony left Number Ten for the last time. Mrs Blair was known as 'Mrs B', and there is a memento with an elegant bookcase she had installed in Lady Thatcher's former study – a carving of six bees, including a small one for 'Mrs B'.[10]

John Major worked at the Cabinet table, while Tony Blair preferred to work in 'the den', a small room he commandeered off the Cabinet Room. It is reached through twin white doors that lead off the Cabinet Room to the right as you enter. This is where he would famously thrash out difficult decisions with a few close allies, from the invasion of Iraq to top-up fees for university students, seated on two sofas and a couple of easy chairs with coffee on a table by the fireplace. Blair's 'sofa-style' of government without civil servants present and official notes of the meetings being taken was later heavily criticized in the report on the intelligence failures leading up to the Iraq War by Lord Butler, the former Cabinet Secretary during the Thatcher and Major years. When he took over power from Blair, Gordon Brown vowed to end 'sofa government' and, by the time of the foot-and-mouth outbreak in August 2007, he had taken over the large suite upstairs where Lady Thatcher used to relax in the evenings. Her settee and easy chairs had been removed and it was turned into a bare workmanlike office. The wall behind his desk was covered in maps of Surrey where the outbreak had occurred. However, he never abandoned the downstairs 'den' and introduced a desk, a computer and a wide-screen television where Brown, a former journalist, habitually watched breaking news on

Sky News while punching away at a keyboard, writing his own speeches, something with which Blair was uncomfortable. Brown, according to insiders, would sometimes walk angrily through the connecting corridors to the press team to remonstrate with them about their failure to counter some news headlines with which he disagreed. He also never threw out the sofas from the 'den'.

Unlike his secretaries of state, the Prime Minister also has no private WC. 'It is a bit disturbing to go into the gents on the ground floor and find the PM next to you,' said one Downing Street insider. 'On one occasion, I walked into the gents and found Anji Hunter [Blair's gatekeeper at the time] comforting a Cabinet minister who had burst into tears because she was being demoted. They had gone into the gents because there was nowhere else. I made a hasty retreat. But it was a bit odd.'

But that may be changing – in 2008 it was discovered by the Conservatives that a planning application had been submitted to Westminster City Council for refurbishment of the gentlemen's toilets in 'The First Lord's Residence'. However, the detailed plan for the PM's loo is 'top secret'. Security has been stepped up considerably since the early 1980s when I sometimes walked along Downing Street late at night and bumped into Sir Geoffrey Howe, the Chancellor of the Exchequer, walking briskly up the 'back stairs' to Number Eleven, having taken his Jack Russell terrier, Budget, for 'walkies' in St James's Park. Number Ten was protected by a friendly unarmed policeman on the door, and Downing Street was open to the public until 1989 when the iron 'Thatcher' gates were installed. Some of her critics said this cut off the Prime Minister from the public in more ways than one, and marked the beginning of the end, but it did stop terrorists exploding car bombs outside the door of Number Ten.

An IRA active-service unit was forced to find an ingenious way round the basic security defences of Downing Street when they made an attack on 7 February 1991. The attack had originally been intended to target Lady Thatcher, but after she was brought down by her own Cabinet the IRA army council decided to allow it to continue to make their point. It was one of the most audacious assassination attempts on a British Government since Guy Fawkes. Like the IRA Brighton bomb in 1984 against Margaret Thatcher and some members of her Cabinet, it came close to succeeding.

At 10 a.m. the Prime Minister, John Major, was chairing a meeting of the War Cabinet in the Cabinet Room when the two mounted guards on duty outside Horse Guards in Whitehall were startled by three loud bangs. Three mortars flew out through the roof of a white Transit van parked at the corner of Whitehall by the Banqueting House and arced over the roof of the Cabinet Office towards Downing Street. It had been gently snowing when the IRA unit had parked their van at a carefully calculated angle to point their home-made missiles at the heart of the government. The IRA men had already slipped away as their mortars soared over the frightened horses in the twin sentry boxes at Horse Guards. Two dropped harmlessly on a patch of grass at the back of Downing Street and failed to go off but the third slammed into a cherry tree outside the windows of the Cabinet Room in the back garden of Number Ten and exploded with a shattering blast.

Inside the Cabinet Room, the Cabinet were studying the secret papers of the American bombing campaign on Iraq in the First Gulf War to free Kuwait from Saddam Hussein. There was a moment's pause as the glass of the elegant windows to the Cabinet Room exploded inwards. Foreign Secretary Douglas Hurd recalled: 'Strangely, I noticed there was not any glass between the Cabinet Room and the garden of Number Ten. I thought, "Funny – I haven't noticed that before – for some reason they must have taken it out." Then you heard the noise.'[11]

Some members of the Cabinet automatically ducked for cover, but Charles Powell, Major's foreign policy adviser, grabbed the Prime Minister by the shoulders and pushed him underneath the Cabinet table. Major said: 'We got down under the table and then there was a tremendous aftershock and we heard the windows being blown in and then the sound of what seemed like a second mortar.'

One civil servant said later that there was a huge splinter of glass that flew across the room and stabbed the wall like a dagger.

Hurd said: 'Nobody knew what to do. What do Englishmen do when they are being mortared in the Cabinet Room? It wasn't clear.'

Major, in his undemonstrative way, suggested they should continue their meeting in another room. 'I looked around and there was the Cabinet Secretary and there was the rest of the Cabinet crouching under the table . . . We waited there a moment until the aftershock and then we got up and I asked people to check to see what damage was done. Then I said, "I think we had better start again, somewhere else".'

The attack was to have far-reaching consequences for Major and his ministers, however. While Number Ten was being repaired, Major and his Cabinet had to decamp to Admiralty House, where Major lived for a time. That is how Major and a few of his most senior ministers came to be in Admiralty House in September 1992 when they were hit by the financial crisis that became known as Black Wednesday. The run on the pound started by George Soros, an international financier, proved far more lethal than the IRA's improvised bombs. It blew apart Tory claims of competence on the economy and contributed to the humiliating general election defeat in May 1997. They do not claim it would not have happened if they had been in Number Ten, with its modern communications, but ministers have admitted they were left without so much as a radio in Admiralty House to monitor the fast-moving scene in the city.

The secret work on Downing Street after the attack included the installation of blastproof windows, and the replacement of the famous front door with a bombproof replica, complete with the brass letterbox still bearing the title of the First Lord of the Treasury. Probably the most famous door in the world, the original door to Number Ten Downing Street was placed in the Churchill Museum at the Cabinet War Rooms after the IRA attack. The new one is steel and, according to officials, it is regularly removed for buffing up and replaced with a copy. It is so heavy that it takes eight men to lift it. There are no keys to the door, but security staff are on duty around the clock to open it, viewing visitors through a security monitor just inside the door.

In spite of the improvements, President George W. Bush's secret service advisers were appalled to find Downing Street was still wide open to attack when they carried out their own secret survey prior to the President's visit in November 2003. Vans and lorries were still allowed into Downing Street to drop off deliveries of parcels and produce for the Number Ten kitchens. A hydraulic ram was put in the road to stop a suicide lorry bomber, but their report, dubbed 'Operation George' by Number Ten insiders, led to a far more radical solution being considered inside Downing Street by Blair's security advisers. One central complaint by the CIA was that everyone, from heads of state to delivery vans, had to use the same entrance to the street itself. A £30 million scheme to create a delivery and staff entrance to Number Ten inside St James's Park was proposed. There would be a heavily fortified tunnel leading under the park road to the Downing Street complex for deliveries and staff, leaving the entrance to Number Ten for purely ceremonial occasions.

The survey also found that offices at Number Ten were 'overcrowded', lighting was 'poor', air conditioning nonexistent and that there were smells of sewage from the drains, which had always been a problem. The redevelopment would create an office in Downing Street 'in keeping with the head of government' and capable of turning it into a White House-style 'world stage'.

The White House security review of Number Ten has raised the question of whether it is still 'fit for purpose'. The Cabinet Office is gradually emerging as an office of the Prime Minister in all but name. As Number Ten Downing Street becomes less capable of coping with modern demands, more Downing Street staff, including some of Gordon Brown's key special advisers, have been moved into the Cabinet Office, causing Cabinet Office civil servants to be moved down the road to 22 Whitehall, which has resulted in others being 'bumped' into offices in Admiralty Arch. Sir Gus O'Donnell, the Cabinet Secretary, uses the 'secret' Tudor passage most working days to walk from his office on Whitehall to have talks with the Prime Minister at Number Ten.

Lance Price, a former Number Ten aide, told me: 'I always thought it was completely incredible that the government is run from what was a private house in Downing Street. It is an extraordinary anachronism that the British Prime Minister in the twenty-first century should work from this building simply out of tradition.'

Blair hinted at the limitations of Number Ten in a series of interviews with the historian Simon Schama for the Downing Street website shortly before he left office.

I think I am right in saying that Gladstone would do his own correspondence from time to time – he might have had a few secretaries to help him. But the concept would be completely alien to him of having a couple of hundred people [in Downing Street] . . . However, that is the modern business of being a prime minister. Therefore, the trouble is that Downing Street at the moment is perched a little uneasily between being the formal, state, visible outward expression of Britain and the place where you receive people, and a functioning workplace.

It is not a new complaint. A guide to the capital – *The Face of London* by Harold Clunn – published in 1932 said: 'No 10 Downing Street . . . can hardly be regarded as consistent with the dignity of [the Prime Minister's] high office on the one hand or the capital of the British Empire on the other. Having regard to the magnificence of most of the adjacent buildings, one might reasonably expect the British nation to provide its leading statesmen with an equally fine residence.'

At 2 p.m. on 27 June 2007, after a carefully choreographed handover of power with Tony Blair, Gordon Brown became the fifty-second prime minister since Robert Walpole in 1735 to enter Ten Downing Street, and he promised change. But changing the address of the First Lord of the Treasury was not on this agenda. It is likely that the Tardis-like Georgian town house, built on shaky foundations by a 'perfidious rogue', will continue to be both the home and the headquarters of the Prime Minister.

# 7

# NELSON AND THE ADMIRALTY

'Before this time tomorrow I shall have gained a peerage
or Westminster Abbey.'

Nelson, on the eve of the Battle of the Nile,

1 August 1798

In March 1798 a carriage deposited a handsome but battered naval officer and a woman in the courtyard of the Admiralty in Whitehall. Rear Admiral of the Blue, Horatio Nelson, had upset the seating arrangements of Lady Spencer, wife of the First Lord of the Admiralty, for the dinner in the ground-floor dining room at Admiralty House by insisting on bringing his wife, Fanny Nisbet. Lady Spencer's dinners were restricted to serving officers but she relented in the case of Fanny.

Nelson had lost the sight in his right eye on 12 July 1794 in an action in Corsica, when a French cannonball hit sandbags and showered his face with pebbles, ripping out half his right eyebrow

– although, in spite of the popular image of Nelson, he never wore an eyepatch. In July 1797 he had lost an arm to the surgeon's knife after a disastrous attack on Santa Cruz, Tenerife. His wife's son by her first marriage, Josiah, a young lieutenant in Nelson's ship, had saved his life by tying a tourniquet round his shattered limb after his elbow was hit by a musket ball. Nelson despaired of a future career in the navy after he lost his right arm but concealed his fears when, using his left hand for the first time, he had scrawled a note to the Admiralty from his ship, the *Seahorse*, at Spithead asking for leave. Dated 1 September 1797, it said:

> Sir, I have the honour to acquaint you of my Arrival here agreeable to orders and which the enclosed is a copy and I have to request their Lordships permission to go on shore for the recovery of my wounds. I have the honour to be Sir, Your most obedient servant, Horatio Nelson.'[1]

Lady Spencer later confided in Lady Shelley that when she saw her gallant guest for the first time in the drawing room at Admiralty House, he appeared a 'most uncouth creature':

> He had just returned from Tenerife, after having lost his arm. He looked so sickly it was painful to see him and his general appearance was that of an idiot; so much so that when he spoke and his wonderful mind broke forth, it was a sort of surprise that riveted my whole attention.[2]

After being won over at their first meeting, Lady Spencer had invited Nelson almost daily to Admiralty House, and they became firm friends. She was the eldest daughter of the Earl of Lucan, and had a reputation for her beauty, intelligence and haughtiness. Her husband, George, the 2nd Earl Spencer (a forebear of Lady Diana

Spencer, Princess of Wales), was a Whig and had succeeded Pitt's father, the Earl of Chatham, as First Lord of the Admiralty three years earlier. His sister was Georgiana, who married the Duke of Devonshire, and was a great Whig society hostess at the time. Lady Spencer had encouraged her husband to invite to dinner all the most senior captains on their return to England or before important operations at sea, but she made it a rule never to invite wives. In the spring of 1798, her husband, no doubt with no small persuasion from his wife, had at last given Nelson command of the Mediterranean fleet. It was, said Lady Shelley, 'to the great annoyance of the Admiralty Board, the ministers and Pitt himself'. On the eve of his departure in March, Lady Spencer invited Rear Admiral Nelson once more to dinner. She told Lady Shelley that Nelson said, out of deference to her 'no wives' rule, he would not beg for his wife to be allowed to accompany him, but 'if I would take notice of her, I would make him the happiest man alive'.

He said he was convinced that I must like her. That she was beautiful, accomplished; but, above all, that her angelic tenderness towards him was beyond imagination. He told me that his wife had dressed his wounds and that her care alone had saved his life. In short, he pressed me to see her with an earnestness of which Nelson alone was capable.

Lady Spencer altered the seating plan, and it turned out to be a charming evening. 'Fanny' sat happily next to the Rear Admiral, cutting up his food while he chatted amiably in the intimate dining room about his exploits, the threat of the French and Spanish fleets, and his tactics. Lady Spencer said Nelson had been all attentive towards his wife, acting more like a 'lover'. 'He handed her to dinner and sat by her, apologizing to me, by saying that he was so little with her that he would not voluntarily lose an instant of her society.'

Nelson had married Mrs Frances Nisbet, the widow of a former apothecary from Coventry with a five-year-old son, on the rebound from an impetuous love affair with another married woman on the island of Nevis during a tour in the West Indies in 1787. Before he left for Portsmouth, Lady Spencer says he told her, 'if he fell, he depended on my kindness to his wife – an angel whose care had saved his life!'

The next time he dined with 'Fanny' as guests of Lord and Lady Spencer at Admiralty House would be very different. It was two years later, and his devotion to his 'angelic' wife had turned to contempt. Nelson, as headstrong in love as he was in battle, was captivated by Emma Hamilton, the wife of Sir William Hamilton, Britain's ambassador to Naples. Nelson had returned to England as the conquering hero of the Nile, but his love affair with Emma Hamilton had caused a scandal all over London, including at the court at St James's.

Emma Hart, the daughter of a Cheshire blacksmith, had gone to London and scratched her living from the age of sixteen in a variety of menial jobs, exploiting her looks, including performing as a 'sex goddess' for a quack sex therapist in the 'Temple of Health and Hymen' in Pall Mall, at a house that was later taken over by the War Office. She had a string of lovers, including Sir Harry Fetherstonhaugh, the son of an MP who owned Uppark and had built the house in Whitehall that was later to become the home of the Melbourne set, now the headquarters of the Scotland Office. She is reputed to have danced naked on Sir Harry's table, but he dumped her when she became pregnant and she fell into the arms of another ruthless lover, the Hon. Charles Greville, second son of the Earl of Warwick and the heir to his uncle Sir William Hamilton. She fell deeply in love with Greville, but despite her sexual attractions Emma, uneducated and poor, was ditched by him when he secured the promise of marriage to a wealthy aristocrat, the Hon. Henrietta

Willoughby, the eighteen-year-old daughter of Lord Middleton. Henrietta's father was fooled into thinking Greville's address in Portman Square showed he was a gentleman. Greville persuaded his uncle, from whom he hoped to inherit a small fortune, to allow Emma to stay the summer in Naples with him. The elderly diplomat, who was thirty-three years her senior and whose first wife had died, was reluctant but quickly fell under Emma's spell. Emma – advised by Greville to oblige his uncle's demands for sex – held out until she had secured her own promise of marriage from Sir William, and quickly learned to play the part of ambassador's wife, becoming fluent in Italian, and providing political gossip from London from Greville to pass on to Queen Maria Carolina. Given to acting and striking attitudes in classical tableaux, the theatrical Emma threw herself at Nelson when he returned victorious from Egypt to Naples with his fleet in September 1798.

Nelson had chased the French fleet across the Mediterranean for nearly five months, encountering criticism in the newspapers at home, before sighting the French – thirteen ships of the line and four frigates – moored in a defensive line across Aboukir Bay, near the mouth of the Nile, on 1 August. That day he toasted his captains, whom he called his 'Band of Brothers', in the cabin of the 74-gun *Vanguard* and said: 'Before this time tomorrow I shall have gained a peerage or Westminster Abbey.' It was not the first time he went into battle shouting 'Glory or Westminster Abbey!' but he was wrong. His tomb was to be at St Paul's.

Although there were only a few hours of daylight remaining, he ordered an immediate attack. In a display of brilliant seamanship, some of his leading ships sailed inside the defensive line to annihilate the French, culminating in the awesome explosion of the 120-gun flagship *L'Orient* with 1,010 men on board. Napoleon's threat to Britain's trade in India died with them. Victory complete, Nelson set sail for Naples to refit, and sent the captain of the *Mutine,* the

Hon. Thomas Capel, with his despatch to the Admiralty. It seems incredible today but it took two months for Capel travelling overland from Naples to reach the Admiralty building in Whitehall with the news. Earl Spencer, who had been heavily criticized for his support for Nelson and his failure to find the French ships, was leaving the Admiralty when he was handed Nelson's despatch and was so relieved by its contents he collapsed. Lady Spencer exultantly penned a note almost incoherent with excitement to Nelson:

> My heart is absolutely bursting with different sensations of joy, of gratitude, of pride, of every emotion that ever warmed the bosom of a British woman on hearing of her country's glory – and all produced by you, my dear, good friend . . .

Lady Spencer told the hero of the Nile that his victory had caused so much excitement in London that after leaving the Admiralty Capel had been followed by a mob of several thousands, 'huzzaing the whole way'. London was 'mad' with joy, she said. Guns were firing as she was writing, illuminations were being prepared, and Nelson's name was echoing from street to street across Whitehall. Nelson had been injured by langridge – rusty old nails and bits of metal like shrapnel – as his ship had sailed into battle, and had thought he had suffered a fatal wound, when a flap of skin fell over his eye. It turned out to be a flesh wound to the scalp, but Emma fell on him as an injured hero when he returned to her port in Naples. Her ageing husband commissioned a portrait of the victorious hero by a local artist, which now hangs in the Admiralty Board Room at Whitehall. It shows Nelson's hat pushed oddly back from his forehead because of the pain from the wound that was still healing.

Nelson had been given the peerage he expected, as Baron Nelson of the Nile, but remained in the Mediterranean for another year, during which time he fell hopelessly in love with Emma. News of their affair caused outrage when it reached London, and, by the time he was recalled to Whitehall, Emma was already pregnant with his child, Horatia, probably conceived on board *Foudroyant* during a Mediterranean cruise.³ Blissfully unaware of the storm at home, Nelson travelled overland with the Hamiltons, where he was fêted across Europe, on a journey that lasted from July to November 1800. Nelson appeared completely oblivious to the social scandal he had caused when he returned to London, insisting his affair with Emma was entirely platonic, in spite of her being heavily pregnant. Lady Spencer invited the Hero of the Nile to dine at Admiralty House once more and out of politeness also invited Fanny. It must have been the dinner from Hell. Lady Spencer told Lady Shelley that this time he treated Lady Nelson 'with every mark of dislike and even of contempt . . . He never spoke during dinner and looked blacker than all the devils.'

His mood cannot have been improved by the royal snub he received earlier that day, when Nelson had gone with Sir William Hamilton to a levee at St James's Palace. They had gone without Emma because the Queen would not allow her to be presented at court. Nelson was introduced to the King, but he had brusquely turned aside when Nelson presented himself and made disparaging remarks about the unauthorized foreign medals with which he decorated himself. They included the glittering Neapolitan Order of St Ferdinand, given for 'saving' the royal family after the Battle of the Nile, the diamond aigrette known as the Chelengk, or Plume of Triumph, which he wore in his cocked hat, a medal presented by the Sultan of Turkey, Selim III. The Sultan described the Chelengk as a 'blaze of brilliants, crowned with vibrating plumage and a radiant star in the middle'. It had a clockwork mechanism that could be wound up like a pocket watch to make it shimmer.

During the dinner, Lady Nelson nervously shelled some nuts for Nelson and put them into a glass but her husband, in a furious sulk, pushed it away with his left hand so violently that it hit a dish and smashed. There is a story in Admiralty House that Fanny fled into an anteroom – now used to store chairs – and burst into tears. Lady Spencer said that when they retired to the drawing room across the entrance hall, while the men savoured their port and cigars, Lady Nelson confided in her 'how she was situated'. Fanny has had a bad press. Recent histories have suggested that Fanny's failure to engage with his career in the navy (Nelson was furious that she had carelessly packed the wrong clothes on one tour of duty), the fact that they never had any children, and her bitterness over his affair with Lady Hamilton contributed to the breakdown of their marriage. Research by Nelson expert Colin White on seventy-two letters sent by Lady Nelson to Nelson's London agent, Alexander Davison, has revised our view of her. They show she was bewildered by her husband's cruel behaviour but did everything she could to win Nelson back, even after his affair with Lady Hamilton. There was little she could do, though. Emma was about to produce Nelson's only child and, a few weeks after Horatia's birth in February 1801, Nelson and his wife finally parted.

The ground-floor dining room at Admiralty House is virtually unaltered since Nelson sat there fuming at his wife. It is intimate and dark, decorated with deep-red damask wallpaper, and the table, which can comfortably seat ten, is dominated by a magnificent chandelier. The walls are lined with portraits of successive secretaries to the Admiralty Board, including the bewigged and portly Samuel Pepys, who was responsible for reforming the navy's ship-building and supplies. Today the portraits include William Marsden, who received the news of the Battle of Trafalgar; John Barrow, who commissioned most of the voyages of exploration of the nineteenth century; and Evan Nepean, to whom Nelson wrote his first letter with his left hand after having his right arm amputated. There is also a portrait of the balding John Wilson Croker, Secretary to the

Admiralty and a Tory politician to whom Southey's biography of Nelson – written just eight years after his death – was dedicated. Croker became such a fixture at the Admiralty he was jokingly known as the one-man Admiralty Board.

The dining room is on the ground floor to the left of the front door to the house, which is in the left-hand corner of the courtyard. It is lit by a large window divided into three sections by two Ionic pillars, while against the wall opposite is a monumental sideboard for the First Lord's servants to serve at table. There is a grand fireplace on the north wall, decorated with an heroic figure in a lion skin wielding a hefty club while a volcano erupts in the background. Directly opposite is the door in the centre of the south wall, taller than the other six doors in the room. It leads to a room with a barrel-vaulted ceiling, painted Wedgwood blue, into which Fanny is said to have fled in tears.

Lord Spencer was a Nelson supporter, but he was replaced as First Lord of the Admiralty by Earl St Vincent, formerly Sir John Jervis, and there was some 'history' between the two men. Nelson had fought alongside Jervis against the Spanish at the Battle of St Vincent on 14 February 1797. Jervis took his title from the victory, but Nelson took the glory. He had boarded two enemy ships, and had been lionized in London with a cartoon depicting 'Nelson's patent bridge for boarding first raters'. St Vincent, now in his mid-sixties, had tired of Nelson's self-indulgent egotism, his pursuit of fame, and his passion for Lady Hamilton. One way of courting fame was to have your portrait drawn by an artist, like a modern-day society photographer, for reproduction in the popular prints. St Vincent wrote disparagingly to the socialite Lady Elizabeth Foster, later to become Duchess of Devonshire after Georgiana's death: 'That foolish little fellow Nelson has sat to every painter in London. His head is turned by Lady Hamilton . . .' St Vincent even refused to attend Nelson's state funeral – a shocking snub by one of the most senior naval commanders then alive – and acidly wrote: 'Lord Nelson's sole merit was animal courage, his private character most disgraceful in every sense of the word.' Lady Hamilton, said St Vincent, was a 'diabolical bitch'.

During a short respite in the Anglo-French war, Nelson created a homely *ménage à trois* with his mistress and her ageing husband (plus their daughter) at Merton Place, a house he had bought in the country (now in the suburbs of London) with an ornamental canal he called the Nile. William Hamilton died on 6 April 1803 in his wife's arms, holding Nelson's hand. The following month, after a year of peace, Britain declared war again on France, and Nelson, as Commander-in-Chief of the Mediterranean fleet, spent two years at sea blockading the French fleet.

Pitt had been replaced by one of his protégés, Henry Addington, after resigning over Irish representation in the Commons, but kept up withering fire on the government for its lack of preparedness for war. Pitt savaged Earl St Vincent's conduct of the Admiralty, declaring: 'Between his Lordship as a Commander on the Sea, and his Lordship as First Lord of the Admiralty, there is a very wide difference.' Pitt's biting criticism contributed to Addington's downfall, and, on returning to Number Ten as Prime Minister, he replaced Earl St Vincent with his old drinking partner, Henry Dundas, Viscount Melville, as his First Lord of the Admiralty. But Pitt suffered a shattering blow when, with the casting vote of the Speaker, the Commons voted to impeach Melville for alleged misappropriation of navy funds during an earlier period when he was the Admiralty Treasurer. Melville was later cleared, but resigned, and Pitt was said to have taken the blow more heavily than any of Napoleon's victories. Pitt collapsed at the Commons at the start of the illness that would claim his life. Jamming his hat on his head, Pitt's friends helped him back to Downing Street. Napoleon, meanwhile, assembled an army of 100,000 men at Boulogne with 1,000 transport ships, spreading alarm through southern England at the threat of imminent invasion.

Nelson was summoned to meet the ailing Pitt at Downing Street to discuss the crisis and told the Prime Minister that nothing short of the total annihilation of the combined Spanish and French fleet under Villeneuve would do, but that would require every available British warship. It is also claimed he tried to turn down command of the British fleet in favour of Collingwood, saying, 'Sir, I wish it not. I have had enough of it, and I feel disposed to remain quiet the rest of my life . . .' There is scepticism about the accuracy of this account, but it is easy to imagine Nelson – having spent a career preparing for an heroic death – feeling fate was beckoning now at the wrong time in his life. He was shortly to celebrate his forty-seventh birthday, and had become settled to domestic life at Merton Place with Horatia and Emma. Pitt, however, needed Nelson and the message they were dreading came on the morning of 2 September 1805, when Captain Henry Blackwood, who had been taking part in the blockading of Villeneuve's French fleet, arrived at Merton en route to the Admiralty in a post-chaise with news that over thirty French and Spanish ships had been sighted in Cadiz harbour. Nelson put his business in order and embarked on a hurried round of ministerial meetings in Whitehall, including with Lord Barham, who had succeeded Melville as First Lord of the Admiralty in May 1805, to discuss his plans for an attack on the combined enemy fleets. He also called on Lord Castlereagh, the Minister for War and the Colonies. The visit to Castlereagh's office in Downing Street brought Nelson and a rising star in the army, Major General Sir Arthur Wellesley, together for an extraordinary chance meeting for the only time in their lives. A watercolour by J. C. Buckler in 1827 shows the office where they met. It was housed in a three-storey terraced building, in the left corner of the cul-de-sac, then known as Downing Square. The Government whips' office, which later occupied No. 12 Downing Street by the steps down to

St James's Park, liked to claim the meeting took place there, but the Foreign Office historian Kate Crowe has discounted this claim. She has shown that the Colonial Office occupied No. 14 Downing Street, which was demolished in the 1870s when Scott built the new Colonial Office at the other end of Downing Street.

Wellesley, before being made Duke of Wellington, had already gained a reputation for his generalship with a series of spectacular and bloody victories in India where his brother, a close friend of Pitt, was Governor-General. They included the defeat of the Tippu that destroyed lingering French ambitions that had persisted after the Battle of Nile. Nelson, whose sickly, whey-faced complexion, grey hair and missing right arm had made him the most famous icon in England, was instantly recognized by Wellesley. But Nelson failed to recognize the long-nosed Wellesley when they found themselves sitting together in a little waiting room to the right of the front door.

Nelson treated Wellesley to a resumé of his victories at sea, like a showman performing for an audience. Wellesley later confided to Croker that he had been shocked by Nelson's bombastic performance but, like Lady Spencer, was forced quickly to revise his view. Croker noted Wellesley's account in his diary:

> He entered at once into conversation with me, if I can call it conversation, for it was almost all on his side and all about himself and, in reality, a style so vain and so silly as to surprise and almost disgust me.
>
> I suppose something that I happened to say may have made him guess that I was **somebody** and he went out of the room for a moment, I have no doubt to ask the office-keeper who I was, for when he came back he was altogether a different man, both in manner and matter.

When Nelson returned, Wellesely said the 'charlatan style had vanished':

> He talked of the state of this country and of the aspect and probabilities
> of affairs on the Continent with a good sense, and a knowledge of
> subjects both at home and abroad, that surprised me equally and
> more agreeably than the first part of our interview had done; in fact,
> he talked like an officer and a statesman . . . I don't know that I ever
> had a conversation that interested me more. If the Secretary of State
> had been punctual and admitted Lord Nelson in the first quarter of
> an hour, I should have had the same impression of a light and trivial
> character that other people have had, but luckily I saw enough to
> be satisfied that he was really a very superior man; but certainly a
> more sudden and complete metamorphosis I never saw.

Nelson also called on the Prime Minister for a final time. Pitt, although ill, came outside his house in Downing Street to see Nelson into his carriage, an honour that Nelson found peculiarly gratifying, saying Pitt would not have done it for 'a prince of the blood'. Pitt, sick with gout, brought on by years of heavy drinking of port, would be dead within six months. His physician Sir Walter Farquhar said he had died of 'old age at forty-six as much as if he had been ninety'.

Emma was heartbroken at Nelson's impending departure, and before his last farewell for Portsmouth they went through a 'marriage' sacrament together attended by Lady Spencer's mother-in-law. Once on board *Victory*, reunited with the captains he called his 'Band of Brothers', Nelson focused on defeating the combined French and Spanish fleet, and explained his novel plan to break the enemy line, saying in a letter to Emma: 'When I came to explain to them the 'Nelson touch' it was like an electric shock.'

Nelson's surgeon Beatty was alarmed to see he was wearing the famous four stars on his left breast as the *Victory* sailed into battle on 21 October 1805. Topped by the star of the garter, they were once described by Sir John Moore as making Nelson look 'more like the Prince of an Opera than the Conqueror of the Nile'. Beatty raised the risk with his officers, but they decided the only man who could tell him to remove his medals was his plain-speaking servant, Tom Allen, who was not on board, something Allen regretted for the rest of his life. Nelson undoubtedly knew that, as his flagship almost locked yardarms with the *Redoubtable*, he was making himself a target for the sharpshooters in the top trees of the enemy ships. Nelson's tunic was already splashed with blood from Thomas Whipple, his eighteen-year-old secretary who was cut to pieces by a cannonball as he paced the deck with Hardy, the captain of the *Victory*. Grenades were exploding about them as they walked on, but suddenly Hardy realized he was alone and looked round to see Nelson on his knees supporting himself with the fingertips of his left hand on the deck. He told Hardy he had been shot through the spine. 'Hardy, I believe they have done it at last,' he gasped.

Nelson's everyday 'undress' uniform, at the National Maritime Museum in Greenwich, shows the small hole slightly forward on the left shoulder where the musket ball entered. It is directly over the centre of the medals. The gaudy stars made him a marked man, and easy to identify, but did the marksman line up his sights with medals to hit him in the heart and, with the heaving of the decks, miss his target by a few inches? The fatal scene on board *Victory* was later depicted in vivid detail on the base of Nelson's Column raised by public subscription: an older sailor is pointing at the rigging and directing a young midshipman with a musket to fire at Nelson's assassin. On the monument, the British sailor with the musket is undoubtedly black, revealing the international composition of her crew. Nine West Indians were listed on board the *Victory* at the battle but none was in Southey's account of the death of Nelson. Southey reported that the quartermaster of *Victory* shouted to two midshipmen, 'That's he, that's he,' and pointed to a sniper in a glazed cocked hat and white frock in the mizentop of the French warship. But, as he did so, the quartermaster was shot in the mouth by the sniper and fell dead on the deck:

> Both the midshipmen then fired, at the same time, and the fellow dropped in the top. When they took possession of the prize, they went into the mizentop and found him dead; with one ball through his head and another through his breast.

A fast schooner, the *Pickle*, carried Collingwood's despatch from the battle but it took fourteen days to reach the Admiralty. It was delivered by a young naval officer at 1 a.m. on 5 November to William Marsden, the First Secretary, who later recorded being told: 'Sir, we have gained a great victory but we have lost Lord Nelson!'

Marsden had trouble finding the room in which eighty-year-old Lord Barham, the First Lord of the Admiralty, was sleeping. When he entered the room with a candle and drew back the curtain, Barham awoke and said: 'What news, Mr M?'

Marsden later told his wife that Barham 'received the account of the important victory with all the coolness and undisturbed tranquillity of an octogenarian'. Barham sat up the rest of the night, composing reports to the King, the Prince of Wales, Pitt, members of the Cabinet and the Lord Mayor of London, who communicated the news to the shipping interests at Lloyd's coffee house. When news reached the rest of London, there was rejoicing at the lifting of the threat of invasion, but an outpouring of grief at Nelson's death that was unmatched until the death of Diana, Princess of Wales, in 1997.

Nelson had given instructions that he did not wish to be thrown overboard so his body was pickled in a barrel of brandy, mixed with camphor and myrrh, and lashed to the main mast of the battered *Victory* for its return to Greenwich more than a month later. It lay in state for three days in the painted hall at Greenwich before being carried in a flotilla of ornate barges on a freezing, suitably solemn 8 January 1806, when even the clouds were black. The ceremony from Greenwich to Whitehall was re-enacted for the 2005 anniversary of Trafalgar but nothing could revive the sense of loss in the nation. In 1806 there were ten gunboats, sailing two and two, nine state barges draped in black containing mourners, Admiralty officials, and Heralds of Arms, bearing Nelson's arms as a viscount. The third barge, carrying the body, was covered in black velvet, with plumes of black feathers, and was rowed by sixteen seamen from the *Victory*. Guns fired as the procession passed the Tower but, amid rumbles in the heavens, there was a chilling shower of hailstones as the coffin – with a band playing the dead march and the gunboats firing every two minutes – was lifted at Whitehall Stairs and carried under leaden clouds by six admirals across Whitehall to the Admiralty. Nelson's coffin had been made by a ship's carpenter out of the main mast of *L'Orient* and was carried with him on board in his cabin after the Nile. It rested a cold night in the captains' waiting room to the left of the entrance that he would have used when he was alive, waiting to see their Lordships in the Board Room upstairs. The next day there was another elaborate ceremony of national mourning, including a huge cortège and heavy funeral carriage carved like the prow and stern of the *Victory*. 'When the Coffin was brought out of the Admiralty,' Nelson's nephew wrote in his diary, 'there seemed to be a general Silence and every one appeared to feel for the Death of so noble and such a good Man.' In St James's Park, behind the Admiralty, admirals and captains cursed in the confusion to find their carriages for the procession, which was so long that its head arrived at St Paul's before the rear had left Whitehall. At the end of the four-hour service, Lord Nelson was lowered into his tomb immediately below the dome. His black marble sarcophagus was the one that had been commissioned by Cardinal Wolsey but confiscated by Henry VIII and had lain unused for three centuries at Windsor. In a final fitting act of defiance, Nelson's sailors, instead of furling the ensign they were carrying to place it on the coffin, tore off a large piece of the flag and ripped it into strips, which they stuffed into their jackets as keepsakes.

Today the Admiralty is like a shrine to Nelson's memory. In the entrance hall of Admiralty House stands an ornate black stove decorated with the prows of sailing ships. It was made to celebrate Nelson's victories in imitation of a Roman monument marking their naval victories over Carthage. It was once lit on the orders of Churchill, when he was First Lord of the Admiralty, ignoring the advice of his staff. The fire split the belly of the stove and filled Admiralty House with choking black smoke. Visitors stepping through the front door of the Admiralty under the enormous portico are greeted by an original smaller version of the Nelson statue on the famous column in Trafalgar Square. The captains' waiting room, a small room with a Georgian glass door and a fireplace, where Nelson's body lay overnight before his state funeral, is filled with Nelson memorabilia, including souvenir prints of his funeral carriage and the procession. Up the worn wooden staircase to the first floor, there is a bust of Nelson over a door to the left, with the Queen's initials, ER II, on either side.

The door to the Admiralty Board Room, at the top of the stairs, is unadorned by any Nelson memorabilia. But the room it conceals is one of the hidden gems of Whitehall. Given its history, it also could be argued it is the most important room in Whitehall. It was from this room that Nelson's battles were directed, the slave trade was protected then stopped, the great discoveries of Cook and Darwin in HMS *Beagle* were conducted, and where a simple clockmaker, John Harrison, came to plead for the £20,000 prize (about £2.6 million at 2007 prices) for discovering the answer to the problem of longitude that was to test his patience and his health for the rest of his lifetime.[4] The room is dominated by the table and red leather chairs made in about 1788. The chairman of the Board, the Lord High Admiral or First Sea Lord, traditionally sat at the centre of the table. But the 24-stone George Ward Hunt (First Lord 1874–7) had a section cut out at the head of the table to accommodate his stomach. When John Prescott took over the Admiralty offices as part of the Cabinet Office complex as Deputy Prime Minister, he conducted Cabinet committee meetings in this room. At his first meeting, he pointed down to the half-moon cut out from the table and said: 'Don't tell the press.'

The feature that makes this room such an astonishing sight is a wind dial over a circular map of the world, surrounded by a spectacular display of carving. The dial above the Charles II fireplace was put in to show the Sea Lords which way the wind was blowing before they ordered the fleet to set sail in the Solent, and it is still in working order. The dial, dating from 1708, is connected to a weathervane on the roof, and swings around from east to west like the finger of a clock. Before the invention of the electrical telegraph, a large wooden semaphore was stationed on the roof of the Admiralty to send urgent messages to the fleet. They were relayed by teams of signalmen stationed on prominent points such as churches, some of which still fly the White Ensign to commemorate the fact, all the way down to Portsmouth. A message from the Admiralty Board Room in Whitehall reached Portsmouth in twelve minutes. The dial can be disconcerting, when the arrow swings. One of Prescott's ministers told me they were engaged in a heated discussion about student loans in a Cabinet committee in the room when the arrow moved around the dial, momentarily interrupting their argument.

To the left of the fireplace there is a white dot on the wall, known as the Nelson Spot. A myth has grown up that the Board measured Nelson's height at this mark, and used it as the minimum entry level for young lieutenants into the navy. It is true this mark at five foot four inches was fixed as the minimum height requirement for naval officers under the 1847 regulations, and was used in interviews for candidates. This was not Nelson's true height, however. The bloodied knee breeches that were cut off Nelson by the surgeon in the gloomy 'cockpit' below decks do seem to be no bigger than a boy's and arguments have raged over how tall Nelson actually was. Colin White, Director of the Royal Naval Museum, Portsmouth, where Nelson's flagship *Victory* is moored, told me that the argument was put to rest during conservation work on his uniform. 'It is now agreed he was about five foot six or seven – in other words, the average height for his time . . . The Nelson Spot was an agreeable fancy but does not accurately show his height as an adult.'

In fact, Nelson was never interviewed for his lieutenancy in this room. When Nelson entered the navy as a spindly boy he was interviewed before the full might of the Navy Board – including his uncle, Admiral Suckling – but that was at the Navy Board office in Seething Lane, where the victualling of the fleet was ordered, and where Pepys had lived and worked, not the Admiralty Board in Whitehall which was responsible for the operational strategy of the navy.

The Board Room also contains a long-case clock made in 1697 by Langley Bradley, a contemporary of Tompion, that has kept time for the masters of the navy in the same room for nearly 300 years. A silver inkstand was introduced by the Duke of Clarence, another First Lord of the Admiralty, and the candlestick on the fireplace is a replica of one used by Nelson. Among the artefacts on display is Pepys's velum appointment in 1662 as Clerk of the Acts when he was Secretary to the Admiralty Board; Lord St Vincent's personal copy of the navy regulations, which he wrote; and a manuscript note by President Theodore Roosevelt at the Allied Bazaar in New York dated 1917 saying: 'Let us not owe our shameful safety to the British Fleet; let us do our own fighting.'

But it is the carving by the English genius of the art Grinling Gibbons that delights the eye. The wind dial is supported by two miraculously carved panels on either side, festooned with flowers and fruit mingled with nautical instruments in all their detail. The carvings are thought to have been rescued from an earlier Admiralty building on the site dating from 1695, and were transferred when the present building was completed in 1725. The nautical instruments include a wooden copy of a mariner's sextant, used for establishing longitude before the introduction of ships' clocks, and Gunter's quadrant, designed by the English mathematician Edmund Gunter in 1623 to find local time at sea by sighting either the sun or a bright star at night. They were in general use in the navy in the seventeenth century and some are the only contemporary facsimile models now in existence, and are so finely carved they can be removed and articulated. The carvings along the top are symbolic and represent the Admiralty anchor, the Sword of Victory and the Trumpet of Fame, surmounted by the crown and laurel leaves; in the centre is the 'Eye in Glory', which a civil service guide innocently says 'is an ancient sign which can be seen on the Pyramids and the one used by the Stuart Kings to signify their belief in the Divine Right of Kings', but the 'all-seeing eye' is also a Masonic symbol. Prominent Masons included Christopher Wren, the King's surveyor, who became a 'brother' in 1691; conspiracy theorists may see its presence in the carving as evidence of Masonic influence at the heart of the Admiralty.

The Admiralty was built on the site of Wallingford House, which had been the home of the vainglorious George Villiers, the Duke of Buckingham, the Lord High Admiral until his assassination in 1628. The site was chosen by Wren but the design was by a navy man, John Evans. Within twenty years, rapid growth in the bureaucracy of the Royal Navy led to a requirement for more office space – a familiar problem in Whitehall. Shops on Whitehall and part of the Spring Gardens were acquired for expansion and in 1723 the first Admiralty building was demolished to make way for a new building designed by Thomas Ripley, who had succeeded Grinling Gibbons as Master Carpenter, and Sir John Vanbrugh, the celebrated architect, as Comptroller of Works. The Admiralty complex – the first purpose-built government offices in Britain – included some town houses but they were taken over as offices as the paperwork of the navy increased. The Admiralty accommodated the First Lord, the Admiralty Secretary and Second Secretary, four Lords Commissioners and around forty-five administrators, plus many servants and clerks who had to work by candlelight in the basement. In 1768, the First Lord, Earl Howe, asked Lord Chatham, the Prime Minister, for funds to build 'a few rooms wherein I might dwell in greater privacy' and work began on Admiralty House using land acquired to the south of the block.

Ripley's building appears grand to an untutored eye but was castigated as a 'most ugly edifice' by Horace Walpole for lacking proper classical proportions, and Vanbrugh said every time he saw Ripley's name in public he laughed so much he 'had like to beshit himself'. But it was not Ripley's fault. If you stand outside today and look through the black security gates on Whitehall, you see the problem – his intended portico with classical dimensions would have covered up the top-floor windows. The Admiralty, which wanted to use all the available space, had little time for classical sensitivities and produced a simple solution. Ripley was ordered, despite his protests, to raise the columns carrying the portico over the windows, and to hell with the classical proportions of the pillars. Both the Admiralty and the architect became a laughing stock for the critics. The Admiralty's embarrassment was later covered up by a stone screen designed by a young Scottish architect, Robert Adam, with his first major work in the capital. Adam's screen was regarded as a masterpiece, and he added humorous naval touches including sea horses, hippogriffs – half horse, with the wings of an eagle and the head of a griffin, as Harry Potter fans would know – and the prows of two ships, a Roman galley and the latest navy frigate, with a gun port open and a cannon sticking out. They are best viewed from the top of one of the London double-decker buses that queue outside to the traffic lights at Trafalgar Square. It also provided relief for the Sea Lords for another reason, however. According to a civil service briefing note, 'This masterpiece . . . was designed to defend their Lordships of the Admiralty from the unwelcome attentions of mid-eighteenth-century seamen, many of whom harboured grudges and would wait outside to confront their superiors.'

In 1826, an 'in and out' entrance was added to allow easier access for the carriage of the First Lord of the Admiralty, the Duke of Clarence, later King William IV, whose name is remembered today by the sign of the Clarence pub across the road at the corner of Whitehall and Great Scotland Yard. Adam's screen was restored to its original design in 1923. Around 1890, the massive extension to the Admiralty building – the one festooned with radio masts enclosing the north side of Horse Guards Parade – created more modern offices for the staff of the Admiralty and a new suite of offices for the First Lord of the Admiralty.

In October 1911, the panelled offices in the 'new' building on Horse Guards were used by Winston Churchill as First Lord; his naval maps are still on the walls, protected by wooden doors. Churchill, still only in his thirties, threw himself into the task with his characteristic gusto, touring the fleet in the Admiralty yacht, the *Enchantress*, to immerse himself in the detail. He found the Admiralty ill-prepared to match the growing threat of the Kaiser's navy, and the lack of cooperation with the War Office suggested a lack of commitment to prepare for the all-out war he feared was inevitable. He replaced three of the four Sea Lords in his first year at the

Admiralty and set about building a new generation of battleships, the enlarged Dreadnaughts, equipped with fifteen-inch guns. Ever restless, he also ordered the fleet to switch from coal power to oil and, seeing the strategic importance of oil, successfully pushed for the British takeover of the Anglo-Persian Oil Company to ensure the supply of fuel in times of war. He was forced to resign after his plan to force a route through the Dardanelles by using naval power alone failed, and led to the disaster of the landings at Gallipoli when Commonwealth forces, notably Australians and New Zealanders, were slaughtered. Lord Fisher, the First Sea Lord, though an old ally of Churchill, resigned, forcing Churchill to quit a month later. Churchill, astonishingly, gave up high office to serve in the mud on the front line in France (perhaps to restore his self-belief), but still blamed Fisher for his own downfall and the failure of his long-term strategy in the Dardanelles.

In the 1930s Churchill kept up a one-man campaign against Neville Chamberlain's policy of appeasement with Hitler from the backbenches, but at the outbreak of the Second World War Chamberlain recalled him from the political wilderness. In an extraordinary act of reconciliation, he reappointed Churchill to the post he had held in the First World War, as First Lord of the Admiralty. Churchill recorded:

I sent word to the Admiralty that I would take charge forthwith and arrive at 6 pm. On this, the Board were kind enough to signal the Fleet, 'Winston is back'. So it was that I came again to the room I had quitted in pain and sorrow almost exactly a quarter of a century before, when Lord Fisher's resignation had led to my removal from my post as First Lord and ruined irretrievably, as it proved, the important conception of forcing the Dardanelles. A few feet behind me, as I sat in my old chair, was the wooden map-case I had fixed in 1911, and inside it still remained the chart of the North Sea on which each day, in order to focus attention on the supreme objective, I had made the National Intelligence Branch record the movements and dispositions of the German High Seas Fleet.[5]

The building was used in the 1980s for the Northern Ireland Office and the then Secretary of State for Northern Ireland, Peter (now Lord) Brooke proudly showed me Churchill's naval maps when he invited a few journalists to his room for a drink. It is now used to house intelligence staff under the Foreign Office and the historic room where Churchill ran the navy is sadly out of bounds to the public.

The 'Admiralty' was abolished as a separate department in defence reforms in 1964 and made part of the Ministry of Defence, when the title of Lord High Admiral – which had been no more than a personal title at the time of the Restoration[6] – passed to the Queen. Admiralty House, attached to the Admiralty building, is now used for grace-and-favour flats for senior Cabinet ministers, but it was originally home to the First Lord of the Admiralty. The staircase by Samuel James Cockerell splits into two at the first floor, and twists in an elegant spiral to the upper floors below a demilune skylight. Churchill occupied the whole house when he was brought back by Chamberlain in 1939.

The upper floors were turned into flats for ministers after Churchill's time at the Admiralty, and John Prescott and his wife Pauline were allocated the top-floor flat, a palatial suite overlooking Horse Guards reached by a very rickety lift. The apartment – a suite of rooms with a galley kitchen, large dining room facing Horse Guards Parade, living room and a bedroom – had previously been occupied by the Tory Defence Secretary, Michael Portillo, and the Prescotts were amused to find a canopy over the bed in pink silk when they arrived, but had it removed. Margaret Beckett was below them and sometimes complained about Prescott's heavy feet thumping on her ceiling. I was invited by the Deputy Prime Minister to one of his small gatherings to watch the Trooping the Colour from his windows. Prescott, a lover of jazz, turned up the volume on his CD of Ella Fitzgerald to drown out the sound of the marching bands below. They did not have butlers or cooks, and the Prescotts provided their own food for the small luncheon party from Marks & Spencer in Oxford Street. They also paid a notional rent for the flat out of his ministerial salary and Prescott, a former Cunard waiter, did the cooking in the galley kitchen.

His most famous culinary efforts were before the 2005 general election when he secretly hosted private dinners for Gordon Brown and Tony Blair in the dining room at his flat to discuss a deal between them for the handover of power. Prescott produced his own cottage pie. Brown complained the chair at the huge highly polished table was too low, so Prescott replaced it. He asked Blair whether he wanted a higher chair. 'No – Gordon's always looked down on me,' Blair quipped. Prescott always denied acting as a broker between the two men. He told me he was 'just holding their coats' while they settled their differences.

The Admiralty complex was refurbished between 2000 and 2003 at a cost of £29 million. It was part of a £60 million scheme announced in 1998, before Prescott had persuaded Blair to allow him to create his own Whitehall department as Deputy Prime Minister, that would create a huge department stretching from Downing Street to Admiralty Arch, with a break for Horse Guards. In all, about 400 Cabinet Office staff were taken out of the Treasury, and the cross-Whitehall machinery of Downing Street was consolidated into a single immense unit. Most of the buildings in Whitehall appeared untouched from the outside, but the former Glyn Mills bank at 22 Whitehall was completely gutted. Beyond its glass doors, a modern glass atrium was thrown over the back of the building covering a

Georgian courtyard so it could be connected to the Admiralty. From the outside it looks like a nondescript bank, but inside it is a riot of wood, steel and glass. Linking the range meant that Prescott could walk all the way from Admiralty House to Admiralty Arch in the Mall without getting his feet wet. At the height of the firemen's strike, when Prescott wanted a trade union leader to slip out of his office without being spotted by the press, his aides found there were at least fifteen alternative exits he could have chosen, and probably more when the secret Cold War tunnels and the old Admiralty building on the Mall – now used by the intelligence services – were included. The Admiralty building on the Mall, used as the Northern Ireland Office during the Thatcher period, was connected by a bridge to Admiralty Arch to increase the office space of the Cabinet Office complex.

Admiralty Arch conceals two houses. It was commissioned by Edward VII in 1906 to create a main processional route from Buckingham Palace to Trafalgar Square, but completed in 1911 after his death. The three gates were the biggest in Britain and the central gate is closed to all traffic apart from the Queen. The millions of people who pass by have not the slightest clue that the north side of the Arch contains two grace-and-favour town houses. They were intended for the First Lord of the Admiralty and the First Sea Lord, but the First Lord in 1909 – a now-forgotten Liberal, Reginald McKenna – kicked up a fuss about being moved out of his historic house in Whitehall and won the backing of the Liberal Cabinet under Herbert Asquith. The First Lord's magnificent house – the larger of the two, with an entrance porch on the Charing Cross elevation – was allocated instead to the First Sea Lord at the time, Sir Arthur Wilson. It had nine bedrooms and two bathrooms plus rooms for servants, but the tradesman's entrance was put in the wrong place, because it lacked direct access to the servants' quarters. They also had to install a spiral staircase to allow the butler to reach the front door from below stairs without having to be seen crossing the grand entrance hall. Before the refurbishment began, offices in the Arch were used in 1998 by Prescott to house sixty homeless people. It caused an outcry and it was not repeated. The entire Arch is now used as civil servants' offices.

The ground-floor rooms at Admiralty House where Lady Spencer entertained Lord and Lady Nelson are now available to ministers and defence chiefs for hire. Prescott used it for an office Christmas Party on 19 December 2002, at which he was photographed laughing, dancing and carrying his diary secretary Tracey Temple in his arms. In April 2006, the same photographs were splashed across the front pages of most newspapers after Prescott, sixty-seven, confessed in the *Daily Mirror* to having had a two-year affair with Ms Temple, forty-three, that started at the Admiralty party. He considered quitting because of the scandal but was persuaded against it by his loyal wife. In October 2006, Prescott apologized to the annual Labour Party conference and said he would go when Blair stood down the following year. In the summer of 2007, Prescott hired the ground floor of Admiralty House one more time with a jazz band for close friends and loyal staff; this time it was for his leaving party. But the 'Prescott sex scandal' at Admiralty House was nothing compared to what went on two doors away at the Scotland Office.

# DOVER HOUSE – THE MOST NOTORIOUS ADDRESS IN LONDON

'Mad, bad and dangerous to know.'

Lady Caroline Lamb on Byron

A hunched figure hurried down the stone steps, through the passage to the public entrance of the House of Commons, and darted out into the cold damp November air enveloping the old Palace of Westminster. The boy was dressed in breeches, shirt and coat, and appeared agitated. He dodged between the horse-drawn carriages of MPs and wealthy visitors to Parliament, and negotiated the dung-strewn New Palace Yard across Bridge Street into Parliament Street and Whitehall. The boy broke into a trot past the end of Downing Street and the Treasury on Whitehall, and slipped breathlessly into the entrance of Melbourne House.

Once inside, the boy startled the butler by throwing off his coat and racing up the stairs. Lady Caroline Lamb, six days after celebrating her twenty-first birthday, was exhilarated by her own daring in defying the rules of the House of Commons to see her husband make his maiden speech. Women were banned from the public gallery in Parliament, so Caroline had borrowed her brother's clothes to gain entrance to a man's world, and it would not be the last time. She enjoyed 'cross-dressing' but there was a wild, untameable spirit about 'Caro' that would ultimately prove her downfall.

The stuffy rules of Westminster held no fear for Caro. Until the 1834 fire which destroyed the medieval Parliament building, the MPs met in St Stephen's Chapel in Westminster, facing each other in pews, adversarial-style, and there was no place for women, who did not even have the vote. The public gallery that was reserved for men ran down the sides of the chamber, supported on slender pillars. Women were, however, permitted to gain admission to the 'ventilator' in the roof space over the chamber through a special arrangement with Mr Bellamy, the deputy housekeeper of the Commons, who also provided meals for MPs. Today his name is remembered in a Commons researchers' cafeteria at 1 Parliament Street called Bellamy's, but the restriction of women to the ventilator room had long been forgotten by the time a Victorian chamber was built with a ladies' gallery in which women could gaze down on their male legislators from behind a discreet screen to avoid their presence disrupting the business of the House. No more than eight women could sit by the ventilator at a time, and they had to get an admission ticket from an MP.[1] There they could look down through a hole by the chain that held the central chandelier and, if they were fortunate, catch a glimpse of MPs' heads below. Frances, Lady Shelley, described what it was like in her diary: 'I found myself in a room about eight feet square resembling the cabin of a ship. There was a window to admit air, two chairs, a table and a thing like a chimney in the centre. This was the ventilator, which opens into the body of the

House of Commons. Through it sound ascends so perfectly that with attention, not a word is lost . . .'[2] That was not good enough for Caroline. Her husband, William Lamb, the recently elected MP for Leominster and heir of Lord Melbourne, was due to make his maiden speech, and she was determined to be there in the chamber to witness it.

Melbourne House, now called Dover House and the London base for the Scotland Office, is the squat building with a small pillared portico, sandwiched between the Cabinet Office and Horse Guards, that is completely ignored by the tourists who crowd into the yard at Horse Guards to see the daily Changing of the Guard. Inside, however, it is an elegant mini-palace, with airy views over St James's Park, and it was once the social centre of the Whig world, with a glittering salon for the political stars of the day, presided over by William's shrewd and ambitious mother, Lady Melbourne. For a time in the Regency period, it was the most notorious address in London.

Everything had changed for William when his older brother Peniston died of consumption on 24 January 1805 at Melbourne House in Whitehall. Lord Melbourne was grief-stricken – Peniston was widely believed to be the only one of his six children that he had fathered – and William now stood to inherit the family fortune and title. He was twenty-five, and as his brother lay on his deathbed, comforted by his mistress, William, one of the most eligible bachelors in London, decided he now had the financial prospects to propose to someone with whom he had been in love for nearly four years – Lady Caroline Ponsonby. Caroline was a member of the Spencer dynasty on her mother's side. They were married in June 1805 and settled down to a life of happily married bliss in rooms on the top floor at Melbourne House. In January 1806 William won a seat as the Whig MP for Leominster, and had waited nearly a year before making his maiden speech in the Commons. It was a doubly auspicious moment, and it is understandable that it was one his wife would not want to miss, as William had been chosen for the honour of proposing the response to the King's Speech at the State Opening of Parliament. Hansard, the official report of Parliament which had recently been started by Cobbett, conveys the combination of boring routine and grand pomp that surrounded William's debut in the annual grand ceremony that is little changed today:

> Friday, November 19 – At 4 o'clock, Mr Quarnie, yeoman usher of the black rod, appeared at the bar, and in the name of the lords authorized by virtue of his majesty's commission, required the immediate attendance of the commons in the house of peers to hear the commission read. The speaker, and nearly all the members present, attended . . .

When the MPs returned to their chamber, the King's Speech, which had been delivered in the Lords by the Lord Chancellor in George III's absence, was read out again by the Speaker of the Commons. The King's Speech was grave, in keeping with the mood of the times: the joy of Trafalgar in October 1805 had given way to grief over Nelson's death, and England was again imperilled by Napoleon. Undaunted by the setback at sea, Napoleon had marched east to his most brilliant victory, over the combined forces of the Austrians and Russians at the Battle of Austerlitz. The self-proclaimed Emperor had entered Berlin in 1806 and issued a decree blockading Britain and her two allies from all trade with the Continent of Europe, threatening all British travellers with imprisonment as prisoners of war, and the seizure of all ships, goods and mail.

The response to the Queen's Speech today by the two backbenchers picked for the honour is supposed to be non-political and, above all, amusing. As he rose to address the Commons for the first time, Lamb could have been forgiven for being less than cheerful. A shadow had hung over Whitehall and Melbourne House in particular in 1806. The mourning clothes for Nelson's state funeral, which started outside their windows in January, had been barely cast off when the Prime Minister William Pitt suddenly died, plunging Whitehall once more into mourning.

William's first child had also died. He was away campaigning to win his seat in Leominster when Caroline went into labour prematurely. The child struggled for life after a difficult, painful birth, but died before William could return to Melbourne House. They were still grieving for the loss of their baby when the Melbourne household was convulsed by the death of Caroline's aunt, Georgiana, the Duchess of Devonshire, at the age of forty-eight. She died after a long debilitating illness that had robbed her of her celebrated looks.

However, politically, for William there had been a silver lining with the cloud over Pitt's death. King George III, who hated the Whigs, reluctantly agreed (in a period of respite from his madness) to the creation of a coalition, known as 'The Ministry of All the Talents'. To a great Whig family like the Melbournes, it was like creating a Cabinet of friends and lovers.

Lord Grenville, a former ally of Pitt who had refused to serve in his last government after forging an alliance with Fox, became Prime Minister. Pitt's long-term opponent Charles Fox was appointed Foreign Secretary. Charles Grey, Lord Howick, was made First Lord of the Admiralty and the Whig wit, playwright and cheerleader, Richard Brinsley Sheridan, ageing author of Georgian society farces such as *The Rivals* and *School for Scandal*, replaced George Canning as Treasurer of the Navy. Grey had fathered a daughter by Georgiana, and had had an affair with Sheridan's second wife, Hecca, while Sheridan, jealous and duplicitous, had had a long-running affair with Caroline's mother, Henrietta Spencer, Lady Bessborough. Henrietta also had two illegitimate children by Lord Granville, who later married one of her nieces, Georgiana's daughter Harriet, known in the family as 'Harryo'.

However in September 1806, Fox, the Whigs' leading light, followed his old rival Pitt to the grave, dying of dropsy – accumulation of fluid in the body, usually associated with liver disease and heavy drinking – and the Whigs' sudden ascendancy came to an equally abrupt end. Within a year they were out of power, and remained in Opposition for twenty-five years.

Sitting in the narrow public gallery of the House of Commons, on the edge of her seat to look down on the benches below, Caroline watched William rise in his place to begin the speech he had rehearsed with her, marching round their private apartments on the first floor at Melbourne House. He began with a statesmanlike summary of current affairs. She knew every word. Hansard recorded:

> The Hon William Lamb (son of lord viscount Melbourne) rose. He said, that unfortunately the gloom cast over the meeting of parliament by the continuation of the disturbance of that system under which Europe had enjoyed the highest tranquillity and happiness was by no means either novel or extraordinary: a disturbance, which sufficient experience had ascertained, went to the complete destruction of ancient and venerable estates, at least to a degradation of them so humiliating as to leave little choice between that and their complete destruction.

He continued with a rallying call which would be echoed 150 years later in similar circumstances by Churchill:

> Although every successive disaster prepared the mind in some measure for the present state of affairs; yet it was not without the utmost awe and inquietude that we could behold the period, so long menaced, at length arrived: a period when the power of the enemy was predominant and unlimited over the greater part of Europe, and when Great Britain, with the exception of two powerful allies

was left unsupported and compelled to rely for its security on those resources on which, he was confident, we might rely implicitly – the natural courage and the unparalleled spirit of the people.

As cries of 'hear, hear' echoed in the chamber, Caroline slipped out of the gallery and dashed back to Melbourne House. Once inside the pillared entrance hall, she raced up the wide main staircase and turned sharp left on the first floor to scale the narrow staircase to the Lambs' upper-storey apartments to change. Caro's bedroom was in the centre of the house at the back, overlooking the trees of St James's Park and Horse Guards Parade below. There was a connecting door to the adjacent room and two more onto the passage, across which William had the master bedroom. Today there is conjecture about precisely which room was hers, but it can only have been the elegant room facing St James's Park, now used as the London headquarters for Scotland Office civil servants. There is an alcove, ten feet wide and eight feet deep, with a desk and shelves, and almost certainly this is where her bed would have stood. To the right, between a door and her bed, is a narrow room with a door that would have served perfectly as Caroline's walk-in wardrobe.

There was to be a small party for the Whig politicians among whom William was now a rising star. She hurriedly stripped out of her brother's clothes and stepped into one of her many fine gowns for her husband's return with his friends and supporters. She was late, and her absence had been noticed by her mother-in-law.

Earlier, the ladies of Melbourne House had gathered in the elegant, glittering drawing room, up the grand staircase at the entrance to the house, to welcome the men back from the Commons in triumph, but there had been no sign of Caroline. Servants said she had disappeared and, when it was reported that she had returned, Lady Melbourne, William's redoubtable mother, wanted to know where she had been. At first Caroline said she had been at Lady Holland's.

However, the truth came out that Caroline had persuaded her brother Willy, then nineteen, to loan his sister his clothes and she had been escorted to the Commons by a family friend, Mr Ross. Lady Melbourne was furious. 'Bess' (Elizabeth Foster, the Duke of Devonshire's mistress who had lived in a *ménage à trois* with Georgiana and her husband) was at Melbourne House that night, and recorded the drama in her diary:

> There was great anxiety. Caroline Lamb was missing! We guessed she had been to the House of Commons but she pretended she went to Holland House. She was not come back to Whitehall and Lady Melb. was angry; however, she said that if William did not disapprove, she would say nothing more . . .[3]

It was regarded in the household as another tiresome example of Caroline's wilful and exhibitionist behaviour. She had been born into one of the great Regency aristocratic houses of the age – the Spencer family – and had been brought up with her aunt's children in London at Devonshire House, a huge pile overlooking Green Park, when the three great society women of the day, Georgiana, Lady Holland and Lady Melbourne, were already in spreading middle age.

'Caro' was born on 13 November 1785, the daughter of Frederick Ponsonby, Viscount Duncannon, and his vivacious wife Henrietta Spencer. Her mother was the daughter of John, first Earl Spencer, and Caroline could not have had more impeccable Whig connections – her uncle was the second Earl Spencer, who became Nelson's staunchest supporter as First Lord of the Admiralty, two doors away from her home at Melbourne House, and her aunt was Georgiana, who had married one of the richest men in Britain, William Cavendish, the fifth Duke of Devonshire. The Devonshires' country seat was at Chatsworth, but Devonshire House in Piccadilly was to be part of the social circus in which Caro was to shine. As a child she was a tomboy, much given to tantrums, which were overlooked or tolerated by her mother. She was called Ariel, Squirrel, and Young Savage but was known as Caro by her mother. In later life, her violent public outbursts were taken as a sign of madness.

Caroline was a drama-queen, who recorded one of her 'scenes' at Melbourne House in her journal:

Then came my fracas with the page, which made such noise. He was a little *espiègle*, and would throw detonating balls into the fire. Lord Melbourne always scolded me for this, and I, the boy. One day I was playing ball with him. He threw squibs into the fire, and I threw the ball at his head. It hit him on the temple, and he bled. He cried out, 'O my Lady, you have killed me!' Out of my senses, I flew into the hall and screamed, 'Oh God, I have murdered the page!'

She was artistic, composed poetry, and would later cause a scandal with her very public love affair with the poet Byron and her first novel *Glenarvon*, a thinly veiled attack on the Melbournes, dashed off in a fever of despair at Byron's rejection of her. Today she would be regarded as a 'wild child' but her reckless contempt for convention was to become her curse. Caro was said to be 'attractive without being a beauty', with a slight boyish figure. Her waiflike looks would have been fashionable in the twenty-first century, but compared to the bosomy beauties of her own day she was regarded as strange. Her androgyny, however, and her love of cross-dressing in her own page's uniforms, later attracted Byron. She had fair curly hair, and a soft voice that possessed great charm. She had, according to a family friend, a 'fascination that was peculiarly hers', a quality that would be called charisma today. The Duke of Devonshire's heir, Lord Hartington ('Hart'), grew up with Caro and was enchanted by her, but Caro turned him down. Instead, on 3 June 1805, Caroline, nineteen, married William Lamb at 2 Cavendish Square, the London house owned by the bride's parents, Lord and Lady Bessborough. To accommodate the newly-weds, Lady Melbourne and her husband moved downstairs into the ground-floor apartments used by the previous owner, the Duke of York, the second in line for the throne, and gave the Lambs their rooms on the second floor, with Caroline occupying the airy bedroom in the centre overlooking the trees of St James's Park to Buckingham House in the distance.

When Lady Caroline arrived at Melbourne House it had been at the centre of Whig society for more than a decade, presided over by William's formidable mother, Lady Melbourne. Elizabeth Milbanke had married into relatively new money when she wed Sir Peniston Lamb. The Lamb family's country retreat was Brocket Hall in the rolling countryside of Hertfordshire, twenty miles north of London. The neoclassical stately home – now a hotel and conference centre with a Nick Faldo golf course – was built in 1760 for Matthew Lamb, Peniston's father, a barrister and politician who had amassed a fortune from the law and his marriage to the heiress Charlotte Coke, from whom he inherited Melbourne Hall, Derbyshire, that was to lend its name to the family title. Elizabeth had set all her energies to advancing her husband's social standing by becoming one of the great society hostesses of the age. She created a grand salon in the family mansion in Piccadilly to rival those of the other great society hostesses, Georgiana, the Duchess of Devonshire, and Lady Holland at Holland House. In the style of the times, she also took a string of lovers, including King George III's two sons, George, the Prince of Wales (the future George IV), and the younger prince, Frederick, the Duke of York. While she produced an heir for her husband, William, Lady Melbourne's second son and her daughter Harriet were widely believed to have been fathered by the one great love of her life, George, the third Earl Egremont. He was a patron of the artist Turner and owner of Petworth, a stately home with rolling parkland in West Sussex, now given over to the National Trust. A second daughter, Emily, was by Francis, the Duke of Bedford. A third son, Frederick, was named after his father, the Duke of York, and her fourth son, George, after *his* father, the Prince of Wales.

As Elizabeth climbed the social ladder on her back, her husband accepted the rewards of her service to the Crown – an hereditary peerage as the First Viscount Melbourne – and embraced her 'natural' children by other men as his own. William was brought up at the family mansion in Piccadilly but the Duke of York, a frequent visitor, had taken a fancy to their home and when he married Princess Frederica of Prussia in 1791 suggested to his mistress, Lady Melbourne, an extraordinary house swap – Melbourne House for York House, the Duke's residence next to Horse Guards in Whitehall. The ever-obliging Lady Melbourne agreed, and the Melbournes took over the lease of York House in October 1792, when it became known as Melbourne House. The Duke was a serving officer in the army, and proved a genial though inexpert general. His statue towers above the steps at Carlton House Terrace but he has become more famous as the butt of the nursery rhyme for his indecision in leading a campaign in Walcheren, Holland in 1793–5:

> The Grand Old Duke of York;
> He had ten thousand men.
> He marched them up to the top of the hill
> And marched them down again.

One of those men was a young Arthur Wellesley, who became the Duke of Wellington, and never forgot the military lesson learned under the Duke of York in Walcheren, saying that it taught him 'what one ought not to do, and that is always something'.

When the Duke of York had acquired the house in Whitehall it had a plain, though pleasing, front, with a small courtyard where coaches could turn, and a simple entrance on the ground floor. It was an ideal town house for an MP: handy for the Commons, a five-minute walk away; Downing Street was around the corner to the right; the social court of the King at St James's Palace was a short stroll across St James's Park; and it was convenient for the nearby gentlemen's clubs in St James's including Brooks's, home to the Whigs. It had been built for Sir Matthew Featherstonhaugh MP in 1755 on land once occupied by Henry VIII's recreation area, near the old Cockpit Lodgings, on designs by James Paine, the same popular architect of the period who designed Brocket Hall for William's grandfather. Architects drawings of Paine's completed Whitehall house are today displayed in the first-floor bedrooms, now offices occupied by civil servants. Emma Hamilton is reputed to have visited the house when she was having an affair with Sir Matthew's son, but it was not grand enough for the Duke of York.

Prince Frederick commissioned Sir Henry Holland, the architect who was at that time working on the nearby neoclassical Carlton House for the Prince of Wales, to remodel York House after he acquired it in 1788. Holland kept the core of the Paine design for the house but threw a stone stairway to the first-floor apartments inside a spacious rotunda, thus creating the impression of a grand staircase leading to the fine drawing rooms where the Duke would hold court and entertain his guests. The Duke's private apartments were arranged below in the garden rooms, where the offices had been, with French windows onto a small garden and Horse Guards Parade. Holland extended the old north wing towards the parade ground to allow access to the Duke's ground-floor bedroom from the library. His suite of rooms included a hot bath, a cold bath, water heater and WC between a new valets' room, an inner dressing room and wardrobe, and the Duke's bedchamber. Outside, the west elevation onto Horse Guards Parade was covered in rusticated Portland stone with a large three-light centre window within an

arched recess divided by Ionic columns. It was ideal for the Duke
while he presided over the Horse Guards next door. The stables at
the side were no longer accessible after the house was extended with
the rotunda at the front and permission was granted to knock down
an old Lottery office across Whitehall next to the Banqueting House
to create a coach house directly opposite Melbourne House at a cost
of £2,730 (£142,037 at 2007 prices).

However, after moving to the Melbourne's house in Piccadilly,
the Duke of York and Albany quickly separated from his new wife,
and the house was later converted by Holland into flats when it was
mortgaged to Coutts Bank by the Duke to clear debts. It was renamed
The Albany after the Duke to lend it cachet, and remains one of
the most exclusive and expensive addresses in Mayfair. The Duke
did leave one lasting memento of his time at York House: a field
marshal's baton and coronet, emblazoned in gold leaf against a
white background, in a frieze above the door to his ground-floor
bedroom.

Two hundred years later, the Duke's ground-floor apartments
were taken over temporarily by John Prescott, the Deputy Prime
Minister, while he was awaiting the completion of the Cabinet
Office complex for his own Whitehall department. The rooms had
been restored to their Regency splendour with green wallpaper and
elegant soft furnishing. Prescott held a number of committee meetings
in the room that had been the Duke's bedroom, and the sight of the
Duke's coronet over the doorway raised a few eyebrows among
Prescott's Cabinet colleagues. It was also while he was working 'in
the basement' at Melbourne House that Prescott is said to have first
met Tracey Temple, the Whitehall secretary with whom he later
had a scandalous affair.

Overall, Holland had created a mini-palace for the Duke that
was home to the Melbournes for the next thirty years. Under its
new chatelaine, Melbourne House quickly became a Whig alternative

salon to the much duller court of George III at Windsor or, when the House of Commons was sitting, St James's Palace. The Prince of Wales, who in the Hanoverian tradition could not abide his father, was part of the regular circle who collected like moths to a flame at Melbourne House when Lady Melbourne was in her prime.

The young Lambs kept open house for the next generation of Whiggish friends and gave balls for the new craze of the waltz in the elegant ballroom overlooking Horse Guards Parade. The room where ladies in ballgowns twirled on the arms of their men is now the main office of the Secretary of State for Scotland, although it is sometimes used for receptions to promote Scottish tourism. The Lambs received visitors morning and afternoon, and gave glittering dinner parties lasting until the early hours of the morning, when the guests would sometimes descend the broad flight of stone stairs to Lord and Lady Melbourne's apartments below for supper and to see the dawn break over St James's Park.

After schooling at Eton, William Lamb had become one of the most dashing men in London, with dark good looks, black curly hair and a romantic, somewhat detached manner, partly caused by his shyness in public. He was a follower of Beau Brummell, the dandy who took three hours to tie a cravat, and adopted the fashion for shorter hair, which was seen as sympathetic to the French Revolutionaries, earning him a scolding from his father for cutting his hair too short. William, who spouted the extreme Foxite views on the tyranny of the monarch, George III, and the blunders of British diplomacy over America, shocked even his Whig-supporting parents by suggesting that the best thing for Britain was to be defeated by the enlightened Bonaparte.[4] He had plenty of opportunities to observe the sparkling wit of his mother's brilliant circle of guests and became an excellent mimic of both Pitt and Lord North. His childhood hero, Charles James Fox, and his acolyte Sheridan were among the frequent visitors to Melbourne House. Sheridan had satirized

Georgiana as the spendthrift Lady Teazle in his play *School for Scandal* and had drawn on her friend Lady Melbourne for Lady Sneerwell.

Elections were rumbustious affairs compared to today's heavily policed polls. The two high-society ladies notoriously canvassed votes for Fox by offering kisses to the voters, and they were lampooned in satirical cartoons of the day. Under William's mother, Melbourne House became a centre for political opposition to the Pitt administrations and King George III. Lady Melbourne was a courtesan with political acumen, a quality she demonstrated one night when the Prince of Wales was dining at Melbourne House. Alarming news reached their Whitehall dinner party that an attempt had been made on the life of George III at the theatre in Drury Lane. The Prince of Wales, whose appetite was astonishing even to Georgian eyes, initially refused to leave the table, but Lady Melbourne prevailed on him to go to his father. He returned to Melbourne House before midnight, thanking her for her advice.[5]

Sheridan congratulated William after his maiden speech, but William never excelled as an orator and his was to be a plodding rather than meteoric career. He was forty-eight before he entered government, partly because of his marriage to the wayward Caroline.

Beyond London, the Industrial Revolution was taking place and fortunes were being made by tradesmen and entrepreneurs, who soon would be demanding parliamentary representation with the Reform Bill, but in the salons around St James's, the land-owning Whig aristocracy were enjoying their golden age. In 1808, to celebrate the birth of Augustus, the Melbourne's grandson, Melbourne House was lit up for a glittering gathering of VIP guests headed by the Prince of Wales. By now, Sheridan had become a dishevelled, drunken pest to Caroline's mother, his former lover, who feared he was a threat to her daughter, and attempts were made to keep him out of the christening party, but at 5 p.m. he slipped up the main staircase with the Prince of Wales, who had agreed to be the child's godfather. Sheridan managed to get a seat opposite Caroline and when it was suggested that they play her favourite game – writing impromptu verse in turn after each other (like a round from BBC Radio's *I'm Sorry I Haven't A Clue*) – Sheridan penned these lines:

> Grant Heav'n, sweet Babe thou mayst inherit
> What Nature only can impart –
> Thy Father's manly sense and spirit,
> Thy Mother's grace and gentle Heart;
> And when to Manhood's hopes and duties grown,
> Be thou a prop to thy great Sponsor's throne.

It was passed to Caroline to read and add her own verse, something she excelled at. Inexplicably, Caroline said she felt unwell and, with a frightened look, hurried from the room. Her mother acidly completed the next verse, and returned it to Sheridan to read out loud:

> May he who wrote ye verse impart
> To thee sweet baby whom he blesses
> As shrewd a head, a better heart
> And talents he alone possesses.

Sheridan quickly amended her lines, and read out: 'A wiser head, as pure a heart, And greater wealth than he possesses.'

Caroline was bored with Melbourne House. She was depressed by miscarriages; her son proved to be mentally backward and given to fits. She violently quarrelled with William, who appears to have shocked his wife soon after they were married by displaying an interest in flagellation, a taste he may have acquired at Eton. She had an affair with Sir Godfrey Webster, Lady Holland's son by her first marriage, and mixed with the 'wrong' types – Lady Wellesley (no connection to Arthur, later the Duke of Wellington) who was a dubious French 'noblewoman', and Lady Oxford, an ageing siren – which distressed her mother and infuriated her mother-in-law. She was bored with her society, the conspicuous wealth, the rides along Rotten Row, the parties and the masques at Melbourne House, where she would appear one minute dressed as a page in a rough red wig and boys' shoes, the next as a harlequin – she confided in a letter she had 'jumped like a Harlequin, laughed heartily and had no mercy on anyone'. She appeared at one Melbourne House masque dressed as the Whiggish cleric Sydney Smith.[6] She was bored by the hypocrisy of the Devonshire set, and disillusioned by the war in the Peninsula against Napoleon – Frederick Ponsonby, her brother, who was to become a hero at Waterloo, had returned injured from Talavera, full of bitter hatred for the betrayal of Britain by her Spanish allies. Most of all she was bored with convention, her marriage vows, her mother-in-law and the stuffy Melbourne circle. Then Byron limped up the grand staircase of Melbourne House, into her life.

1812 – the year in which America declared war on Britain and Napoleon retreated from Moscow – was declared the worst year in history by the BBC in January 2008; it was also the year in which the Industrial Revolution sparked civil unrest, the Luddites were brutally put down for breaking machinery, the Napoleonic wars had led to high taxes, and the Prime Minister, Spencer Perceval, was assassinated. But in Caro's closed and cosseted world it was the year that Byron exploded on to her stage.

It is hard today to understand the impact that a work of poetry could have on such a small, rarefied elite – no CD could match it today – but the appearance of Byron's heroic tale of disillusionment and doomed youth, *Childe Harold's Pilgrimage,* chimed perfectly with Caro's mood and electrified the aristocratic elite of Caro's London. *Childe Harold* was based on Bryon's own grand tour through the wild countryside of Portugal and Spain, and made its author an overnight sensation. Lady Caroline Lamb was among the first to read the book when an advance copy was delivered in March that year to Melbourne House by Samuel Rogers. He was a banker-poet who was acting for the publisher John Murray as an agent with contacts to promote it, and the epic poem could not have been more perfectly designed to seduce her. She told Rogers she wanted to meet Byron, whose picture she had admired. Rogers said the writer was ugly, a nail-biter with a club foot, but she would not be put off, and went to meet him at Lady Westmoreland's ball. Seeing him surrounded by admirers, Caro turned her back on Byron. Intrigued, and offered a calling card, Byron made his way to Melbourne House the next day where the first-floor ballroom was in full swing with a waltzing party when he arrived. He hated dancing because of his club foot, but Caroline presented an exciting challenge, and he was intrigued by the woman he had only met the day before. Before he reached the first floor, he tripped on the stairs.

'When he literally tripped up the stairs of Melbourne House (he read the omen gloomily), holding a rose and a carnation for Lady Caroline in his bitten fingers, he may have been advertizing a passion less for passion itself than for its counterfeit, sensation,' Frederic Raphael speculated in his biography of the poet.[7] The wall to the left of the staircase is today fitted with a sturdy rope. When I visited Melbourne House I was told by the housekeeper it was known as 'Byron's Rope' and had been installed to assist the poet up the stairs.

Caro, like Byron, was a self-obsessed wild romantic, and was intoxicated both by his epic poem that had made him the first celebrity poet, and by his appearance – a strong brow, nose and sensual mouth, coupled with a fashionably pale complexion. She later wrote that his pale face would be 'my fate' and claimed to have coined the phrase 'mad, bad and dangerous to know' about Byron's darker side.

Byron spent the greater part of every day in Caroline's room on the upper floor at Melbourne House and within weeks they had become passionate lovers. They travelled to parties together in Byron's coach, and she would suddenly arrive in his rooms disguised theatrically as a page, dressed in a plumed hat and tight scarlet pantaloons with a silver-laced jacket. They had highly charged lovers' tiffs – he was jealous of her waltzing; she was appalled that he had gone in May to Newgate Prison to witness John Bellingham, the deranged tradesman who had murdered Perceval, being 'launched into eternity' for his crime. But within four months, their passionate love affair – for Byron at least – had burned itself out. Its impact, however, would stay with Caroline for the rest of her life.

Caroline, who was becoming increasingly desperate in her pursuit of her lover, discovered that Byron kept curls from his conquests' hair in annotated folds of tissue paper. On 9 August, she sent him a love letter with a very personal gift for his collection of 'trophies' – her light-coloured pubic hair.

The letter read:

> I asked you not to send blood but Yet do – because if it means love
> I like to have it. I cut the hair too close & bled much more than
> you need – do not you the same & pray put not scissors points near
> where *quei capelli* grow – sooner take it from the arm or wrist –
> pray be careful . . .

The gift was inscribed in lovers' code:

> CAROLINE BYRON – August 9th 1812
> NEXT TO THYRZA DEAREST
> & MOST FAITHFUL – GOD BLESS YOU
> OWN LOVE – RICORDATI DI BIONDETTA
> FROM YOUR WILD ANTELOPE

Biondetta ('little blonde' – a title Caro gave herself in her love affair with Byron) was a devilish spirit who appeared as a woman dressed as a page and seduced a 25-year-old man in the mystical novel *Le Diable Amoureux* (The Devil in Love) by Jacques Cazotte. Biondetta was accompanied by a white spaniel, which in Marlowe's *Doctor Faustus* represented the devil.[8] In a book of quotations, poems and stories, which she kept almost like a scrapbook, Caroline wrote that Biondetta was 'a small spaniel Bitch whom Lord Byron took a fancy for as he saw it bounding wildly along in company with a thousand other dogs'. Biondetta is taken up by Lord Byron but soon neglected, and then completely forgotten.

It was normal for lovers of the period to exchange locks of their hair, but never quite like this. The wild antelope appeared to those around her to be becoming unhinged. Lady Bessborough, Caroline's mother, was a witness to one scene, writing on 12 August, just three days after Caroline sent her pubic clippings to Byron:

I was at White Hall in the morning, trying to persuade Caro to come with me to Roehampton, and let William join us on the Friday to go to Ireland. She was in bad humour and in the midst Lord Melbourne came in reproached her for some of the strange things she does. She answered so rudely, so disrespectfully, that I was frightened and ran to call Lady Mel. We returned instantly together but met Lord Melbourne on the stairs, pale as death, screaming to the porter to stop Caroline. It was in vein [sic]; she had disappeared in a moment, too quick for the servants who ran out after her, to guess which way she had turned. I cannot tell you my agony yet I believed for a long time what Lady M. thought probable, that after the first impulse of anger was over she would return. I drove up and down Palt [Parliament] Street in every direction I thought she could have gone, and returned in despair when Lord Melbourne told us she threatened him with going with

Lord Byron and he 'bid her go and be' but did not think he would take her.

Lady Bessborough burst in on Byron at his private apartment, but he suggested Caroline might have another lover. Caroline, who had bribed her coachman, was eventually found by her mother hiding at a doctor's house, having pawned her jewellery with a mad plan to elope or, if Byron could not be persuaded to join her, leave England for good.

Byron had dismissed Lady Melbourne as a 'hack whore of the last century', but as he turned for help to extricate himself from his increasingly embarrassing liaison, he discovered that Lady Melbourne was far more agreeable to him than at first she had seemed; more worldly-wise and cynical than Caroline or the Devonshires, she was more to his taste. Even at the age of sixty-two, Lady Melbourne possessed the charm and more than a trace of the faded beauty that had made her the lover of two princes.

In November 1812, Lady Melbourne received a note from the poet: 'I presume that I may now have access to the lower regions of Melbourne House from which my ascent [to Lady Caroline's bedroom] has long excluded me.'

As a lifelong matchmaker, she conceived of a plan to break Byron from Caro by having Byron married off to her niece, Annabella Milbanke. It was in the ballroom at a waltzing party that Annabella had first seen Byron as he watched from the sidelines the ladies who twirled in their high-waisted dresses to the strains of the small orchestra. The impending marriage of Byron tipped the scales for Caro. She publicly cut herself with a knife at Lady Heathcote's waltz and supper party on 5 July 1813 after Byron had made a sarcastic remark about her waltzing ability. She had been asked by a young beau whether she would dance, and turned to Byron, half-mockingly, to ask 'permission', now that their affair was over, saying: 'I conclude I may waltz now?'

Byron replied woundingly: 'With everyone in turn, why not?'

When she had finished the dance, he praised her 'dexterity' at waltzing, which she regarded as an insult. Furious, she melodramatically seized a knife from the buffet.

Byron said: 'Do, my dear, but if you mean to act a Roman's part, mind which way you strike. Be it at your own heart – not at mine.'[9]

While their private feud raged, the war against France had been going well for the allies. The despair of 1812 was replaced by the year of celebrations of 1814, when Napoleon was exiled to Elba, Wellington returned to London to be garlanded as the conquering hero of Europe, and British troops burned down the White House in Washington. In London, in June, the Prince Regent, the Prime Minister Lord Liverpool, Marshal Blucher, Prince Metternich and Tsar Alexander I reviewed 12,000 troops in Hyde Park, there was a re-enactment of the Battle of Trafalgar, and Wellington was officially welcomed back at Buckingham Palace by the Regent. But a week later, Caro, still demanding attention, made a scene at the Duke of Wellington's triumphal ball attended by 1,700 people at Burlington House. Such melodrama could be overlooked but the publication of her novel *Glenarvon* – a thinly veiled satire of her family and friends – outraged society, and made her a social outcast. William was humiliated by having the book on the tables of the grand houses he visited, but Caroline, by constantly winning over her husband, blocked repeated attempts by his family to isolate her in a formal separation. Lady Melbourne and Caroline's own mother Henrietta produced illegitimate children in such profusion they were called the 'children of the mist', so why did they draw such little scandal, while Caroline's affairs caused such disgust? The answer was provided by Lady Melbourne herself in a letter to her daughter-in-law after observing Caro with her then lover Webster at a party:

I see you have no shame or compunction for yr past conduct every action every impulse of your mind is directed by Sir Godfrey Webster – I lament it, but as I can do no good I shall withdraw myself and suffer no more croaking upon your hurt – Yr behaviour last night was so disgraceful in its appearances and so disgusting in its motives that it is quite impossible it should ever be effaced from my mind. When one braves the opinion of the World, sooner or later that will feel the consequences of it . . .

Lady Melbourne's son remained devoted to Caroline throughout their married life and, in spite of the pain her affairs had caused him, life went on at Melbourne House almost as normal, including canvassing at elections. Lady Shelley, writing in her diary in February 1820, described a tumultuous and violent election in which William's brother George, another Whig, was defeated. The violence was like nothing we see today on the hustings. Lady Shelley recorded:

A most scurrilous hand-bill has appeared today, raking up all the old stories of Melbourne House! Lady Caroline Lamb is in all the happiness and in all the anxieties of canvassing, and takes all the greasy voters in her carriage to the hustings, apparently forgetting that she fancied herself dying a week ago! She is now reanimated and, as the probability of success gains strength every day, I conclude we shall hear no more of her palpitations till the whole bustle is over . . .

John Cam Hobhouse, a radical who had been on the *Childe Harold* tour with Byron, later exultantly described how 'the mad skeleton [Lady Caroline] rode her a—e bone off, kissed, canvassed and cuckolded but all in vain and the bit of fig leaf which half hid her nakedness was torn off and flung in her face'.

On 4 March, when the polling was reaching a climax, Lady Shelley recorded in her diary that there were riots around Melbourne House, and the party's committee rooms at a house in nearby Henrietta Street were set on fire by the mob.

> I am just returned from Melbourne House where I found that instead of being in a state to receive congratulations, they were in a state of the greatest anxiety about Mr G Lamb who had been driven from his committee-room by the mob ... While I was at Melbourne House, Lavendar, the police officer, came in to tell them where Lamb was, and to say that a detachment of the Life Guards had been sent to escort him home. The Guard had been doubled at the Horse Guards to protect Melbourne House; and measures were taken at Brooks' Club to fill the house with constables, strong sedan-chairmen, and gentlemen of the ring ...
>
> Lady Caroline Lamb's carriage also was attacked. Lady Caroline immediately got out and harangued the mob thus: 'You are all Englishmen, therefore you will not attack a woman. I am not in the least afraid of you.' The mob did not insult her but insisted upon her servants taking off their colours with Lamb's name on them.

Byron was romantic even in death. He drowned at Missolonghi in Greece in 1826, and his body was brought back to London in July. It lay 'in state' for two days in the first-floor front drawing room of a house at 25 Great George Street – now the Institute of Civil Engineers – where the corpse was described by an onlooker:

> Wrapped in a blue cloth cloak, and the throat and head were uncovered. The former was beautifully moulded. The head of the poet was covered with short, crisp curling locks, slightly streak with grey hairs, especially over the temples, which were ample and free from hair, as we see in the portraits. The face had nothing of the appearance of death about it ... the expression was of stern

repose. How classically beautiful was the curved upper lip and the chin!

Lady Caroline Lamb never became Lady Melbourne. She died in her room at Melbourne House in January 1828, aged forty-two, five months before the elderly Lord Melbourne died and her husband inherited the title.

In middle age, William, the consensus politician who quietly made his way up the rungs of power, became Queen Victoria's first Prime Minister. She was eighteen and he was forty years her senior, but she became emotionally attached to Melbourne until she met Albert.[10] She regarded the second Viscount Melbourne as a father figure – a portrait of him at about this time by Edwin Landseer hanging outside Commons Committee Room Eight shows a kindly man, with a smiling expression, bouffant hair and handsome muttonchop sideboards, set off by a crimson coat and yellow waistcoat. Melbourne resigned office, and the Tory leader Robert Peel was appointed Prime Minister, but the Queen refused to follow tradition by replacing her ladies-in-waiting who were the wives of Whig ministers with Tory ladies. The 'Bedchamber Crisis' led to Peel refusing to serve as Prime Minister and Melbourne was returned to office. Victoria became devoted to Viscount Melbourne because he never talked down to her, and confided to her diary: 'Such stories of knowledge; such a wonderful memory; he knows about everybody and everything, who they were and what they did. He has such a kind and agreeable manner; he does me the world of good.' But she also noted his vanity, complaining he dyed his hair too black.

Melbourne never lived in Downing Street and in 1830, two years after Caroline's death, he moved to South Street and sold Melbourne House to George Agar-Ellis, a young MP with Liberal views who was playing a leading role in founding the National Gallery with the creation of Trafalgar Square. In 1831, Ellis became Lord Dover, and though it has no connection to the port the property took the name Dover House by which it is known today. After the death of Ellis's widow in 1885, it was taken over by the government as part of the growing civil service empire in Whitehall to match the growth of empire abroad. Gladstone could have taken the house as his residence instead of Number Ten Downing Street but turned down Dover House because it was too grand. So it was that the Melbourne name was wiped from the memory in Whitehall, but Victoria's first Prime Minister was remembered in one place – in the capital city of the state of Victoria, Australia.

A civil service guide to Dover House by Eric Miller records that it survived a near miss with a bomb that hit the old Treasury building at the Cabinet Office during the Second World War, and that it was used by Viscount Montgomery when the establishment of NATO was being planned after the Second World War.

Since devolution to the Scottish Parliament, the Scotland Office in London has become a political backwater. Dover House last took centre stage when it was the backdrop for the announcement by the then Scottish Secretary, the late Donald Dewar, in 1998 that he was going to run for the post of First Minister in the new Scottish Parliament. Jack Straw, then Leader of the Commons, held court there on Tuesday 23 January 2007, at a reception for lobby journalists that I attended. He gossiped with journalists over white wine about the burning issues of the day, including the impending resignation of Prime Minister Tony Blair, and the candidates for the possible leadership contest to replace him.

Upstairs, in Room 9/2 where Caroline's bed once stood, all that is left to show this once was the apartment in which she conducted her notorious love affair is a portrait of Byron propped on a mantelpiece. But Caro 'the Sprite' may have left a more lasting impression. One civil servant who works there told me that working late at night in her former bedroom on papers for the Scotland Office, she heard a loud rustling noise like a lady's dress. 'It was so loud that I stepped out into the corridor. I thought someone had a lady's dress on and it was rustling, but there was no sign of anyone. I asked the porter whether he had been playing a joke in a dress, but he knew nothing about it,' she said.

# WELLINGTON AND HORSE GUARDS

'The scum of the earth.'
Wellington on volunteer troops

Late on the evening of Wednesday 21 June 1815, a chaise and four, with three captured French standards ('eagles') poking out of the windows, clattered into Downing Street. The carriage was occupied by Major Henry Percy, one of the Duke of Wellington's aides-de-camp, and he had orders to deliver Wellington's hurriedly written despatch on the outcome of the Battle of Waterloo to Lord Bathurst, Secretary of State for War and the Colonies.

A small crowd had followed the coach, jubilant as the news spread, shouting 'Victory!' and – unlike Trafalgar – 'Wellington is safe!' Percy had no time for the plaudits from the crowd. He was in a tearing hurry and had not found Bathurst at Horse Guards so had taken the initiative to deliver the despatch to the Prime Minister, Lord Liverpool, at his official residence, Number Ten Downing

Street. The noise of the crowd had roused Charles Arbuthnot, the Secretary to the Treasury, from his Treasury desk in Downing Street to see what all the commotion was about. He assumed it was a mob protesting at the hated Corn Laws, which had forced up the price of bread. Seeing Percy, the eagles and the cheering throng, Arbuthnot told the major that Liverpool and his Cabinet were dining at Lord Harrowby's in Grosvenor Square. Grateful for someone to help him, Percy invited Arbuthnot to join him, and they set off for the home of the President of the Council, at 44 Grosvenor Square in Mayfair. It was then a four-storey town house dating from 1727, but was later demolished to make way for the present Millennium Hotel and Shogun sushi restaurant.[1] As they raced through clubland along St James's Street and Piccadilly, Percy gave Arbuthnot an eyewitness account of the bloody battle that had taken place on the road to Brussels at the village of Waterloo, three days earlier on Sunday 18 June. Percy was the only one of Wellington's ADCs to have escaped injury. He had travelled night and day to deliver the despatch and was still wearing his uniform, stained by the blood and brains of a fellow officer who was killed by his side as they watched the battle unfolding with the Duke. Percy had left Brussels for Ostend on the 20th carrying Wellington's despatch with orders to get it as quickly as possible to Horse Guards. Percy had ordered a ship to take him to England but before it could reach the mouth of the Thames Estuary, it had been becalmed off the north Kent coast and he had had to clamber into a rowing boat, which at last ran up on the sandy beach in the sleepy little bay at Broadstairs at about three o'clock in the afternoon of the 21st. Percy had then commandeered a fast chaise to carry him, and the first news of the battle, along the old Dover road to London.

Wellington's precious despatch had been folded inside a purple velvet sachet given to Percy by a dancing partner at the Duchess of Richmond's ball on the eve of battle in Brussels, which was attended by most of Wellington's senior officers before news came that Napoleon, who had escaped from exile on Elba, was on the march. Wellington had prepared to intercept Napoleon's forces at Quatre Bras on the road to Brussels, but had been surprised by the speed of the French advance, rushing away from the ball declaring, 'Napoleon has humbugg'd me, by God!' Now a third of the ninety-four officers who were at the ball lay dead or wounded.

The irrepressible Lady Caroline Lamb was among the fashionable ladies drawn to the excitement of war and had attended Lady Richmond's ball herself. It appealed to her Romantic love of drama and tragedy, as she wrote later: 'There never was such a Ball – so fine and so sad. All the young men who appeared there shot dead a few days after.'

Caroline's own brother, Frederick Ponsonby, one of Wellington's outstandingly brave cavalry officers, was one of those stripped and left for dead on the battlefield that day. The story of his miraculous escape was preserved in the diaries of Lady Shelley. He had defied death in the sieges during the long march through the Peninsula War into France, but at Waterloo Ponsonby was hacked by sabres in both arms, and knocked off his horse by another sabre cut to the head. He reported: 'Recovering, I raised myself a little to look around, being I believe at that time in a condition to get up and run away, when a Lancer passing by exclaimed, *"Tu n'es pas mort, coquin,"* and struck his lance through my back. My head dropped, the blood gushed into my mouth; a difficulty of breathing came on, and I thought all was over . . .'[2]

Believing the officer dead, a French skirmisher robbed him, but a French officer found him still alive, gave him brandy and propped his head up on a knapsack, a kindness that he said saved his life. Another French skirmisher used Ponsonby as a shield as he fired over him while chatting gaily to him. Towards the end of the battle, he was ridden over by allied Prussian cavalry and his body roughly searched by a Prussian looking for plunder. Near to death, Ponsonby was discovered by a British soldier of the 40th Foot, who stood guard over him during the night. He was carried away in a cart, and was eventually nursed back to health by Caroline. There were many stories of personal sacrifice and remarkable escapes, but few as dramatic as Ponsonby's that day. Ponsonby remained in the army for the rest of his life. After Waterloo, he went on half pay, and was appointed as a visiting field officer to the Ionian Islands, before being made Governor of Malta, a post he held until 1835. He married Lady Emily Bathurst, daughter of the third Earl Bathurst the war minister, and they had three children. He died suddenly in 1837 at a pub in Basingstoke.

The Cabinet had been in a state of high agitation over their dinner. London had been rife with rumours of the battle all day, with reports that Wellington had been defeated. The banker Nathan Rothschild had received the first outline of Wellington's victory twenty-four hours earlier, on Tuesday 20 June, from an agent he had hired to bring back news that enabled him to make a fortune on his investments. He had passed on his report to the Cabinet the following morning, but refused to give details of its provenance – possibly little more than his agent observing the jubilation among the French royal family exiled in Ghent – leaving Lord Liverpool and his ministers with little option but to regard it with scepticism, until Wellington's official report was in their hands.

Percy and Arbuthnot arrived excitedly at the Earl of Harrowby's house at about 11 p.m. with the banners and three of Napoleon's eagles, which had been carried into battle on long poles in the style of Roman legions by Bonaparte's crack regiments. They were the most highly prized military trophies for British officers to capture but they were too long to keep inside the coach. Liverpool had already left the dinner and was heading back to Whitehall where he had a town house but was stopped by the news of Waterloo. The

Prime Minister ordered his carriage to be turned around, and rushed back to Lord Harrowby's house.

Lord Harrowby's fourteen-year-old daughter Mary had been roused by the commotion downstairs and stood at the head of the stairs, transfixed by the spectacle below. Mary saw Percy in his bloodstained uniform and dusty boots plunging into her father's anteroom with a cry of 'Victory! Victory!' Arbuthnot gave the Cabinet a brief summary of the official account, ending with the words: 'In short, the French Army is entirely destroyed.' Harrowby, the senior minister in charge of running the machinery of government in Liverpool's Cabinet, remained cautious, saying, 'I beg your pardon, Mr Arbuthnot – but not exactly – I think you are going a little too far.'

But even Harrowby's scepticism dissolved when he opened the purple velvet sachet and read the despatch aloud to the Cabinet. Liverpool returned and took Percy off by coach to convey the news to the Prince Regent, the future George IV, and lay the French eagles at his feet. Earl Bathurst, who had been dining with Earl Grey, had also heard the news as it spread across London and hurried by coach to Lord Harrowby's house.

The Prince Regent was attending a soirée at 16 St James's Square, then the home of Edward Boehm and his ambitious socialite wife. The Prince was with his brother, the Duke of York, and Lord Castlereagh, Liverpool's Foreign Secretary, who had recently represented Britain in the carve-up of Europe at the Congress of Vienna, after the exile of Napoleon to Elba. Lady Brownlow, in her *Slight Reminiscences of a Septuagenarian*, recorded seeing Percy's coach with its three captured 'eagles projecting out of the windows' arrive outside Lord Castlereagh's house in the square, where she was spending a quiet evening with Lady Castlereagh, before hurrying off to Mrs Boehm's. They both put on wraps and followed.

The ladies had left the dining-room, and I learnt that Major Henry Percy had arrived, the bearer of despatches from the Duke of Wellington ... The despatches were being then read in the next room to the Prince, and we ladies remained silent, too anxious to talk, and longing to hear more. Lord Alvanley was the first gentleman who appeared, and he horrified us with the list of names of the killed and wounded.[3]

In his journal, Percy recorded:

Came up from Dover in a chaise and four with three eagles out of the window. They were too long to be shut in it. Went ... to the Prince Regent (before he came home) at Mrs. Boehm's in St. James's Square. Prince much affected. All London thrown into agitation—people quitting balls and assemblies as the news was conveyed of the wounds or deaths of relatives. Many ladies fainted. There was a rumour, before the news came, of a great battle and retreat, and even defeat. People were much depressed; therefore the reaction was immense.

Percy was instantly promoted to lieutenant colonel by the Prince Regent, but the events that night marked the apogee for Mrs Boehm's salon. Her husband later went bankrupt and in 1820 the house was taken over by the East India Club, which remains there today.

Percy was kept at Mrs Boehm's until 2 a.m. by the princes, and was invited to breakfast with the Duke of York at Carlton House in the morning. However, he rose too late and, according to one report from the Percy family, went to Horse Guards to meet the Duke at the parade ground

... where immense numbers were assembled, and where all the windows and tops of houses were thronged with people, expecting the eagles and colours were there to be presented to the Duke. When Henry Percy alighted, there was a long-continued cheer, and the band changed to 'See the Conquering Hero comes'. The Duke immediately took Henry to the Horse Guards, where he remained till late in the afternoon. Though he was not wounded, his uniform was entirely stained with blood.

After Waterloo, Wellington became estranged from his Irish wife, Kitty Pakenham, a member of the Longford family, and spent most of the next three years holding 'court' in Paris, attracting leading society ladies of the time including the irrepressible Lady Caroline Lamb (whom he called 'Calantha' after the heroine in her novel *Glenarvon*), Lady Frances Shelley, with whom Wellington had an affair, and Harriet Arbuthnot, the beautiful wife of the Treasury Secretary who had accompanied Percy on his errand with the captured eagles.

When he returned to London, Wellington bought Apsley House from his brother Richard for the princely sum of £42,000. It was known as 'No. 1 London', because it was the first house to be encountered after passing the toll houses on the road from Knightsbridge, and the Duke used it as his town house for the rest of his life. It was built between 1771 and 1778 by John Adam for Henry Bathurst, the first Baron Apsley, and it was here that Wellington held huge banquets and balls, and showed off the glittering prizes of his victory. He complained that Kitty was so dull she turned away his society guests, so asked Harriet to act as his hostess, sparking rumours that she was his mistress.

The Duke was appointed Master-General of Ordnance in Liverpool's Cabinet on 26 December 1818. Wellington was a natural choice. Through India and the Peninsula War, he learned to take meticulous care of planning his campaigns, even down to replacing heavy field kettles with lighter tin versions that his troops could carry to save space on his baggage wagons.

He used his seat in the House of Lords to speak of the dangers of French revolution being brought to Britain and in 1827, after the death of the Duke of York, he took on the role he had been made for. He became the Commander-in-Chief of the British armed forces, and moved into the C-in-C's office with the Venetian window above the archway at Horse Guards, Whitehall. He was head of the British Army, then numbering 151,000 men, but his duties included hearing the appeals for support from the widows of officers, as depicted in a painting of Wellington in his room during a second term in the post in 1845. The C-in-C is standing at his distinctive circular desk, waving a quill pen in conversation with a woman in a black bonnet who is pointing to a small boy, probably her son, next to her. John Wilson Croker, the Secretary to the Admiralty, wrote in his diaries that Wellington told him: 'I am in my proper place, in a place to which I was destined by my trade. I am a soldier, and I am in my place at the head of the army, as the Chancellor who is a lawyer, is in his place on the woolsack . . .'

Horse Guards was almost the personal fiefdom of the monarchy when the Duke of York ran the army. The Life Guard had been created nearly 200 years before to protect the life of Charles I from the growing unrest in the streets of London before the outbreak of the English Civil War. The Tudor tiltyard was chosen as their base for its strategic importance because it controlled the road to Parliament from the city and was directly opposite the Court Gate entrance to the royal Palace of Whitehall.[4] On 28 December 1641 the Lord Chamberlain recorded in his accounts that a royal warrant had been issued to 'Mr Surveyor for ye building a Court of Guard before Whitehall'. However, a month later, Charles I fled to Oxford, leaving the Parliamentary army in control of London and the Palace of Whitehall.

The execution of Charles I led to fears of more civil unrest in Whitehall, and Cromwell's Council of State ordered the Surveyor of Works, Edward Carter, 'To build a guard house in the Tiltyard near the wall of St James's Park for better accommodation of the soldiers. Also to make up the gallery door next St James's Park and set a lock to it.' The doorway to the Tiltyard Gallery was the same through which Charles passed on his way to his beheading at the Banqueting House.

A year later, Sir Arthur Haselrig, one of the MPs who Charles I had tried to apprehend in Parliament, was ordered by Cromwell's council to raise a regiment of horsemen to patrol the northern border territory and two regiments of foot soldiers. They became the Coldstream Guards, after the border town where they were recruited. The horse regiment was taken over in 1651 by Colonel James Berry, whose standard was blue, which led to the regiment adopting the colour and the name 'the Blues'. It was not until 1969, after the Labour Government ordered defence cuts that, now mechanized, they were merged with the most senior cavalry regiment of the line and became the Blues and Royals.

The Commonwealth issued orders to the troops to 'take care that no clamorous women nor spies be permitted to come within the walls' of the palace. The riches of the royal palace were ransacked to pay for the army, billeted round about its gates, but after an attempt on his life in 1656 Cromwell ordered his own Life Guard cavalry to be installed with stables in a new guard house within the walls of Whitehall, leaving the Life Guard of Foot in the tiltyard.[5]

After the death of Cromwell, Pepys witnessed the arrival at Whitehall of Monck's forces from Scotland, with Haselrig's Coldstream Guards and Berry's blue-coated cavalry 'in very good order with stout officers'. The Restoration of the monarchy in 1660 also saw the return of the old Tudor palace to something like its former glory, with the reinstatement of rescued valuables to the staterooms, and repair to the fabric treated so badly by Cromwell's soldiers. Lawns were returfed, courtyards repaved and swept clean, pictures rehung, galleries regilded, and gardens replanted. Monck's troops had to formally surrender their arms at the Tower in 1661 but they were immediately granted their weapons again and reformed as a force loyal to the Crown. Thus, the first standing army in the history of Britain was created, laying the foundation of the modern army. It is from this point that the Household Cavalry trace their roots. Troops of guards formed under the banner of the King, the Duke of York, and the Duke of Albemarle became the Life Guard, responsible for protecting the monarch. The Royal Regiment of Horse eventually became the Blues and Royals. The King's Royal Regiment of Foot Guards and the Lord General's Regiment of Foot Guards respectively became the Grenadier and Coldstream Guards.

The first Horse Guards building to accommodate the cavalry on its present site was completed in 1664, with mounted sentries much as they are today. The 'Old Horse Guards' building lasted a hundred years, but was replaced in 1753 with the Palladian building seen today. It was designed by William Kent, the same architect who was commissioned to create a new Treasury building on the site of the old Cockpit. Kent's design for Horse Guards – completed after his death by his friend and assistant John Vardy – looks harmonious to the modern eye. Architectural historian Arthur Kutcher[6] in 1978 said the octagonal Baroque-scrolled lantern dome and cupola, together with the stone cupolas of the Ministry of Defence (the old War Office) in Whitehall from 1907 and the black pavilion roofs of the Whitehall Club of 1875, 'form a remarkable skyline ensemble, best seen from the bridge across the lake in St James's Park. This is one of the six central London views the Greater London Council would like to see preserved.'

He would not say that now. The view has been joined by the incongruous giant wheel of the London Eye. However, Kent's building too was criticized in its day as 'heavy and tasteless' and ridiculed because the archway was too low to accommodate the twelve-feet ten-inch-high sovereign's gold state coach, still in use today. The solution was found by lowering the road, though it could not be widened, and when it scraped through for the first time, it lost a door handle and a door glass.

The new Horse Guards building housed the Foot Guards to the north and had stabling for sixty-two horses of the Horse Guards to the south. The old Horse Guards clock had a reputation for accuracy shared by Big Ben today, but when the new building was created the clock was in bad repair and a new one was installed in 1768 by London's oldest clockmakers, Thwaites & Reed. The face may be unique in Britain, having Roman numerals for the hours and Arabic numerals for the minutes. The '10' above the 'II' is blacked out to mark the time of execution of Charles I.

It is also likely that the old street sign for the Tiltyard Coffee House was transferred to the new building by the man licensed to run the establishment, John Fry, the Foot Guards' sutler. The tradition of having a licensed premises open to the public as well as the guards inside Horse Guards started at its inception when it was called The Monck's Head and continued well into the Victorian period, as the Tiltyard Coffee House. It ran over three floors with a cellar, a tap room, a lower tap room, and upper tap room. Drinkers would pore over the latest scandal sheets, and get into arguments about the relative merits of Napoleon or Wellington with members of the guards over a quart of gin. There were fights, and prostitutes were attracted by the prospect of easy money, and the Horse Guards coffee house became so notorious that there were repeated attempts to close it down. When the police were formed, they were forbidden from entering the premises on the grounds that it was part of a military establishment. In 1850, a combination of Victorian high moral principle and bureaucratic disapproval condemned the 'common public house' to closure. It was turned into officers' quarters and its magnificent-sounding 'five-motion beer machine in a neat Spanish mahogany case brass-mounted and with ivory tipped handles' was dismantled, never to be seen again.

Wellington's happy sojourn at Horse Guards ended when, in quick succession, Lord Liverpool suffered a stroke, Canning, his successor, suddenly died of fever probably caught at the freezing Windsor funeral for the Duke of York, and Goderich, appointed Prime Minister to fill the gap, resigned. In 1828 Wellington was appointed as Prime Minister and he rode his old warhorse Copenhagen into Downing Street to show the smack of firm government. A natural authoritarian, whose feelings about his Cabinet were echoed later by Lady Thatcher, the ex-soldier complained his ministers wanted to debate rather than obey his orders.

'What is the meaning of a party if they don't follow their leaders? Damn 'em,' his Victorian biographer Philip Guedalla recorded. 'They agree to what I said in the morning and then in the evening start up with some crotchet which deranges the whole plan.'

Croker wrote in his diaries that he found Wellington buried in paperwork and complaining that the private jealousies of his ministers left him no time to look after the country's affairs: 'All my time is being employed assuaging what gentlemen call their feelings.' Wellington was obsessed by the threat of revolutionary republicanism crossing the channel from France to infect England, and had supported the brutal suppression of protests in 1819 by Manchester weavers on St Peter's Fields, later the site of the Manchester Free Trade Hall, that in a bitter twist after Waterloo became known as the 'Peterloo' massacre. Though he supported Catholic emancipation, he was never liberal in his thinking, and vehemently opposed the Reform Act of 1832 that widened the franchise. He entertained at Downing Street with Harriet Arbuthnot acting as his society hostess, but they had become soulmates, judging by her diary entries. On 7

November 1830, just a few days before Wellington was removed as Prime Minister, Harriet wrote in her journal:

We hear the radicals are determined to make a riot. The King gets quantities of letters every day telling him he will be murdered. The King is very much frightened and the Queen cries half the day with fright. The Duke is greatly affected by all this state of affairs. He feels that beginning reform is beginning revolution, and therefore he must endeavour to stem the tide as long as possible, and that all he has to do is to see when and how it will be best for the country that he should resign. He thinks he cannot till he is beat in the House of Commons. He talked about this with me yesterday.

Wellington's popularity as a military hero quickly turned to public scorn as he appeared out of step with the times. The mob stoned his windows at Apsley House so often that he had iron shutters fixed to them, earning him the satirical nickname in the scandal sheets of the 'Iron Duke', by which his admiring troops had known him. Wellington's loyal wife was on her deathbed at Apsley House when the mob attacked again.

On 28 April 1831 Wellington wrote to Harriet: 'I learn from John [his servant] that the mob attacked my House and broke about thirty windows. He fired two blunderbusses in the air from the top of the house, and they went off.'

The next night, after another attack, the Duke wrote again to Harriet: 'I think that my servant John saved my house, or the lives of many of the mob – possibly both – by firing as he did. They certainly intended to destroy the house, and did not care one pin for the poor Duchess being dead in the house.'

When Harriet died of cholera, Wellington felt her loss so much that he invited her husband Charles to live at Apsley House. Charles

Arbuthnot stayed there for the rest of his life as Wellington's personal assistant.[7] The Duke's happiest time was perhaps his second term at Horse Guards as C-in-C for the decade 1842–52. He set the army on the long march of reform to becoming a professional fighting force, but he was by nature a conservative, and refused to end flogging to maintain discipline in the armed forces, saying that, while Britain had a volunteer rather than a conscript army, only 'the scum of the earth' would join.

Wellington also maintained the purchase system in which young men could purchase a place in the army as officers, just as he had done as a young man, but he caused consternation in 1849 by issuing a memorandum from Horse Guards requiring officer candidates to pass an examination at Sandhurst in History and Geography, Algebra and Logarithms, Euclid, French and Latin, Field Fortification, Orthography and Calligraphy. It began the move towards a better-educated, professionally trained army, but it did not come soon enough to prevent the scandalous incompetence of the British military chiefs in the Crimean War.

The proud traditions of Horse Guards that produced heroes like Ponsonby also helped to create the Charge of the Light Brigade and the chaos of the Crimea. Wellington's biographer Elizabeth Longford said the Duke must bear a heavy responsibility for the army's general 'unpreparedness' to face the conflict:

> The failure of this former master of detail and miracle of foresight was due to a variety of causes. He was old. He suffered from a historical hangover, shared by many other people, which made him see the British Army as an anomaly . . . There was also the national drive for economy ever since Waterloo which prevented him from saving the Royal Wagon Train from disbandment; one of the gravest loses to Crimean soldiers.[8]

The soles of the soldiers' boots fell off in the Crimean mud, while tents, made in Spain for sunnier climates, let in the rain. Change was forced on the army chiefs at Horse Guards after Wellington's death, partly as a result of the fearless despatches from the front at the Crimea by the first 'modern' war correspondent, William Howard Russell of *The Times*, and the reforms for the care of casualties demanded by the Lady of the Lamp, Florence Nightingale. Lord Cardigan's 'cherry bums', the Light Brigade, were paraded proudly around Horse Guards before they set off for the Crimea, and Lord Raglan wanted to preserve them in a 'bandbox'. Long before they vainly charged down Tennyson's 'Valley of Death', *The Times* bewailed 'the shortness of their jackets, the incredible tightness of their cherry-coloured pants', which made them as ill-equipped for war as 'the female hussars in the ballet of Gustavus'.[9] Russell, however, laid the blame for the heroic catastrophe of the Charge of the Light Brigade at the door of the chiefs at Horse Guards for the disastrous decision to put the brothers-in-law, the cavalier Cardigan and the loud-mouthed Lucan, in conflict, with Lucan as the divisional commander, and Cardigan in charge of the Light Brigade.

Russell wrote:

Lord Lucan was a hard man to get on with. But the moment the Government of the day made the monstrous choice of his brother-in-law Lord Cardigan as the Brigadier of the Light Brigade of the Cavalry Division, knowing well the relations between the two officers and the nature of the two men, they became responsible for disaster; they were guilty of treason to the Army – neither more nor less.

The bumbling, well-meaning Lord Raglan, who had lost an arm as Wellington's military secretary at Waterloo and still sometimes mistook his French allies in the Crimea as the enemy, eventually took the overall blame.[10] But he was not the last British military officer to be vilified for incompetence. General Haig sits proudly on horseback on his statue opposite the front gates of Horse Guards, but was regarded by the historian and former Tory defence minister Alan Clark as an uncaring donkey who led Britain's lions to the slaughter in the First World War.[11] Clark, a gloriously provocative mixture of Thatcherite Tory and animal-rights campaigner, called for Haig's equestrian statue to be removed from Whitehall, condemning his lack of competence and compassion as compared to Wellington's record of care for his men.

It is unlikely the Iron Duke would have welcomed Clark's praise. Wellington was heavily criticized for failing to praise his officers, such as his second in command at Waterloo, Henry Paget, in his post-Waterloo despatch, although that may have been due to bad blood between the two men. A dashing cavalry officer, Paget, the Earl of Uxbridge, who had a reputation as a rake, had eloped with Lady Charlotte Wellesley, wife of Wellington's brother Henry. Despite the difficulty this caused with Wellington, he was put in charge of the British heavy cavalry at Waterloo and led the charge on 18 June that checked the French *corps d'armée* under D'Erlon. He had his leg smashed by grapeshot from one of the last French cannons to be fired in the battle, while he sat on his horse next to Wellington.

Paget is said to have looked down and said, 'By God, sir, I've lost my leg!' Wellington put down his telescope, studied Paget's leg and said, 'By God, sir, you have!'

What was left of his shattered limb was amputated in the field hospital. Five days later Paget was created the first Marquess of Anglesey by the Prince Regent, and finished his service in 1852 as Colonel of the Horse Guards.[12]

Wellington discouraged familiarity with the men, making him appear cold and haughty. Having regained his popularity in old age, however, the old warrior Wellington followed a daily routine that attracted tourists like those today to see the Changing of the Guard. Wellington's beloved horse Copenhagen died in 1836. But he ordered a cavalry horse to be made ready by his groom, at precisely 4 p.m. each day, and stepped down an internal flight of stairs directly from his office above the Horse Guards arch to the yard to mount his horse for the short ride home along The Mall to Apsley House, untroubled by the traffic around Hyde Park today. The staircase he used is now gone, but the space can still be seen in a store cupboard behind the counter at the Horse Guards Museum.

After his death in 1852, the Iron Duke's body lay in state in his coffin in the Horse Guards Audience Room overlooking the Parade, and his funeral cortège on 18 November started from the parade ground. His room remains the office of the major general commanding the Household Division in charge of 'London District', and Wellington's original round desk is still in use. It was valued on the BBC TV *Antiques Roadshow* in 2007 as being worth more than £100,000. There are other mementoes of Wellington in his room at Horse Guards, including his death mask. His office above the archway at Horse Guards remains out of bounds to the public, but at least the doors have been opened to a fascinating corner of the stables for the Household Cavalry – the regimental museum.

The Horse Guards Museum, which cost £5 million, is designed to show the Household Cavalry regiments are not bandbox troops, but fighting men with a history of valour. The exhibits include some bizarre items, such as Henry Paget's articulated artificial leg, which became the model for prosthetic limbs for the armed forces into the twentieth century. There is also a macabre copy of the skull of Corporal John Shaw, whose heroic death at Waterloo so inspired Sir Walter Scott that he had a cast made of Shaw's skull, which is now on show. Shaw, a former prize fighter, was six foot three inches tall and weighed fifteen stone, and carried on fighting the French on the battlefield with his bare hands after his sword had been broken to the hilt, until he too was cut down. His fame was so great that Shaw was referred to in Dickens's *Bleak House*: 'I'd give a fifty pound note to be such a figure of a man . . .' Just what a fine figure of man he was can be seen from a very explicit nude study of Corporal Shaw who, like other guardsmen, was in the habit of posing naked as models for ladies' drawing classes at the nearby Royal Academy.

The Waterloo exhibits include the tail of the favourite bay mare shot from under Captain Edward Kelly, of the 1st Life Guards, another hero of the battle. A biographical note portrays Kelly as boastful, like the fictional hero of the *Flashman* books by George Macdonald Fraser, saying his letters home were an invaluable record but 'increasingly describe a man desperate to obtain greater recognition for his exploits at Waterloo'. A famous painting by James Tissot in the exhibition appears to show *Flashman* made flesh. It is the portrait of Lieutenant Colonel Frank Burnaby, lounging insouciantly on a sofa, in a pose that the museum note says 'conveys an impression of upper-class life in the Household Cavalry'. Burnaby, with a black, waxed moustache and a red stripe down the seam of his uniform trousers, his forage cap tossed to one side among some books, has one hand raised airily as if describing his exploits.[13] He was physically powerful, an explorer, balloonist, journalist and would-be politician, in addition to being a superlative field soldier who commanded the Blues at Horse Guards. He had thrilled Victorian audiences in 1876 with an account of his exploits on horseback through Russian Asia, *A Ride to Khiva,* which made him famous. But Burnaby's death would never have come out of the *Flashman* 'memoirs'. On 17 January 1885, Burnaby went down heroically trying to rescue his troops in hand-to-hand fighting against the Mahdi's army in the Sudan.

Undoubtedly the most popular 'exhibit' is the living daily routine of the stables at Horse Guards, which can be viewed by the public through toughened glass, as the horses of the Cavalry Regiment are mucked out and groomed for the day's sentry duty. Each of the horses has a squadron number stamped by the farriers on a front hoof and, like cars, they are named by a letter of the alphabet according to the year in which they joined the regiment. The black horses and the greys are mostly bought in Ireland as four- or five-year-olds, and the steadiest horses are used by the standard bearers, who have to lower flags by the heads of their mounts, or for the bandsmen, who need horses that are not frightened by loud bangs on the kettledrums or crashes on the cymbals. Horse Guards is the official gateway to Buckingham Palace and St James's Palace, and there is a list of members of the Royal Family and a few politicians, who still carry the modern-day equivalent of an 'Ivory Pass' – first issued after the Restoration – entitling them to go through the archway in their armour-plated limousines to escape the London traffic. The Foot Guards on duty there also salute passing guards officers, who habitually wear brown trilbies off duty. You may wish to see if you can provoke a salute, but you need a smart suit, a regimental tie and a very straight back.

The museum was opened on 12 June 2007 by Queen Elizabeth II after a pageant on Horse Guards Parade featuring 220 horses and men, 2 mounted bands, 50 historic and contemporary armoured vehicles – and 2 camels. Highlights included a re-creation in full of the coronation procession of King Charles II and the fifty-yard cavalry charge that preceded the capture of the French eagle by the Royal Dragoons at Waterloo, one of those carried to Downing Street by Percy.

The pageant was the sort of spectacle that Elizabeth I would have enjoyed on the same spot over 400 years before on the Tudor tiltyard. Today, the Guards have modern demands, such as front-line service in Iraq and Afghanistan, as Prince Harry – a member of the Blues and Royals – demonstrated in 2008. But they are still the Queen's bodyguards, who would be the last line of defence in the event of a coup attempt.

In June each year, discreet invitations go out to MPs, special advisers and media around Whitehall and Westminster from the secretaries of state, who are lucky enough to have private offices overlooking Horse Guards, for the Beating of the Retreat, the ceremony once used to summon troops back to camp at night. With the windows open, and wine glasses in hand, guests around Whitehall spend a pleasant summer evening in convivial conversation while the bands of the Household Cavalry blast out their marching tunes on the parade ground. Sometimes, they are too convivial. When the Northern Ireland Secretary's private offices were in the former Admiralty building at the north end of the square, a message was sent up by the officer commanding the guards to 'stop the bloody racket'. The Northern Ireland Secretary meekly obliged.

For the soldiers based at their Knightsbridge barracks, the Trooping of the Colour, to celebrate the official birthday of the sovereign in June after two nights of Beating the Retreat, marks the culmination of the 'silly season' of parades and ceremonial duties. It is a tradition that has been going on since the birthday parade for Queen Elizabeth I. Sentry-box duty may look like a form of torture today but according to Barney White-Spunner, a former guards officer and the author of the definitive history of Horse Guards,[14] it used to be coveted by the men because 'it finished at 4 p.m. and constantly attracted the attention of passing women, some of whom were known to drop notes in the men's boots, suggesting future liaisons'.

Tradition hangs heavy over Horse Guards but Prince Charles, the Prince of Wales, is one of the few who have helped to shake it out of one of its ruts. He was enjoying a convivial dinner with senior officers of the Household Cavalry when the Prince asked why were there no blacks in the Guards? The heir to the throne, known for his liberal attitudes, said he thought it odd that when he looked around outside his home at Buckingham Palace there were no black soldiers on duty. The shocked silence that followed was broken by an officer who suggested that they were not good under fire.

'They didn't do too badly at Isandlwana,' said Prince Charles.[15]

Charles was a friend of David Rattray, the historian and epic storyteller, who was an expert on the battle and a guide at Isandlwana, where he was sadly murdered in January 2007. Rattray had escorted the Prince around the battlefield in the northwest corner of KwaZulu-Natal, where the Zulus killed 1,200 British soldiers on 22 January 1879. The battle was the same day that the garrison at the small station of Rorke's Drift was attacked by overwhelming forces, later to be portrayed in the film *Zulu* with Michael Caine. The Prince had his wish. Ethnic minorities have since been recruited to the elite ranks of the Household Cavalry.

Some bastions to change remain in place. The Queen may be the Colonel-in-Chief, and her daughter, the Princess Royal, the Colonel of the Blues and Royals, but women are not permitted to serve as guards in the Household Cavalry. On a tour of Horse Guards, I was told that they once had a veterinary officer who was a woman, and there are a couple of women in the band of the Household Cavalry (they wear the jockey cap and highly colourful uniform) but they are not allowed to become full members of the Guards. That does not mean, though, that women never guard the Whitehall entrance to Horse Guards. Tourists who take a closer look outside Horse Guards in the summer may find that the soldiers on sentry duty are women. They are members of the King's Troop of the Royal Horse Artillery, who perform ceremonial duties including firing gun salutes and providing gleaming black horses and a gun carriage for state funerals. They take over guard duty at Horse Guards from the Household Cavalry during their August break, and it can only be imagined what the Iron Duke would say about that.

# 10

## PAM'S PALACE – THE FOREIGN AND COMMONWEALTH OFFICE

'The Civil Service is a bit like a Rolls-Royce – you know it's the best machine in the world, but you're not quite sure what to do with it.'

Former Foreign Secretary R. A. 'Rab' Butler

The face of Whitehall might have been very different today if Lord Palmerston had not had his way over the design for the Foreign Office.

Britain was a global superpower in the middle of the nineteenth century when the Government announced an international competition for a new Foreign Office building from which it could rule its empire. A total of 218 schemes were submitted. None of the designs was accepted by the parliamentary committee overseeing the project but the third runner-up, George Gilbert Scott, who had submitted a scheme for a Victorian Gothic palace, so impressed the judges that he was appointed as the official architect for the project.

The Victorians were in the grip of a Gothic revival, and a Gothic-style Foreign Office would have been the height of fashion. Public buildings such as the Palace of Westminster and Manchester Town Hall, interior designs by Augustus Pugin and William Morris, literature and the Pre-Raphaelite school of painting, were all heavily influenced by the passion for an earlier courtly age before the Industrial Revolution that had delivered the Victorians their wealth built on coal, steel and factories. Scott was a devotee of the Gothic revival school and the work of Pugin, who had worn himself out designing every detail, from tiles to door locks, for the glorious Gothic interiors of Charles Barry's Houses of Parliament. The Westminster Palace was then nearing completion within a stone's throw of the site allocated for the Foreign Office in Whitehall and Scott proposed a design for the Foreign Office to echo Barry's Gothic fantasy rising across Parliament Square.

The son of a Buckinghamshire vicar, who by his mid-forties was already a prolific restorer of medieval churches and designer of Victorian workhouses, Scott proposed a building that, like the Palace of Westminster, was adorned with gilded spires and heavily decorated arches, trefoils and quatrefoils set around a central square which was open to Whitehall. However, the Prime Minister, the third Viscount Palmerston, dismissed Scott's Gothic palace as 'the barbarism of the Dark Ages' and made it clear that if he did not produce a 'more pleasing' design, the Government would hand the brief to another architect. Scott wanted the commission so reluctantly shelved his Gothic design and proposed a compromise: a Foreign Office in the Byzantine style. Palmerston was implacable and turned this down too as 'a regular mongrel affair'.[1] Scott's rejected Byzantine design was the inspiration for another of his landmark buildings – his crowning masterpiece, the recently refurbished Midland Grand Hotel at St Pancras railway station in north London. Palmerston believed in the civilizing influence of the British Empire around the world, and wanted a building that represented the highest standards of that other great imperial power, the Roman Empire. Scott dutifully delivered an Italianate palace on Whitehall and decorated it with statuary in Roman togas to underline the message that Victorian England was a power like no other the world had seen since the ancient Romans. They included a statue of Britannia, who stands benignly surveying the traffic from the top of the Foreign Office, flanked by four female supporters, all draped in Roman togas. Other figures in niches around the building are also swathed in cloaks made to look like togas, to draw the Palmerstonian parallel between Imperial Whitehall and ancient Rome.

Palmerston's victory over Scott came at an important stage in the development of Whitehall. Had Palmerston not had his way, Scott's Gothic scheme could have held sway over later buildings in Whitehall, including the War Office and the Government Office on Great George Street (GOGGS, now the Treasury) and, through them, in the twentieth century, the Ministry of Defence main building. As a result of Palmerston's intervention, Whitehall came to be dominated by the restrained English Palladian architecture we see today. It may have suited the repressed character of the Victorian pen-pushers who ran the empire behind cliffs of Portland stone, but it left Whitehall with a far less exuberant skyline than Scott would have liked.

In Palmerston's day, the Foreign Secretary would have entered the Foreign Office through the gates in Downing Street, and his carriage would have drawn up to the right, by the impressive stone staircase in the northwest corner of the inner courtyard. Inside, you find an opulence expected of the rulers of the empire. A grand double staircase with statues and busts of former Foreign Secretaries (including Charles James Fox, Salisbury, Clarendon and Ernest

Bevin) leads up to the second floor. Here, Scott created the main ministerial offices and the ornate reception rooms, which he wanted to become 'a kind of national palace, or drawing room for the nation', but it was a drawing room on a monumental scale. Foreign Office ministers were given palatial rooms to match their lofty thoughts, with 22-foot-high ceilings. They were so vast that civil servants complained about their echoing halls. One official protested: 'I not only cannot hear what others say to me, but very often I cannot hear what I am saying myself.'

The former Foreign Secretary in the Major Government, Lord Hurd, rated it as the best foreign ministry building in the world. 'I think the Foreign Office beats the Quai d'Orsay. The French Foreign Ministry is very splendid – probably has more gold in it – but it just slightly overdoes it. The State Department in Washington has pillars, pleasant rooms and nice pictures but it doesn't have the style. The Kremlin is terrific, with tremendous style, but I prefer the Foreign Office.'[2]

Lord Hurd liked working in the Foreign Secretary's room, which occupies the northwest corner of the Foreign Office, because it has windows facing both St James's Park and Horse Guards Parade and is light and airy, in spite of its rich green wallpaper. His predecessor, Lord Howe, who helped to bring down Lady Thatcher with a lethal resignation speech attacking her for undermining Britain's policy on Europe, recalled that the window to the Foreign Secretary's lavatory offers the only view of both Nelson on his column and the statue of Lord Mountbatten in the small garden at the side of Number Ten.

The Secretary of State's room was first used for a reception party hosted by Prime Minister Benjamin Disraeli for the height of Victorian society, including the Prince and Princess of Wales, before the rest of the Foreign Office was completed. Mrs Disraeli considered Downing Street 'so dingy and decaying' that she used the new building, but the reception rooms were not finished, so the guests were ushered into the Secretary of State's room. Lord Salisbury, when he was Prime Minister and Foreign Secretary at the end of the nineteenth century, shared Mrs Disraeli's dislike for Downing Street and chaired Cabinet meetings in the Foreign Office, using the middle room of the reception suite – now the Locarno dining room – as his office.

The decoration of the Secretary of State's office, including the walls with gold stars on a green background, was designed by Scott with his favourite firm of interior decorators, Clayton and Bell, who specialized in church interiors and stained-glass windows. The Foreign Office was opened in July 1868, and Lord Stanley, later the Earl of Derby, became the first Foreign Secretary to occupy the Secretary of State's room. Lord Curzon disliked the heavy folded drapes that made it look like a 'boarding-house'. It too was painstakingly restored in the refurbishment of the Foreign Office in the mid-1980s.

The late Robin Cook, Tony Blair's first Foreign Secretary, once showed me the view from the windows of his large room, overlooking the street lights around St James's Park, and repeated the story that it was on this spot that the Foreign Secretary Lord Grey of Falloden was standing in 1914 at dusk on the eve of the Great War and said: 'The lights are going out all over Europe; we shall not see them lit again in our lifetime.' Cook had Grey's classic book on fly-fishing and a bust of Bevin, the socialist Foreign Secretary in the post-war Labour Government, by his desk. Bevin broke with tradition by signing his official letters with blue ink from his large silver fountain pen, which he called 'The Caber', instead of red ink normally reserved for Foreign Secretaries. Cook was witty, acerbic, egotistical, vain, and did not 'suffer fools gladly' but was widely regarded as having one of the sharpest minds in the Blair Government. But he also created jealousy and animosity among colleagues. On his arrival at the Foreign Office, after announcing an 'ethical foreign policy', he removed a large painting of a Nepalese prince from over the fireplace in the Foreign Secretary's room as not in keeping with Labour's post-colonial view of the world. He replaced it with a breakfast scene by the modern painter John Bratby from the Government Art Collection. The Bratby painting was later replaced with a mirror. One of Cook's former ministers told me it was 'so Cook could look at himself'. This story about Cook has entered the mythology of Whitehall. In fact, the mirror was restored to its original location by his successor Jack Straw. The Foreign Office also boasts a Victorian map room with maps that fold out from a range of drawers and an elegant galleried library with its own archive and a twenty-foot-long stuffed snake, an anaconda, said to have been a gift from a bishop in what is now Guyana.

Scott's original design would have created a pleasing pedestrian plaza open at its eastern side onto Whitehall but his brief changed as Palmerston's government added more departments (including the Home Office, then responsible for a wide range of domestic policy), enclosing the site. The gradual evolution of the complex enclosed an elegant inner courtyard, with the entrances to the four government departments at each of the corners, beneath pillared porticos like four great private town houses. The main entrance to the Foreign Office in the northwest quadrant faces the former India Office on the southwest corner. The former Colonial Office in the northeast quadrant faces the entrance to the former Home Office, and together they share the Whitehall frontage. It is worth standing in Whitehall outside the front of the Foreign Office to study the decorative sculptures above the rush-hour traffic. They reveal the clear split between the 'Home' and 'Foreign' sides of the Foreign Office. While the Foreign Office ruled the empire, the Home Office was responsible for a ragbag of domestic policy, such as the factory acts, in addition to public order, crime, immigration, courts and prisons. The frieze of sculpted figures to the left of the great doorway on Whitehall spell out the advantages of British rule at home: Law, Agriculture, Art, Commerce and Literature, exemplified by busts of great figures in Britain's history, including James Watt, inventor of the first commercial steam engines; writer Francis Bacon, believed by some to be the real author of Shakespeare's work; and the artist Joshua Reynolds, the celebrated portrait painter. To the right of the front door, the continents at one time administered by the Colonial Office – America, Australasia and Africa – are represented by ample female figures. The Victorians clearly had a thing about large breasts: they all have nipples like organ stops. Africa is represented by a native woman with a broken manacle on her wrist, signifying the end of the slave trade. Australasia is demurely covered, and accompanied by two cheerful kangaroos and two sheep. Above them on the second storey are busts of the adventurers Cook, Franklin, Drake and Livingstone (a hero of Victorian England), and the anti-slavery reformer, Wilberforce. The connecting bridge from the Foreign Office to the HM Revenue and Customs building across King Charles Street – designed to underpin the coherence of the Renaissance face of Whitehall – is decorated with figures representing the work of local government, which was also housed in the Foreign Office building.

The India Office, which extends beyond the line of the Foreign Office on the park side, is heavily populated with statuary of long-forgotten figures from India, but the most revealing is the statue of Clive of India, who stands proudly surveying St James's Park above the steps at the end of King Charles Street. The plinth carries plaques depicting his military victories in India, and a moody study of Clive walking alone in the mango tope before the battle at Plassey adds to the image of the lone hero. The bronze statue designed by John Tweed in 1912 was moved to the Clive steps in 1916. Today, with a revisionist view of history, Clive stands uncomfortably as a symbol of British colonialism. In his television series *A History of Britain,* historian Simon Schama accused Robert Clive of hijacking British foreign policy, describing him as a ruthless, corrupt young-man-on-the-make, who went to India to create business for the East India Company and ended up founding an empire. In 'The Wrong Empire' Professor Schama argues persuasively that it was never the intention of Walpole, whose genius was in creating wealth through peace, or of William Pitt Senior to get into the costly business of empire-building in Asia. Their colonial interests lay in the lucrative plantations in the Americas, and had George III and the North Government listened to Pitt's entreaties for a compromise they would never have lost America to independence, nor created an empire in the Indian subcontinent. French competition and personal greed drove Clive – a one-time small-town thug who ran an extortion racket among shopkeepers in his Shropshire home town of Market Drayton – to conquer parts of India by a combination of military strength and bribery. Clive was an employee of a commercial trading company, but broke the influence of the French over their client state governors, the mainly Muslim nawabs, as the Mughal empire declined, to further its financial interests. Clive made his name and his fortune after an uprising by Siraj-ud-Daula, the Nawab of Bengal, led to prisoners being held in the 'Black Hole' at Calcutta. With opinion at home fired up, Clive retook Calcutta, went upriver with Royal Navy ships and defeated the Nawab's army of 34,000, including war elephants, at Plassey on 23 June 1787. Clive was outnumbered ten to one but won by the simple expedient of bribery with the promise of the throne to a subordinate of the troublesome Nawab. Clive 'modestly' took £250,000 as a reward (about £25.1 million at 2007 prices), making him overnight one of the richest men in Britain, and he was fêted at home with a peerage as Baron Clive of India. It marked a line in sand for British foreign policy in India that was to be jealously guarded by the state and its civil service apparatus for almost the next two centuries. The merchants who founded the Honourable East India Company were granted a Royal Charter for the monopoly of British trade with Asia by Queen Elizabeth I in 1600, but the company's role in India was replaced by direct rule by the British Government under the India Act of 1858 after the Indian Mutiny. The sale of the company's headquarters in the City financed the budget for the new India Office in Whitehall and Scott faced another blow to his professional esteem when he discovered that the East India Company's surveyor Matthew Digby Wyatt had been given the brief to design the India Office that was to be attached to his Foreign Office. They reached a gentlemen's agreement in which Wyatt would design the interior of the India Office while Scott would design the exterior. Wyatt's budget – boosted by private finance – was considerably more than Scott could lavish on his interiors. Wyatt could afford to indulge himself in dazzling interior designs and rescued statues and fireplaces from the company's former building to recreate a Mughal palace in Whitehall, colourful enough to impress any visiting nawab, with decorative details picked out in gold leaf. There are twin dark-oak doors to the oval office of the Secretary of State for India – occupied by Meg Munn, a foreign minister in the Brown Government, until October 2008. It is said these were to allow two Indian princes to enter simultaneously, to avoid diplomatic embarrassment over who should take precedence. The relatively small office has two fireplaces to ensure that, once inside, Indian princes were protected from the cold of British summers, but the eye quickly rises to the extravagant, domed ceiling covered with gold leaf. The ceiling was covered with cream paint in the 1960s, but like the rest of the Foreign Office has since been fully restored to its radiant glory.

The centrepiece of the former India Office is its lofty inner courtyard overlooked by three storeys of offices, with richly decorated columns, balustrades and arches. Wyatt had worked with Paxton on the Crystal Palace and had a hand in the elegant roof of Paddington Station. He used the latest Victorian technology – including girders and Hartley's patent rolled plate glass manufactured in Sunderland – to throw a glass roof supported by cast iron over the courtyard in 1868, a year after it had been used for a reception for the Sultan of Turkey. In a nice detail from the age of steam, some of the interior windows open and close on a rail with miniature train wheels. Wyatt's roof created a weatherproof space that anticipated today's fad for 'atriums' in public buildings. The Victorian plate glass has been replaced by Pilkington's hi-tech Sunkool glass but the stone brackets supporting the balustrades still spell out his memorial: 'This court was built AD 1866, MD Wyatt Architect'. It was renamed Durbar Court in 1902 when it was used for some of the coronation celebrations for King Edward VII. The India Office continued until the end of direct rule with independence in 1947 but the Durbar Court proved highly popular as a place for ministerial parties in the 1980s after it was refurbished in the Thatcher era, with hot curries being served to the guests. Chris Mullin, Minister for Africa in Tony Blair's government, had a room overlooking Durbar Court in which he received his guests. They were usually impressed, but the well-oiled diplomatic machine sometimes missed a gear, such as the time Mullin was due to bid farewell to the Ambassador of the Sudan before he returned to his country. 'I asked him how he had enjoyed his two years. He said, "I have only been here for six months." So I said, "Well, I hope the peace agreement is holding." He said, "What peace agreement?" There were worried looks from my officials, so I said, "Who are you?" And he said, "I am the Ambassador to Brazil – who are you?"'

Until the end of the eighteenth century, the Foreign Office was divided between the Northern Department (covering the Holy Roman Empire, Scandinavia, Holland and Russia) and the Southern Department (covering France and the Latin countries), with two

Secretaries of State. Their staff were crammed into two houses at Cleveland Row, conveniently close to the diplomatic court at St James's Palace.[3] This division ended in March 1782 when Lord North resigned as Prime Minister over the loss of America and was replaced by Rockingham, who rightly recognized that the Earl of Shelburne and Charles James Fox could not work together. Rockingham created the Home Office under Shelburne from the Southern Department and put Fox in charge of the new unified Foreign Office, with his playwright sidekick (and MP for Stafford) Richard Brinsley Sheridan as his under-secretary. The Home Office at first occupied the Board of Trade offices on the site of the former great indoor tennis court on Whitehall, now the Cabinet Office stretching between Downing Street and Dover House. In 1793, the Foreign Office moved to Lord Sheffield's house in Downing Street and by the 1820s more houses were acquired for the expanding Foreign Office staff in Fludyer Street, which ran parallel to Downing Street off Whitehall, on the site of Pepys's Axe Yard. Numbers 13–14 Downing Street became the office of the Secretary of State for War and the Colonies in 1801 after the loss of America had made the role of Secretary of State for the (American) Colonies redundant.

The area to the west of Whitehall was honeycombed by narrow streets where Scottish and Irish MPs had lodging rooms; pubs such as the Cat and Bagpipes prospered and all manner of trades were conducted cheek-by-jowl with the burgeoning civil service. Duke Street, which was obliterated by the Foreign Office, ran along the park side, linking the end of Crown Street with Charles Street, Gardeners Lane and George Yard (both also now buried beneath the Treasury). While the ground was cleared for the new offices, Number Ten looked out onto wasteland and shored-up Foreign Office houses, which were described by the Foreign Office librarian and archivist Sir Edward Hertslet in his lively memoir *Recollections of the Old Foreign Office* as looking 'unsightly, not to say undignified'.

The building of the Colonial and Home Offices required the demolition of part of King Street – which had been a thoroughfare for at least four centuries – between Charles Street (now King Charles Street) and Downing Street. It left a small wedge of property near Parliament Square between King Street and Parliament Street that would finally disappear with the building of what is now the Treasury. Foreign Office staff temporarily decamped to palatial houses in Whitehall Gardens until the new offices were completed to Palmerston's wishes in 1868. The growth in the bureaucracy of the Foreign Office was surprisingly slow, partly because Foreign Secretaries insisted on dictating policy to their 'scribes' rather than having an army of advisers. Castlereagh, Canning and Palmerston all ignored the opinions of their staff, which numbered only forty a century after the Foreign Office was created. Diplomatic careers in the FO were looked on as the preserve of the public-school elite. Professor Peter Hennessy says the Foreign Office remained the stronghold of the aristocracy well into the twentieth century. Algernon Cecil in *British Foreign Secretaries* described the Foreign Office as the 'last choice preserve of administration practised as a sport'.[4] A large Foreign Office building was needed, says one guide to the building for civil servants, because: 'It was only possible to accept the job of Foreign Secretary if you owned a large London house in which to accommodate offices for staff and be able to entertain on a lavish scale.'

Palmerston had dominated foreign affairs for nearly two decades through turbulent years of coalition governments before becoming Prime Minister in 1855 at the age of seventy-one – the oldest man ever to take on the office. 'Pam' was so abrasive that he was nicknamed 'Lord Pumicestone' and was heartily disliked by Queen Victoria. He succeeded Lord Aberdeen, who was brought down by the incompetence over the Crimean War and public outrage at the reports in *The Times* of the suffering of British soldiers. A Tory who changed sides to the embryonic Liberal Party over his support for the 1832 Reform Act that extended the franchise to more men (though not women) and Irish emancipation, Palmerston also used the Navy to enforce the end of slavery, though he remained neutral during the American Civil War and he was ready to use force abroad in the British national interest. He pursued the Opium Wars against China, securing Hong Kong as a colony and became associated with 'gunboat diplomacy' when he threatened to use the Royal Navy against Greece to protect a British citizen. The diplomatic row it caused nearly brought him down, but Palmerston's promise that a British subject would always be protected abroad proved enduringly popular with the public, and perpetuated the myth that the British passport requiring foreigners to 'allow the bearer to pass freely without let or hindrance' would be reinforced if necessary by force. The Downing Street website describes him as 'jingoistic' but his sympathizers insist he was misunderstood and sought peace through deterrence.

Palmerston's foreign policy would find an echo in Tony Blair's policy of liberal interventionism and his doctrine of 'international community', which Blair outlined in a speech in Chicago in 1999. Dismissing the traditional principle of non-intervention in the internal affairs of sovereign states, the Prime Minister said the global community had a moral duty to intervene against Slobodan Milosevic in Kosovo, and Saddam Hussein in Iraq: 'Now our actions are guided by a more subtle blend of mutual self-interest and moral purpose in defending the values we cherish. In the end, values and interests merge. If we can establish and spread the values of liberty, the rule of law, human rights and an open society then that is in our national interests too. The spread of our values makes us safer.'

The attacks on the World Trade Center, New York, on 11 September 2001 reinforced Blair's conviction that states have a duty to intervene in the affairs of other sovereign states, even if they are not directly threatened by war, to protect the West from the global threat of terrorism. Asked what was the essence of 'Blairism' in 2007 as he handed over power to Gordon Brown, Blair said: 'Liberal interventionism. I'm a proud interventionist.' His policy was described as dangerous by some leading commentators, and its consequences for overstretched British forces worried senior military figures, one of whom said to me: 'If we invade a country, we have to stay there. As Colin Powell (former US Secretary of State) said, 'If you break it, you keep it.'

Blair also used the doctrine to justify retrospectively the British and US invasion of Iraq in 2003 over which Robin Cook resigned from Blair's government as Leader of the House of Commons. The failure to find Saddam Hussein's alleged weapons of mass destruction, which were the immediate justification of the war, embroiled the Blair Government in a far-reaching controversy about the use of intelligence to justify political ends that two inquiries, by Lord Hutton, the former Northern Ireland judge, and Lord Butler, the former Cabinet Secretary, have not settled. The Foreign Secretary sits at the centre of Britain's international intelligence web, receiving reports from ambassadors across the world, but the Prime Minister remains in charge of intelligence. The head of the Joint Intelligence Committee reports direct to the Prime Minister rather than the Foreign Secretary.

The Prime Minister of the day also takes final control of major foreign policy decisions when diplomacy has failed, as Eden did on Suez, Thatcher did on the Falklands War, and Blair did on Iraq. But the dangers arise when the advice of the experts in the Foreign Office and the intelligence services is ignored or manipulated. The Foreign Office had a long tradition of expertise in the Middle East – its Persian section was known as 'the camel corps' – but insiders were alarmed at the extent to which the Foreign Office appeared to be sidelined by Downing Street in the run-up to the Iraq conflict.

In his report on the intelligence failings prior to the Iraq War, Lord

Butler coined the phrase 'sofa government' to describe Blair's preference for taking decisions at casual meetings in his Downing Street den with a few close acolytes without civil servants being present or official notes being taken. Officials at the Foreign Office also found it alarming that a unit under Alastair Campbell, Blair's 'spin doctor' at Number Ten, had been set up inside the Foreign Office to run the public-relations operation surrounding the Iraq War. It was called the Coalition Information Centre (CIC) and was responsible for the so-called 'dodgy' dossier, which was pushed under the doors of journalists – including mine – at a hotel in Washington when I was covering a US trip by Blair in the build-up to the war. It later emerged that it contained reports cut and pasted from the internet to sustain claims that Saddam possessed weapons of mass destruction. The CIC had a room overlooking their masters in Downing Street. Foreign Office sources told me few of the key meetings on Iraq took place at the Foreign Office, a view confirmed to me by the former International Development Secretary, Clare Short, who resigned from the Cabinet after Cook over the failure to honour promises about the regeneration of Iraq following the war. 'There were Cabinet papers but they were never circulated,' Short told me on 6 June 2008. 'There were a number of meetings but Tony would say, "Don't worry – we will go to the UN." But then you were in the period of the rush to war and there was never a proper Cabinet discussion.'

The Foreign Office, attracting the cream of the public-school elite, traditionally was seen, in Rab Butler's term, as the 'Rolls-Royce' machine in Whitehall. Andrew MacKinlay, a Labour member of the Foreign Affairs Committee, believes the Iraq War was the latest in a series of Foreign Office blunders that led to wars in the twentieth century including Suez and the Falklands War – for which the Foreign Secretary Lord Carrington resigned. MacKinlay's committee questioned Dr David Kelly, the weapons expert who committed suicide after the Iraq War, about the allegations that the Government had 'sexed up' the intelligence on Saddam's weapons of mass destruction. He accuses the Foreign Office of an 'unerring ability to send out the wrong signals'. He said: 'The Foreign Office has a reputation for being a Rolls-Royce. I think it's more of a Ford saloon.'

Intelligence officers – 'spooks' – occupy the top floor of the Foreign Office and an intelligence desk is manned twenty-four hours a day to keep the Foreign Secretary informed of developments around the world at any time. Broken sleep is one of the occupational hazards of being Foreign Secretary, wherever they are in the world. The Foreign Secretary is allocated the grace-and-favour country house at Chevening in Kent, and an apartment at Carlton House Terrace – it was used by Lord Howe, but Jack Straw preferred his London private residence and Margaret Beckett had a grace-and-favour apartment in Admiralty House.

A display case in one of the corridors inside the Foreign Office holds an Enigma machine, the device that helped Britain break the Ultra code and keep ahead of the Germans during the Second World War. Sometimes traitors slipped through, such as Donald Maclean, who joined the Foreign Office during the Second World War. He was a member of the Cambridge Communist spy ring with Guy Burgess, Kim Philby and Anthony Blunt during the Cold War. MI6, the 'James Bond' service they infiltrated, now has its headquarters across the river in Vauxhall but is linked to the Foreign Office, while MI5, based on Millbank, generally operates with the Home Office, although their roles are no longer strictly limited to overseas and home counter-espionage. British embassies have intelligence officers attached to them, and one of the most closely observed is the British embassy in Moscow, an elegant sugar merchant's house, which is constantly under surveillance from the Kremlin across the river. Officials there assume that every conversation – even those in the ambassador's bedroom – can be overheard by bugging devices that pick up vibrations from windows, unless they take special counter measures by holding conversations in a special room. The Foreign Office also relies on the UK listening post, GCHQ, and 'our friends' in the CIA.

Euro-sceptics will always believe the Foreign Office is in the business of surrendering British interests to Europe such as with the Lisbon Treaty in 2008. Tory Euro-sceptic David Davis was given responsibility for Europe by John Major to reassure like-minded colleagues after the damaging battles over the Maastricht Treaty. Pictures on his office wall at the Foreign Office at the time included the Duke of Wellington, which he joked was to upset the French when they visited him.

During the First World War, at his own expense Sir Sigismund Goetze painted the murals above the entrance staircase to the Foreign Office that today are seen as even more offensive to European sensitivities. They trumpeted the achievements of the British Empire, represented by a voluptuous Britannia, the 'warmonger', leading the allies against Germany and shaking hands with her allies France and India at the end of the Great War – Germany had been included after the armistice but was painted out and replaced by India. However, the murals were viewed as too bombastic by Lord Curzon, a Viceroy of India in Victoria's reign and Foreign Secretary between 1919 and 1924, and there was a move to have them painted out. They were rescued after a site visit by the Cabinet under Lloyd George, then Prime Minister, and still greet visitors on the main staircase today. Lloyd George, a notorious womanizer, is said to have admired Britannia and told the Cabinet: 'Well, gentlemen, whenever I have entered this building, I always thought I was entering a tomb, now I begin to see light.' The pro-European Lord Howe shares Curzon's view of the murals: 'I was astonished. I often wondered what would have happened if the Americans had put a similar thing in the Pentagon. It is still there now. It is quite extraordinary but no one has said you are terrible war-mongers.'

In 1925 the Foreign Office was chosen as the location for the signing ceremony of the pact that would supposedly end European conflict for ever after the Great War – the Treaty reached at talks in the Swiss resort of Locarno on Lake Maggiore. The Treaty had one lasting effect as the Foreign Office rooms were renamed the Locarno Rooms after the event, but the pact was broken when Hitler, exploiting the sense of bitter injustice in Berlin, repudiated the agreement by annexing Austria, thus paving the way for the Second World War. Hitler's Luftwaffe damaged many buildings around Whitehall, but the Locarno Rooms survived intact during the Blitz. However, post-war austerity and a plan in the 1960s by Geoffrey Rippon, then Tory Environment Secretary, to demolish the Scott building to make way for a new grandiose Whitehall plan (discussed in the Postscript) nearly did what the Luftwaffe had failed to achieve.

Even the official history of the Foreign Office sounds a note of outrage about the dilapidated state of the once glorious gilded interiors: 'Lack of money, post-1945, and dislike of anything Victorian helped to reduce grandeur to squalor, and many of the fine areas were lost to sight behind false ceilings and plasterboard partitions . . .'

The famous Durbar Court in the India Office was covered with temporary huts housing what was then the Communications Department. The once elegant Locarno Rooms were split into small offices, and staff recalled seeing fragments of the ceiling or the decoration of the walls peeping between the partitions. There was no central heating and diplomats had to thaw themselves by the fires in their offices before beginning work in the winter, and they had only one bucket of coal a day to keep them warm. One civil servant described how fog used to creep into the building during the London 'pea-soupers', making the damp offices as eerie at night as a set for a Hitchcock thriller. But the public outcry at the Rippon plans led to the offices being designated as a Grade I listed building and the start of a more cost-effective scheme for their restoration. The rolling programme of refurbishment – aided by painstaking research to restore the interiors to their original colours and condition – was launched under Margaret Thatcher in 1984 and ended in 1997 as Labour took office. It cost around £100 million but it produced 25 per cent extra usable space for far less than the cost of demolition and rebuilding. Overseen by experts at English Heritage, the stunning Victorian stencil decoration in the Locarno suite was fully restored. High up in a corner of the grand staircase to the Foreign Office, four squares of a chocolate-brown colour were preserved to show visitors just how dirty the ceiling had become.

Security surrounding Number Ten has closed the public entrance to the Foreign Office through Downing Street for all but state visits. The Downing Street entrance was used by Tony Blair and the US President George W. Bush to walk back to Number Ten after a press conference in the Locarno Suite in the Foreign Office. Chris Mullin, then Foreign Minister with responsibility for Africa, was standing on the steps of the former India Office across the quadrangle as the two leaders walked by. A critic of the Bush administration and the author of the conspiracy thriller *A Very British Coup* about the military overthrow of a socialist government, Mullin was surprised when Bush pointed at him, and waved vigorously as though he was an old friend. That night, Blair was hosting a meeting of ministers and Mullin asked the Prime Minister why Bush had waved at him. 'I told him you were his greatest fan,' smiled Blair.

Scott was under orders to save money when he extended the building in 1875 to the Parliament Street frontage, which left the corridors and staircases of the Colonial and Home Offices relatively plain. With Palmerston now dead, he indulged his taste for Gothic architecture by incorporating some Gothic window arches and lavish gilding and stencilling. It was a small act of defiance but Palmerston had the final say over the look of Whitehall for the next 100 years.

## The Home Office

The large entrance on Whitehall of the building now known as the FCO was for 102 years the front door to the Home Office. The Home Secretary's gloomy office was up the grand staircase. It had a large fireplace, but none of the refinements of the Foreign Office or the India Office. The Home Office grew from thirteen men and 'a necessary woman' in the 1830s to a staff of over 35,000, mostly in the prison service, by the late 1980s. Among the staff it shared with the Foreign Office were the Decipherer of Letters, and the Secretary of the Latin Language – a post once held by John Milton. By 1910 typewriters had replaced the pen for most correspondence. 'The first lady typists had come in amidst much head-shaking and trepidation. The telephone was installed in 1882 – though internal speaking tubes remained in use until the 1920s. Coal fires remained in use in the Whitehall building until the 1960s,' says the official history of the Home Office in the Public Record Office. Robert (Bobby) Peel – who created the police or 'bobbies' – is probably the most outstanding Home Secretary, and Melbourne also served as Home Secretary, but after the move into the Scott building the most famous minister to occupy the palatial Home Secretary's suite of offices was Winston S. Churchill. He was Home Secretary in the Liberal Government under H. H. Asquith, though he only remained there for a year. As a restless man of action, he took personal command of one of the most notorious anti-terrorist operations ever mounted by the Home Office: the armed siege in Sidney Street in London's East End. It happened in January 1911, after a group of burglars who had been trying to tunnel into a jeweller's shop were cornered in a lodging house. Three police officers had been killed by the gang, and anarchist literature found in a hideout suggested they were Latvian revolutionaries attempting to finance an uprising in Russia. It was later rumoured they included a shadowy figure known as Peter the Painter, Peter Piatkov, who it was claimed by some became better known as Lenin. Churchill ordered in army marksmen, but could not resist leaving Whitehall to direct the siege himself. There are extraordinary photographs of Churchill, wearing a top hat and large black overcoat with an astrakhan collar, standing on the corner of Sidney Street while puffs of smoke show that an exchange of fire is taking place. The house caught fire, two bodies were discovered, but 'Peter the Painter' was never found. Film of the incident shows Churchill flinching as a bullet zinged through his top hat. Files at the Public Record Office say Churchill regretted taking personal control of the operation because it was seen as grandstanding.[5] It did not restrain Churchill's hand, however. In August 1911, the Home Secretary put down a dockers' strike in Liverpool by sending a warship, HMS *Antrim*, into the docks. The marines fired on the strikers, injuring eight people. In a foretaste of the 1926 General Strike, Churchill also faced down a threatened rail unions' strike by mobilizing 50,000 troops, and despatched troops to the Welsh coal mines at Tonypandy – an action for which the miners never forgave him. In October 1911, Asquith moved Churchill to the Admiralty as First Sea Lord to prepare the navy for war in Europe.[6]

Until 1965, when Britain abolished the death penalty, the Home Secretary had the power of life and death over condemned prisoners. He did not actually sign a death warrant but confirmed an execution by writing the words 'the law must take its course' on the condemned prisoner's file. He also exercised the power of the Royal Pardon on behalf of the Queen. Clare Short, before starting her political career as an MP, was a young civil servant in the Home Office and remembers that numbered cards with black edges were put on the Home Secretary's mantelpiece to remind him of the countdown to the next hanging. The last men to be hanged in Britain were Peter Anthony Allen in Walton gaol and Gwynne Owen Evans in

Strangeways, Manchester, on 13 August 1964 for killing a householder during a burglary. The last Home Secretary to approve the two final executions was the Conservative Henry Brooke, who was much troubled by it. Brooke supported the backbench bill in 1965 by Sydney Silverman abolishing the death penalty for most categories of murder, providing it was reaffirmed by Parliament, which it was in 1969. Short was at the Home Office when the late Roy Jenkins was Labour Home Secretary. In his autobiography, Jenkins described taking over as Home Secretary in the Wilson Government on 22 December 1965 with a commitment to reform, and running into the civil service brick wall of his permanent secretary, Sir Charles Cunningham. It provides a masterclass in minister-mandarin relations, worthy of *Yes Minister*, the television comedy series about Whitehall. 'Sir Charles', as he was universally known in Whitehall, was a liberal, Jenkins recalled, but 'had become the guardian . . . of a certain Home Office approach to life which I was convinced had to be broken if future Home Secretaries were to avoid the St Sebastian-like fate of [Henry] Brooke and [Frank] Soskice [Jenkins's predecessors as Home Secretary]'.[7] 'CC' burst into tears at their showdown, but it was wasted on Jenkins, and Sir Charles retired early in 1966. The Home Office moved out to a new office block at 50 Queen Anne's Gate in 1977, now the home of the Justice Department. The Home Secretary's former office is now a largely forgotten part of the Foreign and Commonwealth Office, though it is used once a year by the Home Secretary and the Queen as a retiring room on Remembrance Sunday, when the Queen and her ministers lay wreaths in Whitehall at the Cenotaph, the monument dedicated to those killed in wars. George Dugdale in *Whitehall Through the Centuries* says the Cenotaph, erected in 1920 and designed by Sir Edward Lutyens, the architect more usually associated with fine country houses and the building of the capital of New Delhi, 'is to this country what the Arc de Triomphe is to France'. Hidden from view to those outside are lines of red chairs by the front door to the former Home Office for VIPs to view the ceremony when the massed bands and veterans lead a march past.

Today, the front door is permanently locked, and the bell-push untouched. There are ornate foot scrapers either side of the great front door, and beyond those, in alcoves on the front wall, metal semicircular hoops to deter muggers from loitering in the corners. A few paces away are the most photographed red telephone boxes in Britain. They have a family connection to the great George Gilbert Scott building that is now the FCO. The K2 telephone boxes were designed by G. G. Scott's grandson, Giles Gilbert Scott, who also designed the Anglican Cathedral in Liverpool, Battersea power station and the Bankside power station, now Tate Modern.

# 11

# THE WAR OFFICE –
# FROM HAIG TO HOON

'Good morning, good morning!' the General said
When we met him last week on our way to the Line.
Now the soldiers he smiled at are most of 'em dead,
And we're cursing his staff for incompetent swine.
'He's a cheery old card,' grunted Harry to Jack
As they slogged up to Arras with rifle and pack
. . . But he did for them both by his plan of attack.

*The General*, Siegfried Sassoon (1886–1967)

Geoff Hoon, the Defence Secretary, sat in Lord Kitchener's chair in the centre of a huge, oak-panelled office at the northern end of Whitehall and parried my questions with ease. We were sitting in the historic Secretary of State's suite of offices in the old War Office, the Portland-stone-fronted Whitehall office with a big wooden entrance door a few paces from the Clarence public house on the corner of

Great Scotland Yard, and it was the run-up to the US–British invasion of Iraq in the first weeks of 2003. I had raised some of the doubts being expressed by families of the soldiers and defence experts about the adequacy of the army's kit, including body armour and radios, with which they were to be sent out to fight the war. He said he had been assured by the service chiefs that the troops would be properly equipped if they went into battle and measures had been taken to minimize 'blue on blue' incidents, deaths by so-called 'friendly fire' from American 'tankbuster' planes. I reported in the *Sunday Telegraph* on 19 January 2003:

> Mr Hoon said he took the responsibility of sending men and women to war seriously and that all steps would be taken to ensure that they were properly equipped. Among the new material available to British forces is communication equipment enabling troops to speak directly to their US counterparts on the battlefield to avoid a repeat of the 'friendly fire' killings in the last Gulf War.

Events were to raise questions about those assurances from the defence chiefs, and not for the first time. The former private office of the Secretary of State for War is up a grand pillared marble staircase that divides and turns past the first floor to the second. In an anteroom were cases of ceremonial curved knives and other artefacts that spoke of Britain's imperial past. The room is panelled in dark, richly carved oak and the chairs are leather, the perfect setting for an Edwardian military chief in riding boots of shiny leather to run the armies of an empire. It lost some of its grandeur in the 1960s when it was modernized – the interior was painted blue and white like a piece of Wedgwood china, and the chandeliers were replaced by strip lights – but the room was restored to something like its original splendour before Hoon took it over. Richard Haldane – after whom the suite is named – was the first to occupy the room, which looks down on Whitehall over the front door of the War Office. He was made Secretary of State for War in 1905 by Henry Campbell-Bannerman, and it was Haldane who created the general staff in 1906 and the Territorial Army the following year. Haldane was moved to the Lord Chancellor's office by Herbert Henry Asquith when he became Prime Minister. Asquith briefly occupied the War Secretary's chair himself as a stopgap in 1914 before the outbreak of the First World War, until Lord Kitchener of Khartoum took over. Kitchener, at sixty-four, had vast military experience which made him the natural choice of leader for the war: he was a national hero for leading the counter-offensive in the Sudan after the failure to save General Gordon in Khartoum in 1885 that so displeased Queen Victoria. His fame was spread by Winston Churchill, then a young lieutenant and budding war correspondent, who had wangled his way into Kitchener's force to write a book on the campaign in the Sudan by appealing directly to the Prime Minister, Lord Salisbury, a friend of Churchill's father. It led to Churchill taking part in the last cavalry charge against the dervishes of the Mahdi at the Battle of Omdurman on 2 September 1898.[1] Kitchener had also led British forces in the Boer War but, by the time he was called from Egypt to the office of War Secretary in Whitehall, the Field Marshal was out of touch with modern mechanized warfare. He was reluctant to take on the post but, persuaded to do so by Asquith, threw himself with great energy into recruiting men for the front for the war against Kaiser Bill, with the iconic poster of himself – so much parodied in the careless 1960s – with a mad eye, walrus moustache, the accusing finger, and the caption: 'Your Country Needs You'. Kitchener correctly forecast a long war that would cost millions of lives but, according to the editors of Asquith's letters to Venetia Stanley, Kitchener 'was too old to change and he had gone a little to seed. "A fatted pharaoh in spurs . . . garrulously intoxicated with power" was Rudyard Kipling's judgement after a visit to Cairo in 1913.'[2]

Venetia was an aristocrat and socialite, the daughter of Lord Sheffield, with a string of admirers. She was twenty-five when she met and captivated Asquith, who was fifty-eight. He began a torrent of correspondence with her, unaware that she was also being courted by his political secretary, Samuel Montagu. His letters to Venetia, a sultry beauty with whom he had fallen in love, were sometimes written during Cabinet meetings in the Great War. They were highly revealing and published in 1982, but he destroyed her letters to preserve confidentiality. The correspondence ended in 1915 when Venetia told the Prime Minister she was marrying Montagu. On 12 May – while he was under attack in the press over reports of German atrocities – Asquith replied:

> Most loved –
> As you know well, this breaks my heart.
> I couldn't bear to come and see you.
> I can only pray God to bless you – and help me.

Asquith's letters to Venetia who died in 1948 offer a remarkable insight into his Cabinet. He confided in Venetia that his appointment of Kitchener was a 'hazardous experiment' but on 6 August 1914 wrote enthusiastically from Downing Street to her: 'K is already throwing great energy into his job; already today he has undertaken to raise another 100,000 Regulars! It will be amusing to see how he gets on in the Cabinet.'[3]

Kitchener's call to arms was answered by workmates, families, groups of young men from the same villages, towns and cities, some from the same occupations, from gardeners in great houses to bankers and solicitors, who were all recruited into the same battalions to encourage comradeship. They became known as the 'Pals Battalions' and, when they went over the top to die in France, the youth of whole communities in England was cut down. It was an experiment in recruiting that was never to be repeated. To compound the misjudgement of Kitchener's appointment, Douglas Haig was put in charge of 1 Corps in France under Sir John French at the start of the Great War, and in little over a year, on 19 December 1915, replaced French as Commander-in-Chief of the British Expeditionary Force (BEF). Haig had royal connections and influence, which helped his rapid rise from Oxford and the staff college at Sandhurst to become the Director of Military Training at the War Office in 1906, sharing one of the offices for military chiefs a few doors away from Haldane's suite. He was a cavalry officer but Professor Tim Travers argues Haig also inherited other traits from the nineteenth century: 'Since both sides were technically much the same, the decisive elements were morale, determination, and the will of the commander.'[4] Military strategy had hardly changed since Waterloo. However, a belief that victory was owed to the brave, a view shared by Nelson, was to prove hopelessly out of date when the forces were faced with the weapons of modern warfare, the machine gun and the high-explosive shell.

When I interviewed Hoon in Kitchener's office, the War Office had long been abandoned by the defence ministers, and left to the shadowy defence intelligence service (DIS), whose staff of 4,500 intelligence officers included Dr David Kelly, the expert on weapons of mass destruction who committed suicide in the 'war of spin' after the war in Iraq. Hoon and his chiefs of staff had been decanted back into the old War Office while the main Ministry of Defence building in Whitehall underwent total renovation. He was serious about wanting improved communications and body armour for the men, but it later emerged that soldiers had been killed for the want of body armour, and a unit of Red Caps had been massacred because, among other things, they lacked the communications to call in the nearby Paras for help. In an earlier age, these could be brushed aside as the casualties of war, but in the age of the BlackBerry, and embedded reporters, it led to the chiefs of the armed services once more being cast by the parents of the dead as the donkeys in charge of lions – just as Kitchener and Haig had been ridiculed in the musical *Oh! What a Lovely War*, based on Alan Clark's acerbic history of the First World War.

The War Office was supposed to bring a new professionalism to the British armed forces when it was completed in 1906. From Tudor times, the monarch had controlled the army through the Secretary-at-War. In 1794, at the start of the Napoleonic wars, a Cabinet post of Secretary of State for War was created to put a politician in charge of the armed forces, answerable to Parliament, but the army continued to be run by the Commander-in-Chief. The duplication of responsibilities was a recipe for inertia, until Edward Cardwell, who became Secretary of State in 1868, introduced far-reaching reforms that created the foundations for the modern Ministry of Defence. He made the Commander-in-Chief subordinate to the politician and moved the C-in-C out of Wellington's office at Horse Guards into the first War Office, which occupied a group of ramshackle houses at 80–91 Pall Mall, where the RAC Club stands today. Cardwell's junior minister and 'enforcer', Lord Northbrook, the Parliamentary Under-Secretary for War, had to use all his political guile to overcome a rearguard action from the C-in-C, Queen Victoria's first cousin the Duke of Cambridge, against being moved out of his office at Horse Guards. The Duke, who had gone to the Crimea with his own cordon bleu chef,[5] was so incensed with the move that he continued to address his letters from 'Horse Guards, War Office'.[6] The post of C-in-C was not abolished until 1895 when the Duke finally retired. He still sits on his horse outside Horse Guards and the sculptor has captured his rather pompous air.

The stench from the cesspit at the Pall Mall buildings made a move from there imperative. It was so unpleasant that it was reported as early as 1860 that mortality rates among the civil servants were about the 'same level as an Ashantee campaign'. The Thames, too, was noxious, and the Great Stink of 1858 when Parliament was suspended because of the smell from the river led to an ingenious solution by the engineer Joseph Bazalgette. He built two great intercepting sewers flanking the river, one on each bank, and covered them over with a promenade and gardens to form Victoria Embankment on the north side and the Albert Embankment on the south. The Metropolitan District line was also under construction at the time, so it was built alongside the new sewer below ground level but left open to the skies to allow the steam to escape. This explains why clouds of smoke can be seen curling from the ground in many prints of the Embankment at the time. The mammoth engineering enterprise benefited the city, but led to the destruction of some of the historic houses by the river at Whitehall Gardens on the site of the old Tudor Palace of White Hall.

Defence chiefs lobbied for a new army headquarters and there were plans to incorporate the War Office into the Foreign Office, but the space was taken by the India Office. A plan to demolish the historic Admiralty House for a new War Office was turned down, and it was decided in 1896 to acquire the land near the Banqueting House at Whitehall Place for the purpose. The commission was handed to William Young, an architect who had specialized in country houses and whose only public building was the Glasgow City Chambers. However, he was a follower of the English Renaissance style and he was under orders to design a building that would fit in with the Banqueting House, the Adam screen to the Admiralty, the old Treasury, the Home Office, and the recently completed Foreign Office, which Sir George Gilbert Scott (under sufferance) had delivered along classical lines. The aim was to enhance the impression that Victorian Whitehall was a harmonious landscape of grand buildings dressed in matching Portland stone, following the classical principles of Sir John Soane, but it enhanced the impression of Whitehall as a featureless canyon suited to its purpose of housing faceless bureaucrats. There was even a proposal to link the War Office with the Banqueting House by an Italianate decorative screen, but that was fortunately dropped. Young had a difficult site to contend with. It was a trapezium and he died before the building was completed, but his design, carried out posthumously by his son, ingeniously used four immense cupolas to produce a visual balance to the exterior, which was dressed in the ubiquitous Whitehall façade of Portland stone. To overcome the waterlogged ground, a huge concrete tank thirty feet below the road level was created, providing two basement floors beneath five upper floors.

The aim of the new War Office was to bring the combined command of Britain's land-based war machine within one purpose-built ministry for the first time. Opposite the Secretary of State's room were the Permanent Under-Secretary's office and three interconnecting War Council rooms in the centre of the Whitehall Place front, with the Chief of the General Staff's room above the quadrangle entrance. All these rooms are oak-panelled and had brass 'electroliers', electric chandeliers which were replicas of those at Hampton Court. The hidden gems in the War Office are the 200-year-old fireplaces, which are Georgian and were brought from the Pall Mall War Office and Buckingham House. The building eventually cost £1.2 million, three times the original estimate.[7] In 2007 it was reported that the old War Office building might be put on the market by the MoD as surplus to requirements for an estimated £35 million.[8] Those who occupied the Defence Secretary's office overlooking Whitehall included David Lloyd George (1916) and Winston Churchill (1919–21). One of the last was John Profumo, who was brought in by the Conservative Prime Minister Harold Macmillan in 1960 to promote the new 'regular army' after conscription ended, but was forced to resign three years later in the spy-and-sex scandal involving 1960s icon, Christine Keeler.

T. E. Lawrence (Lawrence of Arabia) was employed in the War Office in the Great War as part of MO4, the Geographical Section, to use his local knowledge to produce, among other things, a large-scale map of the Sinai. With the onset of the 1914–18 war, the General Staff left for France and Flanders, and the War Office was populated mainly by retired officers from the reserves, and hordes of Boy Scouts acting as messengers. The War Office became so overcrowded that the great hall at Alexandra Palace and the National Liberal Club were requisitioned as War Office annexes. From that moment, armed forces chiefs wanted a bigger, better building and cast around for another site. Whitehall planners had already agreed on a site for a new major public office initially for the Board of Trade – the land occupied by the fine houses in Whitehall Gardens that were already largely used as civil service offices. It was planned to extend the new office as far as the Victoria Embankment but, after a row, it was agreed to keep the building in line with the front of the National Liberal Club. The architect Vincent Harris won a competition as early as 1913 to design the building, but it was held up by the First World War and the interwar depression.

It was not until 1938, with war looming, that the houses at Whitehall Gardens were finally demolished to make way for a new defence building, and the foundations of the old royal palace were revealed for the first time. Whitehall then resembled an enormous *Time Team* dig with the scrape of trowels rending the air as archaeologists furiously tried to uncover historical detail before the site was lost for ever in a sea of concrete in the rush to complete a secret defence bunker on the site before the Blitz. They laid bare the outlines of the Palace of Whitehall, and Wolsey's former wharf with the later enlargement of the embankment by Henry's builders. The outbreak of the war prevented construction of the rest of the building, but two underground bombproof citadels were finished before work stopped.

Needing more space than the War Office could offer, the Ministry for War had taken over two local hotels, both popular with American visitors in the 1930s: the Victoria and the Metropole in Northumberland Avenue. They were constructed on the site of one of the last great privately owned mansions and gardens in Whitehall, Northumberland House, built in the reign of James I and demolished around 1876. The Metropole was created in 1883 for Frederick Gordon, a restaurant owner, who had successfully branched out into the hotel business with the coming of the railways. It was his third hotel and sister of the surviving Metropole in Brighton. The Victoria did not have running hot water in rooms, but the Metropole was sumptuously fitted out and in its heyday offered guests live sound feeds from West End theatres on headphones. It has remained in defence hands more or less ever since. Over half a century later, the baroque interior with '*Midnight Follies*' in large letters over one door provided a surreal setting for press briefings about the conflict in the first Gulf War before being closed up again. Unloved and neglected, 'the building's ostentatious interior – marble columns, chandeliers and richly ornamented carvings, was desecrated by layers of grey paint' by the MoD, according to historian Graham White. In February 2008 it was reported to have been bought by a Dubai state-controlled company for £130 million, and is awaiting demolition.[9]

At the outset of the Second World War, Leslie Hore-Belisha, a Liberal and former Transport Minister who had cut deaths with a road-crossing beacon, was a surprise appointment by Neville Chamberlain as Defence Secretary, replacing Duff Cooper, who was popular with the troops. Hore-Belisha occupied the Haldane Suite, but struggled to reconcile Chamberlain's policy of appeasement and his own belief that conscription – so long avoided in Britain – would be needed. Now remembered only for the Belisha beacon, he was suddenly sacked in January 1940, by Chamberlain in the early months of the war, in complex circumstances. These included radical democratic reforms to the army that upset the upper classes, who were furious to find their sons reduced to the ranks, but there was also shameful anti-Semitic feeling – possibly fuelled by a desire to placate Hitler even after war had been declared – against a Jew being allowed to serve in the Cabinet. In his diary for 6 January 1940 Chips Channon, a Chamberlain supporter, recorded:

> A cabal was formed of people on the General Staff – but they could think of no way to oust him until they hit on the brilliant idea of roping in, of all people, the Duke of Gloucester, as a professional soldier. He took up the cause and told his brother the King. The Crown decided to intervene dramatically, and sent for the PM . . . The PM, startled by the King's complaint, gave in and that turned the scales. Hitherto, the PM, though aware of the movement, had supported Leslie. On Thursday he sent for him to come to No. 10 – and Leslie, unsuspecting went: they had a long talk during which the PM asked Leslie to accept the Board of Trade. Belisha was staggered, and asked why (evidently he had not believed my too-mildly-worded warning). Then he was told, as gently as the PM could do it, that he must go. Leslie demanded an hour in which to make up his mind, and went for a walk in St James's Park. He could hardly believe what he had been told, and was, of course, quite unaware of the Royal intervention. Later he refused the offer of the Board of Trade and made it plain that he would never serve under Chamberlain in any capacity again, because he no longer trusted him.'[10]

Hore-Belisha was replaced by a more conventional Conservative, Oliver Stanley, the younger son of the Earl of Derby, who had held the war ministry post in the First World War, but within three months Chamberlain had been ousted and replaced by Churchill, and Stanley was out of office. In May 1940, following the German invasion of France, Churchill appointed Anthony Eden as Secretary of State for War in his coalition War Cabinet. Eden, who had resigned from Chamberlain's Cabinet as Foreign Secretary in protest at his policy of appeasement, had briefly rejoined the army with the rank of major at the outbreak of war. His tenure of the Haldane Suite at the War Office lasted only seven months, however, as he was moved back to the Foreign Office in December, and served for most of the war loyally supporting Churchill, who took command of most of the crucial decisions on foreign affairs himself. The trusted former Tory Chief Whip David Margesson was made War Secretary by Churchill after Eden. Margesson privately admitted to John Colville, Churchill's private secretary, that he doubted he was up to the job. Churchill took close control of the war effort, firing off detailed memos on his pet plans, and Margesson lasted until the setbacks of 1942, including the fall of Singapore to Japan, when he had to go. Colville recorded going to see Margesson at the War Office in his diary for Thursday 30 January. 'I thought the War Office a horrid crowded place, but the Secretary of State's room is by contrast rather distinguished and its occupant gains in dignity by the fact that one has to walk the whole length of the room before one reaches his desk (a technique, as I pointed out to him, much utilized by foreign dictators).'[11]

An old copy of the wartime *Picture Post* in the MoD archives brilliantly illustrates life at the War Office in the 1940s with a photograph of a minister carrying a gas mask arriving at the front door to be saluted by the chief porter wearing a top hat. Some concessions were made for the war, including rushing down to the basement bomb shelters when there was an air raid, but the Edwardian style of life inside the War Office went on largely as before, even during the Blitz. Viscount Slim, appointed Chief of the Imperial General Staff (CIGS) after the war, described arriving one

*The Palace of Whitehall* by Hendrick Danckerts, *c.*1677. The view is from St James's Park showing Charles II's coach, the Old Horse Guards building and the park stairs leading down from the Tiltyard Gallery.

*Whitehall* by Thomas Sandby, *c.*1750, viewed from the Westminster side near Downing Street looking towards the Holbein Gate.

Dover House, now the Scotland Office. In 1812, known as Melbourne House, it became notorious during a brief but stormy public affair between Lady Caroline Lamb and Lord Byron, a frequent visitor.

Entrance hall to Dover House, a centre of Whig society in the early 1800s. 'Byron's Rope' – reputedly added to assist the club-footed Lord Byron up the steps – is on the left of the staircase.

A door of the room in the ground floor apartments used by the Duke of York and later by Lord and Lady Melbourne. These rooms were used as offices by John Prescott, the former Deputy Prime Minister, who chaired Cabinet committee meetings in the room through this door.

Lady Caroline Lamb's bedroom, now used as an office for a civil servant in the Scotland Office. One civil servant said she had heard the rustling of a dress while she was working here late at night . . .

The Changing of the Guard has been going on for three and a half centuries, the Guard first having been introduced by Charles I as his personal bodyguard.

The changing face of the Horse Guards: a black soldier on duty.

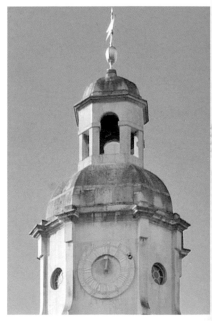

Detail showing the Horse Guards clock. The number blacked out was in memory of Charles I, who was beheaded nearby in Whitehall at 2 p.m.

Durbar Court in the Foreign Office. The India Office was designed by Matthew Digby Wyatt who had worked on Paddington Station and used Victorian engineering for the glass atrium roof in 1868 and sliding windows on runners resembling the wheels of steam engines.

The Secretary of State's room, India Office, has unique twin doors. They were reputedly designed by the architect, Wyatt, to allow two Indian princes of equal rank to enter the room at the same time.

Secretary of State's room, the Foreign Office, used by successive ministers from Lord Stanley to David Miliband.

The Cabinet Room, Number Ten Downing Street. The boat-shaped table was introduced by Harold Macmillan to enable him to keep an eye on his ministers.

The small figure of a thatcher was included in the gilded plasterwork above the door from the Terracotta Room to the Pillared Room in Downing Street as an homage to Margaret Thatcher by architect Quinlan Terry.

VE Day, 8 May 1945: Winston Churchill mingles with the jubilant crowds on Whitehall after delivering his victory address from the balcony of the Health Ministry (left). Two months later the people voted him out of office . . .

chilly November morning in 1948 wearing a black overcoat and homburg hat: 'I walked up the main steps of the War Office to be confronted by the tall frock-coated Head Porter in his gold-banded top hat. He looked down at me and I looked up at him; there could be no question which of us was the more impressive figure . . .'[12]

By the early 1950s, the monstrous MoD main building had risen in the middle of Whitehall to dominate the skyline and dwarf the Banqueting House. Pevsner described the ten-storey office block as a 'monument to tiredness'. There were some concessions to the historical importance of the site: five rooms from the houses the builders had demolished – Pembroke House, Cromwell House and Cadogan House – were dismantled and incorporated in the MoD building as conference rooms on the third and fourth floors. Queen Mary's steps were revealed and preserved for the public to see in the gardens on the Embankment outside the MoD. The most remarkable rescue, however, was hidden from public view. Wolsey's wine cellar was painstakingly moved on steel rollers and lowered, as described in Chapter One, into the bowels of the MoD building. In 1954, the north part of the building was ready for the Board of Trade and statues of Earth and Water by Sir Charles Wheeler were placed over the north door. These were meant to be complemented by similar figures to represent Air and Fire at the south door, but these were dropped when that end of the building was taken over by the Air Ministry in 1958–9. In 1964, the three armed services were merged into a unified Ministry of Defence, and the Board of Trade was forced to vacate the north end to make way for the arrival of defence chiefs and their civil servants from the War Office, Horse Guards, the Admiralty and their outlying offices around London. By the 1980s, the pre-First World War design for the building, with hundreds of small rooms creating a rabbit warren, was hopelessly out of date, and a major refurbishment programme was launched to make all the main floors open-plan. The private-finance deal cost

£2.3 billion over thirty years, and more than three miles of interior walls were demolished in the makeover. The defence chiefs, the Secretary of State for Defence, and the Minister of State for Defence are the only ones left with doors to their own offices in the MoD. Sir Jock Stirrup, the Chief of the Defence Staff, decorated his walls with pictures of battles: the Battle of Chillianwallah in the second Sikh War and the Battle of Gujarat in January and February 1849. The heavy losses and the incompetence of the British commanders at Chillianwallah horrified Victorian opinion back home, but the setback was soon expunged by victory over the Sikhs at Gujarat. Sir Jock told me they were a reminder of the need to learn from military mistakes. While the conduct of the 3rd King's Own Light Dragoons was held up as a paragon, some claim the slur on the courage of the other cavalry brigades may have sewn the seeds for the heroic disaster of the Charge of the Light Brigade in the Crimean War five years later.

Down below on the ground floor, in the echoing pillared entrance hall with its terrazzo marble walls, coffee bars were created for the defence civil servants, and the walls were hung with brightly coloured abstract murals that would not upset any visiting delegations who might be offended by pictures of British victories. In spite of the move to open-plan offices, around 3,500 oak doors were fitted at a cost of £1,200 each. There were also ergonomic chairs for the civil servants, which cost £1,000 each.

## Whitehall Beneath the Streets

More secret work went on during the refurbishment that was never declared in public. Hundreds of feet underground, the twin citadels that survived the Blitz were converted into a single deep bunker capable of withstanding a nuclear blast on London. It is from this top-secret nuclear bunker that the defence of the realm will be carried out in the immediate aftermath of a surprise attack on London. Rooms were allocated to Tony Blair, then Prime Minister, and his Director of Communications Alastair Campbell. Cherie Blair, the PM's wife, would have been allowed in, but in her memoirs Mrs Blair reveals that Downing Street staff were graded red, blue, green or orange, according to whether they were to be admitted to the bunker. 'Alastair was in the Red group, but Fiona (Millar, his partner) was in the Green group and I thought no way is Alastair going to come in with us and leave Fiona and his kids at home if there's a nuclear Armageddon.'[13] Under instructions from security officials, she took some of her children's clothes, games and books down to their quarters in the nuclear bunker, just in case, with Jackie, the children's nanny, but they both agreed it was so 'spooky' it would 'freak them out' and the children never got to visit their bunker. It is part of an extensive underground system that was constructed under the whole of Whitehall during the Second World War and upgraded during the Cold War. It has also spawned an industry on the internet about 'Secret Whitehall', and it is difficult to sift myth from reality. Fictional Cities, a website dedicated to exploring the underground secrets says:

There are several rumoured escape tunnels from Buckingham Palace. One is said to run under Green Park to the Piccadilly Tube line, giving the royals a speedy escape route to Heathrow. Another is said to give access to the Victoria Line – which runs under the Palace – for a similar escape, and one is said to lead to Wellington Barracks just over the road. More likely is the tunnel running along the Mall to the underground citadel called Q-Whitehall which is rumoured to stretch as far north as Holborn. Supposed evidence of this complex is the huge extractor fan outside the Gent's toilets in the ICA, which the ICA say is nothing to do with them, and the top-secret fortress on the corner of the Mall and Horse Guards Road which is said to be an entrance to Q-Whitehall. This complex also probably connects to 10 Downing Street via the atom-bomb-proof bunker which was built under the Ministry of Defence building at a cost over £110 million in the early 1990s.

Senior civil servants with secrets clearance have confirmed to me that much of this is right, and a major tunnel complex does exist. One tunnel runs from the creeper-clad fortress on Horse Guards Parade – known in Whitehall as HMS *St Vincent* – underneath the QE2 Centre by Westminster Abbey to another bunker underneath the former Department of Environment building, now the site of the new Home Office in Marsham Street.

Stephen Smith, author of *Underground London: Travels Beneath the City Streets,* told me: 'The Whitehall tunnel was built in the early years of the last war to provide a secure route for communications cables linking the various war rooms along Whitehall, notably the Central Cabinet War Room. It was later extended to the new Rotunda citadels in Monck Street. It originally carried only cables but I believe it was later enlarged to provide a safe way for people to move between the citadels. The tunnels were extended in the 1950s to provide access to the MoD main building and a telephone exchange under Horse Guards.'

I blundered across part of the network in the 1980s before the QE2 Centre was built, when surface parking was allowed for Westminster pass holders on the site. Approaching a lift on the lower level of the car park, I found a surprised uniformed guard, and noticed the lift went down several floors, not up. The Marsham Street bunker was originally two gasholders that were demolished in 1937, creating two conveniently large holes in the ground that were seen as the ideal base for a secret government bunker during the Second World War. Subterranean Britannica, a website with an extensive history of the bunker, says it was a wartime base for home security and also the air ministry intelligence department, but late in the war when London faced attack by Hitler's V-rockets; an underground retreat, codenamed 'Anson', was created there for the Prime Minister, his wife and senior officials with direct links by tunnel to Whitehall. Winston Churchill clearly feared that the Cabinet War Rooms, now open to the public, were not proof against Hitler's secret weapons.

An underground railway station at Down Street was allocated for Churchill and the Cabinet and they did hold some meetings there. The red-brick façade for the station still exists – part of it is a newsagent – and the bunker, which was used by the underground railway executive committee for meetings during the war, remains largely intact. But Churchill did not like the uncomfortable cramped conditions, which included twin baths and twin toilets. A diagram of 'Anson' at Marsham Street shows that the Prime Minister and his wife had the luxury of separate bedrooms, and there was a bedroom for Churchill's private valet. There were also rooms for Colonel Ives, the camp commandant; General Ismay; General Hollis; the Prime Minister's personal typist; Commander Thompson of the Metropolitan Police; and the typist pool; in addition to a Cabinet room, map room, a dining room and the PM's study. The only outward sign today are the telltale concrete air intakes but the existence of the bunker is the main reason why the building had to remain in government hands when the three towers of the former Department for the Environment above it were demolished and replaced by an ultramodern Home Office building. It is still covered by the Official Secrets Act but it is believed the tunnel network provides an escape route in times of crisis for the Prime Minister, Cabinet and senior officials to a regional bunker via the Tube network.

The Citadel at the corner of the Mall and Horse Guards Parade is without doubt the ugliest building in Whitehall and not even Virginia creeper can soften its brutalist appearance. It was built in 1940 and designed by W. A. Forsyth to survive a 1,000lb bomb. It resembles the viewing platform used by successive Soviet presidents at the Kremlin in Red Square above Lenin's Tomb, but houses a communications system. It is attached to the Admiralty headquarters – bristling with naval aerials on the roof – which, during the Thatcher Government in the 1980s, was used as the Northern Ireland Office. I was told the complex is now occupied by Foreign Office intelligence staff, and is on the restricted list, out of bounds even to journalists, but cranes over the Citadel in 2007 suggest that it is still being modernized.

There is still wild speculation about the tunnels under Whitehall. It is not true – as far as I can discover – that the Prime Minister could walk from Number Ten to the Commons for Prime Minister's questions through a secret underground network of tunnels. A network of tunnels does exist under the road through the heart of Whitehall, with branches to all the key Whitehall departments, but it was designed for communications, not ministers.

'The Prime Minister *could* walk underground along Whitehall, but he'd have to crouch,' one Whitehall official told me. 'They are not meant for walking around.' However, there is a secret tunnel from Downing Street under the bustle of Whitehall to the major bunker under the MoD main building. The MoD bunker, as deep underground as the ten floors above, is provisioned every month, with army-style bunks on which to sleep. Like Mrs Blair, the former Labour Defence Minister Peter Kilfoyle was also escorted deep down into the bunker as part of his ministerial duties by a senior officer of the armed services. They descended many metres beneath the remains of the Tudor palace where Wolsey first held court, and Henry VIII danced with Anne Boleyn.

'We went down a lift and then a flight of steps. We went along a corridor through huge blast doors into the Battle Room. It would be able to take a direct hit on London. I said, "I don't think I would want to be down here . . ." He was a bit taken aback. He said, "But, Minister, someone has to give the orders." I said, "To whom?" It was a little like *Dr Strangelove*.'[14]

There are persistent stories that an identical pub to the Red Lion – the Whitehall pub frequented by civil servants – but called the Rose and Crown, was re-created 120 feet beneath the Wiltshire countryside in a nuclear bunker that was to house the government and 4,000 civil servants in the event of the Third World War. It is true that the Churchill Government in the 1950s secretly ordered the building of a 35-acre nuclear bunker at a quarry near Corsham codenamed 'Burlington' and 'Turnstile'. It had wide streets and offices, a restaurant with industrial-sized kitchens, a bakery, a well-equipped hospital with dental surgeries, and a broadcasting studio for the BBC to broadcast emergency messages, survival advice for those left on the surface, and the last programmes that civilization would hear. The bunker was made obsolete by the development of more powerful intercontinental ballistic missiles and was declassified by the Thatcher Government. There are internet guides to the empty tunnels, which are big enough to drive down and resemble the set for the climax of a *James Bond* movie.

The *Daily Telegraph* reported in 1999:

Burlington, as the radiation-proof bunker near Corsham, Wilts, was known, was a replica of Whitehall with a 'Main Road' running through it and every ministerial department represented. There was even a version of the Red Lion, the Whitehall pub, but the name was changed to a more rural-sounding Rose and Crown.

John Doherty was one of the engineers who built the bunker 100ft beneath the ground in an old quarry. He said: 'You could just open the door of the pub and walk in off the pavement. It had a large front window. But how they were going to get the beer down there I didn't know.'

The bunker was designed to allow Britain to communicate with regional command bunkers around the country and the White House after a nuclear attack – it had a vast telephone exchange – and to enable leaders to control the country from the Prime Minister's map room where Prime Ministers from Harold Macmillan to Margaret Thatcher would be briefed continuously by MI5 and MI6. It was completed in 1961 just before the Berlin Wall was finished, prompting a Whitehall memo which said: 'In view of the international situation, the Treasury is pressing ahead as rapidly as possible with plans for occupation of Burlington.'

Journalist Duncan Campbell, who uncovered documents about the bunker, said: 'They were expecting a precautionary phase prior to nuclear attack which would have been expected to last around two weeks. Then there was "a destructive phase" lasting one to two days; a "survival phase" of a month and then a reconstruction phase of about a year.'

Sadly, there is no evidence today that the pub existed – there are no bright brass hand pumps on a bar, and red velvet seating – but rumours persist that for the select band of Whitehall mandarins the Red Lion/Rose and Crown was going to be the last pub in the universe.

# 12

## THE CABINET OFFICE
## AND THE TREASURY

'It is like the worst kind of municipal mayor's parlour.'
Ken Clarke on the former Chancellor's room at the
Treasury.

Sir George Downing was a brilliant bureaucrat despite his duplicity.
When he returned from The Hague, Downing brought with him
the secrets of financial control of the revenue that had made the
Dutch such a prosperous nation, and dangerous enemy.

King Charles II replaced the traditional role of Treasurer with
a commission and made Downing its Secretary. The Treasury
Commissioners moved from the Exchequer in Westminster to offices
in the King's Privy Gallery in the Palace of Whitehall before moving
again to the Cockpit Lodgings across the road, where they were to
stay for nearly 300 years.

Downing introduced a range of reforms including the centralization of tax collection – ending the system where taxes were collected by private agents – and the issuing of government bonds to raise money for the impoverished Crown, but the most important was the assertion of control over all other departments by the Treasury Commissioners. In June 1667 it was ordered 'that the several [i.e. departmental] treasurers ... do forebear making any payments without directions from the Commissioners of his Majesty's Treasury'. This principle – that even if money has already been voted by Parliament all expenditure must have specific Treasury approval – remains in force today.[1]

In 1703, the Cockpit offices were also the scene of the extraordinary and tense negotiations that led to the historic union (the Scottish Nationalists still say sell-out) between Scotland and England. Like the Downing Street talks that were to take place three centuries later to bring peace to Ireland, the two sides engaged in 'proximity' talks: two sets of commissioners sat in separate rooms at the Cockpit, refusing to meet face-to-face, and communicated their proposals to each other in writing. The English had one powerful weapon hanging over the Scots – trade. The Scots had lost a fortune in a wild adventure in New Caledonia, just south of Panama, where they had planned to create a colony called Darien and control a new trade route between the Pacific and the Atlantic. It was not as mad as it seems – later, the Panama Canal would make a fortune – but the investment of the Darien shareholders died with the settlers in the inhospitable Panama swamps. In Whitehall, the English commissioners led by William Cowper demanded that, in return for financial assistance, the Scots should accept the succession to the joint Kingdoms of Scotland and England by the House of Hanover when Queen Anne died. The Scots, led by Lord Seafield the Scottish Lord Chancellor, desperate for finance, agreed, but demanded a right to free trade, not only with the rest of the UK but also the plantations in North America and the West

Indies that were previously barred to them. The deal was done in three days, eased with a payment to the Scots of £398,085 to offset the compensation demands by the Darien shareholders. That was the price of Scottish independence.

British trade under Walpole was making the nation prosperous, but the Treasury offices in the Cockpit were in so 'ruinous and dangerous' state that in 1732 the Lords of the Treasury sanctioned the building of a new office on the site at a cost of £8,000. William Kent, a Yorkshireman famous now for stately houses and gardens, with the support of his patron Lord Burlington, won a commission to rebuild the Treasury on Whitehall.[2] The new Treasury was finished in 1736 at a cost of £20,000, twice the estimate. By the time it was ready for the civil servants, the tradition had been started for an annual Budget, a word derived from the term *bougette* – a wallet in which either documents or money could be kept. The boardroom in Kent's Treasury building overlooking the gardens at Downing Street is still in existence, behind the bland façade of the Cabinet Office at 70 Whitehall. It is reached by the same Cockpit Passage along which Henry had taken his courtiers to watch him play tennis.

The room where the Treasury Commissioners met is now known prosaically as Conference Room A. It contains an odd collection of furniture: a rich red and gilt throne made in 1739 for George I; over Kent's mantelpiece is a bust of Spencer Perceval, the only British Prime Minister to be assassinated – shot dead at the Commons by a businessman demented by debt and who thought the Government had a duty to help him; and, in the centre of the room, a rectangular table with a table within it. The inner table is decorated with carvings of the shamrock, the rose and the thistle to celebrate the union with Ireland in 1800. For a long time after the completion of the new Treasury office, Treasury letters still bore the address of the Cockpit, which had been demolished. In the 1820s, Sir John Soane was asked to create a new building for the Board of Trade

303

in front of the Treasury building on Whitehall – the site now occupied by the Cabinet Office and the Privy Council Office at the corner of Downing Street. He proposed a Palladian building, 82 feet long with heroic archways over both ends of Downing Street that were never built.

The ceremonial role of the Privy Council has hardly changed from the King's council in the Middle Ages. Its members still swear an oath of allegiance and promise to 'keep secret all matters committed and revealed unto you or that shall be treated of secretly in Council'. They alone have the right to the title 'Right Honourable' before their names. Politicians, such as the Leader of the Opposition, are given Privy Council membership so they can be briefed on 'Privy Council terms' on delicate issues of defence or foreign affairs. This is done to avoid disputes escalating in public that may involve information better kept secret. The entire council, now about 420 members, is rarely called together, except to proclaim a new monarch, or hear the monarch give consent to a royal marriage, but a handful of government ministers have a regular audience of the Queen, usually at Buckingham Palace, where by tradition they must remain standing. Privy Council business mainly involves approving 'orders in council', which has raised anxieties about it being used to circumvent full parliamentary scrutiny. Its judicial members also hear appeals against the death penalty from the former colonies, but that role is being taken over by the new Supreme Court of Justice.

In the basement of the Cabinet Offices is the suite of rooms, now known collectively as COBRA, the nerve centre at the heart of Government, where emergencies are handled by a small team of ministers and senior Whitehall civil servants augmented by intelligence, police or military officers as circumstances dictate. One civil servant who has worked there said: 'It is a bit like *Dr Strangelove*. There were maps of Britain, transparent, with back lighting. At the back are cubicles with ISDN lines to radio stations so they can broadcast directly from the room if necessary. Tables are in a square with a gap in the middle.' It is popularly believed that COBRA stands for Cabinet Office Briefing Room A. In fact, the acronym was COBR and the 'A' was added by a hassled press officer who wanted to answer queries about the name for the press. The correct title for the room is actually Cabinet Office Briefing Room F, but the government has allowed COBRA to stand. It sounds better in a crisis.

Soane was plagued by worries over his soaring estimates for the new Whitehall building, caused by changes to his brief, and his work was cut short. The new Board of Trade office, with a handsome portico supported by Corinthian columns, was completed in 1827 and became an important landmark in Whitehall, echoing Soane's other landmark building, the Bank of England. But critics complained that the old Tudor tennis court on Whitehall which Soane's building joined was unsightly and needed to go. In 1844 Sir Charles Barry, architect of the Victorian Gothic Houses of Parliament, was commissioned to finish the job Soane had started. Barry's Parliament building is exuberant but his brief for Soane's Board of Trade fell like a dead hand on his project – Soane's elegant pillared façade was dismantled and rebuilt. A faint shadow of its former glory can still be seen but the handsome portico was destroyed and the remaining pillars set back into the stone façade.

The reconstruction cost £44,976 18s 9d – way over budget – and caused a row with the Treasury which was later to occupy it. The biggest loss to posterity however was Henry's historic indoor tennis court, which was finally demolished. Some fragments were miraculously preserved inside the skin of the new building, including the northeast tower discussed in Chapter Two and one of the stone arched windows resembling those of a church, which once let light into the court below. It was preserved behind a protective Perspex screen, largely due to a report on the importance of these fragments in 1962 by Michael Green, former Inspector of Ancient Monuments.

Chancellors who occupied the Kent Treasury included the younger William Pitt, who introduced the new system of income tax in his Budget of December 1798 – a few months after Nelson destroyed the French fleet at Aboukir Bay – as a temporary measure to pay off the national debt from the war. It was introduced on a sliding scale from nought below an income of £60 to 10 per cent for incomes over £200 and was abolished after the war against the French, but was reintroduced by Peel and has been with us ever since. The Treasury expanded into the Whitehall block previously occupied by the Board of Trade, and stayed there through the return to the Gold Standard under Winston Churchill (Chancellor 1925–29), the battles with his leading critic John Maynard Keynes (whose theory of economic planning was adopted after the Second World War), the General Strike and the Depression, until bomb damage in the London Blitz in 1940 forced officials to decamp about 400 yards along Whitehall to the Government Offices Great George Street (GOGGS). On 14 October 1940 a high-explosive bomb landed in Treasury Green and caused blast damage throughout Downing Street. The Paymaster General's office in Whitehall, next to Horse Guards, was almost completely demolished by another bomb as Churchill was dining with friends in the garden room under the Cabinet Room in Number Ten. Sir John Martin, former Parliamentary Private Secretary to Churchill, recalled: 'the mess in the house was indescribable – windows smashed in all directions, everything covered with grime, doors off hinges, and curtains and furniture tossed about in a confused mess'. Another high-explosive bomb fell on the Treasury building in a raid on 17 October, exploding inside an air-raid shelter, wrecking fine Georgian rooms at the front of the block and displacing stone columns on the Whitehall façade. Kent's rooms were remarkably unscathed, but the Treasury had to move.

The construction of the GOGGS block at the turn of the nineteenth century at the end of Whitehall by Parliament Square wiped the last link with Henry VIII's Tudor palace from the map of London by finally erasing King Street, the thoroughfare that had lasted for over 500 years. Courtiers and civil servants who had lived in King Street included Lord Howard of Effingham, the High Admiral who fought against the Spanish Armada in spite of being a Catholic, Edmund Spenser, author of *The Faerie Queene*, who died penniless there, and Cromwell's aged mother. A drawing from the Victorian period shows King Street as a delightful muddle of Dickensian cottages, pubs and shop fronts, where the Old Curiosity Shop would not have been out of place. It all went in road widening to create the modern Parliament Street, and the only trace of King Street that remains is a small brass plaque on a balustrade of the building, now HM Revenue and Customs, in Great George Street.

The architect John Brydon came to London in 1866 to run the drawing office for Norman Shaw, the architect responsible for New Scotland Yard at Cannon Row, near the Commons, and had earned a reputation for public buildings after designing three London hospitals, Chelsea Town Hall and the Bath Pump Room extension. He also showed his versatility by designing a villa in St John's Wood for the French Impressionist painter James Tissot. But for the GOGGS building, started in 1898, he shamelessly plagiarized the drawings that Inigo Jones had produced for Charles I more than 250 years before. Copying a corner of Jones's grand design, Brydon created a classical building based on a rectangle encompassing a grand circle – like a double Bath crescent. Today it is known by Treasury civil servants as 'the drum' and marks the invisible demarcation line between the Revenue and Customs half of the building, with a front door at 100 Whitehall and the new Treasury with the door at the back, at 1 Horse Guards Road, giving the Treasury a new acronym, 1HGR. Horse-drawn carriages once used it, but the 'drum' is now the most elegant car park in Whitehall.

Brydon died before it was finished, but the completion of the building by a lesser talent, Henry Tanner, drafted in from the Office of Works, led to criticism of the building by the president of the Royal Institute of British Architects as 'poor' and Lord Robert Cecil as 'ugly'. Tanner used Mazzano marble from quarries at Brescia for the entrance hall and staircases in King Charles Street, Great George Street and Parliament Street, which also was paved in 'Irish Green' marble.[3] Miles of corridors and small rooms were plain and painted utilitarian light green. Tanner included one feature that was to prove valuable – a concrete frame for the basement in the second phase of the building on the St James's Park side which would prevent it collapsing if it was bombed. This was reinforced with a concrete skirt to deflect bombs, which can still be seen bulging out from the back wall of the building. That is why it was chosen for the Cabinet War Rooms, where Churchill secretly conducted the Second World War and which are now open to the public.

Other rooms in the GOGGS building were taken during the war by the Air Ministry, and the largest room on the first floor overlooking King Charles Street was commandeered by 'Bomber' Harris, the controversial head of Bomber Command responsible for carpet bombing in Germany who is now the subject of a debate over whether there should be a statue to his memory. The Department of Health was allocated the front of the building, including the large committee room with a balcony, which is today sometimes used as a cinema for civil servants. It was from this balcony overlooking the corner of Whitehall that Churchill made his VE Day address to the cheering crowds filling the street and Parliament Square. The Treasury, which moved in after the Blitz made Kent's Treasury offices uninhabitable, occupied the offices on the north side, overlooking King Charles Street, but the building suffered one serious structural problem – it was built over the River Tyburn and suffered from rising water in the basement. Kenneth Clarke, Chancellor of the Exchequer in the Major Government from 1993 to the election defeat in 1997, hated the Treasury building and the Chancellor's room, which is listed for preservation.

Bomber Harris's room on the first floor, overlooking King Charles Street, was used by all the Chancellors of the Exchequer from the war, including Labour's Hugh Dalton and Stafford Cripps to Clarke's luckless predecessor, Norman Lamont, who was sacked by Major in 1993, a year after 'Black Wednesday', along with his youthful special adviser David Cameron, later to become leader of the Conservative Party. After Labour came to power in 1997, Gordon Brown decamped to a small room towards the rear of the building.

Clarke told a Commons committee of inquiry in 2000: 'It is like the worst kind of municipal mayor's parlour.' He added: 'It is an awful building and it has water rising in the cellar. My flippant reaction when I was told the water was rising in the cellar and that, therefore, we needed tens of millions of pounds to rebuild it was that we would get round to that when the water reached my room.'

He complained the Victorian builders ran out of money and could not even finish the caryatids on one side. 'It is a poor imitation of that magnificent Foreign Office building next door,' said Clarke, who wanted to demolish the whole edifice and replace it with a building to enhance Parliament Square, but was told: 'English Heritage have listed everything.'

Clarke's plan was to pay for the rebuilding by leasing the front half of the Treasury to a hotel group. Had it worked, the current Chancellor would be sharing his building with American tourists, and the mandarins of Whitehall did not like the sound of that. The plan was stalled until the election, and Gordon Brown found the problem of the waterlogged Treasury high in his in-tray.

Brown arrived determined to focus on reforms, and he had no

time for capital spending on the Treasury building, but he had embraced a new financing concept of the private finance initiative (PFI) and he eventually decided that a lease-back deal would set an early example for the rest of Whitehall to follow in public-sector schemes with private finance, such as schools and hospitals. The contract was won by a consortium of builders called Exchequer Partnerships, who completely gutted the Treasury building and rebuilt the interior as a 50,000 square-metre open-plan modern office. Today Cripps would not recognize it. The Treasury has the feel of a rather upmarket hotel – like Clarke had envisaged but without the tourists. Beyond the reception desk, there is an inner courtyard with a calming ornamental pond, though it is not the Tyburn seeping up. The problem with the river still exists but it is handled by pumps in the basement. A corridor runs around the whole building, which used to delineate the Treasury with red lino. The red lino has been replaced by more subtle colours but there is now an invisible dividing line between the Treasury at the back and HM Revenue and Customs at the front in Whitehall. Brown used the Chancellor's room when he first arrived in 1997, but, after the Treasury was modernized, moved out of Clarke's hated oak-panelled 'mayor's parlour' with its own washroom to a modest office at the back of the building.

'Gordon took the smallest office on the corridor. That is what he is like,' said one of his Treasury colleagues. His successor, Alistair Darling, took a slightly bigger room overlooking the park.

A ground-floor room at the Treasury overlooking St James's Park is also used at 11 a.m. most weekdays for briefings of parliamentary lobby journalists by Number Ten officials on the Prime Minister's day and to make announcements which set the midday bulletins.

The Red Lion pub that stands opposite HM Revenue and Customs in Whitehall became notorious with lobby journalists during the Blair period of office as the 'Treasury Annexe', because it was frequented by Treasury civil servants after work. A brewhouse called the Red Lion had stood near its present site at 48 Parliament Street for over 600 years and a plaque at the side of the pub claims it dates from 1435, although the existing Victorian pub dates from around 1897.

The Red Lion became briefly famous, however, when Charlie Whelan was Gordon Brown's 'spin doctor' at the Treasury and was overheard by two Liberal Democrat press officers in the bar shouting into his mobile phone to a BBC *Newsnight* reporter that *The Times* first editions would be reporting Gordon Brown was going to rule out Britain's entry into the euro for a Parliament. This was sensational, market-moving news, and it caused the first big controversy of the Blair Government. It was seen as a deliberate attempt by Brown to bounce Blair, who wanted the option kept open. Alastair Campbell insisted in his diaries, *The Blair Years*, that it was more Whitehall 'cock-up' than conspiracy:

> I suddenly realised that because I had not really checked and double-checked with TB [Tony Blair], we had briefed an enormous story on the basis of a cock-up . . . TB asked if we had ruled out EMU [economic and monetary union] this Parliament. Yes, said Charlie. 'Is that not what you want?' 'No, it is not,' said TB.

Campbell decided in the aftermath to put the regular morning lobby briefings at 11 a.m. each day on the record to counter any further off-the-record briefings from the Treasury 'Annexe' by Whelan. One senior Whitehall official told me: 'Alastair had had talks with Richard Wilson [Cabinet Secretary]. He persuaded Blair Charlie could not go on the record, so he [Campbell] should.'

He added: 'We used to go to the Red Lion after our "prayer meetings" at Number Ten [strategy meetings with Campbell] but Charlie had turned it into his front office. It was put pretty much out of bounds after the Whelan affair.'

# SCOTLAND YARD

I'm not a butcher
I'm not a Yid
Nor yet a foreign skipper
But I'm your own light-hearted friend
Yours truly, Jack the Ripper.
                                    Anonymous

In early 1887, a careworn police officer joined the overworked detectives in the small office at A Division at Great Scotland Yard. Detective Frederick George Abberline, forty-four, had been promoted as Inspector First Class from H Division covering Whitechapel to the Whitehall office. For him it was a considerable step up from life in the East End, tracking the low-life criminals in the murky, teeming warrens around Whitechapel. The Scotland Yard office was just off Whitehall, around the corner from the Clarence public house, and for the past three years a special team of detectives in

A Division, known as the dynamite branch, had been trying to apprehend a group of Irish-American bombers who had been responsible for a string of bomb outrages, including one outside their office. It had caused only external damage but a well-known archway over the street had to be demolished, the remains of which may be seen today high up on the side of the pub. The bombers had left the device as an audacious calling card for the team who were trying to track them down.

Even today's Special Branch in the Metropolitan Police would have been stretched by the bombing campaign for Home Rule in Ireland. In all twenty-one bombs had been exploded in the capital, including by the side of the Home Office in Great Charles Street and even at the foot of Nelson's monument on Trafalgar Square, to spread terror and attack the symbols of the British establishment.[1] The need to apprehend the bombers was heightened by a growing fear of anarchists from Eastern Europe planting bombs in the city.

But the public panic caused by the fears of terrorism was overshadowed by a string of brutal murders in Whitechapel that were to traumatize Victorian society and dog Abberline for the rest of his days. All the victims appeared to be prostitutes but the murders were unusually bestial and when a letter was received in a news agency from someone claiming to be the killer, signed 'Jack the Ripper', they fired the public imagination. The first to die was Mary Ann (Polly) Nichols, murdered on Friday 31 August 1888. Annie Chapman was murdered on Saturday 8 September, followed by Elizabeth Stride, murdered on Sunday 30 September, Catharine (Kate) Eddowes, also murdered the same day, and Mary Jane (Marie Jeanette) Kelly, murdered on Friday 9 November.[2]

Inspector Fred Abberline was about five feet nine inches tall with dark-brown hair, hazel eyes and the obligatory soup-strainer moustache. His colleagues said he had the air of a bank manager with an eye for detail. He was born in Dorset but had grown to know the alleyways of Whitechapel like the veins on his hand, and because of his local expertise he was put in charge of the Scotland Yard investigation into the murders. The killings became a national obsession after an anonymous letter, written in red ink to imitate blood, was sent by the 'murderer' to the Central News Agency. Addressed 'Dear Boss', and dated 25 September 1888, the letter, now in the Public Record Office at Kew, was the first to be signed Jack the Ripper and taunted Abberline.

I keep hearing the police have caught me but they wont fix me just yet. I have laughed when they look so clever and talk about being on the right track. That joke about Leather Apron gave me real fits. I am down on whores and shant quit ripping them till I do get buckled. Grand work the last job was. I gave the lady no time to squeal. How can they catch me now. I love my work and want to start again. You will soon hear of me with my funny little games. I saved some of the proper red stuff in a ginger beer bottle over the last job to write with but it went thick like glue and I cant use it. Red ink is fit enough I hope ha ha. The next job I do I shall clip the ladys ears off and send to the police officers just for jolly wouldn't you. Keep this letter back till I do a bit more work then give it out straight. My knife's too nice and sharp I want to get to work right away if I get a chance. Good Luck. Yours truly. Jack the Ripper. Don't mind me giving the trade name Wasnt good enough to post this before I got all the red ink off my hands curse it No luck yet. They say I'm a doctor now. ha ha.

A few days later a postcard smeared with blood and written apparently in the same handwriting arrived at the news agency referring to a double murder the night before. Hoax letters were also sent to Scotland Yard. One said, 'I'm not a butcher, I'm not a Yid, nor yet a foreign skipper. But I'm your own light-hearted friend, yours truly, Jack the Ripper.' One letter, believed to be genuine, was posted on 16 October (with part of a kidney, which it claimed to be from Kate Eddowes) to George Lusk, the head of a vigilante committee in Mile End.

Abberline, later played in films by Michael Caine and Johnny Depp, never caught 'Jack' but fuelled the conspiracy theories that abound about the killings after he retired, stoking speculation that it could have been a surgeon acting for Prince Albert Victor (later the Duke of Clarence), the grandson of Queen Victoria and second in line to the throne at the time. One theory is that the wayward 'Eddy', as he was known, who had been in the habit of visiting the prostitutes in Cleveland Street in the East End, had fallen in love with the 25-year-old Mary Kelly, a beautiful Irish woman, and she had to be silenced by her murder to stop the scandal getting out. The other killings, it is claimed, were carried out to conceal the motive. It is also claimed that Abberline was prevented from revealing the identity of the killer by an Establishment cover-up. Abberline fuelled the rumours of a cover-up after he retired to the relative tranquillity of Bournemouth in his native Dorset. He left the Met in 1892 and joined the private American detective agency, Pinkerton's, as the head of its European office, but in retirement is said to have told the writer Nigel Morland: 'You'd have to look for him, not at the bottom of London society at the time but a long way up.' But if Abberline did know the secret of the Ripper murders, he took it to the grave. He died at 195 Holdenhurst Road, in Bournemouth, in 1929 at the age of eighty-six.

Other experts in Ripper theories say at other times Abberline suggested that George Chapman, a barber in the cellar of a Whitechapel pub, was the killer and Abberline's remarks have to be viewed with considerable scepticism. On 29 September 2001, Deputy Assistant Commissioner John Grieve of the Metropolitan Police unveiled a blue plaque to Frederick Abberline on the front of the house where he died. It was during a Ripper conference in the town, which underlines the lasting fascination with the Ripper and Scotland Yard's most famous unsolved case.

After the Ripper murders, the name 'Scotland Yard' stuck to the Metropolitan Police, particularly its detective branch, wherever it moved. It took its name from the yard at Whitehall that had been known as 'Scotlande' for over a thousand years. A Tudor chronicler in 1548, Nicholas Bodrugan, referred to the Saxon King Edgar, King of England from 959 to 975, asking King Kenneth II of Scotland

... once every yere to repaire unto him into England for the making of laws ... to which end this Edgar gave him a piece of grounde upon whiche this Keneth builded a house ... ye house is decaied but the grounde where it stode is called Scotlande to this day.

The area that was nominally Scotland stretched from Horse Guards Avenue north to roughly where the Clarence public house stands today and east to the old line of the Thames. A map by John Agas in 1550 clearly shows Scotland Yard as part of the Palace of Whitehall. Some land known as 'Scotlande' had been incorporated thirty years earlier by Wolsey with the expansion of York Place and again by Henry VIII for the enlargement of his palace. Henry's eldest sister, Margaret Tudor, was the last of the Scottish royalty to live at Edgar's house in Scotland Yard. She arrived in 1516 when she sought refuge in England after being deposed as regent of Scotland. Wolsey arranged for her to live in the old lodgings traditionally given to the kings of Scotland until her return to Scotland after a peace brokered by him a year later. By the reign of Elizabeth, the ancient Scottish house at Whitehall had been allowed to fall into ruin. There was an important wharf and dock in Scotland Yard, which stood approximately where Northumberland Avenue and Whitehall Place meet today by the former Metropole Hotel. The wharf was used to supply the palace with coal, wood and other goods and the yards were to carry on their role for 500 years, eventually becoming the Ministry for Works in 1851. Scotland Yard was quickly established under Henry as an area for offices of state. It was split into three courtyards, surrounded by modest houses in the Tudor style for servants employed in the palace, and there was a public right of way from Whitehall to the wharf through a gateway on the thoroughfare near where Great Scotland Yard stands today.

A plan of Whitehall in 1670 shows Scotland Yard contained the Yeomen of the Scullerys, the Cofferers Office, the King's Lock Smith, the Fish Larder, the King's Herb House, the Coach House and Stables, the Scalding House, the Confectionery, the Poulterers Office, and the small beer buttery overlooking the river. But the most important lodgings and offices in Scotland Yard overlooked Whitehall and were occupied by the King's Surveyor, Inigo Jones, and his successors Sir John Denham and Sir Christopher Wren. Sir John Vanbrugh occupied the offices when he was the King's Comptroller of Works and his much-ridiculed 'goose pie' house was also built near this site. The three courtyards, which were occupied like mews properties attached to the court, developed separately as Great, Middle and Lower Scotland Yard. A clock house, which stood where Great Scotland Yard is now, was used to regulate the work of the small workshops in the yards. It was demolished in 1812 to make way for the Marshalsea Court, the debtors' court, when the court was moved from the City. Charles Dickens's father John was sent from the court to the Marshalsea debtors' prison at Southwark in 1824 like Micawber in *David Copperfield*. The court in Whitehall was abolished in 1849 and its offices were taken over by the Metropolitan Police.

The first recognizable police force was created in the 1750s by Henry Fielding, magistrate and author of the bawdy satirical novel

*Tom Jones*, with his blind brother John, also a magistrate, from their headquarters in Bow Street. They were actually more like early detectives who dashed to the scene of a crime, and became known as the Bow Street Runners.

The Marine Police for the Thames were officially the first police force to be created, in 1798, but the mob riots surrounding the funeral of Queen Caroline, felt by the public to have been wronged by the Establishment like Princess Diana in our age, led to Parliament looking seriously at the need for a uniformed force, other than the army, to tackle civil unrest. Robert Peel had attempted to introduce a civil police force in Ireland, known as the Peelers, in 1814[3] and he tried to do the same on the mainland but encountered opposition from campaigners who said a police force would infringe the civil liberties of Englishmen. It was not until 1828, when Peel was again the Home Secretary, that he made progress through another parliamentary committee to create a police force for London. Wearing blue tailcoats and top hats, the first thousand of Robert Peel's new police began their inaugural patrol on the evening of 29 September 1829 from their new police office at 4 Whitehall Place.[4] Their blue tunics drew all sorts of name-calling from the public, including the 'raw lobster gang', but the names that stuck included 'peeler' and 'bobby'.

Whitehall Place became the home of A Division of the Metropolitan Police and it also took over responsibility for issuing cab licences, a practice that could be traced back to the issuing of a licence to operate sedan chairs in London in 1626. Nothing is left of the Victorian CID office where Abberline hunted the Ripper. The offices were demolished to make way for the building of the former Ministry of Agriculture, Fisheries and Food on Whitehall, though one building has survived. A small Georgian house, No. 1 Great Scotland Yard behind the Clarence public house, and now a solicitor's office, stands in splendid isolation, dwarfed by the taller buildings around it. In Abberline's day it was used as a store for prisoners' possessions that had been seized by the police as part of their detective work. The store was the forerunner of the so-called 'Black Museum' of crime, now held in two rooms on the first floor of New Scotland Yard, the Metropolitan Police Headquarters off Victoria Street, Westminster. Capturing the atmosphere of the early store, one room contains an extensive collection of weapons used in Victorian crimes, in addition to the death masks of prisoners hanged at Newgate Prison. A second room contains items connected to royalty, bank robberies, espionage, sieges and a number of notorious twentieth-century murder cases including John Christie, Dr Crippen, Dennis Nilsen, and the last woman to be hanged, Ruth Ellis. Today the Met is very coy about its 'Black Museum', afraid that its contents will be used to sensationalize crime, and it is closed to the public, but it is used for lectures, and to chill the blood of visiting VIPs.

Scotland Yard, as the Met had become popularly known, moved in 1890 from its cramped premises to a new purpose-built office block by the architect Norman Shaw just off Parliament Street, with a famous entrance which can be seen down the side of the Red Lion pub. It was to have been the site of a new opera house, between Cannon Row and the Embankment, to eclipse the Albert Hall, Covent Garden and La Scala, Milan, but the foundations cost a fortune because of flooding, and it was never completed. The Norman Shaw building was made from granite hewn from a quarry on Dartmoor by prisoners, and for the next century it was to become famous as New Scotland Yard. The entrance, with a distinctive two-tone archway, was featured in the 1950s cult television series *Saber of London*, with 'fast' Jaguar saloon cars from the 'flying squad' roaring out of the gates with their bells ringing in pursuit of villains. It has a more sedate role now, as a side entrance to Parliament. The Norman Shaw buildings once occupied by detectives are used as private offices for MPs, with a walkway into the new atrium extension to Parliament, Portcullis House. The MPs also have a gym in the basement and there is a subterranean route under Bridge Street to the Commons. The Met and its detective branch moved to its present modern office block in 1967 but the name on the revolving sign still says New Scotland Yard, although the Metropolitan Police Headquarters is actually in Broadway.

The offices of A Division were replaced in 1911 by a new recruiting office for the War Office – three years before Kitchener made his personal appeal – but Victorian stables of the mounted branch of the Metropolitan Police are still in use. An unusual feature is that the stables are on the first floor. The horses have to be led up a steep ramp to their stalls and get light from small windows. Next door is the former fire station, and if you stand back in the link road to Whitehall Place you will see a Victorian tower standing incongruously against the modern London skyline, which was used by lookouts before the advent of the telephone. The fire station was opened in 1880, when the fire engines were drawn by horses, and closed in 1922. During the Second World War it was requisitioned as an intelligence and interrogation centre.

## Spies

Whitehall Court, around the corner from Whitehall Place, was home to the first modern British spies – continuing a tradition that goes back to Queen Elizabeth's spymaster at the Palace of Whitehall, Sir Francis Walsingham.

Architects' drawings I have seen in the MoD archive show that a rear entrance to the War Office in Whitehall Court – kept separate from the rest of the War Office building – was reserved for the secret intelligence officers. The government had created the posts of Director of Military Intelligence and Director of Naval Intelligence at the War Office in 1887 to gather information on foreign military strength, but the post of DMI was abolished in 1904 and counter-espionage was handed to the War Office's Military Operations Directorate. A Cabinet Committee of Imperial Defence (CID) chaired by the Prime Minister and including the Chiefs of Defence Staff was created to oversee strategy and policy. It ordered a review of intelligence measures to counter the growing threat of German spies and espionage, and in 1909 Sir Charles Ottley, Secretary to the CID, recommended that a Secret Service Bureau in Whitehall should be set up. It was actively supported by Richard Haldane, Secretary of State for War at the War Office. Commander Mansfield Smith-Cumming, a fifty-year-old Royal Navy officer, was put in charge of the foreign section (later to become the Secret Intelligence Service, MI6)[5] and Captain Vernon Kell took command of the home section (later to become the Security Service, MI5).[6]

Cumming moved into an office in the War Office and rented flat 54 at No. 2 Whitehall Court – the block of flats conveniently at the rear of the War Office. Cumming, who became known as 'C' because he always signed his memos with his initial in green ink, had only a short walk across the road to his secret place of work. The central tower where he had his flat is now part of the Royal Horseguards Hotel and let to tourists, who stay there without realizing they are staying in the room once occupied by the true boss of the first real James Bond. Cumming later expanded his domain into more flats at Whitehall Court, writing in his diary on 23 May 1916, 'moved to a new office'. You can spy on C's eyrie if you stand at the corner near the statue of five soldiers, a memorial to the tank crews of the Second World War, and look up at the roofline. There is nothing to mark it out as a spy headquarters, however. The only plaque on the wall of Whitehall Court displays a portcullis and the letters 'SMW'. This is the parish boundary sign of St Margaret's, Westminster – its mate is painted on the underside of the arch at Horse Guards – and it marked the point where it joined the parish of St Martin-in-the-Fields after Henry VIII's seizure of Whitehall from Wolsey.

In a Dimbleby lecture in 2004, Dame Stella Rimington, then Director General of MI5, said, 'Spy fiction from Kipling's *Kim* through John Buchan to John Le Carré . . . has led to the creation of many myths – and some lurid speculation – about our work.' In fact, John Buchan, the first Baron Tweedsmuir, a Scottish Unionist MP and author of the enduring spy novel *The 39 Steps*, the film version of which climaxes in the clock tower of Big Ben, worked for MI5. In 1916, a year after the publication of his novel, his tenth book, he joined the Army Intelligence Corps and wrote speeches for Sir Douglas Haig before becoming Director of Information – a propaganda role – under Lord Beaverbrook. In the run-up to the Second World War, he is believed to have worked once more for the Security Service in press liaison dealing with disseminating information to journalists, but died after a stroke in 1940.

In January 1917 codebreakers in room 40 in the Admiralty building deciphered an intercepted message that helped change the course of the First World War. The note, from the Kaiser's Foreign Minister Arthur Zimmermann to the German Ambassador in Mexico, contained a promise to help Mexico 'to regain by conquest her lost territory in Texas, Arizona and New Mexico'. It was passed to the US President Woodrow Wilson and two months later the Americans entered the war.

Whitehall Court remained the MI6 headquarters until the end of the First World War. But when it expanded again, MI6 moved out of Whitehall into secret offices around London, including Broadway near St James's Park Tube station, eventually settling in the offices at Vauxhall Cross, the flesh-coloured building south of the River Thames which resembles a cheap hotel. MI5 later moved to Thames House, Millbank, where it remains today. In the fashion for openness under the Blair Government, MI5 has lifted the cloak, and according to its own website has thrown away the dagger. It says it is a myth that it carries out assassinations: 'It is claimed from time to time that we have been responsible for murdering individuals who have become "inconvenient" in some way. We do not kill people or arrange their assassination. We are subject to the rule of law in just the same way as other public bodies.'

# 14

# WINSTON AND WHITEHALL

'The hour has come; kill the Hun.'
Churchill's message to the nation in the event of
invasion, but never broadcast

On the evening of 20 May 1940, as the blackout curtains were going up, Winston Churchill turned the War Cabinet to the last item on its worrying agenda – the defence of Whitehall itself.

Ten days earlier, Hitler had launched the invasion of Belgium, Holland and France, using Panzer tanks to spearhead his new style of land war, blitzkrieg (lightning war). On the same day that Hitler's forces smashed across the borders in a huge sweeping move to circumvent the French Maginot Line, Churchill achieved his lifetime ambition to become Prime Minister. Churchill later wrote: 'I felt as though I were walking with destiny and all my past life had been but a preparation for this hour and these trials.' But his conviction about his 'destiny' was not shared by others. Although the policy of appeasement towards Hitler followed by his predecessor Neville Chamberlain had patently failed, there were still many adherents, and some in Churchill's coalition war Cabinet, such as Lord Halifax the Foreign Secretary – while admiring his courage – still had grave doubts about Churchill's judgement and his conviction that Britain could defeat Hitler.[1]

The night before, at 9 p.m. on Sunday 19 May, Churchill had made his first broadcast on BBC radio to the nation as Prime Minister from Whitehall. It was intended as a call to arms at the hour of Britain's greatest peril, but it was so stark that it risked spreading panic among those grimly listening to the Home Service on their Bakelite wireless sets at home that night.

> I speak to you for the first time as Prime Minister in a solemn hour for the life of our country, of our Empire, of our Allies, and above all of the cause of Freedom.
>
> A tremendous battle is raging in France and Flanders. The Germans, by a remarkable combination of air bombing and heavily armoured tanks, have broken through the French defences north of the Maginot Line, and strong columns of their armoured vehicles are ravaging the open country, which for the first day or two was without defenders . . .

He told the British people he was convinced that the French would stand firm with Britain, casting the long shadow of their history aside to defend democracy and freedom across Europe.

> This is one of the most awe-striking periods in the long history of France and Britain. It is also beyond doubt the most sublime. Side by side, unaided except by their kith and kin in the great Dominions and by the wide Empires which rest beneath their shield – side by side, the British and French peoples have advanced to rescue not

only Europe but mankind from the foulest and most soul-destroying tyranny which has ever darkened and stained the pages of history.

Behind them – behind us – behind the Armies and Fleets of Britain and France – gather a group of shattered States and bludgeoned races the Czechs, the Poles, the Norwegians, the Danes, the Dutch, the Belgians – upon all of whom the long night of barbarism will descend, unbroken even by a start of hope, unless we conquer, as conquer we must; as conquer we will.

However, in spite of Churchill's optimism, there were fears inside the War Cabinet that the French would capitulate, leaving the British Expeditionary Force (the BEF) exposed to the encircling might of Hitler's Panzer divisions. In a conclusion that must have left his listeners in little doubt that an invasion was imminent, Churchill called on everyone to do their best when the time came to defend these islands:

Today is Trinity Sunday. Centuries ago, words were written to be a call and a spur to the faithful servants of Truth and Justice. 'Arm yourselves, and be ye men of valour – and be in readiness for the conflict, for it is better for us to perish in battle than to look upon the outrage of our nation and our altar. As the Will of God is in Heaven, even so let it be.'

John Colville, recorded in his diary for that day that it was 'not Winston at his best, not quite the clarion call I had expected'.[2]

Some British intellectuals such as Evelyn Waugh and Malcolm Muggeridge despised Churchill's rhetoric.[3] Historian Kenneth Clark wrote in *Another Part of the Wood:* 'When he writes in a Gibbonian manner, I do not admire his prose.' Today, with the comfort of hindsight, Churchill's wartime speeches promising to 'fight them on the beaches' may seem like windy hyperbole, but he was deadly serious, as the Cabinet was about to learn. War planning for the invasion included a paper written by General Sir Ronald Weeks of the War Office, later to become chairman of Vickers and the English Steel Corporation, laying out tactics from the German point of view. Churchill had prepared a script to be broadcast to the nation in the event of an invasion taking place and Colville read it out at a dinner hosted by Churchill at Chequers on 25 January 1941. Colville wrote in his diary that the high-blown language 'caused much amusement' and Churchill said he would produce a far better one if an invasion happened. Churchill said if he did have to make such a broadcast, he would end it: 'The hour has come; kill the Hun.'

The Blitz on London had not yet started but when Churchill was taken down the steps for the first time to be shown the secret bunker containing the Cabinet War Rooms, under tons of reinforced concrete beneath what is now the Treasury building in Horse Guards Road, one of his aides noted: 'Mr Churchill took his cigar out of his mouth and pointed to the homely wooden chair at the head of the table. "This is the room from which I'll direct the war," he said slowly. "And if the invasion takes place, that's where I will sit, in that chair and I'll sit there until either the Germans are driven back or they carry me out dead".'[4]

Churchill's bodyguard Walter Thompson confirmed that Churchill intended to go down fighting, if necessary. 'He himself intended that he would never be taken alive,' Thompson later recalled. 'He issued direct instructions to me – I was to have his 45 Colt fully loaded. He intended to use every bullet but one on the enemy. The last one he saved for himself.'[5] Churchill's grandson Nicholas Soames, a Conservative MP, in an interview in 2008 told me: 'I am absolutely clear my grandfather would have stayed until the very, very end and would have died fighting. I am not in any doubt about that whatever. He would have died with a gun in his hand.'

Terry Charman, a Churchill expert at the Imperial War Museum, confirmed that view, telling me:

He was serious. He would have handed on the government to somebody else. They would have gone to Canada or the West Indies to carry on resistance. But I think he himself wouldn't have done. He suggested to the French that they should turn Paris into a fortress, which the French refused to do. He makes that point that London could absorb an invading army. His philosophy was always, 'You can take one with you.' I think he himself would have fought to the last.[6]

Mr Charman added:

He would have seen it as ignominious to go to the West Indies or Canada. I suppose in a way if the Germans had been successful, he would have wanted to go. There was almost a death wish in 1945 when everything was signed, sealed and delivered and he was visiting the troops on the Rhine and he came under sniper fire. He showed no concern. Somebody said, 'It's strange – Roosevelt died of a stroke a month later – perhaps Winston should have gone too.' I am sure the scenario in his mind was that he would die manning a Bren gun.

Cabinet papers I have obtained from the national archives and reproduced here in full for the first time show that Churchill planned his last stand to be in Whitehall, on ground steeped in a thousand years of British history, where Edward the Confessor had been crowned, where Elizabeth I had celebrated victory over the Spanish, where Nelson's body had lain in state after Trafalgar, and Wellington had paraded after his victory over Napoleon at Waterloo. To someone with Churchill's historical compass, it was no doubt a source of inner strength to know he was preparing his own last stand on such hallowed ground. In May that year, as German forces reached the coast and Hitler stood watching the white cliffs of Dover through binoculars, Churchill prepared a defensive plan that would turn Whitehall, and its ministries, into an inner fortress. And when the outer walls were breached, he was prepared for street fighting, office by office, room by room, until they found him, in his bunker, with his gun.

He was convinced that, long before a mass invasion by German forces, German Kommando would land by parachute close to Whitehall, possibly in St James's or Hyde Park, or Parliament Square, and try to kill or capture him. Hitler believed that Churchill was out of touch with his own people and his own ministers, raising the prospect of an attempted *coup de grâce*. Churchill appears at No. 49 in the 'Special Wanted List' hurriedly drawn up by SS General Walter Schellenberg, the Nazi intelligence chief, for the Gestapo Invasion Plan of Britain in May 1940.[7] But it was arranged strictly in alphabetical order and there is little doubt that Hitler saw Churchill as the prize whose capture could bring about the collapse of resistance in Britain. Professor Dr Frank Six was put in charge of SS arrest operations in Britain with a headquarters in London to be carried out by six Action Commandos in London, Bristol, Birmingham, Liverpool, Manchester and Edinburgh. He was later sentenced to twenty years in prison at Nuremberg but was released after four years in 1952. Schellenberg's list helpfully gave Churchill's private address at Chartwell Manor, Westerham, Kent, where he could be picked up. Others on the list included Chamberlain, who had put such faith in Herr Hitler's promises of nonaggression; Lord Beaverbrook, owner of the Express group and a minister for aircraft production in the War Cabinet; Churchill's ally Duff Cooper; and journalists who had criticized Hitler, including Vernon Bartlett of the *News Chronicle*, Claud Cockburn and Sefton Delmer of the *Daily Express*, and the cartoonist David Low, '*Karikaturist des Evening Standart*'. Writers who were to be rounded up by the Gestapo included H. G. Wells, Virginia Woolf, Vera Brittain, E. M. Forster, Aldous Huxley, J. B. Priestley, C. P. Snow, Stephen Spender, Noel Coward and Rebecca West. It is likely most would have been shot had Hitler gone ahead with his invasion plan, codenamed Sea Lion. When the list was published after the war, Rebecca West sent Noel Coward a telegram joking: 'My dear – the people we should have been seen dead with.'[8]

After taking office Churchill had issued an instruction that, for one month, he was to remain living in his ministerial apartment at Admiralty House and the Chamberlains would stay at Downing Street, where they lived in the private first-floor apartments. As a result, Churchill convened his first regular War Cabinets in the former library at the Admiralty. It had been hurriedly turned into a map room when he was first reappointed as First Lord of the Admiralty at the start of the war in September 1939 so that he could closely monitor the U-boat threat.[9] Today the one-time map room has been changed back into a living room at Admiralty House in the first-floor flat overlooking Horse Guards, formerly occupied by Margaret Beckett and later used by Lord Falconer. It had been vacated when I visited the flat where Churchill plotted the submarine war.

Churchill had called a late-night meeting of his War Cabinet to his apartment at Admiralty House after his broadcast on 19 May, including Lord Beaverbrook (Minister for Aircraft Production), Anthony Eden (Secretary of State for War) and the Chiefs of the Defence Staff. Churchill was businesslike but even he could not conceal the doubts that Britain could survive the storm when it broke, and Churchill was not the only one to take a 'Gibbonian' view of the peril the nation faced that night. Returning from the meeting, General Edmund Ironside, Commander-in-Chief of the Home Forces, confided in Eden as he mounted 'the ugly staircase of the War Office' to his room: 'This is the end of the British Empire.'[10] The Cabinet had agreed Churchill should make an urgent appeal to the US President, Roosevelt, for twenty-four fighter aircraft to help repel the invasion force, but they may have been surprised how frank he was with the President about the divisions in his Cabinet over the future strategy for the conduct of the war. Colville recorded in his diary:

> The PM sent a telegram to Roosevelt asking for fighter aircraft and implying that without them we should be in a parlous state, even though this country would never give up the struggle . . . I was somewhat taken aback when he said to me, 'Here's a telegram for those bloody Yankees. Send it off tonight'. I duly sent it to Herschel Johnson at the American Embassy and was somewhat annoyed to be woken up at 2.30 am and told that the PM wanted it back to review what he had said . . .

It was not surprising that Churchill lost sleep mulling over his message to the President because it contained a terrible warning to Roosevelt that if he prevaricated, and Britain was beaten, it would damage America's interests. Signing himself 'Former Naval Person', as his did throughout the war in his messages to the President, Churchill had bluntly warned Roosevelt that, although he would never give up without a fight, there were others in his Cabinet who would sue for peace if Britain was defeated by Hitler, and they would use the formidable British fleet as a bargaining counter. Nazi Germany would then become the greatest naval power in the world, threatening even the US trade routes. 'Excuse me, Mr President, putting this nightmare bluntly. Evidently, I could not answer for my successors, who in utter despair and helplessness might well have to accommodate themselves to the German will.'

To survive, Churchill knew that he must be able to repel any lightning strike on Whitehall by German Special Forces, and in one of his first orders after taking office had asked his chief of staff,

Major General Hastings Ismay, to give him a memorandum on the plans for its defence. On 18 May 1940, Ismay sent the plans with a covering memo to Churchill's Principal Private Secretary, Eric Seal: 'The Prime Minister may wish to see the attached paper which shows the arrangements which have been made in accordance with his instructions to safeguard the Whitehall area. A rough sketch map is placed below.'

In his personal diary, Ismay recorded he had walked with Churchill from Downing Street to the Admiralty shortly after Churchill became Prime Minister and there had been a number of people waiting outside the private entrance to greet him. They shouted, 'Good luck, Winnie. God bless you.'

Ismay noted: 'He was visibly moved, and as soon as we were inside the building, he dissolved into tears. "Poor people," he said, "poor people. They trust me, and I can give them nothing but disaster for quite a long time."'

On 20 May, Churchill initialled 'good' at the bottom of Ismay's note, shortly before convening the War Cabinet to discuss the plans. Seated with his senior ministers, Churchill showed no sign of his private fears as he passed around Ismay's rough hand-drawn sketch map of Whitehall. It showed the whole of Horse Guards Parade was to be cordoned off with barbed wire to delay parachutists attacking Horse Guards from St James's Park. The plan was to place machine-gun nests with road blocks at key points around Whitehall to stop commandos and light tanks from getting into the central thoroughfare of Whitehall. They would be positioned on top of Admiralty Arch so they could fire down at German forces either in the Mall or Parliament Square; on the Embankment (near the entrance to what is now Portcullis House, the modern extension of the House of Commons) to block access to Whitehall across Westminster Bridge or down Richmond Terrace from the riverside; and at the east and west corners of Great George Street on Parliament

Square to stop raiders getting into Whitehall from Westminster or from St James's Park. The King's Life Guard was to occupy the upper rooms of the Horse Guards in the archway, near the office once occupied by Wellington, and fire down on German troops or 'Fifth Columnists' – Nazi sympathizers already in Britain who could rise up when the crisis came – attacking them from St James's Park. The Guards could also fire on the enemy as they tried to race into Whitehall past the Banqueting House from Horse Guards Avenue. A Bren gun was also to be placed at the corner of Downing Street with an arc of fire up and down the street. If the raiders succeeded in getting inside some of the Whitehall buildings, the defenders were to seek higher ground inside offices of ministries such as the Home Office, the Colonial Office and the Privy Council Office to avoid being pinned down by covering fire from windows across the road. I have quoted Ismay's plan in full below to give the full picture of the desperate defence the Cabinet was called on to discuss that night.

London Area Operation Order No 2 – 16 May, 1940

INFORMATION.

1. ROYAL MARINES are affording close protection to the
   Admiralty.

INTENTION.

2. To prepare a defensive position for the close defence of
   Government offices in WHITEHALL.

METHOD.

3. Troops.
   Holding Bn Scots Gds will be responsible for defence of this
   sector.

Holding Bn Gren Gds will be prepared to man the defences in emergency and in event of arrival of Holding Bn Scots Gds being delayed.

4. Posts.

Sandbagged posts will be prepared as follows:-

    (i) STOREYS GATE to cover with fire

        (a) West face of Foreign Office

        (b) GREAT GEORGE ST.

        (c) BIRDCAGE WALK

    (ii) Junction GREAT GEORGE ST WHITEHALL S.E. corner of Board of Education offices to cover with fire

        (a) WHITEHALL

        (b) BRIDGE ST.

        (c) Approaches from PARLIAMENT SQUARE

    (iii) SE corner of NEW SCOTLAND YARD on embankment to cover

        (a) East side SCOTLAND YARD and Cabinet Offices

        (b) South side SCOTLAND YARD

        (c) Approaches from WESTMINSTER BRIDGE

    (iv) At Wooden Gate leading to railings at East end of RICHMOND TERRACE to cover approaches from North along EMBANKMENT

    (v) At N.E. corner of HOME OFFICE corner of DOWNING ST and WHITEHALL to cover RICHMOND TERRACE WHITEHALL Northwards

(vi) N.E. corner of WAR OFFICE to cover

> (a) WHITEHALL PLACE
> Eastwards
> (b) WHITEHALL PLACE
> Westwards
> (c) WHITEHALL COURT

(vii) North end of WHITEHALL on West side by traffic lights to cover

> (a) South down
> WHITEHALL
> (b) Approaches from
> TRAFALGAR SQUARE

(viii) Centre of ADMIRALTY ARCH to cover

> (a) Approaches from
> TRAFALGAR SQUARE
> (b) THE MALL

<u>King's Life Guard.</u>

5. King's Life Guard will be prepared to cover HORSE GUARDS AVENUE from windows above HORSE GUARDS ARCH.

<u>Alternative Positions.</u>

6. Holding Bn Scots Gds will carry out recces for alternative positions in windows of buildings in case posts become overlooked by enemy in windows of buildings opposite.

<u>Strength of Posts.</u>

7. Posts will consist of not more than one sec and one Bren gun though it will be necessary to station two Brens at certain posts which have more than two fire tasks.

Road Blocks.

8. Knife rest road blocks will be established at points marked on attached map. Roads will not be blocked till ordered but knife rests will be dumped in position ready to put across.

C.R.E. holds numbers required for each point and these will be issued from R.E. dump RAWLING ST Duke of York's H.Q. in seven dumps around the perimeter of the area.

Holding Bn Gren Gds will provide labour if required on demand by C.R.E.

Wire

9. The following places will be wired under arrangements to be made by C.R.E.

West side of Horse Guards Parade

West side Foreign Office, Home Office and Board of Education Offices.

Centre PARLIAMENT SQUARE.

Sandbags for Posts.

10. C.R.E. will arrange to dump sandbags and sand at positions selected for posts and will notify Holding Bn Gren Gds when work can start. Holding Bn Gren Gds will be responsible for labour for erection of posts but Holding Bn Scots Gds will supervise exact siting and position of loop holes can carry out the tasks required and that protection is given to men in the post from fire from adjacent posts.[11]

A few weeks later, in a secret session of the Commons on 20 June 1940, of which only Churchill's speaking notes survive, he made it clear he believed that, if only Britain could hold on until Roosevelt was re-elected in November, the US would begin freely supporting Britain in the war effort and the country could survive the war. 'All depends upon our resolute bearing and holding out until election issues are settled there. If we can do so, I cannot doubt, the whole English-speaking world will be in line together . . .'[12]

Colville, who did not witness the debate, had trouble driving to Number Ten after the secret session, recording in his diary:

> At about 11.30 p.m. Winston went back to No. 10 taking Alexander [Lord Alexander, First Lord of the Admiralty] and Duff Cooper [Alfred Duff Cooper, ally of Churchill and Minister of Information] with him: 'Two dreadnoughts and a battleship', as he described the party on getting into the car. I had great difficulty in returning in my car owing to the formidable defences of Whitehall, and I found the Grenadiers on duty most unhelpful. Eventually, I more or less forced my way through barriers onto the Horse Guards Parade and had quite an acrimonious '*passage d'armes*' with the officer in charge.[13]

On 21 July 1940 Ismay again wrote a memorandum to the Prime Minister marked 'Secret' about the plans. Churchill had questioned whether the whole of the defence of Whitehall should be handed to the Royal Marines. Ismay gently urged him against the idea on the grounds that to do so would mean taking the Royal Marines away from the main field army, and it would be difficult to find accommodation for the additional men. A total of one hundred Royal Marines were already guarding the Admiralty itself, said Ismay. The King's Life Guard was stationed at Horse Guards and the Whitehall defences were manned by the Grenadier Guards, based at Wellington Barracks.

> The various posts which cover all the approaches to the area are permanently manned, for which purpose two Officers and 156 other ranks are required . . . A Company is ready in (Wellington Barracks) for rapid reinforcement of the area, one platoon being at 15 minutes

notice and the remainder of the Company at 30 minutes notice. If any kind of serious attack developed, the defence would be taken over by the Officer commanding the Battalion.

Ismay sent Churchill a further memorandum on 30 July 1940, which revealed the scale of the attack for which they had prepared – 'light and medium tanks, and infantry by sea or air'. He said instructions had been issued to the officer commanding the London area on 5 July by the Commander-in-Chief Home Forces (General Bernard Paget) in the following terms:

> The actual centre of Government round Whitehall will be considered as the keep of a fortress. The roads leading to the keep will be defended by posts and anti-tank obstacles. These obstacles must not obstruct the free flow of road traffic and will therefore be movable, e.g. steel rails in sockets. In addition, wiring will be prepared which can be fixed when necessary. The fixing of anti-tank obstacles and wire must be possible in one hour.

Ismay also described the dithering that had gone on over the anti-tank measures in St James's Park, which today read like a script from *Dad's Army*. Anti-tank obstacles had been created across the Mall and Birdcage Walk, but when it was realized that the German tanks could use the open ground in St James's Park, the men were then ordered by their commanding officer to extend the anti-tank trenches inside the park. General Paget countermanded this plan, and ordered the 'excavations to be filled up'. Ismay said: 'It is now proposed to construct two concrete pill-boxes in St James's Park and to put a belt of wire across the park parallel to, and on the approximate alignment of the bridge across the lake. This is to prevent access by enemy or by 5th Column snipers to the East end of the park overlooking the Horse Guards Parade.'

Churchill had good reason to be worried about the Luftwaffe targeting Whitehall. The Cabinet agreed in August to send bombers to attack Berlin, in retaliation for the air raids over London, which led to Hitler threatening to 'erase' British cities. Between 7 September and 3 November Churchill said an average of 200 German bombers attacked London every night. For three nights, Londoners endured the attacks with no sound of resistance as anti-aircraft guns were reinforced and the British night-fighters were withdrawn from the skies. Then a huge cannonade of ack-ack guns opened on the German bombers, accompanied by a blaze of searchlights.

Colville noted in his diary for Wednesday 18 September 1940 that Churchill had gone over to the Central War Room (now the Cabinet War Rooms) with Sir Eric Seal, his principal private secretary, leaving Colville and a few of Churchill's close aides including Brendan Bracken to sleep in the Number Ten shelter, which he likened to:

third class accommodation on a Channel steamer – the typists and servants slept on mattresses in the bigger room in the shelter. Enemy aircraft boomed overhead and once or twice I looked out into the garden to watch the shells and the bombs until the falling shell splinters – one of which came unpleasantly near – drove me in. One splinter is embedded firmly in the inside wall of our room as a result of last night's activities.

Unable to sleep, they went to the Central War Room and had a whisky and soda with Seal and the military chiefs but

hurried away to No. 10, a bomb falling close as I entered the Foreign Office arch. Then Brendan and I did some sightseeing, watching the A.A. [anti-aircraft] barrage at work on planes directly over our heads. There was an orange glow as a balloon above us collapsed in flames and then, in the direction of the river, we saw a parachute descending through the moonbeams. 'A parachutist,' said one policeman. 'A pilot escaping; that orange glow was an enemy plane down,' said another (the big fat one who guards the door); but a third said; 'No it is coming down too fast, it's something worse than that.' A few seconds later he was proved right: a landmine exploded on the County Hall [now a hotel on the South Bank] and even the windows in Downing Street and the FO were shattered. Slept uncomfortably in the shelter.

The makeshift bomb shelters under Downing Street had been created during the Munich crisis for the occupants of Numbers Ten and Eleven. The rooms on the garden level had had their ceilings propped up with a wooden under-ceiling and strong timbers. It was believed, Churchill later wrote, that this would support the ruins if the building was blown or shaken down. 'But of course,' he added, 'neither these rooms nor the shelters were effective against a direct hit.' During September, preparations had been made to transfer his ministerial headquarters to the Central War Room, known as 'The Annexe', down the Clive steps near Storeys Gate and St James's Park. But Churchill persisted in relaxing in bed until 10 a.m. at Number Ten wearing a red dressing gown, smoking a cigar and dictating memoranda to his secretary Mrs Hill, who sat with her typewriter at the end of his bed. Colville noted: 'His black cat Nelson, which has quite replaced our old No. 10 black cat, sprawled at the foot of the bed and every now and then Winston would gaze at it affectionately and say, "Cat, darling".'

The Prime Minister insisted also on having convivial evenings at Downing Street, in spite of the danger of the bombing. 'Life at Downing Street was exciting,' Churchill said. 'One might as well have been at a battalion headquarters in the line.' It is hard to imagine his guests, more used to civilian comforts than life in the trenches, shared his enthusiasm. On 14 October he had been dining at Downing Street during an air raid when the old Treasury building on Whitehall by Downing Street received a near-direct hit. Fortunately, the Prime Minister had taken the precaution of dining in the basement of Number Ten behind blast doors. He was entertaining Moore-Brabazon, the Transport Minister, Sir Archibald Sinclair, the Liberal leader who was also a defence minister in the coalition, and Oliver Lyttelton, the President of the Board of Trade. On an impulse, he had also ordered his butler, his cook Mrs Landemare, and servants to go into the basement for safety before the bombs fell. Churchill recalled:

> I had been seated again at table only about three minutes when a really very loud crash, close at hand, and a violent shock showed that the house had been struck.
>
> My detective [Walter Thompson] came into the room and said much damage had been done. The kitchen, pantry and the offices on the Treasury side were shattered. We went into the kitchen to view the scene. The devastation was complete. The bomb had fallen fifty yards away on the Treasury and the blast had smitten the large, tidy kitchen, with all its right saucepans and crockery, into a heap of black dust and rubble. The big plate-glass window had been hurled in fragments and splinters across the room and would of course have cut its occupants, if there had been any, to pieces. But my fortunate inspiration, which I might so easily have neglected, had come in the nick of time.[14]

The underground Treasury shelter across the court had been blown to pieces and the four civil servants who were doing Home Guard duty were killed under tons of rubble. The Treasury was forced to move into the public offices at the corner of Great George Street and is still there to this day. As the raid continued and seemed to grow in intensity, Churchill says: 'We put on our tin hats and went out to view the scene from the top of the Annexe buildings. Before doing so, however, I could not resist taking Mrs Landemare and the others from the shelter to see their kitchen. They were upset at the sight of the wreck, but principally on account of the general untidiness!'

Moore-Brabazon sent a note the next day, thanking him for the 'lively dinner – bombs and all'. From their vantage point with Churchill on the roof of the 'Annexe' (today the Treasury building) above the Cabinet War Rooms they saw Pall Mall in flames. John Martin, a member of Churchill's private office, rang the porter at the Reform Club to ask how things were. 'The Club is burning, sir,' the porter calmly replied.[15]

As the threat of invasion receded, Churchill took respite from the war by watching films of all kinds. He had a private cinema in a basement of Admiralty House – the sign is still visible today, just inside the entrance gates, pointing down a flight of steps to the cinema below ground. Sadly, there is nothing left inside of the cinema that Churchill used. I was told a start was made on refurbishing it, possibly for a media briefing room under John Prescott in 2003, but it was abandoned through lack of money. While I was researching this book, the family of Churchill's wartime projectionist handed to the curators at the Cabinet War Rooms a pocketbook containing brief handwritten details of the films Churchill saw during the middle of the war, both in Whitehall and at Chequers. It is a fascinating list, containing morale-boosting war films alongside Disney's escapist cartoons – Churchill's projectionist ran eight Disneys on Boxing Day 1942. It also reveals that Churchill, who was in the habit of working into the early hours after taking a nap, watched some films after midnight. Pity the poor projectionist. His list occasionally noted Churchill's verdict on some of the movies. His favourite is widely believed to be *Lady Hamilton*, but this notebook shows he had high regard for *In Which We Serve* – Noel Coward and David Lean's movie loosely based on the wartime exploits of Lord Mountbatten and HMS *Kelly*. It starred Coward as the skipper of HMS *Torrin* with a stiff upper lip, and contained a searing attack by the Beaverbrook press on the support for Chamberlain's policy of appeasement – the front page of the *Daily Express* hailing 'No War This Year' is seen floating on the sea, after the ship has been sunk. Clearly propagandist, it earned Churchill's accolade: 'One of the finest films I have seen . . .' Churchill's rating of the film is in brackets – he thought *Bambi* 'very good'.

1942: 1 May PM at Chequers Secret show to PM only at 1.30 am *One Foot in Heaven*. 2 May *Jungle Book, Lost Horizon, Reap the Wild Wind*. 16 May PM at Chequers *Tom Sawyer's Adventures*. 17 May *Sea Hawk* Film Return to Min of Information. 17 July PM's *Pied Piper*. 19 July *Listen to Britain* (1 am). 20th July Mansion House – special news reels. 25th July PM's *The Young Mr Pitt*. 26th *Wild Bill Hicock* Also Churchill Film and news reels. August 28 *Bambi* (VG). August 30 *Goodbye Mr Chips*. Sept 4–7 1942 PM *Kings Row, Gay Sister*. 6 September *First of the Few* (VG) Sept 26 *Yankie Doodle* (Fair) *Sea Wolf* (VG) 2 Oct *In Which we Serve* (PM's comment: One of the finest films I have seen). 3 Oct 1942 *To Be or Not To Be* (excellent film). 4 October *Stanley and Livingstone* (Very good). Chequers weekend with General Smutts *Coastal Command*. *Pride of the Yankies* (Fair) 12 Nov House of Commons *Rio Rita, Young Mr Lincoln* (VG). Dec 6 *The Real Glory* 4.30 pm (VG). 25 December PM – *Dumbo* eveng *Moon and Diamond*. 26 Dec 8 Disneys *La Grande Illusion*. 27 December *Trouble in Paradise*.

1943 28 Feb NO 10 *Nine Men. Once upon a Honeymoon*. March *Desert Victory* (twice). March 19 *Desert Victory*.

The projectionist also noted that Churchill watched the documentary *Stalingrad* twice on 27 and 29 March 1943, but Whitehall was never to see the sort of merciless street fighting in London that defied Hitler in Stalingrad in late 1942.

Churchill's chair in the Cabinet War Rooms at Whitehall bears testimony to the tension he was under. One corner of the armrest has been worn by his ring constantly rubbing over it. But Churchill's coalition War Cabinet was debating the end of the war, long before the end came in sight.

We now have the remarkable record of what each member of the Cabinet actually said, thanks to the release of the personal notes taken by the Cabinet Secretary, Sir Norman Brook, in a series of ordinary government-issue notebooks. They reveal that Churchill was overruled by his colleagues including key Labour members, Labour leader Clem Attlee, Ernest Bevin as Minister for Labour, and Herbert Morrison as Home Secretary, when partisans urged Britain to bomb innocent villages in Germany in reprisal for atrocities against a village in Prague. The Cabinet also discussed in 1942 the question of imposing segregation on black US troops like they would have faced at home – blacks would not have been served at London railway stations, for example – and the Cabinet vetoed the idea, partly because of the fear that it would have led to dissent among Britain's black Commonwealth troops, who had no tradition of segregation and were fighting the war alongside white Britons.

Churchill in late 1942 was already considering how to deal with the Nazi leaders at the end of the war. He put forward a paper proposing a fact-finding commission to identify the Nazi leaders with war crimes, saying, 'The idea of my paper is that you don't pass judgement but collect facts in an authoritative manner. It is important to make a big show of them – publish evidence from time to time to hot up the fires of war. I propose a fact-finding commission, flourish of trumpets, and then I believe Washington will take the initiative.'

The Lord Chancellor, Viscount Simon, a founder of the breakaway Liberal National group, said: 'A similar committee was appointed in September 1914 but it contained no names of offenders.'

Churchill retorted: 'It is my view, Lord Chancellor, that we should consider names now. If Hitler falls into our hands, we should most certainly put him to death. After all, he is not a sovereign, who could be said to be "in the hands of his ministers" like the Kaiser was.'

However, as the Cabinet discussed the details, Churchill made it clear he favoured summary execution for the ringleaders, rather than a trial: 'We must remember that Hitler is the mainspring of evil. The instrument I propose is the electric chair like the one they use for gangsters in America. That would no doubt be available on lease-lend . . .' Brook does not record whether this was taken as a black joke, or not. Sir Norman's notes show Attlee urged Churchill to moderate his views. But Herbert Morrison argued that a 'mock trial' of Nazi leaders would be 'objectionable'. Instead he said it would be 'better to declare that we shall put them to death'. Churchill agreed that a fair trial for Hitler would be a 'farce – they should be treated as outlaws' and said Roosevelt would allow US troops to shoot the Nazi leaders. Churchill said he favoured naming fifty or so Nazis who would be executed, when caught.

As the end of the war came closer, the Labour members of the War Cabinet were in revolt over Churchill's refusal to allow the Beveridge report on the welfare state, including the creation of a free National Health Service, to be implemented before hostilities ceased. Attlee and his colleagues were preparing for the post-war period and Attlee threatened to force a general election before the war was over, but Churchill was implacable. 'Everyone wants it, but can you pay for it?' said Churchill.

On 8 May 1945 – VE (Victory in Europe) Day – Churchill stepped onto the balcony of the Department of Health in Whitehall (now HM Revenue and Customs) to address a cheering multitude of jubilant Londoners and service personnel from around the globe. Hundreds of thousands of ordinary people had crowded into

Whitehall, the heart of the capital and the empire, to celebrate the end of the war in Europe, and cheer 'Winnie' and the Royal Family until they were hoarse. Joyce Trimmer, then seventy-five, recalled for the Museum of London archive being a student on VE Day:

> Armed with borrowed or stolen mascots from various colleges the students marched down Regent Street to Trafalgar Square and toward Whitehall. The crowds were enormous and unbelievably joyful and happy, with hugs and kisses for all, especially servicemen and women. In Whitehall, word quickly went back along the line as we reached the Cenotaph, when there was complete silence as we marched past. The instant respect shown was quite awesome to witness. We then made our way to Buckingham Palace and became part of the huge throng of cheering people outside the gates of the Palace, where we yelled and cheered for the Royal Family, who happily obliged their overjoyed subjects.

From the balcony of the Department of Health, Churchill made his final speech of the war: 'It is the victory of the cause of freedom in every land. In all our long history we have never seen a greater day than this,' said the greatest wartime leader Britain has ever known.

'My dear friends, this is your hour. This is not a victory of a party of any class. It's a victory of the great British nation as a whole.

'God bless you all. This is your victory!'

The crowd roared back, 'No – it is yours!'[16]

Two months later, Winston Churchill was turned out of office, defeated by the democratic system he had fought to defend, in the election of July 1945.

# POSTSCRIPT

A final attempt to remodel the whole of Whitehall was attempted in 1965 with a grandiose blueprint called 'Whitehall – A Plan for the National and Government Centre'. It would have involved the demolition of Victorian and Georgian Whitehall, including the Treasury, Foreign Office and Richmond Terrace. They would have been replaced by a vast modern Whitehall complex, stretching across Parliament Street, with the bureaucrats accommodated in ziggurats – giant stepped blocks, seven storeys high. A road tunnel would have been bored under Parliament Square to create a traffic-free Parliamentary Precinct by the Palace of Westminster.

It was designed by Sir Leslie Martin, architect of the Royal Festival Hall, and would have turned the centre of Whitehall into the kind of concrete jungle that so defaced our provincial towns and cities in the 1960s in the name of modernism. Martin drew up the plans at the request of Sir Geoffrey Rippon, Tory minister for public building, and they were unveiled by Charles Pannell, his Labour successor in the Wilson Government. Fortunately, they excited such a strong powerful outcry from politicians that they were dropped. It has since been claimed that this opposition 'deprives us of a cohesive government centre'.[1] Certainly, the traffic problems persist, but the continued refurbishment of the existing buildings has produced a more sympathetic approach to the modernization of Whitehall. Parliament Street and Whitehall were designated a conservation area in 1969 and most of the buildings were listed for protection, including the nine lamp standards in Downing Street, Queen Mary's Steps, the 1926 statue of Lord Kitchener on Horse Guards Parade, the 1939 air-raid shelter and fortress known as the Citadel on Horse Guards Parade, Nos. 1–8 Richmond Terrace and even the Grade I listed MoD main building standing on the palace where Wolsey entertained Henry VIII. Wolsey's wine cellar under the MoD is now officially an ancient monument, the only one in Whitehall. He would have appreciated that.

# NOTES

Prices and their modern-day equivalents are a vexed issue. They are calculated here from a best estimate of the increase in the prices index but that does not give you contemporary comparisons of value and it is difficult to compare bundles of prices for consumer goods over the centuries. I can recommend the website www.measuringworth.com for further study.

## Introduction: The Seabird Shore

1  p. 12, *Chivalry & Command: 500 Years of Horse Guards*, Brian Harwood, Osprey

2  p. 378, *A Great and Terrible King: Edward I and the Forging of Britain*, Marc Morris, Hutchinson

3  p. 38, *London: The Biography,* Peter Ackroyd, Chatto & Windus

4  p. 9, *The Lost Palace of Whitehall*, Simon Thurley, Royal Institute of British Architects (RIBA)

5  p. 11, *Chivalry & Command: 500 Years of Horse Guards*, Brian Harwood, Osprey

6  p. 57, 'Whitehall Palace and King Street Westminster: The Urban Cost of Princely Magnificence', Gervase Rosser and Simon Thurley, *London Topographical Record* Vol. XXVI.

7  Simon Thurley, note to the author, 4 February 2007

## Chapter 1: The Cardinal's Court

1  *The Richest of the Rich: The Wealthiest 250 People in Britain Since 1066*, Philip Beresford and William D. Rubinstein, Harriman House

2  p. 137, *Thomas Wolsey, late Cardinal: His Life and Death*, George Cavendish, J. M. Dent

3  p. 10, *The Lost Palace of Whitehall*, Simon Thurley, RIBA

4  p. 32, *The Reign of Henry VIII: Personalities and Politics*, David Starkey, Vintage

5  p. 207, *The Six Wives of Henry VIII*, Alison Weir, Pimlico

6  'The special problem of the resiting of an historic building', Lawson Scott White and George Anthony Gardner, *Journal of the Institution of Civil Engineers* No. 7, May 1950

## Chapter 2: Henry VIII's Palace of White Hall

1  *Treatise on the Pretended Divorce between Henry VIII and Katherine of Aragon*, Nicholas Harpsfield, Camden Press

2  *The life of Kinge Henry the 8th from his fallinge in love with Anne Bulloigne to the death of Queene Katheren, his wife*, British Library, Folio 13, Sloane MS 2495

3  p. 240, *The Six Wives of Henry VIII*, Alison Weir, Pimlico

4  p. 168, *The Life and Death of Anne Boleyn*, Eric Ives, Blackwell Publishing

5   p. 44, *Whitehall Palace: The Official Illustrated History*, Simon Thurley, Yale University Press

6   p. 335, *Henry VIII: King and Court*, Alison Weir, Pimlico

7   p. 529, *The Six Wives of Henry VIII*, Alison Weir, Pimlico

8   *Royal Landscape: The Gardens and Parks of Windsor*, Jane Roberts, Yale University Press

# Chapter 3: Queen Elizabeth I's Whitehall

1   p. 291, *Elizabeth*, David Starkey, Chatto & Windus

2   p. 65, *Whitehall Palace: The Official Illustrated History*, Simon Thurley, Yale University Press

3   2 September 1680, *The Diary of John Evelyn*, John Evelyn, Everyman

4   *1599: A Year in the Life of William Shakespeare*, James Shapiro, Faber & Faber

5   p. 200, *The Virgin Queen*, Christopher Hibbert, Addison-Wesley

6   *Chivalry & Command: 500 Years of Horse Guards*, Brian Harwood, Osprey

# Chapter 4: Blood at the Banqueting House

1   *Charles I*, Christopher Hibbert, Weidenfeld & Nicolson

2   A rifle range for staff, peers and MPs was located in a basement of the Commons where Members of the Parliamentary gun club, including women MPs, were able to fire small-bore rifles at targets. It was on the line of the ceremonial search before every State Opening of Parliament, but closed after eighty years amid the outcry against guns after the Dunblane and Hungerford killings.

3   Interview with Prof. Max Hutchinson, *Men of Stone,* BBC Radio 4, 30 June 2007, by Julian Richards

4   *Samuel Pepys: The Unequalled Self*, Claire Tomalin, Viking

5  p. 111, *Lost Treasures of Britain: Five Centuries of Creation and Destruction*, Roy Strong, Guild Publishing
6  Ahasuerus Fromanteel, the first clockmaker in England to make pendulum clocks
7  1 November 1660, *The Diary of John Evelyn*, John Evelyn, Everyman
8  *The Noble Revolt: The Overthrow of Charles I*, John Adamson, Weidenfeld & Nicolson

# Chapter 5: Pepys's Whitehall

1  6 February 1685, *The Diary of John Evelyn*, John Evelyn, Everyman
2  *Charles I*, Christopher Hibbert, Weidenfeld & Nicolson
3  *Invitation to a Funeral*, Molly Brown, www.okima.com
4  *The Map of London from 1746 to the Present Day*, Andrew Davies, Guild Publishing
5  p. 314, *Samuel Pepys: The Unequalled Self*, Claire Tomalin, Viking
6  p. 176, *Monarchy: From the Middle Ages to Modernity*, David Starkey, HarperPress
7  *A History of Britain: The British Wars 1603–1776*, Simon Schama, BBC

# Chapter 6: Downing Street

1  *Samuel Pepys: The Unequalled Self*, Claire Tomalin, Viking
2  p. 21, *No. 10 Downing Street: A House in History*, R. J. Minney, Cassell
3  p. 139, *The Posthumous and Historical Memoirs*, Sir Nathaniel William Wraxall, Vol. II
4  *No. 10 Downing Street: A House in History*, R. J. Minney, Cassell
5  *Manuscripts*, J. B. Fortescue, HMSO
6  p. 221, *William Pitt the Younger*, William Hague, HarperCollins
7  p. 114, *Gladstone*, Roy Jenkins, Macmillan

8   p. 36, *10 Downing Street: The Illustrated History*, Anthony Seldon, HarperCollins

9   p. 322, *Speaking for Myself*, Cherie Blair, Little, Brown

10  p. 323, *Speaking for Myself,* Cherie Blair, Little, Brown

11  *The Major Years*, Blakeway Productions for BBC, 11, 18 and 25 October 1999

# Chapter 7: Nelson and the Admiralty

1   National Archive Admiralty papers, ADM 1/396 (N168)

2   p. 77, *The Diary of Frances Lady Shelley 1787–1817*, Richard Edgcumbe, University Press of the Pacific

3   p. 207, *Nelson: A Personal History*, Christopher Hibbert, Penguin

4   *Longitude,* Dava Sobel, Fourth Estate

5   p. 365, *The Gathering Storm*, Winston Churchill, Penguin

6   p. 108, *Pepys and the Navy*, C. S. Knighton, Sutton

# Chapter 8: Dover House –
# the Most Notorious Address in London

1   *Elite Women in English Political Life c.1754–1790*, Elaine Chalus, Clarendon Press

2   *The Diary of Frances Lady Shelley 1818–1873*, edited by Richard Edgcumbe, University Press of the Pacific

3   *Dearest Bess: The Life and Times of Lady Elizabeth Foster afterwards Duchess of Devonshire,* Dorothy Margaret Stuart, Methuen and Co Ltd

4   p. 40, *The Young Melbourne & Lord M*, David Cecil, Phoenix Press

5   p. 45, *The Young Melbourne & Lord M,* David Cecil, Phoenix Press

6   p. 83, *Lady Caroline Lamb*, Paul Douglass, Palgrave Macmillan

7   *Byron*, Frederic Raphael, Thames & Hudson

8   p. 120, *Lady Caroline Lamb*, Paul Douglass, Palgrave Macmillan

9   p. 72, *Byron*, Frederic Raphael, Thames & Hudson

10  p. 233, *Lord Melbourne 1779–1848*, L. G. Mitchell, Oxford University Press

# Chapter 9: Wellington and Horse Guards

1  *Wellington: Pillar of State*, Elizabeth Longford, Weidenfeld & Nicolson. Note – there are numerous accounts of this event, but I have taken Lady Longford's account, drawing on the diaries of Lady Frances Shelley. I have also drawn on research by Adam Matthew Publications, www.adam-matthew-publications.co.uk

2  p. 183, *The Diary of Frances Lady Shelley, 1787–1817*, edited by Richard Edgcumbe, University Press of the Pacific

3  p. 182–190, 'St James Square: residents', *Old and New London*, Volume 4 (1878)

4  p. 26, *Chivalry & Command: 500 Years of Horse Guards*, Brian Harwood, Osprey

5  Ibid.

6  p. 53, *Looking at London*, Arthur Kutcher, Thames & Hudson

7  p. 314, *Wellington: A Personal History*, Christopher Hibbert, HarperCollins

8  p. 373, *Wellington: Pillar of State*, Elizabeth Longford, Weidenfeld & Nicolson

9  p. 187, *Charge!: A Life of Cardigan of Balaclava*, Donald Thomas, Omega

10  *The Destruction of Lord Raglan: A Tragedy of the Crimean War*, Christopher Hibbert, Penguin

11  *The Donkeys,* Alan Clark, Vintage

12  *One Leg: The Life and Letters of Henry William Paget, the first Marquess of Anglesey*, The Marquess of Anglesey, Reprint Society

13  James Tissot, *Captain Frederick Burnaby*, 1870 oil on mahogany panel 19½ x 23½ inches, The National Portrait Gallery, London

14  p. 446, *Horse Guards*, Barney White-Spunner, Macmillan

15  Anecdote told to the author by the Prince of Wales at a lunch for lobby journalists, Rules Restaurant, 3 December 1985

# Chapter 10: Pam's Palace –
# the Foreign and Commonwealth Office

1 FCO official history, www.fco.gov.uk
2 FCO film, *FCO Past and Present*
3 *FCO buildings*, FCO internal archive
4 p. 29, *Whitehall*, Peter Hennessy, Pimlico
5 Press notice for the Ninth Security Service Records Release, 25–6 November 2002
6 p. 92, *In the Footsteps of Churchill*, Richard Holmes, BBC Books
7 p. 183, *A Life at the Centre*, Roy Jenkins, Macmillan

# Chapter 11: The War Office –
# from Haig to Hoon

1 p. 52, *In the Footsteps of Churchill*, Richard Holmes, BBC Books
2 p. 153, *Letters to Venetia Stanley*, H. H. Asquith, edited by Michael and Eleanor Brock, Oxford University Press
3 p. 158, *Letters to Venetia Stanley*, H. H. Asquith, edited by Michael and Eleanor Brock, Oxford University Press
4 p. 214, *The Oxford History of the British Army*, edited by David Chandler and Ian Beckett, Oxford University Press
5 p. 47, *The Destruction of Lord Raglan: A Tragedy of the Crimean War*, Christopher Hibbert, Penguin
6 p. 114, *Chivalry & Command: 500 Years of Horse Guards*, Brian Harwood, Osprey
7 Civil Service briefing note on War Office History by Lora Scott
8 p. 18, *Independent*, 27 December 2007
9 *Property Week*, 6 February 2008
10 p. 228, 'Chips': *The Diaries of Sir Henry Channon*, Chips Channon, edited by Robert Rhodes Jones, Phoenix

11  p. 299, *The Fringes of Power: Downing Street Diaries 1939–1955*, John Colville, Phoenix

12  p. 13, *The Old War Office Building*, pamphlet published by MoD

13  p. 307, *Speaking for Myself*, Cherie Blair, Little, Brown

14  Peter Kilfoyle, interview with author, April 2008

# Chapter 12: The Cabinet Office and the Treasury

1  p. 25, *Whitehall*, Peter Hennessy, Pimlico

2  p. 71, *The Lost Palace of Whitehall*, Simon Thurley, RIBA

3  'A History of the Building now occupied by HM Treasury' by Neil Cook, internal civil service memorandum

# Chapter 13: Scotland Yard

1  p. 218, *Scotland Yard*, Sir John Moylan, Putnam and Co

2  Research note five, 'Jack the Ripper: the Whitechapel Murders', National Archives

3  p. 28, *Scotland Yard*, Sir John Moylan, Putnam and Co

4  Ibid.

5  p. 32, *MI6*, Nigel West, Granada

6  p. 38, *MI5*, Nigel West, Triad Granada

# Chapter 14: Winston and Whitehall

1  p. 67, *Five Days in London: May 1940*, John Lukacs, Yale University Press

2  p. 109, *The Fringes of Power: Downing Street Diaries 1939–1955*, John Colville, Phoenix

3  p. 30, *Five Days in London – May 1940*, John Lukacs, Yale University Press

4  *Churchill and the Cabinet War Rooms*, History Channel 1995

5  *Churchill's Bodyguard*, film series, Nugus/Martin Productions Limited, 2006

6  Terry Charman, interview with author at Cabinet War Rooms, 28 November 2007

7  *Invasion 1940: The Nazi Invasion Plan for Britain*, SS General Walter Schellenberg, St Ermin's Press

8  *Future Indefinite*, Noel Coward, Heinemann

9  p. 8, *Winston S. Churchill: Finest Hour,* Martin Gilbert, Heinemann

10  p. 107, *The Reckoning*, Anthony Eden, Houghton Mifflin

11  PRO premier 3.263/1 Cabinet papers, 69/1 Defence committee No. 5, 20 May 1940

12  p. 15, *Secret Session Speeches*, by Winston S. Churchill, compiled by Charles Eade, Cassell and Co Ltd

13  p. 140, *The Fringes of Power: Downing Street Diaries 1939–1955*, John Colville, Phoenix

14  p. 306, *Their Finest Hour*, Winston S. Churchill, Penguin

15  p. 843, *Winston S. Churchill: Finest Hour*, Martin Gilbert, Heinemann

16  p. 390, *Winston Churchill's Speeches: Never Give In!*, edited by his grandson Winston S. Churchill, Pimlico

# Postscript

1  *Ziggurats for Bureaucrats*, Ian Rice, The Twentieth Century Society Newsletter, Winter 2003–4

# PICTURE CREDITS

The Royal Palace of Whitehall *c*.1560 © Guildhall Library

Henry VIII's wine cellar © Jaime Turner

Cockpit Passage © Jaime Turner

An exterior wall of Henry VIII's tennis courts: courtesy of the author

The northeast tower of the former Tudor tennis court inside the Cabinet Office © Jaime Turner

Banqueting House © Historic Royal Palaces

The execution of Charles I © Mary Evans Picture Library

Whitehall Palace *c*.1698 by Leonard Knyff © City of Westminster Archives Centre

Queen Mary's steps, part of Wren's terrace ... © Museum of London

The Tudor foundations of the Royal Palace of Whitehall revealed in 1939 © Museum of London

The dining room of Admiralty House © Jaime Turner

The Board Room of the Admiralty © Jaime Turner

A bust of Lord Nelson © Jaime Turner

# INDEX

Abberline, Inspector Frederick, 312,
    313–16, 318
  death of, 315
  plaque unveiled to, 315–16
Abbey Park, 42
Aberdeen, Lord, 269
Abramovich, Roman, 14–15
Ackroyd, Peter, 4
Act of Supremacy, 38
*Acts and Monuments* (Foxes), 49
Adam and Eve stair, 48
Adam, John, 243
Adam, Robert, 151, 203
Adams, Gerry, 67, 173–4
Adamson, John, 119
Addington, Henry, 192
Adjutant General, 115
Admiralty Arch, 181, 207–8, 332
Admiralty/Admiralty House, 57, 114,
    149, 179, 183–6, *passim*, 188–93, *passim*,
    199–209 *passim*, 287, 293, 330
  becomes part of MoD, 206
  Board Room, 188, 199–202
  codebreakers in, 322

Masonry and, 202
  ornate stove in, 199
  recent refurbishment of, 207
  shrine to Nelson's memory, 199
Afghanistan, 255
Agar-Ellis, George, Lord Dover, 234–5
Agas, John, 316
Agas, Ralph, 49
Agincourt, 21
Agriculture, Ministry of, 318
Air Ministry, 293, 308
Albemarle, Duke of, 138
Albert Embankment, 287
Albert, Prince, 234
Alexander I, Tsar, 231
Alexander, Lord, 337
Alexandra Palace, 289
Allen, Peter Anthony, 278
Allen, Tom, 196
Allied Bazaar, 201
Alvanley, Lord, 242
*Ambassadors' Secret, The* (Holbein), 78
America:
  Civil War in, 270

361

early colonists of, 153, 162
War of Independence in, 162, 163
war on Britain declared by, 226
*see also* Roosevelt, President Franklin;
Roosevelt, President Theodore
Amiens, 4
Anglican Cathedral, Liverpool, 280
Anglo-Persian Oil Company, 205
Anjou, Duc d', 84
Anne, Princess Royal, 257
Anne, Queen (daughter of James II),
141, 143–4
Anne, Queen (first wife of James II),
135, 143
Anne, Queen (wife of James I), 96, 98
*Another Part of the World* (Clark), 326
'Anson' underground retreat, 297
*Antiques Roadshow*, 253
*Antrim*, 278
*Anyone For Denis?*, 92
*Apotheosis of King James I, The* (Rubens),
104
Apsley, first Baron, 237, 240, 241, 243
Apsley House, 165, 243, 249, 253
Arbuthnot, Charles, 238, 240–1, 243,
249–50
Arbuthnot, Harriet, 243, 248–9
Armstrong, 'Archy', 91
Army Intelligence Corps, 322
Arthur, King, 20
Arthur, Prince of Wales, 34–5
Arundel, Bishops of, 6
Arundel, Earl of, 98
Ashley, Kat, 74–5
Asquith, Herbert, 164, 208, 277, 278, 283
letters of, 283–4
Assumption Guild, 9
astrology, 60
Attlee, Clement, 153, 173, 344, 345
Avon, Lady, 169, 175
Axe, 9, 123, 157
Axe Yard, 115, 123, 268

Bacon, Francis, 264
Bagwell, Mrs, 128
Bagwell, William, 128

*Bambi*, 343
Bank of England, 100, 305
Bankside power station, 280
Bankside, 132
Banqueting House, 11, 17, 66, 76, 82,
94–5, 98–104, 107, 129, 147, 151, 287
chapel conversion of, 148
Charles I's execution outside windows
of, 113, 119, 157, 245
in Charles I's plans for Whitehall
Palace, 109
fire in, 99–100
glimpsed in Hollar portrait, 109
MoD building dwarfs, 293
MPs petition Cromwell in, 116
new, materials used in, 100
plan to link War Office with, 288
Rubens paints ceilings of, 103–4
traces of fire still shown in, 148
Barham, Lord, 193, 197
Barkstead, John, 156
Barrow, John, 190
Barry, Sir Charles, 11, 259, 305
Barry, Edward, 11
Bartlett, Vernon, 329
Basing House, 108–9
Bath Pump Rooms, 307
Bathurst, Lady Emily, 240
Bathurst, Lord (Henry), *see* Apsley, first
Baron
Batten, Sir William, 127
Battersea power station, 280
Bawdy House Riots, 139
Bazalgette, Joseph, 287
*Beagle*, 199
Bear Gallery, 54
bear-baiting, 54–5, 89
Beatty, Dr, 195, 196
Beauclerk, Lord, 135
Beaverbrook, Lord, 322, 329, 330
Beckett, Margaret, 206–7, 273, 330
'Bedchamber Crisis', 234
Bell pub, 8, 9
Bell Savage, 71
Bell Tower, 75
Bellamy, Mr, 211

Bellingham, John, 228
Bengal, Nawab of, 265
Bennett, John, 10
Benson of Whitehaven, 170
Berlin Wall, 300
Bernini, Gian Lorenzo, 117, 131
Berry, Colonel James, 245
Bessborough (née Spencer), Lady, 214,
    217, 219, 229–30, 231
Bessborough, Lord, 219
Beveridge Report, 345
Bevin, Ernest, 260–1, 262, 344
Bible, 95
Big Ben, 247, 321
Black Friars, 2, 6
'Black Museum', 319
Black Rod, 106
'Black Wednesday', 179, 309
Blackwood, Captain Henry, 193
Blair Years, The (Campbell), 295
Blair, Cherie, 169, 170, 174, 176
    property investments of, 171
    underground bunker and, 295
Blair, Leo, 174
Blair, Tony, 11, 67, 93–5, 161, 169–70,
    172, 174, 176, 181, 276
    'dodgy dossier' and, 272
    EMU and, 311
    impending resignation of, 235
    liberal interventionist policy of, 270–1
    Prescott's private dinners for, 207
    'sofa' government of, 272
    underground bunker and, 295
Blake, Admiral, 123
Bleak House (Dickens), 254
Blenheim Palace, 149
Blitz, 167, 275, 289, 292, 306, 327
    see also Second World War
Bloody Assizes, 141
Blount, Elizabeth, 27, 29
'Blubbering Cabinet', 167
Blucher, Marshal, 231
Bludworth, Sir Thomas, 132
Blues and Royals, 245, 246, 255, 257
    see also Horse Guards; Household
        Cavalry

Blunt, Anthony, 273
    see also spies and espionage
Board of Ordnance, 115
Board of Trade, 268, 289, 291, 293,
    303–4, 305, 306
    see also Treasury
bobbies/peelers, 318
Bodrugan, Nicholas, 316
Boehm, Edward, 241
Boehm, Mrs, 241–2
Boer War, 283
Boleyn, Anne, 9, 22, 25–30, 33–4, 35–8,
    43–7 passim, 56, 59–60, 76
    charges against and execution of, 61
    coat of arms of, 59
    coronation of, 60
    coronation parade of, 90–1
    description of, 33
    Henry marries, 44–7
    Henry tires of, 61
    household staff of, 59
    pregnancy of, 46, 60
    ruthless side of, 30
    in Shakespeare, 25–6
    see also Henry VIII
Boleyn, Mary, 27–9, 33–4, 45
Boleyn, Sir Thomas, 27, 33–4
Bonham-Carter, Violet, 168
Book of Common Prayer, 91
Bosworth, 97
Bow Street Runners, 318
Bracken, Brendan, 339
Bradley, Langley, 201
Braganza, Catherine of, 134
Brandon, Charles, first Duke of Suffolk,
    28, 36, 56, 57
Bratby, John, 262
Braun and Hogenberg, 54
Breda, Declaration of, 126
Britannia, 260, 274
British embassy, Moscow, 273
British Foreign Secretaries, 269
British Library, 45
British Museum, 146
Brittain, Vera, 330
Brocket Hall, 219, 221

Brook, Sir Norman, 344–5
Brooke, Henry, 279
Brooke, Peter, 206
Brown, Gordon, 67, 170–1, 172, 174,
    176–7, 271, 309–10
  Prescott's private dinners for, 207
Brownlow, Lady, 241–2
Bruce, Robert, 3
Brummell, Beau, 223
Brydon, John, 307, 308
Buccleuch, Duke of, 150, 150
Buchan, John, first Baron Tweedsmuir,
    322
Buckingham, Duke of, 6
Buckingham House, 219, 288
Buckingham Palace, 32, 94, 208, 255,
    295, 346
Buckler, J. C., 193
Budget, 303
bull-baiting, 55, 89
Bunell, Madam, 53
Burbage, Richard, 89
Burgess, Guy, 273
  see also spies and espionage
Burghley, Lord, 76, 82, 87–8
'Burlington', 299–300
Burlington House, 231
Burlington, Lord, 303
Burnaby, Lieutenant Colonel Frank, 254
Bush, President George W., 175, 180, 276
Butler, Lord, 176, 271–2
Butler, R. A. ('Rab'), 258, 272
Byng, Sir George, 41, 150
Byng, Admiral John, 150
Byron, Lord, 210, 218, 226–31, 232
  death of, 233–4
  portrait of, 235

Cabinet Office, 8, 45, 52, 67, 138, 143–4,
    180–1, 303, 304–5
  bomb damages, 235
  COBRA beneath, 304–5
Cabinet War Rooms, 167, 296, 308, 327,
    339, 342
Cadiz, 87
Cadogan House, 293

Caine, Michael, 257, 315
Calcutta, 265
Callaghan, Lord, 169
Calvary, 4
Cambridge Communist spy ring,
    273
Cambridge, Duke of, 286
Cameron, David, 309
Campbell, Alastair, 67, 94, 171, 172, 272,
    311
  'dodgy dossier' and, 272
  underground bunker and, 295
Campbell, Duncan, 300
Campbell-Bannerman, Sir Henry, 167,
    283
Campeggio, Cardinal Lorenzo, 35–6
Canaletto, 151, 152
Canning, George, 214, 268
  death of, 248
Cannon Row, 307
Capel, Thomas, 188
Cardigan, Lord, 251
Cardwell, Edward, 286
Carlton Terrace, 172
Caroline, Queen, 160, 318
Carrington House, 149
Carrington, Lord (first Baron), 149
Carrington, Lord (sixth Baron), 272
Carter, Edward, 245
Carteret, Sir George, 127
Castelnau, Michel de, 83
Castlereagh, Lord, 193, 241, 269
cathedral building, age of, 4
Cause of the English Revolution, The
    (Stone), 119
Cavendish, George, 13, 14, 15, 23–5, 29,
    30–1, 35, 36, 37, 47
Cavendish, William, fifth Duke of
    Devonshire, 217
Cazotte, Jacques, 229
Cecil, Algernon, 269
Cecil, Lord Robert, 308
Cecil, Robert, 88
Cecil, William, see Burghley, Lord
Cenotaph, 279–80, 346
Central News Agency, 314

Chamberlain, Neville, 164, 205, 290–2, 325, 329, 330, 343
Churchill replaces, 291
Chamberlain's Men, 80, 89
Chancellor of the Exchequer, origin of, 5
Chandler, David, 113
Changing of the Guard, 212, 253
Channel 4, 53
Channon, Chips, 291
Chapel Royal, 148
Chapman, Annie, 313
Chapman, George, 315
Charge of the Light Brigade, 250, 294
Charing, 2, 6
Charing Cross, 2, 9, 11, 12, 52, 107, 208
Charles I:
  accession of, 102
  bedchamber moved by, 129
  in Civil War, 107–9
  death warrant of, 119–20, 156
  dispersal of properties, treasures and works of art of, 116–17, 157–8
  divine right of kings believed in by, 104
  equestrian statue of, 11
  execution of, 95, 104, 112–15, 247
  flight to Carisbrooke Castle by, 109
  Henrietta Maria marries, 102
  Houses of Parliament summoned by, 104–5
  jester to, 91
  Knyvett moved to make way for, 157
  Life Guard created to protect, 244
  London quit by, 107
  MPs' arrest attempted by, 105–6, 245
  reforms agreed by, 104–5
  retreats to York, 107
  rickets suffered by, 102
  sentence passed on, 110–11
  sporting pursuits of, 103
  strains of marriage of, 102–3
  taken prisoner on Isle of Wight, 109
  taken prisoner in Scotland, 109
  trial of, 110
  Whitehall Palace rebuilding plans of, 109–10
  Whitehall Palace tenure of, 102–7
Charles II:
  caged birds kept by, 139–40
  children sired by, 129
  clocks of, 136
  court moved to Winchester by, 139
  deathbed conversion of, 141
  Declaration of Breda written by, 126
  exile of, 124, 126, 155
  Great Plague fled by, 131
  illness and death of, 139–41
  laying-on-of-hands tradition reinstated by, 130
  mistresses of, 129, 134
  palace alterations ordered by, 130
  Pepys's part in restoration of, 115, 119
  plan to install, 126
  as Prince, 105, 112
  return to England of, 126s
  Rochester banned by, 135
  services offered to Parliament by, 126
  sexual appetite of, 129
  state bedchamber ordered by, 129
  tennis court of, 53
  thwarted attempt to gain throne by, 116
  Treasury Commission created by, 301
  Whitehall Palace tenure of, 129–31, 134–40
Charles V, Holy Roman Emperor, 21, 22, 26, 40, 71
Charles, Prince of Wales, 256–7
Charman, Terry, 328
Chartres, 4
Chase Me Comrade, 91
Château Vert, 27
Chatham, Lord, see Pitt, William (the Elder)
Chelsea FC, 15
Chelsea Town Hall, 307
Chequers, 170
Chiefs of Defence Staff, 321, 330
Chiffinch, William, 136–7
Childe Harold's Pilgrimage (Byron), 226–7
Chinon Castle, Siege of, 6

Christ Church Hospital, 148
Christian IV of Denmark, 98
Christie, John, 319
*Chronicles* (Holinshead), 82
Church of England, 38, 160
Churchill Museum, 180
Churchill, Clementine, 167
Churchill, John, first Duke of
    Marlborough, 143, 149
Churchill, Sarah, 143
Churchill, Winston, 167, 170, 173, 199,
    204–6, 277–8, 288, 291–2, 297, 306, 308
    appeal to Roosevelt by, 331
    Chamberlain replaced by, 291
    films watched by, 342–3
    first prime-ministerial broadcast of,
        325–6
    intended last stand of, 327–9
    lieutenant and budding war
        correspondent, 283
    wartime leader, 324–46
CIA, 180, 274
Cipriani, Giovanni, 151
Citadel, 297–8
City of London Brewery, 148
civil service, 5
*Civitates Orbis Terrarum*, 54
Clarence, Duke of (later William IV),
    201, 203
Clarence, Duke of (Prince Albert
    Victor), 315
Clarenden, Lord, 260
Clark, Alan, 252, 286
Clark, Kenneth, 326
Clarke, Andrea, 45
Clarke, Ken, 301, 309
Clayton and Bell, 262
Clement VII, Pope, 40, 46
Cleveland, Duchess of, *see* Villiers,
    Barbara
Clive, Robert, 264–5
Clowson Stream, 9
Clunn, Harold, 181–2
Coach House and Stables, 317
Coalition Information Centre, 272
Cobbett, William, 163, 213

COBRA, 304–5
Cockburn, Claud, 329
Cockerell, Samuel James, 206
cockfighting, 54
Cockpit Passage, 56, 67, 303
Cockpit, 53, 104, 143, 154, 159, 301, 302,
    303
Cofferers House, 317
Coke, Charlotte, 219
Cold War, 91, 273, 295
Coldstream Guards, 245, 246
Collingwood, Admiral Lord, 192, 197
Colonial Office, 194, 263, 264, 269, 276,
    333
Colville, John, 292, 326, 327, 331, 337,
    339–40
Committee of Imperial Defence, 321
Comptroller of Works, 203, 317
Confectionary, 317
Cook, Captain James, 199, 264
Cook, Robin, 262–3, 272
Cooke, Mr, 128
'Cool Britannia', 94
Cooney, Ray, 91
Cooper, Duff, 290, 329, 337
Corbet, Miles, 156
Corn Laws, 238
Correggio, Antonio da, 117
Corsham, 'Burlington' and 'Turnstile'
    beneath quarry near, 299–300
Cotton House, 110
*Country Life*, 168
court fools/jesters, 90
Court Gate, 7, 82, 88, 148
Coutts Bank, 222
Covent Garden, 101
Coward, Noël, 330, 342–3
Cowper, William, 302
Cranmer, Thomas, 34, 60, 65
Crew, Mr, 125
Crimean War, 250–1, 269, 286, 294
Crippen, Dr, 319
Cripps, Stafford, 309
Crisp, Diana, 127–8
Croker, John Wilson, 190–1, 194, 244,
    248

Cromwell House, 41, 150, 293
Cromwell, Oliver, 108, 110, 113, 114,
    115–16, 154, 157, 173–4, 245
    death of, 118, 124
    Lord Protector title taken by, 116
    MPs petition, 116
    New Model Army, 108
    Parliament dismissed by, 123
    spiked head of, 120
Cromwell, Richard, 124, 126
Cromwell, Thomas, 61
Crowe, Kate, 194
Crown Jewels, 117
Crusades, 1, 6
Crystal Palace, 267
Cunningham, Sir Charles, 279
Curzon, Lord, 262, 274
Cuttance, Captain, 120

Daily Express, 329, 343
Daily Mail, 172, 174
Daily Mirror, 94, 209
Daily Telegraph, 299
Dalton, Hugh, 309
Darling, Alistair, 310
Darnley, Lord, 96
Darwin, Charles, 199
Dashwood, Sir Francis, 162
David Copperfield (Dickens), 317
Davis, David, 273
Davison, Alexander, 190
de Burgh, Hubert, 5–6
death penalty, 278–9
debtors' court, 317
Decipherer of Letters, 277
Declaration of Breda, 126
Declaration of Rights, 144
Defence of the Seven Sacraments (Henry
    VIII), 34
Defence, Ministry of (MoD), 5, 8, 16, 39,
    41, 129, 135, 146, 246, 260, 285, 293–4
    car park at, 150
    unified, 293
    see also War Office; Whitehall:
        underground
'Defender of the Faith' title, 34

Delmer, Sefton, 329
Denham, Sir John, 317
Denmark House, 103
Depp, Johnny, 315
Depression, 306
Derby, Earls of, 262, 291
Devereux, Robert, Earl of Essex, 87–9
    execution of, 89
Devonshire House, 164, 217
Dewar, Donald, 235
Diable Amoureux, Le (Cazotte), 229
Diana, Princess of Wales, 94, 184–5, 197,
    318
Dickens, Charles, 254
Dickens, John, 317
Digby, Lord, 105
Disraeli, Benjamin, Earl of Beaconsfield,
    150, 166, 261
Disraeli, Mrs, 261–2
divine right of kings, 104, 202
Dixey, Phyllis, 91
Doctor Faustus (Marlowe), 229
Dog pub, 128
Doherty, John, 299
Domesday Book, 5
Dover Castle, Siege of, 6
Dover House (formerly Melbourne
    House), 57, 165, 212, 235–6, 268
    see also Melbourne House; Scotland
        Office
Dover, Lord, see Agar-Ellis, George,
    Lord Dover
Down Street, 297
Downing, George, 116, 123–4, 125, 126,
    154–9, 301–2
    baronetcy for, 156
    knighthood for, 155
Downing Square, 193
Downing Street, vii, 143, 153–82 passim
    blast damage throughout, 306
    lamp standards in, 348
    makeshift shelters in, 340
    necessary repairs to properties in, 159
    Number 10 in, see Ten Downing
        Street
    Number 11 in, 170–1

Number 12 in, 171, 172, 192
Number 14 in, 194
renumbering of houses in, 159
Drake, Sir Francis, 264
Drury Lane, 224
*Dry Rot*, 91
Dryden, John, 135
Duck, Dr Richard, 8, 9, 10, 47
Dudley, John, Duke of Northumberland, 69
Dudley, Lord Robert, 54, 84, 85, 87, 89
Dugdale, George, 279
Dundas, Henry, Viscount Melville, 192, 193
Durbar Court, 267, 275
Dürer, Albrecht, 117
Durham, Bishops of, 6
Dyck, Sir Anthony van, 63, 102, 109

East India Company, 265, 266
Eddowes, Catharine ('Kate'), 313, 315
Eden, Sir Anthony, 169, 175, 271, 292, 330
Edgar, King, 4, 316
Edgehill Ridge, 107–8
Edward I, 1–3
    crown of, 60
    death of, 3, 4–5
    inscription on tomb of, 1, 3
    'Longshanks' sobriquet of, 6
    marriage of, 2
Edward the Confessor, 2, 4, 139
    crown of, 117
    shrine to, 3
Edward VI, 7, 69, 73, 77
    birth of, 62
    death of, 70
    depicted in second dynastic painting, 64
    portrait of, 77–8
Edward VII, 208, 267
Eglin, Mr, 125
Eleanor of Castile, 1–2
    tomb of, 2
    destruction of memorial to, 11
    marriage of, 2

Elector Palatine, 105, 108
Eliot (née Pitt), Harriet, 164
Elizabeth I:
    accession of, 75–6
    Alençon and, 82, 83–4
    Anjou and, 84
    barge journey of, 74–5
    bear-bating enjoyed by, 54–5
    birth of, 60
    blackened teeth of, 86
    Catholic plot to assassinate, 84
    Charter for Asian trade granted by, 266
    dancing by, 80
    death of, 90
    depicted in dynastic painting, 64
    Devereux and, 87
    'Golden Speech' of, 89–90
    Hampden House and, 15
    implicated in Protestant plot, 69
    imprisoned in Bell Tower, 75
    intelligence chief/spymaster of, 84, 320
    journey to Whitehall by, 69–71, 72
    Knyvett and, 157
    Mary frees, 75
    musical instruments of, 78
    necessary parsimony of, 82
    pageantry loved by, 85
    palace house arrest of, 72
    people's disillusionment during final years of power of, 96
    pleading letter of, 72–4
    red hair of, 86
    Stone Gallery banquet of, 50
    tantrums displayed by, 76
    wardrobe of, 76
    Whitehall Palace tenure of, 76–90
    Woodstock house arrest of, 75
    Wyatt's letter to, 72
*Elizabeth I*, 78
Elizabeth, Princess, 111, 112
*Elizabeth R*, 74
Elizabeth II, 32, 41, 93–4, 255, 257
    Golden Jubilee of, 169
Elizabeth of York, 63, 96
Ellam, Mike, 171, 172

Ellis, Ruth, 319
*Enchantress*, 204
Endive Lane, 8, 9, 18
Enedehithe (Seabird shore), 1, 5
*England as Seen by Foreigners* (Rye), 55
England–Scotland union, 302
English Civil War, 11, 107–9, 244
  arguments over cause of, 118–19
English Commonwealth, establishment
  of, 115
English Heritage, 276, 309
Enigma, 273
Environment, Department of, 297
Erasmus, 54
Erith, Raymond, 168
Erlon, Comte de, 252
Esher, 14, 37, 47
  Gallery, 47
espionage, *see* spies and espionage
euro, 311
Evans, Gwynne Owen, 278–9
Evans, John, 202
Evelyn, John, 78–9, 116, 117, 129–30,
  130–1, 142, 147, 156–7
*Evening Standard*, 329
Evreux, 4
Ewans, Ralph, 97
Exchequer Partnerships, 310
Express group, 329

*Face of London, The* (Clunn), 181–2
*Faerie Queen, The* (Spenser), 307
Fage, Luellin, 128
Fairfax, Sir Thomas, 108
Falconer, Lord, 330
Falklands War, 15, 153, 169, 271, 272
*Family of Henry VIII, The*, 48
farce, 90–2
Farquhar, Sir Walter, 195
Fawkes, Guido, 96
Fernández de Velasco, Juan, 55
Fetherstonhaugh, Sir Harry, 186
Fetherstonhaugh, Sir Matthew, 221
Fictional Cities website, 295
Field of the Cloth of Gold, 21, 82
Fielding, Henry, 317–18

Fielding, John, 318
Fife House, 149, 150
firemen's strike, 208
First Lord of the Treasury, office of,
  159–60
First World War, 164, 252, 274, 275,
  283–5, 289, 322
  Americans enter, 322
  British Expeditionary Force in,
    285
  Kitchener raises troops for, 284
  'Pals Battalions' in, 284
Fish Larder, 317
Fisher, Lord, 205
Fitzgerald, Ella, 207
FitzNigel, Richard, 5
*Flashman* (Fraser), 254
Fludyer Street, 268
flying buttresses, 4
fools, 90
Foot Guards, 246, 247, 255
foot-and-mouth disease, 176
Foreign Affairs Committee, 272
Foreign and Commonwealth Office,
  258–79, 287, 309, 347
  Cabinet meetings held in, 262
  first telephone installed in, 277
  first typists in, 277
  Grade I listing for, 275
  Locarno Rooms in, 275
  north–south divide in, 267
  opening of, 262
  Palmerston rejects Scott's designs for,
    258, 259–60
  rolling programme of refurbishment
    for, 276
  Scott's designs for, 258–60
  'spooks' in, 273
Foreign Office, 123, 161
Foreign Press Association, 172
Forster, E. M., 330
Forsyth, W. A., 298
Foster, Lady Elizabeth (later Duchess of
  Devonshire), 191, 217
Fotheringhay Castle, 84
*Foudroyant*, 189

Fox, Charles James, 163–4, 214, 215, 223, 224, 260, 268
Foxes, John, 49
Francis I of France, 21–2, 33
Francis, Duke of Bedford, 220
Franklin, Sir John, 264
Fraser, George Macdonald, 254
Frederica of Prussia, Princess, 220
Frederick, Prince, 17
Frederick, Prince, Duke of York, 149, 219, 220, 221, 241, 242–3
    death of, 244
    funeral of, 248
French Foreign Ministry, 261
French, Sir John, 285
French Revolution, 118, 163
Fry, John, 247

Gage, Sir John, 71
Gallipoli, 205
Gardiner, Stephen, 71
Garter jewel of St George, 112, 113
Gascony, 2
GCHQ, 274
Geddington, 11
General Strike, 278, 306
Genoa, Doge of, 137
George I, 160, 303
George II, 66, 150, 160
George III, 213, 214, 223, 224, 265
    attempt on life of, 224
    dull court of, 223
    madness of, 165
    Pit the Younger backed by, 163
George IV:
    as Prince Regent, 231, 241, 242, 252
    as Prince of Wales, 163, 219, 223, 224, 225
George of Denmark, Prince, 143
George, Earl of Cumberland, 89
George, third Earl Egremont, 219
Georgiana, Duchess of Devonshire, 164, 185, 191, 214, 217, 219
    Harriet, daughter of, 214
    Sheridan satirizes, 224
Gerin, 5

Gestapo Invasion Plan of Britain, 329
Gibbons, Grinling, 142, 202, 203
Gilt Chamber, 19
Girls Aloud, 174
Giustiniani, Giovanni, 105
Giustiniani, Sebastian, 20
Gladstone, William, 165–6, 167, 181, 235
Glenarvon (Lamb), 218, 231
Globe Theatre, 54
Glorious Revolution, 144
Gloucester, Duke of, 291
Glyn Mills bank, 207
Goderich, Lord, 248
Godwinson, Harold, see Harold II
Goetze, Sir Sigismund, 274
Gold Standard, 306
Gordon, Frederick, 290
Gordon, General, 166, 283
Gothic revival, 259
government whips, 31–2
Gower, Earl, 149
Gower House, 149
Grafton, Duke of, 134
Grand Remonstrance, 104
Grant, Hugh, 174
Granville, Lord, 214
Great Fire of London, 131–4
Great George Street, 56, 233, 307, 341
    Government Offices at ('GOGGS'), 260, 306, 307
Great Plague, 131
Great Reform Bill, 152
Great Scotland Yard, see Scotland Yard
Great Stink, 287
Great War, 164, 252, 274, 275, 283–5, 289, 322
    Americans enter, 322
    British Expeditionary Force in, 285
    Kitchener raises troops for, 284
    'Pals Battalions' in, 284
Greatorex, Ralph, 134, 138
Greece, British naval threat to, 270
Green, Michael, 306
Greig, Gordon, 172
Grenadier Guards, 246, 337
Grenville, William, first Baron, 164, 214

Gresham College, 135
Greville, Charles, 186–7
Grey, Charles, Lord Howick, 214
Grey, Earl, 152, 241
Grey, Lady Jane, 69, 72
Grey, Lord, of Falloden, 262
Grieve, Deputy Assistant Commissioner
    John, 315
Grosvenor Square, 238
Guedalla, Philip, 248
Guildford, Sir Henry, 23
Gulf Wars:
    First, 178, 282, 290
    Second, see Iraq
Gunpowder Plot, 32, 96–7, 103, 157
Gunter, Edmund, 135, 202
Gwydyr House, 55, 134, 150
Gwyn, Eleanor ('Nell'), 135, 136–7, 139,
    140

Hacker, Colonel Francis, 110, 112, 120
Hague, 123, 126, 134, 155, 156, 301
Hague, William, 165
Haig, General Douglas, 252, 285, 321
    lampooned, 286
Haines, Joe, 171
Haldane, Richard, 282–3, 321
Haldane Suite, 282, 285, 290, 292
Halifax, Lord, 325
Hall, Edward, 27–8
Hamilton, Emma, 186–7, 188–9, 191–2,
    193, 195, 221
    Nelson falls in love with, 188–9
Hamilton, Sir William, 186, 187, 189,
    192
Hammer, Armand, 171
Hampden, Elizabeth, 157, 158
Hampden House, 157, 158–9
Hampden, John, 106, 108, 154, 157
Hampton Court, 14, 19, 37, 63, 135, 288
    art collection at, 64
    Palace, 66
Hansard, 213
Hardingstone, 11
Hardy, Captain, 196
Harman, Harriet, 173

Harold II, 5
Harpsfield, Nicholas, 45
Harris, 'Bomber', 308
Harris, Vincent, 289
Harrison, John, 199–200
Harrison, Major General, 120
Harrowby, Lord, 238, 240
    Mary, daughter of, 241
Harry, Prince, 255
Hartington, Lord, 218
Harvard, John, 154
Harvard University, 154
Harwood, Brian, 58
Haselrig, Sir Arthur, 106, 245
Hastings, Battle of, 5
Hatton, Sir Christopher, 86, 87
Health, Department of, 8, 152, 308, 345,
    346
Heath, Sir Edward, 167, 169, 171
Heathcote, Lady, 230
Hellfire Club, 162
Henbury, John, 9–10
Heneage, Thomas, 43
Hennessy, Professor Peter, 269
Henrietta Maria, Princess, 102–3, 105,
    108
    death of, 131
Henry II, 5
Henry III of England, 1, 2, 4
Henry III of France, 82
Henry V, 21
Henry VII, 49, 79, 96, 97, 116
    depicted in dynastic mural, 63
Henry VIII:
    Anne marries, 44–7
    council moved by, 76
    death of, 65
    declining years of, 64–5
    'Defender of the Faith' title bestowed
        on, 34
    dramatized portrayals of, 20–1
    dynastic mural commissioned by, 62–4
    fall from horse by, 60–1
    at Field of the Cloth of Gold, 21–2
    Holbein's detailed portrayal of, 64
    Jane bears son of, 62

Jane marries, 62
jousting by, 57–8
later reclusive nature of, 64–5
love letters of, 34
'minions' of, 20
Parliament approves seizure of York
  Place property by, 60
power struggle follows death of, 70
second dynastic painting
  commissioned by, 64
tennis court of, vii, 52, 56, 268, 305
tennis played by, 53
Whitehall Palace tenure of, 43–69
wine cellar of, vii
Wolsey a restraining hand on, 20
Wolsey stripped of Lord
  Chancellorship by, 9, 14, 36–7
Wolsey's gift of fool to, 90
Wolsey's New Year's banquet
  gatecrashed by, 23–5, 147
York Place seized by, 6, 14
as younger man, 21
see also Boleyn, Anne; Katherine of
  Aragon; Whitehall Palace: Henry
  VIII's time in
Henry, Duc d'Alençon, 82, 83–4
Henry, Philip, 114–15
Henry, Prince of Wales, 99, 102
Henry, Prince, 111–12
Hentzner, 79
Hentzner, Paul, 79
Herbert, Sir Thomas, 112
Hertford (later Somerset), Lord, see
  Somerset, Duke of
Hertslet, Sir Edward, 268
Hetzner, Paul,
Hibbert, Christopher, 74
Hill, Mrs, 340
History of Britain, A, 265
History of England (Macaulay), 137–8
Hitler, Adolf, 164, 205, 324, 329
  Austria annexed by, 275
  'mainspring of evil', 345
  threat to 'erase' British cities by, 339
HM Revenue and Customs, 56, 264, 307,
  310, 345

Hobhouse, John Cam, 232
Holbein Gate, 43–9 passim, 52, 54, 55–6,
  64–6, 107, 113, 148, 151
Holbein, Hans, 33, 48, 50, 59, 60, 64,
  77–8, 117
  Henry's dynastic mural by, 62–4
  Tate Britain exhibition of work of,
    63–4
Holland, Sir Henry, 221, 222
Holland, Lady, 217, 219
Hollar, Wenceslaus, 49, 67, 108–9
Holles, Denzil, 106
Hollis, General, 297
Home Office, 263, 268, 269, 273, 276,
  277–80, 296, 297, 313, 333
Hong Kong, British acquisition of, 270
Hoon, Geoff, 281–2, 285
Hore-Belisha, Leslie, 290–1
Horse Guards, 57, 58, 133, 134, 138, 159,
  178, 204, 206, 107, 212, 220, 222, 233,
  237, 238, 242, 243, 244, 247–8, 254–7,
  286, 293, 330, 337
  Beating of the Retreat by, 256
  change forced on, 251
  ethnic minorities and, 256–7
  first building for, 246
  Haig's statue near, 252
  horses of, 254–5
  Kent's building for, 246–7
  living daily routine at, 254–5
  Russell blames for Light Brigade
    catastrophe, 251
  Wellington's happiest time with, 250
  see also Household Cavalry;
    Wellington, Duke of
Horse Guards Avenue, 7, 17, 18, 40, 41,
  150, 316
Horse Guards Museum, 253
Horse Guards Parade, 7, 53, 68, 85, 143,
  161, 174, 204, 206, 216, 221, 223, 255,
  296, 297, 348
  wartime plan to cordon off, 332
Horse Guards Road, 296, 307, 327
Houghton Hall, 161
House of Commons, 31, 32, 104, 106,
  210–14, 215

Central Lobby of, 109
Irish representation in, 192
Pitt collapses in, 192
press gallery at, 172
House of Fame, 99
House of Lords:
  Charles II's illegitimate progeny in, 134
  Record Office in, 120
  Rix in, 91
Household Cavalry, 246, 253, 255
  Horse Guards, *see* main entry
  women not permitted to serve in, 257
Howard, Lady Elizabeth, 27, 38, 45
Howard, Lord, of Effingham, 307
Howard, Tom, 155
Howe, Earl, First Lord of the Admiralty, 203
Howe, Sir Geoffrey (later Lord), 177, 261, 273, 274
Humphrey, Nick, 78
Huncks, Colonel, 110, 120
Hunsdon, Lord, 85
Hunt, Mrs, 128
Hunter, Anji, 177
Hurd, Douglas, 178, 179, 261
Huskisson, William, 151–2
Hutchinson, Professor Max, 100, 101
Hutton, Lord, 271
Huxley, Aldous, 330

Imperial War Museum, 328
*In Which We Serve*, 342–3
India Act, 266
India Office, 263, 264, 266–7, 287
  *see also* Foreign and Commonwealth Office
Indian Mutiny, 266
Industrial Revolution, 224, 226, 259
Ingham, Sir Bernard, 171
Ingrams, Richard, 92
Institute of Civil Engineers, 233
Iraq, 255, 270
  'dodgy dossier' concerning, 272

invasion of (Second Gulf War), 175, 176, 271–2, 282, 285–6
  *see also* Gulf Wars; Kelly, Dr David
Ireland, 88
  Catholic uprising in, 105
Irish Republican Army (IRA), 153, 177–8
  Brighton hotel bomb of, 178
  Downing Street attack by, 177–9
Ironside, General Edmund, 330
Islanlwana, 257
Ismay, Major General Hastings, 297
  first Whitehall defence memorandum of, 332–6
  first Whitehall defence memorandum of, verbatim, 333–6
  second Whitehall defence memorandum of, 337–8
  third Whitehall defence memorandum of, 338
Ives, Colonel, 297

Jack the Ripper, 312, 313–16, 318
Jackie (Blairs' nanny), 295
Jackson, Glenda, 74
James I (James VI of Scotland):
  bawdy parties thrown by, 97–8
  bear-bating and, 55
  court jester of, 91
  Gresham sundial of, 135–6
  Knyvett moved by, 157
  love of boys displayed by, 98
  manners of, 95–6
  move to London by, 90
  Whitehall Palace tenure of, 95–100
James II (James VII of Scotland) (formerly Duke of York), 112, 133, 135, 136, 137
  accession of, 141
  escape and return of, 144
  Gwyn granted house lease by, 140
  Matted Gallery apartment of, 129
  navy commanded by, 127, 138
  post surrendered by, 139
  religious tolerance promised by, 141
  weathercock ordered by, 143

Whitehall Palace tenure of, 141–4
William III's forces amassed against,
    143
Jeffreys, Judge, 141
Jenkins, Roy, 165–6, 279
Jervis, Sir John, 191
jesters, 90
John, King, 5
Johnson, Herschel, 331
Johnson, Samuel, 163
Joint Intelligence Committee, 271
Jones, Inigo, 82, 95, 98–9, 100–1, 109,
    117, 307, 317
Jonson, Ben, 91, 98–9
jousting, 57–8, 85
    lances for, 57–8
Judge Marshall, 115
Justice Department, 279
Juxon, William, 113

Karsh, Yousef, 174
Katherine of Aragon, 15, 21, 26–7, 33–5,
    46
    Arthur's marriage to, 34–5
    Henry orders Wolsey to procure
        divorce of, 33
    Wolsey's first secret trial of marriage
        of, 40
Keeler, Christine, 288
Keeper of His Majesty's Back Stairs, 136
Keeper of the King's privy closet, 136
Kell, Captain Vernon, 321
*Kelly*, 342
Kelly, Dr David, 272–3, 285
Kelly, Captain Edward, 254
Kelly, Mary Jane ('Marie Jeanette'), 313,
    315
Kemp, Will, 81
Kempson, Rachel, 74
Kenilworth, 54
Kenneth II of Scotland, 316
Kensington Palace, 145, 148
Kent, William, 161, 246, 303
Keynes, John Maynard, 206
Khartoum, 166
Kilfoyle, Peter, 298–9

*Kim* (Kipling), 322
King Charles Street, 308
*King Henry the Eighth* (Shakespeare),
    25–6, 43
*King Henry the Fourth* (Shakespeare), 81
King's Herb House, 317
King James Bible, 95
*King Lear* (Shakespeare), 98
King's Lock Smith, 317
King's Men, 98
King's Own Light Dragoons, 294
*King Richard the Second* (Shakespeare),
    78
King Street, 6–7, 9, 18, 47, 55–6, 105,
    128, 269
    Charles I carried along, 111
    erased, 307
King Street Gate, 55–6, 66, 122
Kipling, Rudyard, 283, 322
Kitchener, Lord, 281, 283, 284, 348
    iconic poster depicting, 283
    lampooned, 286
Knollys, Sir Francis, 114
Knollys, Lettice, Countess of Essex, 87
Knyff, Leonard, 145
Knyvett House, 157
Knyvett, Sir Thomas, 96–7, 197
Kosovo, 270
Kratzer, Nikolaus, 60
Kremlin, 175, 261, 273, 298
Kutcher, Arthur, 246
Kuwait, 178

Labour, Ministry of, 150
*Lady Hamilton*, 342
Lamb Alley, 8–9, 40, 50
Lamb, Augustus, 224
Lamb (née Ponsonby), Lady Caroline
    ('Caro'), 210–11, 212–13, 214, 215–18,
    224, 225–34, 235, 239
    Byron enters life of, 226
    death of, 234
    mother-in-law's letter to, 231–2
    novel of, 218, 231
    Wellington's nickname for, 243
    William marries, 218

Lamb (née Milbanke), Elizabeth, *see* Melbourne, Lady

Lamb, George, 220, 232, 233

Lamb, Matthew, 219

Lamb, Peniston (Jr), 212

Lamb, Peniston (Sr), *see* Melbourne, first Viscount

Lamb, William (later second Viscount Melbourne), 165, 212–14, 220, 223, 225, 231, 232–5

   Caroline marries, 218

   Commons speech of, 215–16, 224

   Melbourne title inherited by, 234

   Prime Minister, 234

   reinstated to office, 234

Lambeth Palace, 17, 22

Lamont, Norman, 309

Landemare, Mrs, 341, 342

Landseer, Edwin, 234

Laneham, Robert, 54

Laud, Archbishop, 91

Laughton, Charles, 20

Lawrence, T. E. (of Arabia), 289

Lawson, Lord, 169

Lawson, Nigella, 169

Le Sueur, 11

Lean, David, 342

Lee, Dr Rowland, 44

Leemput, Remigius van, 63

Leg pub, 128

Leicester Abbey, 42

Lennox, Duchess of, 118

Lent, 77

Lenthall, Speaker, 106

Leonardo da Vinci, 117

Leviticus, 34

Liberal Club, 150, 289

Liberal Democrats, 119

Liberal National group, 344–5

Liberals, 152, 160, 165, 270

Lichfield, Countess of, 159

Lichfield House, 159, 161

Life Guard, 233, 244, 245, 246, 333, 337

*Life in the Farce Lane* (Rix), 91

*life of Kinge Henry the 8th from his fallinge in love with Anne Bulloigne to the death of Queene Katheren, his wife, The*, 45

*Life of Wolsey, A* (Cavendish), 13

Lincoln Cathedral, 2

Lisbon Treaty, 273

Lithgow, William, 110

Liverpool dockers' strike, 278

Liverpool House, 150

Liverpool, Lord, 149, 231, 237–8, 240, 241

   stroke suffered by, 248

Livingstone, Dr David, 264

Lloyd George, David, 274, 288

Locarno, 275

London Eye, 246

*London Gazette*, 134, 137

*London Topographical Record*, 10

Longford, Elizabeth, 250

*L'Orient*, 187, 198

lottery, 148–9

Louis XII of France, 57

Louis XIV of France, 141

Louise-Renée de Kéroualle (later Duchess of Portsmouth), 135, 139, 140, 151

Louvre, 60, 117, 130, 131

*Love Actually*, 174

Lucan, Earl of, 184, 254

Luddites, 226

Luftwaffe, 151, 153, 275, 339

Lundenwic, 3

Lusk, George, 315

Luther, Martin, 34

Luttrell, Narcissus, 145

Lutyens, Sir Edward, 279

Lyttleton, Oliver, 341

Maastricht Treaty, 273

Macaulay, Thomas, 137–8, 140

Machiavelli, 156

Machyn, Henry, 71

McKenna, Reginald, 208

MacKinlay, Andrew, 272

Maclean, Donald, 273

   *see also* spies and espionage

Macmillan, Harold, 168, 169, 288

Magna Carta, 5
*Majesty* (Starkey), 96
Major, John, 149, 153, 169, 176, 178–9, 273, 309
Manchester Free Trade Hall, 248
Manchester Town Hall, 259
Mancini, Hortensia, Duchess of Mazarin, 140
Mandelson, Peter, 11
Mander, Karel van, 63
Margaret, Queen, 6
Margesson, David, 292
Maria Carolina, Queen, 187
Marillac, Charles de, 65
Marine Police, 318
Marlowe, Christopher, 229
Marsden, William, 190, 197
Marshalsea Court, 317
Marsham Street bunker, 296–7
Martin, Sir John, 306, 342
Martin, Sir Leslie, 347
Marvell, Andrew, 93
Marxists, 118, 119
Mary I, 15, 26, 45, 50, 69–75
    'Bloody Mary' sobriquet of, 45
    death of, 75
    depicted in dynastic painting, 64
    Philip marries, 75
    as Princess Mary, 25
Mary II, 7, 141, 143, 144–5, 146
    accession of, 144
    death and funeral of, 146
    gardening loved by, 146
    Nottingham House (later Kensington Palace) bought by, 145
    Wren's ornate garden for, 150
Mary of Modena, 135, 141, 144
Mary, Princess of Orange (daughter of Charles I), 155
Mary, Queen of Scots, 79, 84, 96
Mary of Teck, Queen, 41
Mary Tudor, 28, 56, 57
*Mask of Beauty, The* (Jonson), 98
Masons, 202
Massachusetts, 154
Master of Bears, 54

Matted Gallery, 50, 129, 135
media:
    Central News Agency, 314
    Channel 4, 53
    *Country Life*, 168
    *Daily Express*, 329, 343
    *Daily Mail*, 172, 174
    *Daily Mirror*, 94, 209
    *Daily Telegraph*, 299
    *Evening Standard*, 329
    Express group, 329
    Hansard, 213
    *London Gazette*, 134, 137
    *News Chronicle*, 329
    *Newsnight*, 311
    *Picture Post*, 292
    *Private Eye*, 92
    *St James's Chronicle*, 53
    Sky News, 177
    *Sun*, 172
    *Sunday Telegraph*, 282
    *Times*, 251, 269, 311
Melbourne, Australia, 235
Melbourne, first Viscount, 212, 219, 223, 229
    peerage accepted by, 220
Melbourne Hall, 219
Melbourne House (later Dover House), 165, 210, 212, 217–20 *passim*, 222–8, 230, 232–3
    name change of, 235
    sale of, 234
    *see also* Dover House; Lamb, Lady Caroline; Scotland office
Melbourne, Lady, 164, 212, 216–17, 219–20, 223, 224, 229–30, 231–2
    Sheridan satirizes, 224
Mencap, 91
Mendoza, Ambassador, 83
*Merry Wives of Windsor, The* (Shakespeare), 89
Merton Place, 192, 193
Metropole Hotel, 290
Metropolitan Police, 297, 316–20
    A Division of, 318, 320
    first recognizable version of, 317

Special Branch of, 313
*see also* Scotland Yard
Metternich, Prince, 231
Meyer, Sir Christopher, 171
Meyers, Jonathan Rhys, 21
MI5, 273, 300, 322–3
*see also* spies and espionage
MI6, 273, 300, 321, 322
*see also* spies and espionage
Michell, Keith, 20
Middleton, Lord, 187
Midland Grand Hotel, 259–60
Milbanke, Annabella, 230
Military Secretary, 115
Militia Bill, 107
Millar, Fiona, 295
Millbank, 273
Millennium Dome, 94
Millennium Hotel, 238
Miller, Eric, 235
Millyng, John, 7–8
Milosevic, Slobodan, 270
Milton, John, 277
'Ministry of All the Talents', 214
Ministry of Defence (MoD), *see* Defence,
    Ministry of; *see also* War Office
Ministry of Works, 317
Mirren, Helen, 77
monarchy:
    Blair's support for, 94
    continued trust in, 119
    Parliament's abolition of, 115
    Parliament's vote to restore, 126
    Restoration of, 11, 107, 117, 155, 245
*Monarchy*, 40, 129
Monck, General George, 124, 125, 138,
    245
Monck's Head, 247
Monmouth Rebellion, 138, 141
Montagu, Edward (later Earl of
    Sandwich), 123, 124, 126, 128, 138
Montagu House, 150, 151, 318
Montagu, Samuel, 284
Monteagle, Lord, 96
Montgomery, Viscount, 235
Montmorency, Duke of, 50

Moore, Sir John, 196
Moore-Brabazon, John, 341, 342
More, Sir Thomas, 34, 60
    becomes Lord Chancellor, 37
Morland, Nigel, 315
Morris, Marc, 3
Morris, William, 259
Morrison, Herbert, 344, 345
Mount Sinai, 4
Mountbatten, Lord, 261, 342
Muggeridge, Malcolm, 326
Mullin, Chris, 267, 276
Munn, Meg, 266
Murray, John, 227
*Mutine*, 187
*My Farce from My Elbow* (Rix), 91

Napoleon, 187, 192–3, 213, 226, 239
    exile of, 231, 241
Napoleonic Wars, 163, 226, 286
*Naseby*, 126
Naseby, Battle of, 108
National Gallery, 234
National Health Service, 345
National Liberal Club, 289
National Maritime Museum, 17, 196
National Portrait Gallery, 60
Navy Board, 126–7
Nelson (cat), 340
Nelson's Column, 196, 261, 313
Nelson, Horatia, 189, 190, 192, 193
Nelson (Admiral Lord), Horatio,
    183–201, 209, 306
    arm lost to, 190
    death of, 165, 196–7, 213
    eye injury to, 183–4
    funeral of, 198–9
    height of, 201
    medals sported by, 189
    peerage awarded to, 188
    state funeral of, 191–2, 214
    tomb of, 187
Nelson, Lady, 183, 185, 186, 189–90, 209
Nepean, Evan, 190
Neville, Sir Edward, 25
Neville, George, 17

New Caledonia, 302
New Labour, 11, 94–5
New Palace Yard, 210
New Scotland Yard, *see* Scotland Yard
Newgate Prison, 228, 319
*News Chronicle*, 329
*Newsnight*, 311
Nichols, Mary Ann ('Polly'), 313
Nightingale, Florence, 251
Nile, Battle of, 183, 186, 188, 189, 194
Nilsen, Dennis, 319
9/11, 270
Nisbet, Frances ('Fanny'), *see* Nelson, Lady
Nisbet, Josiah, 184, 186
*Noble Revolt: The Overthrow of Charles I, The* (Adamson), 119
Norfolk, Duke of, 27, 36
Normans, 5
Norris, Sir Henry, 37, 43
North, Lord, 162–3, 267
Northbrook, Lord, 286
Northern Ireland Office, 206, 208
Northern Ireland peace initiative, 67
Northumberland Avenue, 151
Northumberland, Duke of, 6, 134
Northumberland, Earl of, 28, 29–30
Northumberland House, 151, 290
Norwich, Bishops of, 6
Nottingham House, 145
Nuremberg trials, 329

Oates, Titus, 139
O'Donnell, Sir Gus, 67, 181
Office of the Revels, 80, 82
*Oh! What a Lovely War*, 286
Okey, Colonel John, 154, 156
*Old Gate, Whitehall, The* (Sandby), 66
Oliver, Peter, 118
Olympic Games (2012), 68
Omdurman, Battle of, 283
*One for the Pot*, 91
O'Neill, Hugh, Earl of Tyrone, 88
Opium Wars, 270
Oratory School, 52
Ormonde, Duke of, 138

Ottley, Sir Charles, 321
Oval Office, 175
Overkirk, Lord, 159
Oxford, Lady, 226

Paddington Station, 267
Page, William, 83–4
Paget, General Bernard, 338
Paget, Henry, Earl of Uxbridge (later Marquess of Anglesey), 252, 253
Paine, James, 221
Pakenham, Kitty, *see* Wellesley (née Pakenham), Kitty
Pall Mall, 48, 140, 164, 186, 286, 288
  in flames, 342
Palladio, Andrea, 101
Palmerston, Lord, 258, 259–60, 269–70, 276
'Pals Battalions', 284
Panama Canal, 302
Pannell, Charles, 347
Parkside, 49
Parliament Square, 56, 259, 269, 308
Parliament Street, 56, 210, 211, 269, 276, 307, 308
  designated a conservation area, 348
Parr, Katherine, 70
Patch (fool), 90
Paxton, Joseph, 266–7
Paymaster General's Office, 306
Payne, Tom, 154
Peacock, 158, 159
Pebble Court, 51, 146
Peel, Sir Robert, 150, 234, 277, 306, 318
peelers/bobbies, 318
Pegge, Catherine, 135
Pembroke, Earl of, 97
Pembroke House, 293
Penn, Sir William, 127, 128, 132–3
Pepys, Elizabeth, 122, 132
Pepys, Samuel, 53, 115, 119, 120, 122–7, 131–4, 138–9, 154, 155, 190, 201, 245
  Admiral's Secretary and Treasurer of the Fleet, 126
  Clerk of the Acts to the Navy Board, 126

diary begun by, 124–5
Gwyn captivates, 135
marriage of, 122
move to King Street by, 123
powers of patronage exercised by, 127
sexual conquests of, 127, 128–9
at Whitehall Palace, 122–3
Perceval, Spencer, 226, 228, 303
Percy, Lord Henry, 28–30
Percy, Major (later Lieutenant Colonel)
  Henry, 237–8, 240–3
Percy, Thomas, 97
*Pericles* (Shakespeare), 85
Peter the Painter, 278
'Peterloo', 248
Petworth, 219
Pevsner, Nikolaus, 293
Phayre, Lieutenant Colonel, 100, 120
Pheasant Court, 158
Philby, Kim, 273
  *see also* spies and espionage
Philip II of Spain, 71, 75, 88
Philip, Prince, Duke of Edinburgh, 93–4
Physician, 115
Piatkov, Peter, 278
*Pickle*, 197
*Picture Post*, 292
Pierce, Mrs, 133
Pinkerton's, 315
Pitt, William (the Elder), first Earl of
  Chatham, 162, 185, 203, 265
Pitt, William (the Younger), 162, 163–5,
  192, 195, 306
  collapse and illness of, 192–3, 195
  death of, 165, 214
Plassey, 265
Plymouth, Earl of, 135
Pomfrett, John, 9–10
Ponsonby, Lady Caroline, *see* Lamb (née
  Ponsonby), Lady Caroline
Ponsonby, Frederick (Jr), 226, 239–40
Ponsonby, Frederick (Sr), Viscount
  Duncannon, 217
Ponsonby, Willy, 217
'Popish Plot', 139
Portal, Lord, 16

Portcullis House, 319
Portillo, Michael, 206
Portland, Earl of, 147, 150
Portland stone, 100–1, 142, 281, 287–8
Portman Square, 187
Portsmouth, Duchess of, *see*
  Louise-Renée de Kéroualle
Poulet, Sir Amyas, 35
Poulterers Office, 317
Powell, Sir Charles, 175–6, 178
Powell, Colin, 271
Powell, Enoch, 15
Powell, Jonathan, 176
Prado, 117
Preaching Place, 49, 76–7
Prescott, John, 173, 200, 206–8, 209, 222,
  342
Prescott, Pauline, 206, 209
Presence Chamber, 23, 31, 40, 49, 55, 77,
  80, 89, 101, 147
Price, Lance, 181
prices and their modern-day equivalents,
  349
Priestley, J. B., 330
*Private Eye*, 92
private finance initiative (PFI), 310
Privy Bridge, 17
Privy Chamber, 62, 76, 79
Privy Council, 47, 55, 72
  Office, 304, 333
  unchanging ceremonial role of, 304
Privy Gallery, 46, 47–8, 49, 51, 52, 71, 76,
  78, 107, 113, 301
  Charles II's tennis court in, 53
  glimpsed in dynastic painting, 64
  Henry VIII's mourning in, 62
  new, 142
  open to view, 77
Privy Garden, 49, 51, 76–7, 123, 135,
  147
Privy Stairs, 23, 37, 38, 50, 51, 59, 62,
  103, 107, 144, 147
Profumo, John, 288
Public Record Office, 277, 278, 314
Pudding Lane, 133
Pugin, Augustus, 259

Puritan Protectorate, 122, 123
Puritans, 104, 107, 116, 139, 154
*Pyjama Tops*, 92
Pym, John, 104, 106

QE2 Centre, 296
Quartermaster General, 115
Queen Anne's Gate, 279
Queen's Club, 52
Queen's Gallery, 51
Queen Henrietta's Men, 109
Queen's House, Greenwich, 101
Queen Mary's Steps, 293, 348
Queen's Speech, 89, 106, 213

RAC Club, 286
Raglan, Lord, 251–2
Raleigh, Sir Walter, 87
Raphael, Frederick, 227
Rattray, David, 257
*Recollections of the Old Foreign Office*
    (Hertslet), 268
Red Lion, 299, 300, 310–11
Red Lion brewhouse, 9, 10, 311
Red Square, 298
*Redoubtable*, 196
Reform Act, 248, 270
Reform Bill, 224
Reform Club, 342
Reformation Parliament, opening of,
    37–8
*Reluctant Heroes*, 91
Remembrance Sunday, 279
Renard, Simon, 71
Restoration, 11, 107, 117, 155, 245
Revenue and Customs, 56, 264, 307, 310,
    345
Revisionists, 118
Reynolds, Joshua, 264
Richard, Earl of Warwick, 17
Richmond, Duke of, 135, 136, 151
Richmond, Fiona, 91–2
Richmond House, 151, 152
Richmond, Lady, 239
Richmond Palace, 52
Richmond Terrace, 8, 151–2, 347, 348

*Ride to Khiva, A* (Burnaby), 254
*Rights of Man, The* (Payne), 154
Rimington, Dame Stella, 322
Ripley, Thomas, 203
Rippon, Geoffrey, 151, 275, 347
Rix, Brian, 91
Robbins, William, 109
Rochester, Earl of, 135
Rochford, Lord, 61
*Rocket*, 151–2
Rockingham, Marquess of, 268
Rogers, Samuel, 227
Roosevelt, President Franklin, 331, 336,
    345
Roosevelt, President Theodore, 201–2
Rose Alley, 8
Rose and Crown, 299, 300
Rose pub, 9
Rose Yard, 8
Ross, Mr, 217
Rosser, Gervase, 7
Rothschild, Nathan, 240
Rotten Row, 226
Round Table, Knights of, 20
Roundheads, naming of, 107–8
Roxburgh, Earl of, 105–6
Royal Academy, 254
*Royal Charles*, 126, 138
Royal Dragoons, 255
Royal Festival Hall, 347
Royal Institute of British Architects, 308
Royal Library, 66
Royal Marines, 337
Royal Master of Bears, 54
Royal Naval Museum, 201
Royal Regiment of Horse, 246
Royal United Services Institute, 148
Rubens, Peter Paul, 103–4
rugby World Cup, 2003, 169
Rump Parliament, 124, 125
Rupert, Prince, 108, 135, 136
Russell, Conrad, 119
Russell, John, 10
Russell, Richard, 8
Russell, William Howard, 251
Russell, William, 8, 10

Russian Revolution, 118
Rutland, Earl of, 59, 85–6
Rye, W. B., 55

*Saber of London*, 319
Saddam Hussein, 178, 270, 272
St Albans, Duke of, 135, 140
St Dunstan, 4
St Edward, *see* Edward the Confessor
*St James's Chronicle*, 53
St James's Church, Piccadilly, 143
St James's Fields/Park, 7, 9, 51, 158, 194,
    198, 212, 245, 246, 262
    plan for pill boxes in, 338
St James's Palace, 9, 148, 223, 255, 268
*St John* (Leonardo), 117
St Margaret's parish, 7
    Church, 56
St Paul, 4
St Peter, 4
St Peter's Field, Manchester, 248
St Stephen's Chapel, Westminster, 211
St Vincent, Earl, 191–2, 201
Salem, MA, 154
Salisbury, Lord, 260, 262, 283
Sandby, Thomas, 66
Sandhurst, Royal Military Academy at,
    250, 285
Sandwich, Earl of, *see* Montagu, Edward
Sandys, Lord, 23
Savage, Anne, 43–4
Savorgnano, Mario, 19
Scalding House, 317
Scawen, 128
Schama, Simon, 181, 265
Schellenberg, General Walter, 329
*School for Scandal* (Sheridan), 224
Scotland–England union, 302
'Scotland', London, 18
Scotland Office, 149, 165, 186, 209, 212,
    216, 235
    *see also* Dover House; Melbourne
    House
Scotland Yard, 9, 147, 151, 204, 282, 307,
    312, 314, 316–20
    'Black Museum' in, 319

name of, 316
    *see also* Whitechapel murders
Scott, George Gilbert, 258–61, 262, 263,
    266, 276, 280, 287
Scott, Giles Gilbert, 280
Scott, James, Duke of Monmouth and
    Buccleuch, 134, 137, 138, 141
Scott, Sir Walter, 253
Scottish Nationalists, 302
Scottish Parliament, 235
Scoutmaster General, 116, 124, 154
Seabird Shore (Enedehithe), 1
Seafield, Lord, 302
*Seahorse*, 184
Seal, Eric, 332, 339
Sealed Knot, 113
Second World War, 41, 167, 205, 273,
    275, 290–2, 295, 296, 324–46
    British Expeditionary Force in, 326
    Churchill's intended last stand during,
        327–9
    Gestapo Invasion Plan of Britain
        during, 329
Secret Intelligence Service (SIS),
    *see* MI6
*Secret Love* (Dryden), 135
Secretary of the Latin Language, 277
Secretary of State, office of, 160
Security Service, *see* MI5
Sedgemoor, Battle of, 141
Seething Lane, 127, 201
Selim III, Sultan of Turkey, 189
sentry-box duty, 256
Seven Years War, 150
sewerage, 287
Seymour, Edward, Duke of Somerset,
    103
Seymour, Jane, 59, 70
    death of, 62
    depicted in dynastic mural, 63
    depicted in second dynastic painting,
        64
    Henry marries, 62
    rumours concerning Henry and, 61
    son born to, 62
Seymour, Thomas, 70, 74

Shakespeare, William, 11, 25–6, 43, 78, 85–6, 91
  performances in Whitehall by, 80–1, 89, 98
Shapiro, James, 80, 81
Shaw, Corporal John, 253–4
Shaw, Norman, 307, 319
Sheffield, Lord, 268, 284
Shelburne, Earl of, 268
Shelley, Lady, 184, 185, 189, 211–12, 232–3, 239, 243
Sheply, Mr, 125
Sheridan, Hecca, 214
Sheridan, Richard Brinsley, 214, 223–4, 224–5, 268
Sherwyn, Richard, 122
Shield Gallery, 59
Ship Money tax, 106
Shogun restaurant, 238
Short, Clare, 272, 278
Shrewsbury, Earl of, 30
Sidney Street siege, 277–8
Silverman, Sydney, 279
Simon, Viscount, 344
*Simple Spymen*, 91
Sinclair, Sir Archibald, 341
Singapore, fall of, 292
Sinn Féin, 67, 173
Six, Professor Frank, 329
Skelton, John, 19
Skerrett, Maria, *see* Walpole (née Skerrett), Maria
Skinner, Dennis, 32
Sky News, 177
slavery, 164, 199, 270
*Slight Reminiscences of a Septuagenarian* (Brownlow), 241
Slim, Viscount, 292–3
Slingsby, Mr, 66
Sloane collection, British Library, 45
Smith, Stephen, 296
Smith, Sydney, 226
Smith-Cumming, Commander Mansfield, 321
Snow, C. P., 330
Snow Hill, 66

Soames, Nicholas, 327
Soane, John, 100, 288, 303–4, 305
Sobieski, John, 137
Somers, Will, 90
Somerset (formerly Hertford), Duke of, 70, 73
Somerset House, 103, 131
Soros, George, 179
Soskice, Frank, 279
South Georgia, 153
South Sea Company, 160
Southampton, Duke of, 134
Southampton, Earl of, 88–9
Southey, Robert, 191, 196
Spanish Armada, 79, 83, 84–5
Spanish Inquisition, 71
Special Branch, 313
Spencer, first Earl, 217
Spencer, Henrietta, *see* Bessborough (née Spencer), Lady
Spencer, Lady, 183, 184–5, 186, 188, 189, 190, 209
Spencer, second Earl, 184, 186, 188, 191
Spender, Stephen, 330
Spenser, Edmund, 307
spies and espionage, 320–3
  *see also* MI5; MI6
Spring Garden, 112
Spurs, Battle of, 21
*Stalingrad*, 343
Stanley, Colonel, 146
Stanley, Lord (later Earl of Derby), 262
Stanley, Oliver, 291–2
Stanley, Venetia, 283–4
Star Chamber, 20, 30
Starkey, David, 21, 33, 40, 96, 104, 129
state lottery, 148–9
State Opening of Parliament, 32, 96, 97, 120, 213
Statement Department, Washington, DC, 261
Stein, Rick, 169
Stephenson, George, 151
Steynour's Croft, 7–8
Stirrup, Sir Jock, 294
Stone Gallery, 50, 135, 136, 150

Stone, Lawrence, 119
Strand, 6, 12
Strangeways prison, 279
Straw, Jack, 173, 235, 263, 273
Street, The, 56, 134
Stride, 313
Strode, William, 106
Strong, Sir Roy, 116–17
Stuart, James Francis (son of James II),
    141–2
Stubbs, John, 83–4
Subterranean Britannica website, 296–7
Suckling, Admiral, 201
Suez Crisis, 175, 271, 272
Suffolk, Countess of, 136
Suffolk, Earl of, 155
Suffolk, first Duke of, see Brandon,
    Charles
*Sun*, 172
*Sunday Telegraph*, 282
Supreme Court of Justice, 304
Sussex, Countess of, 134
Sussex, Earl of, 72, 75
Swift, Jonathan, 149

Tailboys, Gilbert, 29
Tanner, Henry, 308
Tanner, Mr, 125
Tate Britain, 63–4
Tate Modern, 280
*Tempest, The* (Shakespeare), 99
Temple, Tracy, 209, 222
Ten Downing Street, 52, 56, 67–8, 159,
    160, 161–82, 237–8, 261–2
    Americans' security fears surrounding,
        180
    armed police officers in, 170
    Blair in, 67, 161, 169–70, 172, 176
    breakfast room in, 169
    Brown in, 172–3, 176–7, 182
    Cabinet Room in, 164, 172–4, 176, 178
    Campbell-Bannerman dies in, 167–8
    Churchill in, 167, 170, 173, 174, 340–1
    colour-grading of staff of, 295
    Disraeli in, 166
    Eden in, 175

Erith's restoration of, 168
    famous staircase in, 174
    first telephone in, 167
    front door of, 179–80
    'ghost' haunts, 169
    Gladstone in, 165–6, 167, 181
    Heath in, 167, 171
    IRA attack on, 177–9
    Macmillan in, 168, 173
    Major in, 176, 178–9
    men's toilets in, 177
    North in, 162–3
    overcrowded offices in, 180
    Pillared Room in, 169
    Pitt the Elder in, 162
    Pitt the Younger in, 163–6
    Policy Unit in, 172
    press lobby in, 172
    private tours of, 170
    sinking foundations in, 168
    staff on payroll of, 172
    Strategic Communications Unit in, 172
    switchboard in, 167
    Terracotta Room in, 161, 164, 169
    Terry's refurbishments in, 168–9
    Thatcher in, 15, 167, 168–9, 173, 175,
        176
    tunnels beneath, see Whitehall:
        underground; Whitehall: wild
        speculation about tunnels beneath
    Walpoles move into, 161
    website of, 270
    Wellington in, 165, 248
    White Room in, 161, 167
    Wilson in, 173, 174–5
Terason, H., 107
Territorial Army, 283
Terry, Quinlan, 168–9
Terry, Walter, 172
Test Act, 139, 141
Thames, as main artery, 16
Thatcher, Denis, 92
Thatcher, Margaret, 15–16, 92, 149, 153,
    167, 168–9, 175, 176, 177–8, 248, 271,
    276
    Howe's resignation speech and, 261

*39 Steps, The* (Buchan), 322
Thompson, Commander Walter, 297, 327, 342
Thorney Island, 3–4
Three Cranes, 132
Throckmorton, Bess, 87
Thurley, Simon, 7, 10, 18, 47, 49–50
Thurloe, John, 155
Thwaites & Reed, 247
tiltyard, 7, 53–4, 55, 57, 244, 245
  etymology of, 57
  *see also* jousting
Tiltyard Coffee House, 247
Tiltyard Gallery, 57
*Times*, 251, 269, 311
Tintoretto, 117
Tissot, James, 254, 307
Titian, 117
*Tom Jones* (Fielding), 318
Tomkyns, Mr, 53
Tonypandy, 278
Torel, William, 2
Tories, 160
Tothill Fields, 4
tournaments, 57–8
  armour for, 58–9
  jousting, 57–8
Tourney of the Inner Temple, 85
Tower Green, 14, 69, 89, 113, 119
Tower of London, 32
  armour displayed in, 58
Townsend, Lady, 150
Trafalgar, Battle of, 190, 213
  Nelson's death at, 165, 196–7
  re-enactment of, 231
Trafalgar Square, 45, 151, 199, 208, 235
Trafalgar Studios, 92
Traitors' Gate, 74
Transport, Department of, 41
*Travels in England* (Hentzner), 79
Travers, Professor Tim, 285
Treasurer of War, 115
Treasury Passage, 143
Treasury, 56, 246, 260, 268, 301–11
  *passim*, 347
  bomb damage to, 306, 341–2

Commissioners, 122, 301–2, 303
  Kent's commission to rebuild, 303
  lobby briefed in, 310
  *see also* Board of Trade
*Treatise on the Pretended Divorce between Henry VIII and Katherine of Aragon* (Harpsfield), 45
Trenchard, Lord, 16
*Trew Law of Free Monarchies, The*, 104
Trimble, David, 173–4
Trimmer, Joyce, 346
Trooping of the Colour, 85, 174, 207, 255
Tudor, Margaret, 316
*Tudors, The*, 21
Tull, Mr, 8
Turk's Gallery, 76, 129
Turkey, Sultan of, 267
'Turnstile', 299–300
Tweed, John, 264
Tyburn River, 4
Tyndale, William, 16

Ulster Unionists, 173
Ultra code, 273
*Underground London: Travels Beneath the City Streets* (Smith), 296
*Union of the Crowns of Scotland and England by the accession of James I of England and VI of Scotland, The* (Rubens), 104
United States of America, *see* America
Usher, Archbishop, 114

Vanbrugh, Sir John, 149, 203, 317
Van Dyck, Anthony, 63, 102, 109
*Vanguard*, 187
Vardy, John, 246
VE Day, 345–6
Veezy, Mr, 125
Verrio, Antonio, 142
Versailles, 130
*Very British Coup, A* (Mullin), 276
vessels:
  *Antrim*, 278
  *Beagle*, 199
  *Enchantress*, 204

*Foudroyant*, 189
*Kelly*, 342
*L'Orient*, 187, 198
*Mutine*, 187
*Naseby*, 126
*Pickle*, 197
*Redoubtable*, 196
*Royal Charles*, 126, 138
*Seahorse*, 184
*Vanguard*, 187
*Victory*, 195–6, 197–8, 201
Victoria and Albert Museum, 78
Victoria Embankment, 16, 287, 289
Victoria Hotel, 290
Victoria, Queen, 42, 66, 234, 283
   Gladstone disliked by, 166
   Palmerston disliked by, 269
*Victory*, 195–6, 197–8, 201
*View of Whitehall from King Street*
   (Hollar), 49
Villeneuve, Pierre-Charles, 192
Villiers, Barbara, 137
Villiers, Barbara, Countess of
   Castlemaine (later Duchess of
   Cleveland), 134, 140, 159
Villiers, Edward, 137
Villiers, George, Marquess of
   Buckingham ('Steenie'), 98, 102, 202
Vincent, Mr, 125
*Virgin Queen, The* (Hibbert), 74
Volary, 140
Vrelant, Paul van, 58

Wagonmaster General, 115
Waldstein, Baron, 78
Wallingford House, 114, 149, 202
Wallingford, Viscount, 114
Walpole (née shorter), Catherine, 161
Walpole, Horace, 66, 161, 203
Walpole (née Skerrett), Maria ('Molly'),
   161–2
Walpole, Robert, 159–62, 265, 303
   long office of, 162
   mistresses of, 161–2
   portrait of, 173
Walsingham, Francis, 84, 320

Walters, Lucy, 134, 138
Waltham Cross, 11
Walton Gaol, 278
War Cabinet, 178, 326, 330–1, 332, 344,
   345
war crimes, 344–5
War Office, 260, 281–94 *passim*
   first, 286
   Haldane Suite in, 282, 285, 290, 292
   Military Operations Directorate of,
     321
   plan to link Banqueting House with,
     288
   *see also* Admiralty; Defence, Ministry
     of
Ward, Dr, 99
Warham, William, 17
Wars of the Roses, 17, 63
Warwick, Earl of, 186
Waterloo, Battle of, 153, 226, 237–8, 239,
   240–2, 252, 253, 254
   *see also* Wellington, Duke of
Watling Street, 3–4
Watt, James, 264
Waugh, Evelyn, 326
Webb, John, 109, 110
Webster, Sir Godfrey, 225–6, 231–2
Wedel, Leopold von, 51, 77
Weeks, General Sir Ronald, 327
welfare state, 345
Wellclose Square, 142
Wellesley, Sir Arthur (later Duke of
   Wellington), *see* Wellington, Duke of
Wellesley, Lady Charlotte, 252
Wellesley, Henry, 252
Wellesley (née Pakenham), Kitty, 243,
   249
Wellesley, Lady, 226
Wellesley, Richard, 243
Wellington Barracks, 337
Wellington, Duke of, 151–2, 165, 193–5,
   220, 226, 231, 237–9, 240, 237–44,
   248–53 *passim*
   appointed Master-General of
     Ordnance, 243
   appointed Prime Minister, 248

Apsley House bought by, 165, 243
death of, 251, 253
despatch of, 237–42
funeral of, 253
'Iron Duke' sobriquet of, 249
mementoes of, 253
painting of, 244, 274
public scorn for, 249
wife estrangement from, 243
Wells, H. G., 330
Wells, John, 92
Welsh Office, 55, 134, 150
West, Rebecca, 330
Westminster Abbey, 1–5, 8, 142, 161
place of ancient power, 3
William I crowned at, 5
Westminster, Palace of, 4, 6, 10, 120, 210, 259, 347
Edward begins rebuilding of, 6
fire at, 22
Westmoreland, Lady, 227
Wheeler, Sir Charles, 293
Whelan, Charlie, 311
Whigs, 118, 152, 163, 212, 214, 221
long opposition of, 215
Whipple, Thomas, 196
White, Colin, 190, 201
White, Graham, 290
White House, 175, 180, 231, 300
White, Rowland, 89
Whitechapel murders, 313–16, 318
'Dear Boss' letter concerning, 314
Whitehall:
Charles I's execution leads to fears of unrest in, 244
designated a conservation area, 348
Eleanor's body carried along, 2, 6
England's first purpose-built office in, 149
final attempt to remodel, 347
fine houses begin to populate, 149–50
Green in, 7
Internet chatter concerning secrets of, 295–6, 296–7
leading statesmen begin to occupy, 150
prestigious nature of, 149
railway station beneath, 297
Scott's Gothic tastes avoided by, 260
Scott's Gothic tastes imposed on, 276
secret nuclear bunker beneath, 295
shops acquired for Admiralty expansion in, 203
underground, 294–300
wild speculation about tunnels beneath, 298
as York Place, see main entry
'Whitehall – a Plan for the National and Government Centre', 347
Whitehall Club, 246
Whitehall Court, 16, 18, 149, 320, 321, 322
Whitehall farce, 90–2
Whitehall Follies, 91
Whitehall Gardens, 150, 287, 289
Whitehall Palace:
cabinet room in, 117–18
cellar beneath, 40, 41
Charles I's plans for rebuilding of, 109–10
Charles I's time in, 102–7, 116–17
Charles II abandons ambitious plans for, 139
Charles II's ambition for complete modernization of, 130
Charles II's time in, 129–31, 134–40
Cromwell's administrative offices, 115–16
Cromwell dies in, 118
Cromwell moves into, 116
Elizabeth I's time in, 76–90
fires at, 7, 39, 41, 63, 99–100, 145–6, 146–8
first revelation of foundations of, 289
glimpsed in dynastic painting, 64
Great Fire of London escaped by, 133
Greatorex's survey of, 134
Henry VIII creates, 6
Henry VIII's time in, 43–69
James I's bawdy parties in, 97–8
James I's time in, 95–101
James II's time in, 141–4
naming of, 10–11

new river wall as part of enlargement of, 50
Pepys's frequent visits to, 127
Pepys's time in, 122–3
rescued valuables reinstated in, 245–6
Roundheads' move to sell, 117
Shakespeare performs in, 80–1, 89, 98
shelving of Wren's plans for, 133
William and Mary abandon, 148
see also York Place
Whitehall Stairs, 16, 17, 198
Whitehall Theatre, 91–2
Whitehall Through the Centuries (Dugdale), 279
White-Spunner, Barney, 256
Wilberforce, William, 164, 264
Wilhelm II, Kaiser, 164, 204, 283
William, Duke of Cumberland, 66
William I (Conqueror), 5
William II (Rufus), 5
William II of Orange, Prince, 143, 155
William III, 102
William III, 7, 141, 144–5, 155
    accession of, 144
    armada amassed by, 143
    asthma suffered by, 145
    Nottingham House (later Kensington Palace) bought by, 145
William IV, see Clarence, Duke of
William and Mary, see Mary II; William III
William of Orange, see William III
Willoughby, Henrietta, 186–7
Wilson, Sir Arthur, 208
Wilson, Harold, 118–19, 173, 174–5
Wilson, Mary, 174–5
Wilson, Richard, 311
Wilson, President Woodrow, 322
Winchester, Marquess of, 72
Windsor Great Park, 66
Windsor, House of, 94, 95
Winthrop, John, 154
Wolsey, Cardinal Thomas, 7–11, 13–26, 28–42, 47, 49, 79, 199, 316
    Anglo-French summit brokered by, 21
    burial of, 42
death of, 42
fool given to Henry by, 90
gold and silver plate of, 38–9
as government of England, 20
Henry gatecrashes New Year's banquet of, 23–5, 147
Henry VIII's divorce and, 33
Kratzer employed by, 60
Percy and, 28–30
personal wealth amassed by, 14–15
Privy Council's old scores against, 47
showman skills of, 22
stripped of Lord Chancellorship, 9, 14, 37
supplications to, 20
treason charges against, 37–8, 42
wine cellar of, 32, 40, 150, 293, 348
York Place left by, 13–15, 16, 37
    see also York Place
Wood, Sir Charles, 152
Woolf, Virginia, 330
World Trade Center, attacks on, 270
World War One, 164, 252, 274, 275, 283–5, 289, 322
    Americans enter, 322
    British Expeditionary Force in, 285
    Kitchener raises troops for, 284
    'Pals Battalions' in, 284
World War Two, 41, 167, 205, 273, 275, 290–2, 295, 296, 324–46
    British Expeditionary Force in, 326
    Churchill's intended last stand during, 327–9
    Gestapo Invasion Plan of Britain during, 329
Woronzow, Count, 164
Wren, Christopher, 131, 134, 139–40, 145, 146, 150, 159, 317
    Masonry and, 202
    new Privy Gallery of, 142
Wyatt, Dixon and Lytton, 8
Wyatt, Matthew Digby, 266–7
Wyatt, Sir Thomas, 71–2, 73
Wyngaerde, Anthonis van den, 50

Yeoman of the Guard, 97

Yeoman of the Scullerys, 317
York House, 7, 149
  becomes Melbourne House, 220
York Place:
  chapel at, 8
  doubling of size of, 17
  extension of, 17, 316
  growing importance of, 6
  Henry and Anne inspect, 38–9
  Henry VIII's seizure of, 6, 14
  Henry wins leave to seize, 60
  home to successive archbishops, 6
  public right of way at, 16
  Shakespeare witnesses name change
    of, 11
  stables at, 32
  village around, 20
  Wolsey's ambitious expansion of,
    17–19

  Wolsey's gold and silver plate found
    in, 38–9
  Wolsey leaves, 13–15, 16, 37
  Wolsey's nobles, servants and scribes
    at, 31–3
  Wolsey orders improvements to,
    18–19
  *see also* Whitehall; Whitehall Palace;
    Wolsey, Cardinal Thomas
York, Archbishops of, 6, 7, 17
York, Dukes of, *see* Frederick, Prince;
  James II
York, See of, 6
Yorktown, 162
Young, William, 287, 288

Zimmermann, Arthur, 322
*Zulu*, 257
Zulus, 257